MARKETS AND THE STATE

This book illustrates essential microeconomic concepts and theories through the examination of related policy formulation in Australia since the 1980s. It provides a fresh approach to the subject of microeconomics from the perspective of both market and government failures.

By looking at how Australia has transformed over the course of time, the book traces and tracks these changes and relates them to the broader microeconomic reforms. It also looks at the structure of Australian economic public policy formulation and process. The book uses standard microeconomic techniques to analyse the impact of these Australian policies and examines the role of government in the implementation of these policies, making it a very useful teaching vehicle for learning about microeconomics and microeconomic policies.

Malcolm Abbott is Associate Professor of Economics at the Swinburne University of Technology in Melbourne, Australia.

MARKETS AND THE STATE

MARKETS AND THE STATE

Microeconomic Policy in Australia

Malcolm Abbott

LONDON AND NEW YORK

First published 2018
by Routledge
2 Park Square, Milton Park, Abingdon, Oxon OX14 4RN

and by Routledge
711 Third Avenue, New York, NY 10017

Routledge is an imprint of the Taylor & Francis Group, an informa business

© 2018 Malcolm Abbott

The right of Malcolm Abbott to be identified as author of this work has been asserted by him in accordance with sections 77 and 78 of the Copyright, Designs and Patents Act 1988.

All rights reserved. No part of this book may be reprinted or reproduced or utilised in any form or by any electronic, mechanical, or other means, now known or hereafter invented, including photocopying and recording, or in any information storage or retrieval system, without permission in writing from the publishers.

Trademark notice: Product or corporate names may be trademarks or registered trademarks, and are used only for identification and explanation without intent to infringe.

British Library Cataloguing in Publication Data
A catalogue record for this book is available from the British Library

Library of Congress Cataloging in Publication Data
Names: Abbott, Malcolm, 1963- author.
Title: Markets and the state : microeconomic policy in Australia / by Malcolm Abbott.
Description: First Edition. | New York : Routledge, 2018. | Includes bibliographical references and index.
Identifiers: LCCN 2017045934| ISBN 9780815379515 (hardback) | ISBN 9780815379522 (pbk.) | ISBN 9781351215626 (ebook)
Subjects: LCSH: Australia—Economic policy. | Australia—Social policy. | Australia—Commercial policy. | Public welfare—Australia.
Classification: LCC HC605 .A23 2018 | DDC 330.994—dc23
LC record available at https://lccn.loc.gov/2017045934

ISBN: 978-0-8153-7951-5 (hbk)
ISBN: 978-0-8153-7952-2 (pbk)
ISBN: 978-1-351-21562-6 (ebk)

Typeset in Bembo Std
by Swales & Willis Ltd, Exeter, Devon, UK

Visit the companion website: www.routledge.com/cw/abbott

CONTENTS

List of figures   *vii*
List of tables   *x*

PART I
Methods and themes   **1**

1   Introduction   3

2   The public policy process in Australia   5

3   Economic policy and efficiency   24

PART II
Economic policy   **45**

4   Industry policy   47

5   Agricultural policy   58

6   Government support for research and development   74

7   Trade practices   83

8   National Competition Policy   94

9   Government business enterprises and privatisation   103

10 Energy policy   138

11 Utility regulation in Australia   159

12 Infrastructure   173

13 Labour market intervention   183

14 Training and education markets   197

PART III
Social policies, environment and taxation   **209**

15 Social policy and the welfare state in Australia   211

16 Health care   225

17 Revenue raising and tax policy   239

18 Environmental policy   261

PART IV
Conclusion   **275**

19 Conclusion   277

Index   *279*

FIGURES

2.1	General government expenditure as a percentage of GDP, Australia, 1980 to 2014	7
2.2	General government expenditure as a percentage of GDP, various countries, 2013	8
2.3	General government fiscal surplus/deficit (+/−) as a percentage of GDP, Australia, 2000 to 2014	8
2.4	General government expenditure areas in Australia, 2013	9
2.5	General government revenue in Australia by type, 2013	9
2.6	Pages of Acts of the Australian Parliament passed per year, 1901 to 2006	11
2.7	Structure of the Australian Government	11
3.1	Equilibrium and perfect competition	30
3.2	Restriction in output to boost prices	31
3.3	Private and social costs of pollution	35
4.1	The effective rate of protection for manufacturing in Australia, 1969 to 2014	53
4.2	The economic effects of a protective tariff	54
5.1	Contribution to GDP by sector, Australia, 1950, 1970, 2000, 2008, 2015	59
5.2	Contribution to exports by sector, Australia, 1950, 1970, 1990, 2008, 2015	59
5.3	Gross farm product at real market prices, Australia, 1960 to 2015	60
5.4	Farmers' terms of trade, Australia, 1956 to 2012	60
5.5	A graphic summary of the farm problem	62
5.6	Price stabilisation buffer stock schemes	64
5.7	Increasing demand for agricultural produce with advertising	65

viii Figures

5.8	A home consumption price scheme	66
6.1	Proportion of GDP spent on research and development, various countries, 2014	79
6.2	Proportion of GDP spent on R&D in Australia, 1984/85 to 2012/13	80
6.3	Proportion of gross expenditure on R&D by various sectors in Australia, 1984/85 to 2013/14	81
7.1	Monopoly solution	85
7.2	Benefits and costs of a merger	89
8.1	Terms of trade, Australia, 1973 to 2015	95
9.1	Annual value of privatisations in Australia, 1987 to 2017	115
9.2	Jurisdiction of privatisations in Australia, 1988 to 2017	116
9.3	Privatisations in Australia by industry type, 1988 to 2017	116
9.4	Government ownership in various countries, 1983	118
9.5	Government ownership in various countries, 2017	119
9.6	Australia Post earnings (before interest and tax)/total assets, 1976/77 to 2007/08	129
9.7	Capital expenditure on Australian airports by the FAC and major airports, 1988/89 to 2010/11	131
10.1	Primary energy consumption, Australia, 1965 to 2015	140
10.2	Fuel shares of primary energy consumption, Australia, 1965 to 2015	140
10.3	Victorian electricity industry structure, 30 June 2016	144
10.4	South Australia: weekly generation by fuel type, 2013/14	146
10.5	Victoria: system demand, 2013/14	147
10.6	Victoria: system demand and spot prices	147
10.7	Fatalities from electrical accidents, various countries, 1989 to 2013	149
10.8	Index of real retail electricity prices, Australia and cities, September 1980 to February 2016	150
10.9	Australian electricity supply industry: numbers employed, 1988 to 2015	151
10.10	Australian average reserve plant margin, 1990 to 2014	151
10.11	Australian net capital investment in electricity supply, 1988 to 2015	152
10.12	System reliability, Victoria, 1990 to 2014	152
11.1	Restriction in output to boost prices	162
11.2	Regulating the price of a natural monopoly	164
12.1	A model showing the short-run price and long-run price and investment decisions for infrastructure	177
13.1	Monopoly power of sellers of labour	184

13.2	Trade union membership as a percentage of all employees, Australia, 1969 to 2015	187
13.3	Unemployment rate in Australia, 1969 to 2016	190
13.4	Total working days lost in industrial disputes, Australia, 1969 to 2016	190
13.5	Real unit labour costs and labour productivity, Australia, 1972 to 2015	191
13.6	Number of deaths from electrical accidents, Australia, 1907 to 2013	193
13.7	Migrant visas issued by the Australian Government, 1983/84 to 2014/15	194
15.1	Australian Government expenditure by function, 2015/16	212
15.2	Australian social spending as a percentage of GDP, 1980 to 2014	217
15.3	Social spending as a percentage of GDP, 2014	217
15.4	Percentage of public social expenditure on means tested programmes, various countries, 2007	219
15.5	Percentage of persons living with less than 50 per cent of median equalised household income, 2010	222
16.1	Expenditure on health as a percentage of GDP, Australia, 1971 to 2014	231
16.2	Public proportion of health expenditure, Australia, 1971 to 2014	232
16.3	Health care costs and the CPI, 1989 to 2015	232
17.1	Sources of Australian Government revenue, 2015/16	241
17.2	Sources of Australian Government revenue, 1978/79 to 2014/15	242
17.3	Effect of a commodity tax on supply	257
17.4	Effect of tax on prices and quantities	258
17.5	Alternative views of tax	258
18.1	Production of a good with negative externalities	262
18.2	Common resources problem	263
18.3	Market equilibrium with and without taxes	264
18.4	Australian CO_2 emissions, 1961 to 2012	269

TABLES

2.1	Pages of Australian Government Acts of Parliament passed per year, by decade, 1900s to 2000s	10
3.1	Government agencies and the Australian electricity industry, 2016	26
4.1	Breakdown of Australian exports of goods and services, 1970/71 to 2014/15	51
4.2	Nominal and effective rates of protection for various industry groups, 1968/69 to 2013/14	52
5.1	Australian agricultural productivity growth, 1977/78 to 2013/14	61
5.2	First agricultural statutory marketing authorities in each state	67
5.3	Marketing authorities/companies with single desk, Australia, 2000 to 2015	70
6.1	Proportion of funding of R&D spending from various sources, various countries, 2010	80
8.1	Average total factor productivity (multi-factor productivity) growth, Australia, 1964/65 to 2009/10	98
8.2	Growth in real GDP per capita, various countries, 1950 to 2010	99
8.3	Effective rates of assistance to the Australian dairy industry, 1970/71 to 1999/2000	100
9.1	Privatisations of government owned enterprises in Australia, 1987 to 2017	104
9.2	Government business enterprises in Australia, 2016	113
9.3	Average total factor productivity (multi-factor productivity) growth, Australia Post and national averages, 1975/76 to 1998/99	129
9.4	Australian growth per annum of GDP, aviation passenger numbers, cargo and productivity indicators, 1940s to 2010s	131
10.1	Primary energy in Australia, consumption by fuel, 2015	139

10.2	Principal electricity generation by fuel type, Australia, 1994, 2015	141
10.3	Approximate breakdown of electricity tariffs, Australia	142
10.4	Economic regulator in each jurisdiction in Australia, 2016	148
10.5	Safety regulator in the electricity industry in each jurisdiction in Australia, 2016	149
11.1	Regulatory agencies in Australia, 2016	160
11.2	Regulatory approaches, Australian water industry, 2014	169
11.3	Non-water, government owned regulated businesses in Australia, 2016	170
11.4	ActewAGL revenue and tariff models, 2009 to 2014	171
12.1	Gross domestic product and gross fixed capital formation in Australia, 1900 to 2015	173
12.2	Planning framework at the state and territory level in Australia, 2017	180
13.1	Migrants by class of visa to Australia, 1988/89, 1998/99, 2008/09, 2014/15	194
14.1	Decomposition of changes in annual average growth rates of GDP per capita, 1980s to 1990s	199
14.2	Expenditure (government and private) on tertiary education as a percentage of GDP (VET and university), 2012	202
14.3	Educational attainment of the workforce (25 to 64 years), 2014	203
14.4	Government higher education expenditure in Australia, 1989 to 2014	206
14.5	Australian higher education funding, 1939 to 2014	207
15.1	Australian social spending as a percentage of GDP, 2014	216
15.2	Summary of Australian Government expenses: social security and welfare, 2015/16	218
15.3	Gini coefficient, after taxes and transfers, various countries, 1975, 1990, 2000, 2010	223
16.1	Health expenditure as a percentage of GDP, and public health expenditure as a percentage of health expenditure, various countries, 2014	226
16.2	Summary of health expenditures, Australian Government, 2015/16	230
17.1	Major legislative changes to tax at the Australian Government level	241
17.2	Government revenue, OECD countries, 2013	242
17.3	Australian individual income tax rates (residents), 2016/17	252
18.1	Carbon emissions (CO_2) in a range of countries, 2012	269
18.2	Examples of taxes on petrol	270
18.3	Examples of emissions taxes and trading schemes, 2017	271

PART I
Methods and themes

1
INTRODUCTION

Ever since the British Government sent the First Fleet to Botany Bay to set up a penal colony the state has played a central role in the regulation of economic activity in Australia. During the nineteenth century, the colonial governments in Australia continued to take on roles for themselves that were uncommon in the United Kingdom. Most prominent then were the large-scale government businesses that were set up in the postal and railways departments. These departments were the forerunners of the government business enterprises that still exist today. Also in the late nineteenth century Australia became an innovator in the field of industrial relations regulation, through the establishment of quasi-legal bodies to regulate labour markets, as well as an innovator in a range of other fields of government activity such as the use of the tariff to protected industry, subsidised immigration, welfare payments to distressed individuals and a range of other activities.

After federation, the state and Australian governments continued to play an important role in Australia's economic life, although the vexed issue of Commonwealth–state government relations complicated matters. Government regulation of economic life in its many forms was not uncriticised before the 1970s, but overall was largely accepted by policy makers and the Australian public in general. Since the problems that beset the Australian economy during the 1970s, however, people have become more willing to question the role of the government in the economic life of Australia and look for better ways of governments regulating activities or alternatively leaving greater responsibilities to private individuals and firms to make choices for themselves about their economic behaviour. Despite this greater questioning, the government still plays a particularly important role in the economic life of the country. Even though there has been a trend towards deregulation and privatisation, governments at all levels still regulate the activities of individuals to a large degree. This activity on the part of governments does not appear to be about to be diminished. Every week that state and Australian parliaments sit, new legislation is passed that regulates the behaviour of individuals when they engage in economic activity. Understanding the economic consequences of this intervention would therefore appear to be an important component for any person wishing to understand the nature of the economic life of Australia.

This book develops a theoretical framework around the notions of 'market failure', 'government failure', private interest theories of government regulation, and welfare economics, and uses it to analyse the regulatory activity of governments in Australia. Broadly speaking, economics is the study of how people make choices about the allocation of resources in the face of unlimited wants and scarce resources. This book is aimed at applying conventional economic theory to the way governments affect how these choices are made and the impact that this intervention has. In the process the intention is to give the reader a better appreciation of the way economic theory has been used in Australia to improve the government policy process. Unlike in the past most major government policies today are scrutinised on economic grounds, their benefits and costs analysed in order to determine just what sort of economic contribution each will make.

Given the considerable scope of government intervention in Australia it would be impossible to cover all of the different areas of government involvement in the Australian economy. Instead the book concentrates on such things as industry policy, competition policy, agricultural policy, privatisation and government ownership infrastructure, taxation, health, and the economics of education and training policy. From this book it is hoped that readers will get a better appreciation of the economic costs of government intervention and understand that government intervention, however well intentioned, often does more harm than good. This does not mean that governments should simply discard their responsibilities but instead should better focus on areas of activity that provide positive benefits to the citizens of Australia while at the same time minimising the costs of such intervention.

2

THE PUBLIC POLICY PROCESS IN AUSTRALIA

Introduction

In Australia, there are three levels of government – national, state, and local – all of which are involved in the formulation and application of microeconomic policy. The Australian Government's[1] responsibilities include such things as financial market regulation, health insurance, telecommunications, postal services, aviation, agricultural policy that involves international trade, corporation law (including the *Competition and Consumer Act*), higher education, trade policy (including tariffs and quotas), immigration policy, and a range of other areas. The state governments exercise regulatory powers over such things as electricity and gas retail, environmental matters, ports and rail, occupational health and safety, liquor licensing, gambling, secondary and vocational education and training and so on. Local government also has powers over such things as local planning and zonal regulations. The demarcation between the three levels is not at all clear cut in some areas, and at times more than one level is involved, such as in the areas of energy policy, education, and industrial relations.

Over the past two decades there has been a trend towards deregulating some areas of government activity. Deregulation refers to the removing of restrictions on prices, output, product standards, types and entry to the market. In recent years, deregulation has occurred in domestic air travel, banking, oil, alcohol, telecommunications, postal services, electricity and gas, and a range of other areas. Despite the deregulatory process governments are still passing new laws and enacting new regulations that seek to modify the behaviour of individuals and businesses. This is especially true in such areas as occupational health and safety and environmental areas.

The purpose of this chapter is twofold. First of all, the purpose is to give a very brief overview of the general nature of the economic role of government in the

6 Methods and themes

post-war era in Australia. The second purpose is to describe the process by which government policy in Australia is formulated at both the Australian and the state government level (Crisp 1983).

Public policy

Public policy involves pretty much whatever the government does to alter the arrangements made by private individuals. By government we mean the ultimate coercive authority of the national state and the institutions constitutionally derived from it. In Australia, as previously mentioned, this means all three levels of government.

From birth to death, our lives are affected in countless ways by the activities of these levels of government. For example:

- We are born in hospitals that are government subsidised, if not government owned. Our arrival is then publicly recorded (on our birth certificates).
- Most of us attend government owned or government subsidised schools.
- At different times, we receive money from the government in the form of unemployment or disability payments, old age pensions or Medicare payments.
- We all pay taxes to the government – income taxes, goods and services tax (GST) and so on.
- Many of us are employed by the government or by government owned institutions such as universities, schools or hospitals.
- What we eat, the appliances we use, how we drive our cars and many of the conditions under which we work are regulated by government.
- Our legal structure provides a framework within which individuals and firms can sign contracts with one another. When there is a dispute between two individuals, the two may turn to the courts to adjudicate the dispute.
- The environment in which we live is regulated by government agencies.

In light of all the different aspects of public policy the Australian economy can be referred to as being a 'mixed economy', where many economic activities are undertaken by private firms, while others are undertaken by the government. There is a third sector as well, made up of community organisations, non-profit organisations and families that make decisions influencing the economy and are part of the economy. Although the predominant interest of this book is still the interrelation between market and state it is well worth remembering that these types of arrangements are also influenced by policy.

The government can alter the behaviour of the private sector (and non-profit arrangements) through a variety of regulations, taxes and subsidies. The questions then arise: Why does government engage in some economic activities and not others? Why has the scope of its activities changed over time, and why does it have different roles in different countries? Does the government do too much? Does it do well what it attempts to do? Could it perform its economic role more efficiently? These are the central questions of the study of the economic relationship between the state and markets.

We are, therefore, interested in the interaction between public and private decision making. A primary interest is the way private decision making is altered by government action. Every act of government substantially alters the allocation of resources and distribution of income and wealth. It in effect alters both the bases on which market decisions are made and the outcomes of market decisions. In some areas governments can 'displace' entirely market decisions through the establishment of government agencies or enterprises. This does then raise the question of how these agencies or enterprises behave, and how they affect private agents. Displacement includes enterprises such as the historical post office and railways along with other organisations such as government schools and hospitals.

In addition to displacement there are, broadly speaking, two main types of public policy intervention: allocative/redistributive and regulatory. Redistributive polices involve such things as social programmes and taxation. Over time there has been a tendency for government expenditure in Australia to rise as a proportion of GDP. Before the Second World War, this proportion fluctuated around 15 to 20 per cent (Butlin *et al.* 1982, p. 5). However, since then it has risen to over 30 per cent (Figure 2.1). Figure 2.2 shows a comparison of this percentage in Australia with that of other countries. Australia stands as being a country with a medium level of government expenditure. In raising this revenue and spending it the government does at times run budget deficits (where expenditure exceeds revenue). As can be seen in Figure 2.3 this has been the case since the Global Financial Crisis in 2008. Figures 2.4 and 2.5

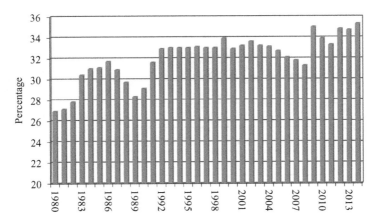

FIGURE 2.1 General government expenditure as a percentage of GDP, Australia, 1980 to 2014

Source: IMF (1980–2014).

8 Methods and themes

provide a breakdown of the main spending and taxation areas of the combined governments of Australia (Australian, state and local). As can be seen the main spending areas are in welfare, education, defence and general services. The main forms of taxation are income and companies tax and the goods and services tax.

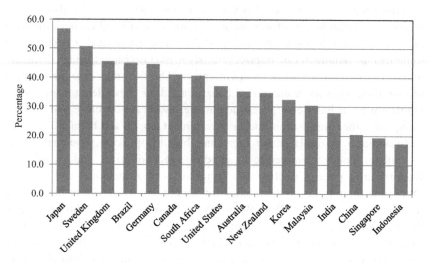

FIGURE 2.2 General government expenditure as a percentage of GDP, various countries, 2013

Source: IMF (1980–2014).

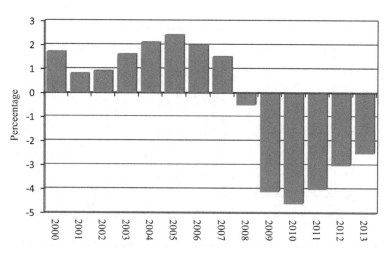

FIGURE 2.3 General government fiscal surplus/deficit (+/−) as a percentage of GDP, Australia, 2000 to 2014

Source: IMF (1980–2014).

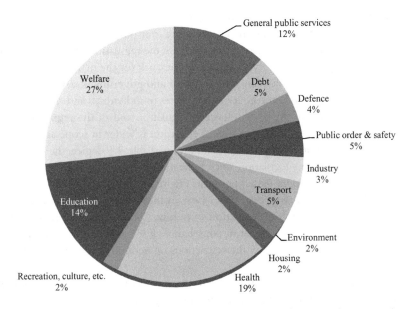

FIGURE 2.4 General government expenditure areas in Australia, 2013 (percentage)

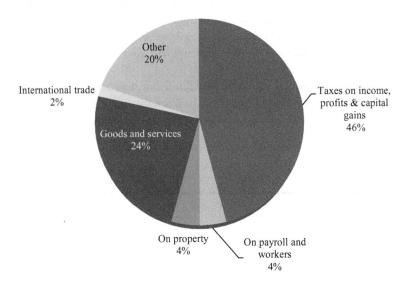

FIGURE 2.5 General government revenue in Australia by type, 2013 (percentage)

As well as displacement and redistribution there is regulation. Regulation is the imposition of laws and other regulators that seek to change the behaviour of private individuals. As Joseph Stiglitz pointed out, 'Government affects private production and is directly involved in production itself. It affects private production through the legal system and regulatory mechanisms, through direct and indirect subsidies, through lending activity, and through publically provided services' (Stiglitz 1989). Governments, therefore, not only engage in taxation and expenditure programmes, but also are involved in the regulation of private activity. Regulation is a political activity. It sets the framework for the market economy by defining the boundaries between private action and government action. It is one of the main ways by which the government relates to individuals and communities. One striking feature of the overall level of regulation and of the regulatory burden in Australia is its growth over time. Legislation is wider in scope and content than regulation, but it can serve as a useful proxy. Table 2.1 depicts the growth in Australian Government legislation since federation, by looking at the number of pages of Acts of Parliament passed per year. Figure 2.6 shows the number of pages of legislation and its growth over time. Bear in mind that state parliaments have also seen a similar growth in legislation over time. The full cost of regulation is much greater than the visible cost of compliance. For much of the economy, the paper-burden cost is dwarfed by the restrictions on economic activity imposed by the regulations.

In analysing the nature and role of government, economists attempt to incorporate an understanding of the limitations of both government and markets. There is agreement that there are many problems that the market does not adequately address; more generally, the market is fully efficient only under fairly restrictive assumptions. The recognition of the limitations of government, however, implies that government should direct its energies only at areas in which market failures are most significant and where there is evidence that government intervention can make a significant difference.

Controversy remains, though, over how limited or how active the government should be, with views differing according to how serious one considers the failures of the market to be and how effective one believes government is in remedying them.

TABLE 2.1 Pages of Australian Government Acts of Parliament passed per year, by decade, 1900s to 2000s

	Total pages	*Average per Act*
1900s	1,072	6
1910s	1,195	3
1920s	1,515	3
1930s	2,530	3
1940s	2,795	4
1950s	5,274	4
1960s	7,544	6
1970s	14,674	9
1980s	29,299	37
1990s	54,573	31
2000–2006	40,266	35

Source: Berg (2007).

The public policy process in Australia **11**

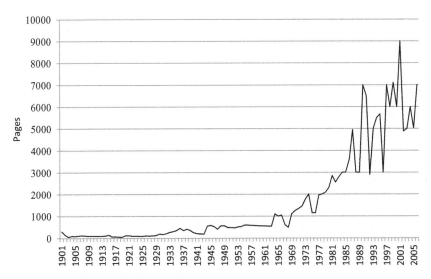

FIGURE 2.6 Pages of Acts of the Australian Parliament passed per year, 1901 to 2006
Source: Berg (2007).

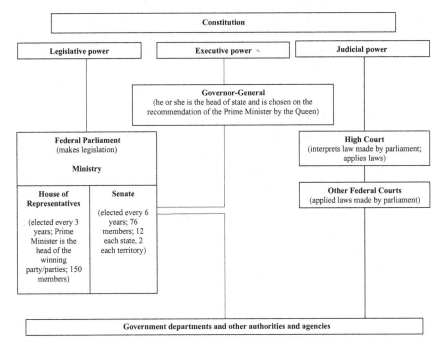

FIGURE 2.7 Structure of the Australian Government

Background and history

Background

In order to understand the nature of government policy in Australia some understanding of the long-term development of the Australian economy is needed. Australia has long been dependent on the exploitation of its natural resources (pastoral, agricultural and mining) to generate exports to foreign markets, while at the same time importing substantial amounts of inputs (capital and labour) and manufactured goods (Ville and Withers 2014). Although the competition of these goods has changed, and the sources of overseas labour and capital, and destinations of the exports have shifted over time, these underlying factors have remained unchanged (McLean 2012).

The first European settlement of Australia took place on 26 January 1788 at Port Jackson (the site of modern Sydney), when the First Fleet arrived to found the penal colony of New South Wales. The colony of New South Wales barely survived its first years and was largely neglected for much of the following quarter-century while the British government was preoccupied until 1815 with the Napoleonic Wars. In the early years of the colony, whaling and sealing were the country's first major export industries. There was a significant increase in the transportation of convicts after 1810, which provided cheap and skilled labour for the colony. As their terms expired, they also added permanently to the free population.

Agriculture was established on the basis of land grants to senior officials and emancipated convicts, and limited freedoms were allowed to convicts to supply a range of goods and services. Although economic life depended heavily on the government Commissariat as a supplier of goods, money and foreign exchange, individual rights in property and labour were recognised, and private markets for both started to function. The first bank in Sydney, the Bank of New South Wales, was established in 1817, which helped to encourage commercial activity. In addition to New South Wales other colonies were established: Van Diemen's Land (Tasmania) (1825), Western Australia (1829), South Australia (1836), Victoria (1851) and Queensland (1859). From the 1850s, these colonies acquired responsible government, and in 1901 they federated, creating the Commonwealth of Australia.

Despite the uncertainty of much of the land tenure, 'squatters' ran large numbers of sheep and cattle over increasing areas of New South Wales. From the 1820s economic growth was based increasingly upon the production of fine wool for markets in Britain and the industrialising economies of Western Europe. To finance this trade a number of banks set up in London in the 1830s. Agriculture, local manufacturing and construction industries expanded to meet the immediate needs of growing populations, which concentrated increasingly in the main urban centres. The opportunities for large profits in pastoralism and mining attracted considerable amounts of British capital, while expansion generally was supported by government outlays for transport, communication and urban infrastructures, which also depended heavily on British finance. As the economy expanded, large-scale immigration became necessary to satisfy the growing demand for workers, especially after the end of convict transportation to the eastern mainland in 1840.

Owing to the increases in income attributable to the gold rush (from 1851 onwards), manufacturing and construction sectors of the economy fared very well. The boom fuelled by gold and wool lasted through the 1860s and 1870s. This boom petered out in the 1890s, and became a full-blown depression from 1893 onwards. During the 1880s trade unions developed among shearers, miners and stevedores, but soon spread to cover almost all blue-collar jobs. Some employers tried to undercut the unions by importing Chinese labour, which led to all the colonies restricting Chinese and other Asian immigration. The 'Australian compact' or 'federation settlement' was created at this time, combining centralised industrial arbitration, a degree of government assistance for primary and manufacturing industries, and the White Australia Policy. This compact or settlement continued after federation in 1901 and was to survive intact up until the 1970s.

The recovery of the Australian economy around the time of federation was based on a combination of a growing national market and the diversification of agriculture. While wool growing remained at the centre of economic activity, a variety of new goods such as wheat, beef, dairy and other agriculturally based produce became a part of Australia's exports. By the 1920s agricultural producers were experiencing profit troubles, and governments, which invested heavily in transportation infrastructure, were not getting the returns they expected. Cutbacks in borrowing and government and private expenditure in the late 1920s led to a recession. The recession itself became worse when internationally nations fell into depressions, which not only cut back on foreign investments to Australia, but also led to a lower demand for Australian exports. Recovery took place in the 1930s based mainly on expansion of the manufacturing sector, assisted by tariff protection, a devaluation of the Australian currency and lower labour costs.

The Second World War encouraged this shift towards manufacturing, but it also raised the importance of the national Australian Government in the management of the Australian economy. Before the war the state governments levied most of the income tax and carried out most welfare programmes, but this changed during the war. In addition a wide range of industries, including motor vehicles, metal processing, textiles, clothing and footwear (TCF) and chemicals, all benefited from government contracts and regulations. Immediately after the war ended Australia continued to be governed by the Australian Labor Party, which adopted a policy of reconstruction based on the principles of government control over key industries. This policy achieved high economic growth, but led to growing political opposition, especially after the failure of the government to nationalise the banking sector in 1948. Political opponents also capitalised on the retention of rationing of food and petrol. As a result, in 1949 the government was replaced at national elections with a more conservative government led by Liberal Party leader Robert Menzies. Under his government more encouragement was given to private industry, but where public enterprise was deemed 'necessary' it was retained, and in some cases expanded.

The previous government's commitment to mass immigration, begun in 1946, was retained, and importantly new trade agreements were signed with nations including West Germany (1955), Japan (1957) and New Zealand (1965), which encouraged a shift of Australia's exports towards non-British markets. In 1955 Australia began exporting coal to Japan, and by 1967 Japan had surpassed Britain as Australia's main market, as resurgence occurred in Australia's mining sector.

The decline in Australia's relative economic performance in the 1970s led to an increased questioning of policy. To some degree the economic programme of governments in Australia over the last 20 years has been to overturn the policies introduced in the previous 30 years. Up until 1970 there was a general trend toward increasing government intervention in the economy, which came to an end with the economic dislocation in the period between 1970 and 1975. An important cause of this trend between 1945 and 1970 was the establishment of Keynesian macroeconomic management principles in the 1940s. John Maynard Keynes's General Theory was published prior to the Second World War in 1936 and quickly became adopted by most Australian economists as the basis of macroeconomics. In 1945, the publication of the Australian Government's White Paper *Full Employment in Australia* (Australia, Parliament 1945) signalled on the part of the Australian Government the acceptance of the responsibility to manage the level of aggregate demand in the Australian economy in order to balance levels of unemployment and inflation (Whitwell 1986). Parallel to this was the application of a monetary policy on the part of the Commonwealth Bank and its successor the Reserve Bank that rested on the application of a complex collection of direct controls (Schedvin 1992).

The perceived success of demand management macroeconomic intervention in the 1950s and 1960s helped to generate an intellectual atmosphere in which proposals for microeconomic intervention based on the notion of market failure received a favourable hearing. This Keynesian tendency reinforced the more traditional Australian attitude of favour towards government control of utilities, arbitration of industrial disputes and a tariff policy that encouraged the development of the country's domestic manufacturing sector.

In Australia, there was a larger degree of government intervention in the economy before the Second World War than in Great Britain or the United States. In Australia since the end of the nineteenth century there has been substantial government ownership and operation of public utilities (Pember Reeves 1902). In Australia, the post office (including telephones), railways, airports and seaports, electricity supply industry and gas supply industry in most states were state controlled, as were enterprises in such areas as aviation, shipping and banking (Butlin et al. 1982). In addition the arbitration system of industrial relations had been developed in the inter-war period and linked to tariff protection of domestic manufacturing. This tariff policy was further linked to immigration policy, as it was felt that expansion of the sector would absorb imported labour and thereby boost Australia's population (Australia, Committee on Economic Effects of the Tariff 1929).

The inter-war period had also seen the establishment of organised agricultural marketing schemes for the majority of Australia's export commodities (the major exception was the wool industry) (Campbell and Fisher 1991). These economic measures were supplemented by social welfare intervention in the form of old age pensions, workers' compensation schemes, child endowments, unemployment benefits, state bank financed housing and expenditure on hospitals and schools.

The success of the Australian manufacturing sector at producing so much of Australia's munitions needs during the Second World War encouraged the view that Australia's national development depended on the expansion of the industrial base. Post-war development plans incorporated a continued desire to expand the population base through immigration, which it was again expected would be employed in Australia's expanding import-competing manufacturing sector.

The result of the perceived macroeconomic success of Keynesian demand management combined with the traditional favour shown toward government intervention was the further development of the 'mixed economy'. As the mixed economy evolved in Australia it typically involved large-scale government involvement in an economy that was predominantly privately owned. The combined government revenue shares of gross domestic product rose to around 35 per cent in the mid-1970s, and the government share of output and employment rose to around 25 per cent (Butlin *et al.* 1982).

This role on the part of the government was accepted by all of the major political parties; points of difference mainly concerned the speed at which government interventionism should be implemented or differences of opinion along the margin. The Liberal/Country Coalition governments that were in office at the national level and in most of the states throughout the 1950s and 1960s advocated a moderate and gradual increase in the role of government, with increases responding to public demand.

This is not to say that there was no criticism of the general trend in economic policy making during the 1950s and 1960s. Some ineffectual opposition included the criticisms of agricultural economists of the dairy marketing schemes in the 1960s (Drane and Edwards 1961; Gruen 1961; Parish 1962) as well as of proposals to establish organised marketing in the wool industry, the opposition and forced resignation of the chairman of the Tariff Board, the economist Leslie Melville (Cornish 1993), in the early 1960s because of his general dissatisfaction with Australia's tariff policy, and the general opposition that the Treasury had to the increases in tariff levels during the 1960s (Whitwell 1986). These criticisms of the tariff policy and agricultural marketing schemes were however ineffectual and largely ignored by the government.

It was only in the 1970s that more notice began to be taken of this criticism of government policy. The worldwide breakdown of Keynesian economic management in the period between 1970 and 1975, and the increases in unemployment and inflation helped to undermine the faith in government intervention. By undermining Keynesian arguments for macroeconomic demand management, criticism also began to be levelled at other microeconomic policy interventions. In addition, the poor performance of the Australian economy during the 1970s meant that more attention was given to proposals to improve this performance. In most countries – including Australia – the first reaction was to switch to a monetarist approach to macroeconomic management, which combined constraints on growth of the money supply with cuts in government expenditure and taxes. The failure of monetarist policies to reignite growth rates and lower unemployment levels gradually led to a switch to microeconomic reform (supply-side reforms), which became the focus of economic debate in the 1980s.

World reforms

The problems of lagging growth rates, high inflation and unemployment hit most Western countries in the 1970s, and reform moves began in a number of countries in the late 1970s. Two countries that had an influence on Australia were the United States and the United Kingdom. Major reform of the regulatory regimes in the United States began in 1978 with the deregulation of the airline industry. This was followed by deregulation of road transport in 1980, and deregulation of natural gas production and partial deregulation of the telephone industry in the early 1980s. In the United Kingdom, the path breaking reforms of the Conservative Party Government of Margaret Thatcher involved the privatisation of utilities starting with telecommunications in 1983. In the United States the emphasis was on deregulation, whilst in the United Kingdom it was on privatisation. This reflected the difference between the forms of regulation in the two countries. In both countries, there were also moves at this time toward financial market deregulation. These deregulatory moves were mainly considered a success.

Australian reform

In Australia, major microeconomic reform began in 1973 with a 25 per cent across the board tariff cut and establishment of the Industries Assistance Commission, whose job it was to evaluate the economic benefits and costs of industry and agricultural protectionism. The passing of the *Trade Practices Act* in 1974 was another major measure, which signalled the intention of the government to regard competition as being a generally beneficial state of affairs and any government intervention that prevented it to be an exception to the general rule. These measures were not the first deregulatory measures that were implemented in the post-war era. Previous measures such as the abolition of wartime rationing controls in 1950, the cessation of import licensing in 1960 or even the ending of the notorious six o'clock closing in the liquor industry in 1966 might all be regarded as examples of microeconomic reform that moved in a pro-market direction. They were all, however, isolated, one-off measures and were not part of any general trend toward microeconomic reform but instead stand out rather conspicuously as exceptions to the general trend of the 1950s and 1960s.

The next major measures did not occur until the early 1980s and the coming to office of the Hawke Labor Government. Following on from the Campbell Committee of Inquiry into the banking industry the Hawke Government implemented financial market deregulation in the early 1980s as well as floating the Australian dollar. By 1988 the Hawke Government was committed to a general reduction in tariffs, and privatisation of the Commonwealth Bank of Australia, QANTAS and Australian Airlines (Abbott and Cohen 2014). In 1990, the two-airline policy was ended and the basis for competition in telecommunications established. Later the Howard Government completed the full privatisation of Telstra and therefore the telecommunications industry, and other major privatisations were undertaken by state governments as well.

Reform of the labour market proceeded later than in other areas but began in the late 1980s. Labour market reform has lurched back and forth a bit, with the Howard Government attempting further changes in the 2000s, which in turn were altered by the Rudd Labor Government after it came to office. One major landmark was the 1993 Hilmer Report on competition policy (Australia, Independent Committee of Inquiry into Competition Policy in Australia 1993). This report led to an extension of competition to areas such as the professions and government owned utilities previously exempted from the *Trade Practices Act* (since 2010 the *Competition and Consumer Act*). It was implemented through a Commonwealth/state government agreement in 1995 known as the Competition Principles Agreement, which committed all governments in Australia to the promotion of competition in markets. Before this agreement was made each of the states pursued quite separate reform agendas.

Throughout the 1980s, 1990s and 2000s therefore there was considerable activity in microeconomic reform right across the spectrum of government activity. In some circumstances this involved the questioning and overturning of policies that had been in place since before the First World War. None of this change in economic policy took place without controversy, and as it often involved large shifts in employment and income there was a great deal of associated concern expressed about the implications of the changes for income equality in Australia. Throughout the twentieth century much of the Australian Government's economic policy has had distributional effects and therefore it is necessary to study the process of Australian economic policy in conjunction with the development of social policy.

The formulation of public policy

Microeconomic policy originates from small groups of individuals promoting the idea of reform generally within some institutional framework (i.e. farmers' groups, trade unions, consumer groups, professional or business groups, or a government department or agency). The idea of reform is promoted by this group and if it is to be successful gathers the support of the public and the media. Politicians then react to the pressure that is brought to bear on them. This pressure is not necessarily external to the political groupings themselves but instead might manifest itself inside a political party, which in turn might adopt it as a major policy plank.

In response to this public pressure government ministers may request advice from their departments or other government agencies. Sometimes policy originates from within a department, but this usually involves adjustments to existing policies rather than the origination of new policies. It should be noted that a similar process takes place at the state level of government as at the national level.

The process of implementing major policies originates with the Cabinet, made up of the Prime Minister and senior ministers (at the state level the Premier and senior ministers). The Cabinet, at both the national and state levels, is the executive body from which the major political proposals and decisions are issued. The Cabinet acts as the final tribunal of policy, and as such is the pinnacle of the political, legislative and administrative structure. It also directs, coordinates and arbitrates on policy conflicts that occur within the government. It is the political executive of government and is made up of ministers of state – members of parliament who have been given the responsibility for a government department or portfolio. The typical ministry at the Australian Government level has around 30 members, some of whom will be members of the Cabinet and others of the 'outer ministry'. The executive itself is a hierarchy with the Prime Minister or Premier and the senior ministers at the apex.

Ministers bring their policy recommendations to Cabinet, which may accept, reject or request modifications to these proposals. Cabinet decisions are made in a political framework. All Cabinet ministers are selected from the parliamentary party of the parties in office and so therefore are all practising politicians. Cabinet ministers are therefore very conscious of, and sensitive to, the political impact that any decisions they make will have on the electorate. Debate and conflict over policy decisions do occur from time to time, but once decisions are made parliamentary traditions and party discipline impose strict rules on Cabinet solidarity and secrecy. The principle of collective responsibility means that ministers are expected to defend government policies in parliament and to the public regardless of the position they took inside the Cabinet room.

In Australia, major government policies are often preceded by a Green Paper, which is a document giving details of a government's intention to legislate. This is followed by a White Paper, which sets out a resolved policy issue. The White Paper on Employment 1945 mentioned previously is an example of an Australian Government White Paper. Alternatively, a government may commission an independent body to study a particular policy problem and make recommendations. The government will then respond to those recommendations. This may be in the form of committees of inquiry, taskforces, commissions or royal commissions, which have in the common that they are temporary extra-governmental bodies established to investigate, consider or research on behalf of governments. Some of these have been especially important in Australian economic policy development, for instance the Australian Financial System Inquiry (Campbell Inquiry) in 1981, which led to the deregulation of the Australian banking sector, and the

Independent Committee of Inquiry into Competition Policy (Hilmer Inquiry) in 1993, which preceded the formulation of the National Competition Policy.

The primary ostensible reason for inquiries is to provide information and advice to the government that is more independent, inclusive and well researched than would normally be available to government. But there are more politically expedient reasons as well. Among other things inquiries can help to delay matters, deflect criticisms, provide support for unpopular decisions, redefine problems or enable a government to change its mind on an issue. To be successful, though, inquiries need to be technically convincing.

In addition to commissions of inquiry and departments there are statutory authorities that carry out a variety of government purposes. These authorities are created by Acts of Parliament and operate at arm's length from the executive and legislature. They are created to fulfil a variety of purposes, including the provision of goods and services, the subsidising of groups and individuals, and the regulation of activities. They may be public service organisations such as the ABC or SBS, the universities or the CSIRO. Others have been established to enforce specific regulations on behalf of the government but are often called upon to give their views on economic questions. Examples of these include the Australian Competition and Consumer Commission (responsible for the enforcement of the *Competition and Consumer Act*), the Australian Prudential Regulatory Authority (responsible for financial market regulation) and the National Competition Council (responsible for the implementation of the Competition Principles Agreement). Others may have been created to carry out particular spheres of social services delivery. Australian governments have also created statutory authorities whose mandate it is to carry out research and to provide advice to the government. The Industries Assistance Commission when it was set up (1974) was designed to develop policy recommendations for the Australian Government. Its successor organisation, the Productivity Commission, has continued this practice, and in recent times governments have used private consulting groups to conduct investigations and make policy recommendations, as well as departmental groups of inquiries, cross-departmental taskforces or even industry task groups especially established to inquire into policy issues. The Australian Bureau of Agriculture and Resource Economics and Sciences is another important agency that investigates specific economics issues and tenders advice to the government. In other circumstances a political party might go to the polls espousing a policy either when it is in government or when it is in opposition. After it is elected to office it might then implement the policy espoused.

To implement a policy decision of Cabinet often legislation needs to be passed through parliament. Once legislation is passed through both houses of parliament (a single house in the case of Queensland) and has received royal assent it becomes law. A policy is then put into effect by a specified department or agency. Legislation often delegates authority to a government agency or department for the issuance of regulations, which determine how the new legislation will operate. The management of each department is the responsibility of the most senior public servants – the department secretaries and associate secretaries or in more recent years CEOs. These managers form the bridge between policy and administration. Ministers also represent their department in Cabinet meetings, putting forward their policy proposals and fighting for their share of resources.

The public service has continual experience in government in contrast to the transitory nature of political leaders of the government. Public servants in departments and agencies therefore can exercise a powerful role in both the shaping and the implementation of policy. Traditionally the public service in Australia followed a bureaucratic-administrative model of rule bound hierarchy. At the top were senior public servants, whose expertise and permanence allowed them to dispense advice to ministers and implement policy in a politically neutral fashion. Control of the public service was insulated from political interference by centralisation of staffing and management responsibility in the hands of the Public Service Board. This approach changed from 1984 onwards when department secretaries were no longer permanent and the Public Services Board was re-created as the Public Services Commission with reduced powers. Secretaries were given greater discretion in managing their department, and greater allowance was given to them in terms of hiring and promotion of staff, known as the New Public Management approach). These changes have occurred across both the state and the national level of government.

The crucial microeconomic policy departments are as follows:

- Treasury. The Australian Government Treasury deals with economic, fiscal and monetary policy, taxation, superannuation, public finance, banking, insurance and currency regulation, foreign investment and foreign exchange. It acts as economic adviser and financial controller, enabling it to participate in virtually all policy making and administrative decisions. As most government policies involve the expenditure of money, the Treasury gives advice to the Treasurer on nearly all new policy proposals. The state government treasuries fulfil a similar function in that they provide economic advice as well as act as financial controller of the government. At the state level, they are often responsible for the overseeing of the government owned enterprises.
- Prime Minister and Cabinet or, at the state level, Premier and Cabinet. These departments tender advice on policy initiatives to the Prime Minister and the Premiers. As the Prime Minister and Premiers are generally the most influential members of their respective cabinets and are generally held responsible by the public for any unpopular policy decisions these central departments generally tender advice on all major policy proposals (and quite a few minor ones).
- Finance – an Australian Government department which is responsible for: budget policy advice and process; government accountability, governance and financial management frameworks; competitive tendering and contracting; shareholder advice on government business enterprises; superannuation for Australian Government employees; government procurement and strategic management of the Australian Government's property estate. At the state levels these responsibilities are generally carried out by the state department of treasury.

- Industry, Innovation and Science – an Australian Government department that gives advice on policy for the development of Australian manufacturing, commerce, and research and science policy. It also administers tariffs and customs. The state government equivalent is generally known under different titles such as State Development, Innovation or Industry.
- Agriculture and Water Resources – the Australian Government department that gives advice on agricultural, pastoral and water management matters. In these areas, the Australian Government mainly has responsibilities in those areas that involve international affairs, and so the department is mainly involved in export promotion, commodity-specific international organisations and activities, administration of international commodity agreements, and administration of export controls on primary industry products.
- Natural Resources, Primary Industries – most state governments have a department that is responsible for primary industries (agriculture, forestry, fisheries and, in some states, energy and mining).
- Education and Training – the Australian Government department responsible for funding education and training programmes. At the Australian Government level this department is also responsible for the national government's education policy. The state governments all have departments responsible for education and training.
- Foreign Affairs and Trade – the Australian Government department responsible for trade relations with other countries.
- Infrastructure and Regional Development – an Australian Government department. State governments generally have a similar department, often called Transport, Infrastructure or similar.

It must be remembered that the development of policy involves a heavy interaction between politicians (both ministers and backbenchers), departmental officials, agency officials, private individuals, consultants and firms. It may also involve formal coordination between the various governments – state and national. The latter is generally carried out through a series of Ministerial Council meetings in the various areas of interest, i.e. Transport Ministers Council, Energy Ministers Council, Education Ministers Council and so on.

It should also be remembered that the media plays a very important role in the process, as it both influences public opinion and conveys public opinion to the government and so therefore influences politicians and through them the policy formulation process. Although it is the politicians who ultimately make the decisions to implement policy change, they are influenced by a range of other groups.

In more recent years in Australia there has been an increasing use of regulatory impact analysis (RIA) to help guide policy reform. This has been used by the Australian Government since 1985, and state or territory government has also made use of it. In 2017 every policy proposal designed to introduce or abolish regulation must be accompanied by a regulation impact statement. These statements set out the problem the regulation or policy addresses, its objectives, different options to achieve them, an assessment of the impact of each option in terms of its costs and benefits, and recommendations of which option will have the greatest net benefit. The costs and benefits may include administrative burdens and compliance costs as well as more complex types of costs and benefits including environmental benefits, distributional effects and impacts on trade. The idea is to make regulation more efficient and effective by having its proponents justify the reasons for its implementation, and for a consideration of the costs and benefits to be provided at an early stage (Harrison 2009, p. 41). In particular, it is hoped that information asymmetries in the demand and supply of regulation are overcome and the process of regulation becomes more open and transparent. There have been criticisms of the process in Australia on the grounds that it has not tended to improve the general quality of regulation in Australia (Australia, Taskforce of Reducing Regulatory Burdens on Business 2006). However, it is part of the general trend in Australia to subject regulatory changes to greater economic scrutiny.

Conclusion

Over the past 30 years there has been an intensified scrutiny of the economic implications of government policy. This originally occurred in response to the poor performance of the Australian economy during the 1970s but has continued until today and has become an accepted part of the policy formulating process. Over the same period government in Australia has come to accept that markets and competition can bring real benefits to consumers and help to raise the wealth of Australians. One of the main causes of the change in attitude was the application of the market failure/imperfection and government failure framework. Economists attempted to try to identify what type of market failure or imperfection government policy was attempting to address and whether it was successful in doing so. They then made judgements about whether government intervention improved the efficient allocation of resources compared to what would have eventuated without such intervention.

Throughout the 1970s and 1980s mainly, previously accepted government policies came to be regarded as simply the result of private interest groups' rent seeking rather than examples of governments improving the efficient allocation of resources though the alleviation of market failures. That is, direct government intervention in markets occurred because government or private interests perceived that it was possible for government to increase the imperfections of the market to the advantage of some private interests. If governments were more concerned about improving the overall economic climate than in satisfying the demands of these private interest groups, then microeconomic reform usually eventuated. Throughout the 1970s and 1980s the weakness of the Australian economic performance helped to persuade politicians and government officials that microeconomic reform was essential even in the face of strong opposition.

Note

1 In the Australian context the national government is often referred to as the Commonwealth Government or, less frequently, the Federal Government or the National Government. In this book when referring to the national government (as opposed to the state ones) the title 'Australian Government' will be used.

References

Abbott, M. and Cohen, B. 2014, 'A survey of the privatisation of government-owned enterprises in Australia since the 1980s', *Australian Economic Review*, vol. 47, no. 4, pp. 432–54.

Australia, Committee on Economic Effects of the Tariff 1929, *The Australian Tariff: An Economic Enquiry*, Melbourne University Press and Macmillan, Melbourne (Brigden Report).

Australia, Independent Committee of Inquiry into Competition Policy in Australia 1993, *National Competition Policy*, AGPS, Canberra (Hilmer Report).

Australia, Parliament 1945, *Full Employment in Australia*, Government Printer, Canberra.

Australia, Taskforce of Reducing Regulatory Burdens on Business 2006, *Rethinking Regulation: Report of the Taskforce on Reducing Regulatory Burdens on Business*, Report to the Prime Minister and Treasurer, Productivity Commission/Regulation Taskforce, Belconnen ACT.

Berg, C. 2007, *Policy Without Parliament: The Growth of Regulation in Australia*, IEA, Melbourne.

Butlin, N.G., Barnard A. and Pincus, J.J. 1982, *Government and Capitalism: Public and Private Choice in Twentieth Century Australia*, George Allen & Unwin, Sydney.

Campbell, Keith O. and Fisher, Brian S. 1991, *Agricultural Marketing and Prices*, Longman Cheshire, South Melbourne.

Cornish, Selwyn 1993, *Sir Leslie Melville: An Interview*, Working Papers in Economic History No. 173, Australian National University, Canberra.

Crisp, L.F. 1983, *Australia's National Government*, Longman Cheshire, Melbourne.

Drane, N.T. and Edwards, H.R. 1961, *The Australian Dairy Industry: An Economic Study*, F.W. Cheshire, Melbourne.

Gruen, F.H. 1961, 'Crying over spilt milk', *Economic Record*, vol. 37, pp. 352–68.

Harrison, M. 2009, *Assessing the Impact of Regulatory Impact Assessments*, SMART Infrastructure Facility – Papers, University of Wollongong, Wollongong.

International Monetary Fund (IMF), 1980–2014, *Government Financial Statistics*, IMF, Washington DC.

McLean, I. 2012, *Why Australia Prospered: The Shifting Sources of Economic Growth*, Princeton University Press, Princeton NJ.

Parish, R. 1962, 'The costs of protecting the dairy industry', *Economic Record*, vol. 38, pp. 167–82.

Pember Reeves, William 1902, *State Experiments in Australia and New Zealand*, Grant Richards, London.

Schedvin, C.B. 1992, *In Reserve: Central Banking in Australia, 1945–75*, Allen & Unwin, St Leonards NSW.

Stiglitz, Joseph E. 1989, *The Economic Role of the State*, Wiley-Blackwell, Oxford.

Ville, S. and Withers, G. (eds) 2014, *The Cambridge Economic History of Australia*, Cambridge University Press, Cambridge.

Whitwell, Greg 1986, *The Treasury Line*, Allen & Unwin, Sydney.

3
ECONOMIC POLICY AND EFFICIENCY

Introduction

As the purpose of this book is to study and discuss the relationship between government and the private sector it draws upon microeconomic theory to help explain the motivation for government intervention and its impact on the performance of the economy in general and industry sectors and businesses. In analysing the relationship between the state and the private sector the question of the economic role of government is raised, in terms of not just the size of the government but also the appropriate tasks for it to undertake and the form any government intervention should take. This is an important issue, as much research indicates that the long-run economic performance of a country is mainly determined by the quality of its public policies and institutional arrangements (IMF 2003; OECD 2003; World Bank 2006). In the Australian case scrutiny of the way government regulates private sector activity has become acutely important. Over the past 30 years the question about whether the costs of regulation of government on business are greater than the benefits of regulation has become paramount. In particular government regulation has been criticised as being more to the interest of private groups rather than the public at large: 'Current interest in industry regulation has been stimulated by political and economic factors. Politically regulation has come to be viewed increasingly as an expression of interest group power. Questions have arisen as to whether regulations are serving the public interest or are merely channelling benefits to particular groups' (Australia, Bureau of Industry Economics 1986).

This criticism followed a very long period of gradual increase in the scope of government intervention in the Australian economy. In the post-Second World War period in Australia there was a steady increase in government spending as a proportion of gross domestic product. This trend indicates an increase in the resources allocated both to the provision of government services and to the subsidisation of private activities. Government expenditure does not tell the whole story, however; legal restrictions were also important. Over the period government intervention through the legal system and regulatory mechanisms also increased. A final important area of government intervention in the Australian case was the practice of operating utilities under government ownership.

In economics the term 'regulation' has a variety of meanings:

1. The first definition involves specific directions – rules administered by a government agency to restrict economic activity, such as prohibition, determination of prices, fixing of output levels, establishment of product standards, types and conditions under which new firms can enter the market, and so on.
2. The second and broader definition involves any intervention in the economy, either by direct control or by financial inducements, which may cause individuals or groups to pursue their interests in ways they might not have chosen otherwise. This means that it might involve such things as taxes and subsidies of all sorts, as well as explicit legislative and administrative controls (Posner 1974).

As governments can influence private sector behaviour through a range of activities besides simply using legalistic measures it would seem prudent to use the latter definition rather than the former.

The key resource of the government is the power to coerce. Regulation is the use of this power for the purpose of restricting the decisions of firms or individuals. The state is the one organisation where membership is both universal and compulsory – except to the degree that individuals or firms can emigrate or avoid regulation. 'The state – the machinery and the power of the state – is a potential resource or threat to every industry in society. With its power to prohibit or compel, to take or give money, the state can and does selectively help or hurt a vast number of industries' (Stigler 1971, p. 3). Public policy, therefore, is not a voluntary action for many people or in many circumstances. We can contrast this with the voluntary exchanges of market transactions, which reflect the preferences of individuals. In a market economy governments fulfil three main allocative purposes (Stiglitz 1989):

1. Government acts as a referee or umpire in the day-to-day affairs of the market system (may enforce rules for fair trading, corporations and contract law).
2. Government acts as a replacement of the market system. It may directly allocate resources and see that goods and services are produced that the market is unwilling to supply.
3. Government acts to redistribute income from some individuals to others.

In the Australian case these activities of government intervention can take place at any of the three levels of government – Australian, state or local. Taken together

26 Methods and themes

individuals and firms can often find themselves very extensively constrained by government regulation. To illustrate this, we could look at an example of a single industry and see the extent to which it is regulated by various government agencies.

The electricity supply industry is one that was substantially reformed during the 1990s and 2000s. This saw the widespread privatisation of government assets in a number of states and introduction of competition into all states. Despite this process governments at all levels are still heavily involved in the regulation of the industry. Table 3.1 lists some of the various government agencies that are involved in the regulation of the Australian electricity supply industry. To simplify matters state government bodies have been taken only from one state – Victoria. In each case the other states have a similar agency to the Victorian ones listed.

This single example gives a good indication of the degree to which governments are involved in the regulation of business activity in Australia. What we now need to do is develop a framework by which we can analyse the impact of government intervention.

Economists and policy

Economists study scarcity – that is, how societies make choices concerning the use of limited resources. They inquire into four central economic questions:

1. What is to be produced?
2. How is it to be produced?
3. For whom is it to be produced?
4. How are these decisions made?

Like all economists, economists who study policy are concerned with these fundamental questions of choice, but their focus is the choices made within the public

TABLE 3.1 Government agencies and the Australian electricity industry, 2016

Area of responsibility	Government agency
Planning – transmission	VENCorp* (intrastate), ACCC (interstate)
Planning – generation	Local council and VCAT*
Planning – emissions	Environmental Protection Agency*
Market operation	NEMMCO
National Economic Access Code	Australian Energy Market Commission
Transmission economic regulation	Australian Energy Regulator
Distribution economic regulation	Australian Energy Regulator
Electrical safety	Workcover*, Energy Safe Victoria*
Consumer dispute resolution	Energy and Water Industry Ombudsman*
Energy concessions	Victorian Government, Department of Human Services*
Industrial relations	Fair Work Australia

Note: * Victorian Government agency.

Economic policy and efficiency **27**

sector, the role of the government, and the ways government affects the decisions made in the private sector.

1. What is to be produced? How much of our resources should be devoted to the production of public goods, such as defence and highways, and how much of our resources should we devote to the production of private goods? Society can spend more on public goods, but only by reducing what is available for private consumption.
2. How should it be produced? Under this question are subsumed such decisions as whether to produce privately or publicly, to use more capital and less labour or vice versa, or to employ energy efficient technologies. Other issues are also subsumed under this second question. Government policy affects how firms produce the goods they produce: environmental protection legislation restricts pollution by firms; payroll taxes that firms must pay on the people they employ may make labour more expensive and thus discourage firms from using production techniques that require much labour.
3. For whom is it to be produced (the question of distribution)? Government decisions about taxation or welfare programmes affect how much income different individuals have to spend. Similarly, the government must decide what public goods to produce. Some groups will benefit from the production of one public good, others from another.
4. How are choices made? In the public sector, choices are made through a political process.

In addressing each of the fundamental economic questions, there are four general stages of analysis: describing what the government does, analysing the consequences of government action, evaluating alternative policies, and interpreting the political forces that underlie the decisions government makes.

1. Knowing what activities the public sector engages in and how these are organised. The complexity of the government's operations is so great that it is difficult to assess what its total expenditures are and what they go for. Further, taxes and expenditures occur at several different levels: in some places, individuals pay not only Australian Government and state taxes but also local government rates and charges.
2. Understanding and, so far as possible, anticipating the full consequences of these governmental activities. The consequences of government policies are often complicated and difficult to predict accurately, and even after a policy has been introduced there is often controversy about what its effects are.
3. Evaluating alternative policies. To do this, we need not only to know the consequences of alternative policies, but also to develop criteria for evaluation. First, we must understand the objectives of government policy, and then we must ascertain the extent to which a proposal meets (or is likely to meet) those criteria.

4. Interpreting the political process. Economists identify the various groups that benefit or lose from a government programme and analyse the incentives facing these groups to attempt to mobilise the political process to promote outcomes favourable to them.

The theory of the firm and markets

Competition

In a market economy, resources are mainly allocated according to the market mechanism (the forces of supply and demand). This market mechanism determines what is produced, how much is produced and at what price. Economists often emphasise the benefits of competitive markets in bringing about an efficient allocation of resources. Overall, they argue, there are welfare advantages to having competitive markets compared to the dominance of markets by oligopolies or monopolies (Pindyck and Rubinfeld 2009).

This view is based mainly on the following proposition. Wealth is created when assets are moved from lower- to higher-valued uses. Value can be measured as the amount that an individual is willing to pay for a good. If large numbers of buyers and sellers of a good or service are brought together in a market and they trade with each other then we would expect the goods and services to move from lower- to higher-valued uses. That is, they would move from those with a lower willingness to pay for the good or service to those with a higher willingness to pay for it. Goods or services would move from those people who value them less and toward those who value them more. When there are no more value (or wealth) creating transactions to be consummated then the allocation of resources is said to be efficient. This level of economic efficiency is often referred to as 'Pareto optimality'. Pareto optimality is a situation where no feasible change can raise anybody's welfare without lowering that of someone else. That is, all of the wealth creating transactions have occurred. One tool for evaluating policy reform is to see if the Pareto criterion is met, i.e. whether someone is made better off and no one made worse off by the application of the policy. That is, resource allocations that have the property that no one can be made better off without someone else being made worse off are called Pareto efficient allocations. Generally speaking, this is unlikely to occur. The application of a government policy generally hurts the interest of somebody. For instance, a tariff on imports raises prices to consumers, the payment of a government subsidy hurts taxpayers, and so on. A generally accepted alternative standard is the compensation principle. The basic idea is that potentially the winners from any policy reform could compensate the losers and still have some gain left over. This is equivalent to saying that the overall economic (consumer and producer) surplus has been increased, even if there has been some reallocation of surplus between consumers and producers.

If voluntary transactions create wealth then anything that disturbs this process – such as a government regulation – must potentially destroy wealth. In general, therefore, the case for a market system in determining the allocation of resources is based on the acceptance of the precept that it leads to the most efficient allocation of resources.

The Pareto principle has several characteristics. It is based on individualistic values. Whenever a change can make some individuals better off without making others worse off, it should be adopted. Most public policy choices, however, involve trade-offs, under which some individuals are better off and others are worse off. The principle of consumer sovereignty holds that individuals are the best judges of their own needs and pleasures.

The fundamental theorems of welfare economics provide conditions under which a competitive economy is Pareto efficient, and under which every Pareto efficient allocation can be obtained through markets, provided that the appropriate redistribution of initial endowments (incomes) occurs. This constitutes what we call economic efficiency.

Economic efficiency

Another way of looking at markets is to consider the implications of competition for economic efficiency. Competition is not about the pursuit of competition for its own sake, but instead effective competition is desirable to promote economic efficiency and in turn high material standards of living. Competition is the driver that promotes economic efficiency, which in turn can be divided up into three different sub-sections.

- Allocative efficiency. In the production process this is the situation where inputs are used in combinations, which minimises costs given the input prices. From a consumer's view, it is the situation where resources are allocated to the production of goods and services that consumers value most highly given input prices.
- Technical (or productive) efficiency. This is the situation where firms have incentives to produce at least cost and production activities are distributed between firms such that industry costs are minimised (i.e. maximum output given inputs).
- Dynamic efficiency. This is the situation where firms have incentives to invest, innovate and improve the range and quality of services they provide. It also means that firms, over time, improve the effectiveness with which resources within a firm are utilised, through the development and use of new technologies and through improved managerial techniques.

The general conclusion is that competition is essential to efficiency. In practice markets do not satisfy the textbook competitive ideal of perfect competition, but it is mostly true that markets generally embody a degree of competition that puts pressure on firms to improve their level of efficiency. Competition does this by promoting the production of goods and services at the lowest average cost of production (technical efficiency) and producing goods and services that consumers value the most (allocative efficiency).

These two aspects of economic efficiency (technical and allocative) can be illustrated using conventional elementary economic techniques. In Figure 3.1a the situation faced by an individual firm in a perfectly competitive market is depicted. As the firm is so small compared to the size of the market it is said to be a price taker. The price the firm has to accept is determined in Figure 3.1b. If demand for a product increases and this leads to the temporary establishment of price at a level above the individual firm's marginal cost (the additional cost incurred in producing an additional unit of output), then society values the good more highly than the resources being put into it. This is the situation of the market price in Figure 3.1b, which is established at P_2. Generally, this situation would lead to an expansion of output to meet this demand either by existing firms in the market or by the new entrance of firms into the market. Prices would therefore be competed down to P_1, where the market price is equal to the lowest point of the average cost curve. At this point the firm has achieved technical efficiency (i.e. least cost levels of production). At the same time the increase in output means that producers are responding to the changes in consumer demand and therefore allocative efficiency is being achieved.

Significant divergence away from competitive conditions can lead to economic inefficiencies, as in the case of monopoly provision (Figure 3.2). Monopolies can potentially maximise profits by constraining output and raising prices above that of marginal costs. In this case, not only is economic surplus transferred from consumers to producers, but a 'deadweight loss' is created. This deadweight loss signifies a

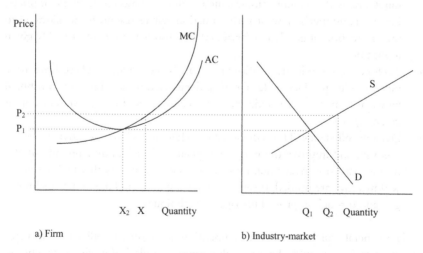

FIGURE 3.1 Equilibrium and perfect competition

Source: Pindyck and Rubinfeld (2009).

loss of wealth compared to what would occur if there were conditions of perfect competition. In this circumstance, there are some consumers who are willing to pay above the marginal cost of producing the item, but these consumers are not being supplied. These consumers in effect value more highly the goods than the resources being put into them. As value and wealth are created by moving assets from people who value them relatively lowly to those who value them relatively highly monopoly provision can mean that not all of the potentially wealth creating transactions have occurred.

An additional source of inefficiency in monopoly provision is that there is less compulsion on the part of the producer to economise on the use of inputs. A lack of competition is often found in combination with a lack of incentive to lower average unit costs to their minimum possible level.

In most markets, perfect competition is probably an unrealisable aim, and often not desirable. Workable or effective competition instead provides guidance for policy makers. Although it is fairly clear that a high degree of competition promotes technical and allocative efficiency these is some doubt over whether perfect competition would promote the greatest possible level of dynamic efficiency. Dynamic efficiency involves the degree to which firms innovate and develop technological improvements over time, in terms both of production processes and of product development. Empirical studies indicate that large firms spend more on research and development but that smaller firms often tend to be more innovative in the use of existing technologies. A further complication is the existence of economies of scale and scope. Economies of scale are where lower average unit costs of production are achieved when progressively larger scales of production are realised. Economies of scope are the situation where lower average unit costs are achieved when a firm produces a range of different products. In achieving scale

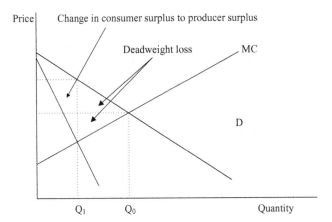

FIGURE 3.2 Restriction in output to boost prices

Source: Pindyck and Rubinfeld (2009).

and scope efficiency it is possible that the conditions of perfect competition would be undermined. Workable competition involves the notion that the firms in the market are large enough to innovate, introduce new technologies and achieve economies of scale and scope so as to be able to reach the lowest possible levels of average unit costs but are still compelled to compete against at least a small number of competitors.

The incentives placed on firms to improve efficiency might be heightened if the barriers to entry into the industry are not prohibitive. The theory of contestable markets stresses the importance of the conditions of entry into an industry. If the barriers to entry are not too substantial, then a dominant firm in an industry may have to innovate and price in an efficiency enhancing manner because of the threat of entry by, if not actual competition from, rivals. This so-called 'contestability' can be a further spur to the achievement of efficient outcomes.

Efficiency versus equity trade-off

As a practical matter, in evaluating alternative proposals we do not detail the impact each proposal has on each individual in society, but rather we summarise its effects by describing its impact on some measure of inequality (or on some well-identified groups) and describing the efficiency gains or losses. Alternative proposals often present trade-offs between efficiency and distribution; to get more equality, one must give up some efficiency. Differences in views arise concerning the nature of the trade-offs (how much efficiency one needs to give up to get some increase in equality) and values (how much efficiency one should be willing to give up, at the margin, to get some increase in equality).

This is a crucial point of public policy making: the so-called efficiency–equity trade-off. If economic policy is about maximising efficiency, whereas social policy is about redistributing income, then it is possible that one can only occur at the expense of the other. Decisions that are made about how best to generate wealth may also have repercussions on how this wealth is subsequently redistributed. One of the central debates about microeconomic reform over the past 30 years has been the extent to which there is a trade-off between efficiency enhancing reform and equity.

Arguments for microeconomic policies

If markets were always effective at allocating resources to their most efficient use, then analysing the economic impact of public policy would be a relatively simple undertaking. In these circumstances, any government intervention that influenced transactions between willing parties would be considered to be wealth destroying. Economists, however, also identify circumstances in which markets may fail to bring about the most optimal distribution of resources and most technically efficient means of production. In these circumstances, it is possible that there may be some justification for government intervention. Identifying these so-called 'market failures or imperfections' does not necessarily mean that government intervention will make things better. In most circumstances a judgement must be made about whether government policies make things better or worse. The existence of market failures and imperfections does however make the practice of judging the economic impact of government intervention more complicated.

Economic arguments for government intervention revolve around overcoming some perceived market failure or imperfection (Bator 1958; Jones 1994; Buchanan and Musgrave 2001; Abelson 2012; Stiglitz and Rosengard 2015). It is important therefore for it to be clear in our minds what the sources of these failures and imperfections are.

Even though the presence of market failures implies that there may be scope for government activity, it does not imply that a particular government programme aimed at correcting the market failure is necessarily desirable. To evaluate government programmes, one must take into account not only their objectives but also how they are implemented.

> It is the central theorem of modern welfare economics that . . . the equilibrium conditions which characterize a system of competitive markets will exactly correspond to the requirements of efficiency. What is it we mean by 'market failure'? Typically, we mean the failure of a more or less idealized system of price-market institutions to sustain 'desirable' activities or to stop 'undesirable' activities.
>
> *(Bator 1958)*

Market failure

First of all are the sources of market failure:

- Externalities. An externality is a cost or benefit that arises from any activity, which does not accrue to the person or organisation carrying out the activity. An example of a negative externality is the damage to the environment, by radiation, river or air pollution, or noise, which does not get paid for by those engaged in the activity (the producers or consumers). External benefits or economies are effects of an activity which are pleasant or profitable for other people who cannot be charged for them. If people, for instance, benefit from the education undertaken by other people then these benefits might be referred to as positive externalities. Externalities are actions of an individual or firm that have an effect on another individual or firm for which the latter does not pay or is not paid.

  > Here the essence of the matter is that one person, A, in the course of rendering some service, for which payment is made, to a second person, B, incidentally also renders services or disservices to other persons (not producers of like services) of such a sort that payment cannot be exacted

from the benefited parties or compensation enforced on behalf of the injured parties (Pigou 1920).

Sometimes economic efficiency can be attained without resorting to government intervention. This can be achieved as follows:

a. By establishing sufficiently large economic organisations, the externalities can be internalised.
b. By establishing clear property rights, private parties can bargain toward an efficient solution, as suggested by Coase (1937).
c. By using the legal system, imposers of externalities can be forced to compensate victims.

There are important limitations to each of these private remedies. For instance, public goods problems and transactions costs impede efficient bargaining solutions in the manner suggested by Coase (1937). These failures necessitate a greater role for government in remedying the problems of externalities.

There are four methods by which the government has attempted to induce individuals and firms to act in a socially efficient manner: fines and taxes, subsidies, tradable permits and regulation. When there is good information about the marginal social cost of the externality (as with pollution), and the fines can be adjusted to reflect those costs, then a fine system can attain a Pareto efficient outcome. Subsidies to pollution abatement, while enabling the efficient level of pollution abatement to be attained, will result in excessive production of the pollution generating commodity. In principle, the gainers under the fine system could more than compensate the losers, but in practice these compensations are seldom made. Thus, the choice of the system for controlling externalities has important distributional consequences. Figure 3.3 is the standard supply and demand curve diagram showing the different equilibrium results from incorporating and not incorporating the costs of pollution.

There are numerous other examples besides pollution of the impact of externalities. For instance, with electrical safety, there are externalities (spillovers) in that electrical contractors and builders do not bear the full cost of electrical fires and accidents involving future occupants or users of a building. Or in the case of banking the collapse of large financial institutions from imprudent and risky loan activity can flow on to the rest of the financial sector as well as other business activity. Instability can be transposed from a failing bank to others as confidence in financial institutions fails (the financial crisis in 2008). There are also examples of positive externalities. R&D and knowledge often can be copied and passed on. In language, the study of the English language by non-first language speakers has large external benefits to English speaking people. Education often has large spillover effects if the education of one person helps others.

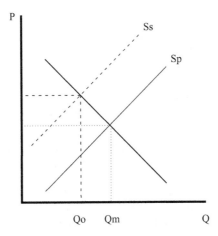

FIGURE 3.3 Private and social costs of pollution

Note: If costs to society are greater than the cost to the supplier (e.g. with pollution) then the market equilibrium (Q_m) leads to too much of the good being produced. Then the supply curve for private costs is S_p, and including social costs is S_s.

- Pure public goods. Pure public goods are goods or services which if they are produced at all are open to use by all members of society. Examples include defence, law and order, and public parks. As no one can be excluded from using them they cannot be provided for private profit (this is the so-called free rider problem). Individuals and organisations for altruistic motives provide pure public goods in some circumstances. Individuals often contribute to the creation of public facilities. More often such facilities are provided by government bodies and are paid for from taxation. They are said to be non-exclusive and non-rival in their use in that people cannot be excluded from consuming them and any single person's enjoyment of the good or service does not come at the expense of others using it (it does not rival them) (Samuelson 1954). Non-excludable means that it is undesirable to exclude individuals from enjoying the benefits of the goods, since their enjoyment of these goods does not detract from the enjoyment of others. Non-rival means that the marginal cost of an additional individual enjoying the good is zero (non-rival consumption). Although there are a few examples of pure public goods, such as national defence, for many publicly provided goods exclusion is possible, although frequently costly. Charging for use may result in the underutilisation of public facilities. For many publicly provided goods, there is some marginal cost of an individual enjoying the good. Although, for example, the marginal cost of an individual using a completely uncongested road may be negligible, if there is some congestion the marginal cost may be more significant.

With pure public goods, private markets either will not supply or will provide an inadequate supply of pure public goods. The problem with voluntary arrangements for providing public goods arises from individuals trying to be free riders and enjoying the benefits of the public goods paid for by others. Developing efficient and effective mechanisms for the provision of global public goods is one of the greatest challenges now facing the international community. For publicly provided private goods, some method of rationing other than the price system may be used; sometimes queuing is used, whereas at other times the good is simply provided in fixed quantities to all individuals. Both entail inefficiencies.

Pareto efficiency requires that a public good be supplied up to the point at which the sum of the marginal rates of substitution equals the marginal rate of transformation. Different Pareto efficient levels of consumption of the public good are associated with different distributions of income. The basic rule for the efficient level of supply of public goods must be modified when there are costs (distortions) associated with raising revenue and redistributing income. It should be noted here that efficient management of the government is a public good in itself.

The non-rivalry of some goods was noted by the American President Thomas Jefferson as long ago as 1813. He noted that: 'He who receives an idea from me receives instruction himself without lessening mine; as he who lights his candle at mine receives light without darkening me' (Jefferson [1813] 1905, p. 333).

- Merit goods. These are goods or services whose consumption is believed to confer benefits on individuals greater than those reflected in the consumer's own preferences. Primary school education might be deemed a merit good. A child might not see the 'merit' in it and therefore not purchase it unless compelled. Conversely some goods might be regarded as demerit goods. That is, the value of them might be less than the value consumers place on them. Addictive habits that injure a person's health such as smoking would be an example.

Market imperfections

Market imperfections are a slightly different category:

- Natural monopoly. This is where an industry embodies large economies of scale such that the efficient level of production for one firm satisfies the entire market demand. In this circumstance, the largest firm can enjoy the lowest possible average unit costs and drive any rival out of business. Often this is the case in network industries (such as electricity, gas, water and sewerage distribution) where capital costs are very high and marginal costs are very low.

- Anti-competitive behaviour. In markets where oligopolies are dominant, it is possible that these firms will collude in order to establish monopoly type conditions in markets.
- Information and transactions costs. Persons or firms might have insufficient information to make decisions that optimise the allocation of resources (Akerlof 1970; Stiglitz 2001). Information imperfections would include the electrical safety example. It is difficult and costly for users to discover whether electrical installation work has been carried out adequately. Consumers often do not know if electricians are qualified and experienced enough to undertake work in the absence of occupational licensing. Users are not always aware of the degree to which the electrical products they purchase are safe. A variety of measures are undertaken to overcome these types of problems, not just in the case of electrical safety but also in the case of other areas. These include such things as:
    - Occupational licensing (doctors, dentists, electricians, plumbers, etc.).
    - Truth in advertising (disclosure, labelling).
    - Product standards.
    - Occupational health and safety standards.
    - Prudential regulation (banks, insurance), to reduce the level of risk to which bank creditors are exposed (i.e. to protect depositors).
    - Systemic risk reduction, to reduce the risk of disruption resulting from adverse trading conditions for banks causing multiple or major bank failures. Measures include capital requirements, reserve requirements and financial reporting.

Government intervention

Problems of government intervention (government failure)

If government regulation is going to enhance economic efficiency, then it seems obvious that there needs to be market failure or imperfection that is preventing the market from achieving an optimal allocation of resources and the achievement of technical efficiency. However, the existence of market failures and imperfections on their own is not enough to justify government intervention. It might conceivably be argued that nearly all markets have some element of failure or imperfection, even if it is only a lack of information on the part of a section of producers and consumers. Government regulation is only justified on economic grounds if a number of conditions are met. First of all, the market failure or imperfection has to be of sufficient importance to create a substantial divergence from the optimal outcome. Second, the government intervention has to be effective at overcoming this market failure or imperfection. Finally, the costs of government intervention have to be less than the costs of the market failure or imperfection. In most cases one or more of these conditions are not met. Often, for instance, government intervention is ineffective at overcoming the market failure or imperfection or the cost of government intervention is so high that it would be better simply to tolerate the market failure or imperfection.

Ineffective government intervention or costly government intervention is often referred to as 'government failure' (Krugman 1983; Buchanan 1988; Shleifer 1998; Tullock et al. 2002; Mueller 2003; Butler 2012). Government failure can be defined as being the case where the allocation of resources brought about by government does not reflect the value of the benefits and costs involved.

Government failure has a number of causes. To begin with government intervention involves the making of decisions by politicians and bureaucrats on behalf of others. These have a tendency to be made with less care and awareness of what the beneficiaries might actually want. There might for instance be a bureaucratic bias towards some form of action, or alternatively avoidance and evasion problems, as well as imperfect information on the part of government officials.

A further important source of government failure is the absence of the discipline of voluntary exchange. That is, the competition that is embodied in markets creates incentives to achieve efficient outcomes that are often absent from public provision. Finally, there might be a bias in the political process. That is, interest groups may use their influence on the political process to achieve outcomes that are desirable to themselves and not necessarily conducive to an efficient allocation of resources.

Large bureaucratic organisations, which provide most modern public services, are beset by pervasive principal–agent problems, with employees as agents having comparatively little incentive to vigorously and thoroughly enact policy set by senior managers and politicians as principals. Wallis and Dollery (1999) simplified the reasons given previously for government failure by referring to them as being examples of 'political (or legislative) failure', where the excessive provision of a public good by vote seeking politicians led to waste, of 'bureaucratic failure', where public servants faced insufficient incentives to act efficiently, or finally of 'rent seeking' behaviour.

Government intervention, therefore, is not a panacea. A judgement must be made about whether the value from government intervention is greater than the costs of the market failure or imperfection. Given the sheer scale of government intervention in the economy it seems unlikely that it is all designed to overcome some form of market failure or imperfection. Instead it often takes place in response to some sort of private interest demand rather than in order to overcome a market failure. In that case it is possible that government intervention leads to a reduction in overall welfare rather than enhancement.

In determining why government intervention takes place there are two competing views, those of 'public and private interest'.

Public interest theory

Before the 1960s the generally held view of regulation by economists was that it was intended to protect the public from the operation of inefficient and inequitable markets. Economic markets were considered extremely fragile and apt to operate inefficiently or inequitably. Government regulation was regarded as being largely costless. The general perception, therefore, was that government regulation evolved not by accident or wilful decisions by corrupt politicians but in response to public needs and to recognised inefficient or inequitable market practices (market failures and imperfections).

Government policies were thought to be designed to increase social welfare. The role of economists was to seek the likely consequences of these policies. Gradually this 'public interest model' attracted criticism. The actual performance of regulatory schemes rarely matched the ideal theoretical model, and the poor performance of regulatory intervention led to the development of the previously mentioned concept of government failure.

The catalyst for this criticism was the slowdown in economic growth, productivity growth and higher unemployment rates which the Australian and other Western economies experienced during the 1970s. The poor performance of the Western economies during the 1970s led critics to argue that the burdens of government intervention were damaging economic performance, and in many countries – including Australia – government regulation came under intensified scrutiny.

Private interest theory

One aspect of this scrutiny was the development of the 'private interest theories of government regulation'.

1. The first version of private interest theory is the capture theory: this is the view that government regulation is usually lobbied for by an industry and designed for its benefit. Alternatively, government intervention might be implemented initially to constrain an industry, but eventually it is 'captured' by the industry and works in its favour. One problem with this theory is its inability to explain government intervention where there are conflicting interest groups. In these circumstances it is not possible for rival groups both to capture government regulation (Posner 1974; Priest 1993).
2. The second version is the economic theory of regulation (Stigler 1971). This approach admits the possibility of capture, but views economic regulation as serving the private interests of politically effective groups. According to this view regulation is provided in response to the demands of interest groups struggling amongst themselves to maximise the incomes of their members. The theory is based on two propositions. The first is that governments can exercise coercive power to give special advantages to various groups. The second is that the expression of this power in economic matters is a product subject to the laws of supply and demand. This power is provided to those who value it most highly. Voters are in effect consumers of government regulation and express their demands by voting and lobbying (both consumer and producer groups).

It is assumed people support policies in their own self-interest. The politicians and bureaucrats who make up government supply government regulation. The political process often works badly in translating preferences into outcomes. Groups with low costs of organising and no free rider problem will be more successful in influencing the political process than groups with higher costs of organising. Policies yielding great benefits to a small concentrated group and losses to a widely dispersed group are likely to be successful. Examples of this would be tariffs on imported motor cars, which benefit a highly concentrated workforce at the expense of the motoring public.

These theories helped to develop the notion of 'rent seeking'. Rent seeking is the spending of time and money by people not on the production and sale of goods and services but rather on trying to get government to change rules so as to make their businesses more profitable (Krueger 1974). Rentiers gain benefits above what the market would have offered, but in the process allocate resources in sub-optimal fashion from a societal point of view.

An associated development is that of 'public choice theory'. It starts from the premise that policy making is influenced by the behaviour of those who themselves are self-seeking. 'We must accept that in government, as in any form of commerce, people will pursue their private interests, and they will achieve goals, reasonably closely related to those of citizens only if it is in their private interest to do so' (Tullock *et al.* 2002). Public choice theory tries to make 'use of economic tools to deal with traditional problems of political science' (Tullock *et al.* 2002). It studies self-interested agents (voters, politicians, bureaucrats) and their interactions, which can be represented in a number of ways – using (for example) standard constrained utility maximisation, game theory or decision theory. Public choice analysis has roots in positive analysis ('what is') but is often used for normative purposes ('what ought to be') in order to identify a problem or to suggest improvements to constitutional rules (i.e. constitutional). Public choice theory modelled government as made up of officials who, besides pursuing the public interest, might act to benefit themselves, for example in the budget maximising model of bureaucracy, possibly at the cost of efficiency. James M. Buchanan and Gordon Tullock coauthored *The Calculus of Consent: Logical Foundations of Constitutional Democracy* (1962), considered one of the landmarks in public choice. Public choice theory is often used to explain how political decision making results in outcomes that conflict with the preferences of the general public. For example, many advocacy group and pork barrel projects are not the desire of the overall democracy. However, it can make sense for politicians to support these projects if it benefits them. The project may be of interest to the politician's local constituency, increasing votes or campaign contributions. The politician pays little or no cost to gain these benefits. Special interest lobbyists are also behaving rationally. They can gain government favours for relatively small investments. They risk losing out to their competitors if they don't seek these favours. The taxpayer is also behaving rationally. The cost of defeating any one government giveaway is very high, while the benefits to the individual taxpayer are very small. Each citizen pays only a few dollars for any given government favour, while the costs of ending that favour would be many times higher. Everyone involved has rational incentives to do exactly what they are doing, even though the desire of the general constituency is opposite. Costs are diffused, while benefits are concentrated. The voices of vocal minorities with much to gain are heard over those of indifferent majorities with little to lose individually.

While good government tends to be a pure public good for the mass of voters, there may be many advocacy groups that have strong incentives for lobbying the government to implement specific policies that would benefit them, potentially at the expense of the general public.

If government intervention is based on private interest pressures and rent seeking rather than as a response to a substantial degree of market failure or imperfection, then there would be expected to be substantial costs imposed not only on particular groups but on society as a whole. The slowdown in economic growth and higher levels of unemployment in the 1970s and 1980s led to a stronger question of the value of government regulation and an intensified interest in determining if government intervention had real public interest benefits. If analysis is to determine if government intervention is efficiency enhancing, then it would seem prudent to begin by simply determining if the government regulation has come about because of some perceived substantial market failure or imperfection or alternatively is simply the result of rent seeking pressure groups attempting to influence the government to act in their favour. If the latter is true, then it is unlikely that the government intervention is efficiency enhancing.

Conclusion

The theory of the firm suggests that competitive markets encourage economic efficiency by compelling firms to act in response to consumer demands and to produce at least cost. Markets however do experience circumstances where they might fail or act imperfectly. In these circumstances it might be possible to enhance efficiency and the wealth creation process through government intervention if the market failure or imperfection is substantial, the government intervention is effective and the government intervention is relatively costless. The efficiency enhancing potential of government intervention is made further unlikely if regulation is enacted in response to political pressures that come from private interest groups rather than some sort of more general public interest pressure or in order to overcome market failures or imperfections. Government intervention, therefore, should be limited to areas where it can best improve efficiency and not be all encompassing. John Maynard Keynes, writing in the first decades of the twentieth century, stated it thus: 'The important thing for government is not to do things which individuals are doing already, and to do them better or a little worse; but to do those things which at present are not done at all' (Keynes 1926, IV, Sec 178:15).

In succeeding chapters, different types of government regulation will be analysed trying to identify if the regulations arose in response to market failures or imperfections or alternatively were a response to private interest groups. Further an evaluation is made about the effectiveness of this government intervention and its ability to improve the allocation of resources within the Australian economy.

References

Abelson, Peter 2012, *Public Economics: Principles and Practice*, McGraw-Hill, Sydney.
Akerlof, George A. 1970, 'The market for lemons: quality uncertainty and the market mechanism', *Quarterly Journal of Economics*, vol. 84, no. 3, pp. 488–500.
Australia, Bureau of Industry Economics 1986, *Government Regulation of Industry: Issues for Australia*, AGPS, Canberra.
Bator, Francis M. 1958, 'The anatomy of market failure', *Quarterly Journal of Economics*, vol. 72, pp. 351–79.
Buchanan, James M. 1988, 'Market failure and political failure', *Cato Journal*, vol. 8, no. 1, pp. 1–13.
Buchanan, James M. and Musgrave, Richard A. 2001, *Public Finance and Public Choice: Two Contrasting Visions of the State*, MIT Press, Cambridge MA.
Buchanan, James M. and Tullock, Gordon 1962, *The Calculus of Consent: Logical Foundations of Constitutional Democracy*, Liberty Fund, Indianapolis IN.
Butler, E. 2012, *Public Choice: A Primer*, IEA, London.
Coase, R.H. 1937, 'The nature of the firm', *Econometrica*, vol. 4, no. 16, pp. 386–405.
International Monetary Fund (IMF) 2003, *World Economic Outlook*, IMF, Washington DC.
Jefferson, Thomas [1813] 1905, *The Writings of Thomas Jefferson*, vol. 13, edited by Andrew A. Lipscomb and Albert Ellery Bergh, Thomas Jefferson Memorial Association, Washington DC.
Jones, Ross (ed.) 1994, *Australian Microeconomic Policies*, Prentice Hall, Sydney.
Keynes, John Maynard 1926, *The End of Laissez-Faire*, Macmillan, London.
Krueger, Anne 1974, 'The political economy of the rent seeking society', *American Economic Review*, vol. 64, no. 2, pp. 291–303.
Krugman, Paul 1983, 'Targeted industrial policies: theory and evidence', in *Federal Reserve Bank of Kansas City*, Federal Reserve Bank, Kansas City MO, pp. 123–55.
Mueller, Dennis C. 2003, *Public Choice III*, Cambridge University Press, Cambridge.
Organisation for Economic Co-operation and Development (OECD) 2003, *The Sources of Growth in OECD Countries*, OECD, Paris.
Pigou, A. 1920, *The Economics of Welfare*, Macmillan, London.
Pindyck, Robert S. and Rubinfeld, Daniel L. 2009, *Microeconomics*, 7th edn, Prentice Hall, Upper Saddle River NJ.
Posner, Richard 1974, 'Theories of economic regulation', *Bell Journal of Management Science*, vol. 5, pp. 335–55.
Priest, George L. 1993, 'The origins of utility regulation and the theories of regulation debate', *Journal of Law and Economics*, vol. 36, pp. 289–323.
Samuelson, Paul 1954, 'The pure theory of public expenditure', *Review of Economics and Statistics*, vol. 36, no. 4, pp. 387–9.
Shleifer, Andrei 1998, 'State versus private ownership', *Journal of Economic Perspectives*, vol. 12, no. 4, pp. 133–50.

Stigler, George J. 1971, 'The theory of economic regulation', *Bell Journal of Economics and Management Science*, vol. 2, pp. 3–21.

Stiglitz, Joseph 1989, 'On the economics of the state', in A. Heertje (ed.), *The Economic Role of the State*, Basil Blackwell, Oxford, pp. 9–85.

Stiglitz, Joseph E. 2001, 'Information and the change in the paradigm in economics', *American Economic Review*, vol. 92, no. 3, pp. 460–501.

Stiglitz, J.E. and Rosengard, J. 2015, *Economics of the Public Sector*, 4th edn, W.W. Norton, New York.

Tullock, Gordon, Seldon, Arthur and Brady, Gordon L. 2002, *Government Failure: A Primer in Public Choice*, Cato Institute, Washington DC.

Wallis, J. and Dollery, B. 1999, *Market Failure, Government Failure, Leadership and Public Policy*, Palgrave, London.

World Bank 2006, *Doing Business 2007: How to Reform*, World Bank, Washington DC.

PART II
Economic policy

PART II
Economic policy

4

INDUSTRY POLICY

Introduction

In Australia industry policy in the past has been a major area of government intervention. The beginning of the movement toward microeconomic reform in Australia came about as a consequence of the debates over tariffs and agricultural pricing policy in the mid-1970s. It seems, therefore, an appropriate place to start our study of each area of government intervention.

Industry policy is a government policy that seeks: 'To achieve the national economic and noneconomic goals of a country by intervening in the allocation of resources among industries or sectors of the country, or in the industrial organization of an industry or sector' (Itoh *et al.* 1988, p. 233). Industry accepts the proposition that there is something particularly significant about the manufacturing sector to a country's economic development. Industry policy, therefore, is generally designed to promote expansion of this sector – or important sections of it such as heavy industry or high-technology industries – even if it is at the expense of other sectors. Some of the main examples of industry policy include such things as customs tariffs on imports, import quotas, subsidies on production and consumption, government purchases of local production, research and development assistance (tax concessions or subsidies), and extension services to industry and agriculture. All of these policies will have resource allocative effects in the sense that they will encourage expansion of the favoured areas of the economy at the expense of those areas that do not receive such assistance.

Economists generally accept that there are benefits of pursuing a free trade policy particularly for small countries that are price takers in world markets. Any industry policy that directs resources into the production of goods and services for which a country like Australia has not got a comparative advantage runs the risk of being wealth destroying. Comparative advantages are important at promoting trade between countries. There are gains from trade because nations possess differences in factor endowments or levels of technology use. A nation, therefore, has a comparative advantage over another at producing a particular good if it can produce that good at a lower opportunity cost.

As pointed out in Chapter 3, government regulation will only be efficiency enhancing if it assists in overcoming some substantial market failure or imperfection. It would appear appropriate therefore to begin by attempting to identify what potential market failures there may be that justify industry policy.

Motivations for government intervention

There are three main arguments in favour of protection based on the notion that there might be a market failure (Salvatore 2012). These are as follows:

1. The infant industry argument. A new industry, which is in its early stages of development, might be unable, temporarily, to compete with established producers abroad. State support of such industries is justified if there are external benefits, for example if the industry creates new skills which can be exploited in other industries, or if the capital market is imperfect and the government is more far sighted than private investors. Temporary assistance may enable the 'infant' to survive its early stages and build up the ability to compete. Difficulties arise in picking those industries that have the scope to compete internationally in the long run, in making choices about protecting particular industries without being influenced by political considerations and in ensuring that the assistance doesn't lead to a stagnation of innovation and efficiency in the industry. It also assumes private investors cannot raise capital internationally or recruit scarce skills overseas.
2. The terms of trade argument. This argument is sometimes referred to as the optimal tariff. An optimal tariff is one that maximises a country's welfare, trading off an improvement in the terms of trade against a restriction of trade quantities. For a small country which is a price taker in international markets the optimal tariff is zero. For a country with monopoly power in its export markets or monopsony power in its import markets the optimal tariff is positive. For instance, if a tariff is imposed it will raise domestic prices of imports and exports. If as an exporter a country has market power then the terms of trade will move in its favour. In practice it is very difficult to implement and requires no retaliation. Generally, it would be accepted that a small country like Australia would have no monopoly power over its exports and no monopsony power over its imports. Therefore, this argument has no relevance for the formulation of industry policy.
3. The strategic trade argument. If it is accepted that, for many internationally traded goods, increasing returns and product differentiation are common, then trade might be said to be imperfect. If a government can assist a local firm to gain a strategically dominant position in international markets, then it might

be able to extract monopoly rents from those markets. Alternatively, governments might subsidise industries that have positive externalities that spill over to other industries in the country. In the Australian case the difficulty with this argument is that the small size of the economy means that it is unlikely that any domestic industry would be able to easily reach the necessary economies of scale to take advantage of imperfect markets. To justify the support of industries that generate externalities not only do they need to be substantial but they also need to be preserved within the country and not flow overseas.

All three arguments have similar problems associated with the practicality of implementation. Interest groups might corrupt the process, governments might have trouble picking firms that are potentially 'winners' in international trade, and the use of any intervention might incite retaliation from other countries.

These problems have long been recognised, and although the nineteenth-century English economist John Stuart Mill was an early proponent of the infant industry argument, he hedged it with many qualifications: 'In a new country a temporary protecting duty may sometimes be economically defensible; on condition, however, that it is strictly limited in point of time, and provision be made that during the latter part of its existence it be on a gradually decreasing scale' (Mill 1865, p. 923). Given the difficulties involved in justifying industry policy using any one of these three arguments, in the Australian case it is probably more remarkable that industry policy was so pronounced for so long rather than that it was dismantled in the 1990s. To understand just why it did eventuate and survive for so long, a little knowledge of the historical background is necessary.

Evolution of trade policy

Throughout most of the twentieth century the main industry policy instrument used by the Australian Government to assist the expansion of the manufacturing sector was that of tariff protection against imports. Before federation of the Australian colonies in 1901 the separate colonies pursued their own tariff policies. Some like Victoria and South Australia were heavily protectionist in their tariff policies, while others like New South Wales tended toward free trade (Pember Reeves 1902). After federation a trend toward tariff protection gradually built up.

The Australian Government's 1908 *Tariff Act* was the first really national protective tariff measure. This tariff also attempted to embody the principle of 'new protection' which linked the defence of wage levels to protection. After the First World War national development arguments became more prominent. In 1921 a *Tariff Act* was passed which extended protection to industries like the steel industry, which had been built up during the isolation created by the First World War (Forster 1964). By this stage free trade groups had been virtually silenced and a policy of protection of manufacturing from imports was regarded as essential to the national development of Australia. A government report in 1929 stressed the effects that the tariff policy had in shifting income, employment and population growth from agriculture and toward manufacturing (Australia, Committee on Economic Effects of the Tariff 1929).

In order to attempt to distance politicians from the tariff setting process a statutory authority known as the Tariff Board was created during the 1920s to provide independent advice to the government on industry assistance. The Board conducted public inquiries into tariffs and subsidies to industry, and reported to Parliament.[1] It only investigated industries seeking protection and when it reported had the tendency to recommend assistance that was sufficient to enable an industry to survive in the face of foreign competition. On the whole, general equilibrium effects were ignored (i.e. the costs of protection to other industries and the general public were not considered).

Manufacturing expansion continued after the Second World War. High growth in consumer demand further stimulated by immigration, isolation from suppliers, and quotas on imports all helped to stimulate growth in the manufacturing sector during the 1950s. Manufacturing's contribution to GDP rose from 18.5 per cent before the Second World War to 28.5 per cent by 1967/68 (Boehm 1971, p. 8; Whitwell 1989). From the late 1960s this proportion declined. By 1990, when the tariff reduction programme was under way, this figure had fallen to 17 per cent. Manufacturing output in Australia during the 1990s continued to rise, but its proportion of GDP, employment and investment declined (reaching only 11 per cent of GDP in 2008; see Figure 5.1).

When the Industries Assistance Commission began to investigate the manufacturing sector in the mid- to late 1970s it found that, compared to overseas industry, Australian industry suffered from low levels of research and development expenditure, low labour productivity, low levels of intra-industry trade, and an overwhelming concentration on domestic markets.

Although isolation from overseas markets was a factor the tariff was generally blamed for the poor performance of manufacturing and economic growth in general. Manufacturing in Australia was stereotyped as being inward looking, complacent, import competing and not export orientated. Despite the considerable resources that had been sunk into manufacturing Australia remained reliant largely on agricultural, pastoral, mining and metal products for generating export income. Table 4.1 provides percentages for some of Australia's major export commodities in 1990/91, 2007/08 and 2014/15 and shows that even at this late period Australia was heavily dependent on these goods for generating much of the country's export income.

In the late 1960s the Tariff Board was still in existence, but in 1971 it changed its approach somewhat when it began to conduct reviews of existing tariffs rather than just newly proposed ones (Rattigan 1986). At the same time, it began to undertake a comprehensive review of all tariffs and analyse them on the basis of their impact on the rest of the economy and implications for resource allocation.

The Whitlam Labor Government implemented a 25 per cent across the board tariff cut in 1973 and in the following year replaced the Tariff Board with the Industries Assistance Commission. The Industries Assistance Commission was

TABLE 4.1 Breakdown of Australian exports of goods and services, 1970/71 to 2014/15 (percentage)

	1970/71	1990/91	2007/08	2014/15
Farm	41.3	18.7	11.7	13.4
Forestry and fisheries	1.6	2.2	1.7	–
Resources	28.1	40.0	49.3	53.2
Manufactures	12.8	14.6	16.3	13.7
Services	16.2	24.5	21.1	19.7
Total	100.0	100.0	100.0	100.0

Source: ABS, Cat. Nos 5302.0, 5303.0; Australia, DFAT (2015).

responsible for reviewing not just manufacturing tariffs and subsidies but agricultural ones as well. The Industries Assistance Commission began a series of reports on industry assistance and in general advocated the lowering of assistance levels. This process began to be implemented in the second half of the 1970s except in the case of the motor vehicles, and textiles/clothing/footwear (TCF). From Table 4.2 and Figure 4.1 it can be seen that the average level of effective protection was lower by the late 1970s than it was in the late 1960s (an effective rate of 24 per cent compared to 36 per cent). The motor vehicle and TCF tariffs were raised in the mid- to late 1970s and so were considerably higher (Table 4.2). This meant that the general dispersion and reallocation effects within manufacturing were higher in the late 1970s than they had been in the late 1960s (Pomfret 1995). Nominal protection levels refer to the extent to which the tariff allows the market price of an import to exceed its duty free price (expressed in percentages). Effective protection measures the percentage change in value added that results from protection (Corden 1971).

Effective rates of protection were lowered gradually throughout the 1980s and 1990s and by the turn of the century had reached trivial levels for all sectors of manufacturing with the exception of motor vehicles and TCF, which were around a quarter of what they had been at peak levels in the 1970s (see Table 4.2). The Australian Government today is committed to gradually abolishing all tariffs on imports under its agreement with the Asia-Pacific Economic Cooperation Group, although there is some debate at present about the pace at which this should take place (Pomfret 1995). The Howard Government for instance delayed the reduction in tariffs for five years between 2000 and 2005, but continued to reduce them after this date. In addition, various Australian governments have negotiated free trade agreements with countries such as New Zealand (1983), Singapore (2003), the United States (2004), Thailand (2005), Chile (2009), Malaysia (2012), Japan (2014), Korea (2014) and China (2015), which has tended to lower the overall level of tariffs.

In terms of policy advice to the government the Industries Assistance Commission was replaced by the Industry Commission in 1990 when it was merged with the Inter-State Commission, which was concerned with transport issues, and the

TABLE 4.2 Nominal and effective rates of protection for various industry groups, 1968/69 to 2013/14 (percentage)

	1968/69 NRP	1978/79 NRP	1978/79 ERP	1989/90 ERP	1999/00 ERP	2001/02 ERP	2013/14 ERP
Food beverages tobacco	13	2	13	4.5	4.6	3.7	3.4
Textiles	14	11	47				
TCF	21	26	143	85.5	23.2	25	8.0
Fabricated metal products	20	12	31	20	4.6	4.1	5.4
Motor vehicles and parts	28	30	81	54.9	14.1	11.2	8.4
Other vehicles	15	15	9	10	−0.6	2.8	0.6
Machinery and equipment	27	13	20	19.8	2.1	3.0	2.8
Miscellaneous manufacturing	25	15	30	24.7	4.7	4.2	4.0
Total manufacturing	15	9	24	16.3	4.3	4.6	4.3
Cotton	100	11	21	6	3	–	–
Tobacco	>250	76	145	80	1	–	–
Wheat	20	−2	−1	0	1	–	–
Sugar	23	−3	−4	16	6	–	–
Fresh milk	68	81	>250	105	>200	–	–
Manufacturing milk	60	5	11	38	19	–	–
Wool	10	2	6	1	3	–	–
Beef	1	1	7	5	1	–	–
Total agriculture	15	4	7	8	6	3	3

Source: Industry Commission; Productivity Commission (2014).

Note: NRP – nominal rate of protection; ERP – effective rate of protection.

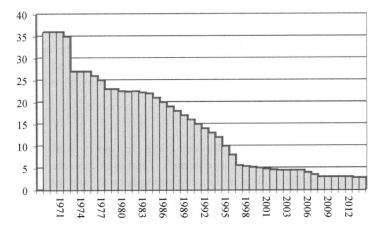

FIGURE 4.1 The effective rate of protection for manufacturing in Australia, 1969 to 2014 (percentage)

Source: Productivity Commission (2014).

Business Regulation Review Unit, which had been established to review regulation. The Industry Commission took over the responsibilities of the Industries Assistance Commission and added to them responsibilities concerning public sector matters such as public housing, utilities, public transport, workers' compensation, charities and professions. The Industry Commission was replaced with the Productivity Commission, which was formed from its merger with the Bureau of Industry Economics and the Economic Planning and Advisory Commission (Freedman and Stonecash 1997).

Regarding the structure of manufacturing tariffs, it seems unlikely that the tariff could be considered an example of overcoming any sort of market failure or imperfection. Australian manufacturers and consumers had no degree of monopoly power in export markets and no monopsony power in import markets and so the terms of trade argument would appear to have been an irrelevancy. As Australian manufacturing behind the tariff wall was entirely domestically orientated the strategic trade argument would also appear to have been irrelevant.

The high level of tariffs granted to the TCF industries is clearly not an example of any substantial infant industry, terms of trade or strategic trade arguments. It is far more likely that the high tariffs received by this industry were a product of public choice reasons such as the high degree of political influence this relatively labour intensive industry had in the 1960s and 1970s. The motor industry is probably a similar case except that some people regarded it as a strategically valuable industry and a symbol of national independence in a way in which they would not have regarded the TCF industries. In the process the infant industry argument was heavily invoked but in reality the industry did not move consciously toward world best practice techniques of production until tariff levels were reduced in the 1980s.

54 Economic policy

The industry policy of the 1960s and 1970s would have to be regarded as being wealth destroying rather than wealth creating, which is why it came under such sustained criticism from the Industries Assistance Commission during the 1970s and 1980s. The next section of this chapter turns to understanding some of the reasons why this policy helped to reduce the economic welfare of Australians.

Effects of a tariff

In order to see why criticism was levelled at the tariff policy it is important to understand the impact tariffs had on consumers. Tariff protection raises the landed price of imports, which enables import competing firms to raise the price to the same extent without losing sales. The higher prices and profits accruing to the local producers attract additional investment into the industry.

It is possible to analyse the results of a tariff on wealth by looking at a simple demand and supply diagram; see Figure 4.2. A tariff on imports will affect domestic consumers, domestic producers and government revenue and in addition create a deadweight loss, which signifies a destruction of national wealth and is the costs caused by the tariff's misallocation of resources.

In Figure 4.2 Dd and Sd are the domestic demand and supply curves respectively. If the economy is an open free trade one and world prices are established below the closed market equilibrium, then the import supply curve would be Sw. With free trade, domestic production would be at the point where the Sw curve cuts the Sd curve. In this circumstance the level of output is the quantity domestically produced. At the point where the Sw curve cuts the Dd curve domestic consumption is set, i.e. at point d. The difference between a and d is the level of imports, and the price in the domestic market is Sw.

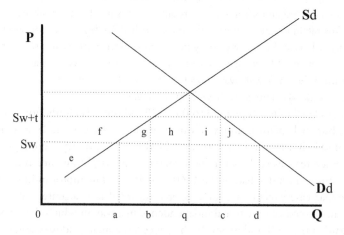

FIGURE 4.2 The economic effects of a protective tariff

Source: Salvatore (2012).

If a tariff (t) is imposed on imports, then the domestic price level will be raised to Sw+t. Local production would respond by rising to b and domestic consumption would respond to the higher price by falling to c. The difference between c and d would be the remaining imports.

As imports are still entering the country and a tax is raised on them government revenue would rise. The amount of this tax would be the size of the tariff (t) multiplied by the level of imports (c−b). In Figure 4.2 this is indicated by the boxes labelled h and i. These two boxes indicate consumer surplus that is transferred to the government.[2] At the same time local producers would enjoy an increase in their producer surplus at the expense of consumers. This increase is indicated by the segment labelled f.

The reduction in consumer surplus is not simply equal to the segments h, i, and f, but also include the segments g and j. These segments indicate consumer surplus that is taken away from consumers but not transferred to producers or the government. In effect some consumers are willing to pay enough to cover the costs of producing the item imported but are unable to do so as the price is artificially increased. This then denotes a deadweight loss or loss in wealth to consumers and the economy as a whole.

In the past the Productivity Commission has used this approach by making use of price and quantity data as well as price elasticities of demand and price elasticity of supply estimations to estimate the size of deadweight losses associated with Australia's tariff policy. In most cases these were found to be substantial and were the basis of the recommendations that tariff levels should be reduced, as they would lead to a higher level of welfare for Australians.

It is also this approach that is used to determine the economic effects of other protective measures such as import quotas and export subsidies. Most textbooks on international economics have explanations of application (see for instance Krugman et al. 2012; Salvatore 2012, chap. 9). Needless to say the results are similar to the analysis when applied to tariffs. Surplus is transferred from either consumers or taxpayers to domestic producers and a deadweight loss is created. In each case the overall impact on national welfare is to decrease it.

The wealth destroying effects of a tariff as depicted in Figure 4.2 are known as partial equilibrium effects, as they only show the impact on wealth in the industry on which the tariff is raised. There are general equilibrium impacts as well that act as a detriment to the economy. In particular, a high tariff on one sector of the economy will lead to a reallocation of resources away from other sectors of the economy. It does this by attracting labour, capital and raw materials away from other areas and therefore raising the prices of inputs to these industries. In the process wealth is reduced not just in the industry in question but in other industries as well.

A final impact that may be important is the dynamic impact on the protected industry. Shielded from competition by the tariff a protected industry has less incentive to improve its performance. This may also encourage it to put more of its efforts into rent seeking activity rather than managerial improvements that raise its performance (Bhagwati 1988).

Given the welfare costs of tariff protection the consensus amongst economists is that the government would do better to try to set a general macroeconomic framework of stability as well as assist in the provision of a skilled workforce, an efficient capital market, stable industrial relations and well-provided infrastructure. In the process efficient manufacturing enterprise would be able to survive and export without being a burden to consumers or to other industries in the economy.

Non-tariff industry policy

In more recent times use of tariff policy has been generally discredited but industry policy still does exist in other forms. Today governments still do from time to time try to favour one industry at the expense of others by providing it with research and development assistance or tax concessions. These measures, although having a lesser impact than tariffs did in the past, still have a distortionary effect on resource allocation similar to the impact of a tariff. They may favour some industries over others and influence the input mix within an industry. They might be justified if it can be shown that the industries targeted have more substantial positive externalities that flow from them through to other firms and industries that do not get assistance and bear the costs of assistance. Difficulties emerge in the estimation of these relative externalities and identifying in which industries they exist, and of course there is also the difficulty involved in ensuring that the positive externalities remain in Australia and don't flow overseas.

Conclusion

Although the Australian public was generally well disposed toward industry policy based on tariffs for national development reasons, in practice the structure of tariffs that arose in Australia seems more to have been determined by governments responding to private interest, public choice style pressures. None of the market failure arguments described at the beginning of the chapter seem to fit the case of industry protection in Australia, so it would have to be concluded that the long-standing tariff policy in Australia did more to reduce rather than increase national wealth. The application of economic techniques of analysis by such bodies as the Industries Assistance Commission would appear to bear this out, and much of the structure and focus of many of the measures were the results of political pressures rather than well-targeted assistance. For this reason the policy could be categorised as being an example of government failure of the political rather than the bureaucratic type.

To some degree the debates surrounding the analysis undertaken by the Tariff Board in 1971 and its successors set the general theme of microeconomic reform in Australia. Reductions in tariffs did help to bring about more competitive domestic markets in Australia. After the formation of the Industries Assistance Commission, however, attention also turned to the functioning of agricultural support schemes. These policies had been in place since the 1920s and began to be reformed during the 1980s at the same time that manufacturing tariffs were substantially reduced.

Notes

1 The Tariff Board survived until 1974, when it was converted into the Industries Assistance Commission.
2 Consumer surplus is an economic measure of consumer benefit, which is calculated by determining the difference between what consumers are willing to pay for a product and what they actually pay (the market price).

References

Australia, Committee on Economic Effects of the Tariff 1929, *The Australian Tariff: An Economic Enquiry*, Melbourne University Press and Macmillan, Melbourne (Brigden Report).
Australia, Department of Foreign Affairs and Trade (DFAT) 2015, *Composition of Trade Australia 2014–15*, DFAT, Canberra.
Australian Bureau of Statistics (ABS), various issues, *Balance of Payments*, Cat. Nos 5302.0, 5303.0, ABS, Canberra.
Bhagwati, Jagdish 1988, *Protectionism*, MIT Press, Cambridge MA.
Boehm, E.A. 1971, *Twentieth Century Economic Development in Australia*, Longman Cheshire, Camberwell VIC.
Corden, W.M. 1971, *The Theory of Protection*, Clarendon Press, Oxford.
Forster, Colin 1964, *Industrial Development in Australia 1920–1930*, Australian National University Press, Canberra.
Freedman, C. and Stonecash, R. 1997, 'A survey of manufacturing industry policy: from the Tariff Board to the Productivity Commission', *Economic Record*, vol. 73, no. 221, pp. 169–83.
Industry Commission various issues, *Assistance to Manufacturing Industries*, AGPS, Canberra.
Itoh, M., Kiyono, K., Okuno, M. and Suzumura, K. 1988, *Industrial Policy in Japan*, Academic Press, New York.
Krugman, Paul R., Obstfeld, Maurice and Melitz, Marc 2012, *International Economics: Theory and Policy*, 9th edn, Addison-Wesley, Boston MA.
Mill, John Stuart 1865, *Principles of Political Economy: With Some of Their Applications to Social Philosophy*, 6th edn, Colonial Press, New York.
Pember Reeves, William 1902, *State Experiments in Australia and New Zealand*, Grant Richards, London.
Pomfret, Richard (ed.) 1995, *Australia's Trade Policies*, Oxford University Press, Melbourne.
Productivity Commission 2014, *Trade and Assistance Review 2013–14*, Productivity Commission, Belconnen ACT.
Rattigan, G.A. 1986, *Industry Assistance: The Inside Story*, Melbourne University Press, Carlton VIC.
Salvatore, Dominick 2012, *International Economics*, 11th edn, John Wiley & Sons, Hoboken NJ.
Whitwell, G. 1989, *Making the Market: The Rise of Consumer Society*, McPhee Gribble, Fitzroy VIC.

5

AGRICULTURAL POLICY

Introduction

Besides industry policy the major area of government regulation that came under intensified scrutiny in the 1970s was that of agricultural policy. Although in the 1970s the level of assistance to the agricultural sector tended to be less than that of the manufacturing sector (see Table 4.2) it was still quite substantial up until the mid-1980s. Extensive government assistance was given to the agricultural sector from the 1920s onward, and its nature was virtually unchanged up until the 1970s. Over the whole of this period there was a substantial long-term reduction in the terms of trade faced by the farm sector. That is, the ratio of output prices to input prices faced by Australian farmers declined. This decline in the terms of trade occurred at the same time as there was considerable government intervention aimed at boosting the incomes of the farm sector. The inability of these measures to stop the long-term decline in rural incomes eventually led to a questioning of their desirability during the 1970s at the same time as inquiries began into the tariff protection granted to manufacturers.

In this chapter we will look at the basis of agricultural policy to see if there are any economic arguments for government support of agriculture. Government support for agriculture has not always been argued in economic terms but has often been advocated for redistributional reasons. The focus of this chapter, however, will be on whether there were any substantial market failures or imperfections that may have justified government intervention. To begin with, the fundamental problem faced by farmers will be addressed. This is followed by a section in which are outlined some of the arguments that have been used to justify government intervention. In succeeding sections, the historical background to the implementation of agricultural policy will be outlined in order to determine the degree to which private interest arguments were the basis of government support to agriculture, and then an assessment of possible market failures and imperfections will be made.

The 'farm problem'

To understand why the farm sector in Australia was so attracted to seeking government assistance to boost agricultural incomes it is necessary to understand the nature of the 'farm problem'. Over most of the past 50 years agriculture has declined in its importance to the national economy in terms of its contribution both to GDP and to exports; see Figures 5.1 and 5.2. After contributing around 30 per cent of GDP in the early 1950s and 90 per cent of exports, agriculture had seen these figures fall to around 5 per cent and 21 per cent respectively by the late 1990s (Figures 5.1 and 5.2). This relative decline in the importance of agriculture to the Australian

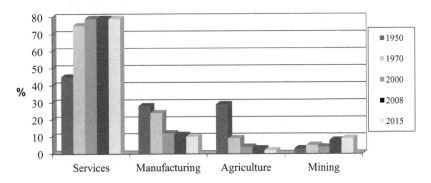

FIGURE 5.1 Contribution to GDP by sector, Australia, 1950, 1970, 2000, 2008, 2015 (percentage)

Source: ABS, Cat. Nos 5206.0, 7113.0, 7503.0.

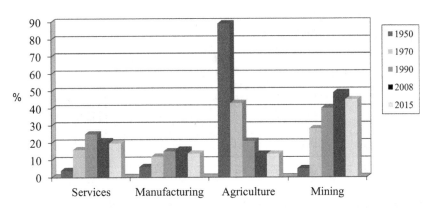

FIGURE 5.2 Contribution to exports by sector, Australia, 1950, 1970, 1990, 2008, 2015 (percentage)

Source: ABS, Cat. No. 5206.0.

economy has been mirrored by a slight decline over the long term in absolute incomes (i.e. over time gross farm product has fluctuated in real market prices but over the long run has very slightly declined in absolute terms; see Figure 5.3).

This decline in farmers' income has been created primarily by the decline in the real terms of trade for agricultural produce (Figure 5.4). This decline in the terms of trade faced by the agricultural sector in Australia is a direct result of the

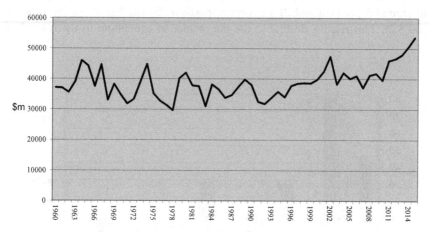

FIGURE 5.3 Gross farm product at real market prices, Australia, 1960 to 2015 ($ million)
Source: ABS, Cat. Nos 7113.0, 7503.0.

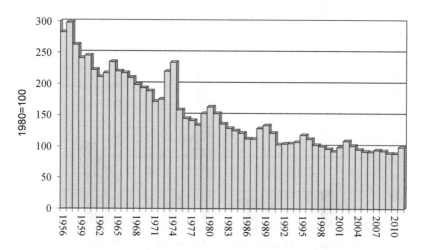

FIGURE 5.4 Farmers' terms of trade, Australia, 1956 to 2012 (1980=100)
Source: ABS, Cat. Nos 7113.0, 7503.0.

so-called 'farm problem'. This problem is a consequence of the interaction between slow growth in demand for agricultural produce and strong supply-side productivity growth.

Demand for Australian agricultural produce has grown over the past 50 years but at a relatively low rate. This was caused by the inelastic nature of demand with respect to both income and prices. As people become wealthier over time they increase their expenditure on food but at a lower rate than their other expenditures so that their total proportion spent on food declines. Demand for food is therefore relatively unresponsive to changes in income. The same is true of price. Despite substantial reductions in the real price of Australian agricultural produce over the long term – as depicted by the terms of trade – growth in demand for Australian produce has been sluggish. This would indicate that demand is also relatively price inelastic. At the same time growth in productivity in the Australian agricultural sector has been steady. Table 5.1 presents productivity growth rate figures for major Australian agricultural crops for a sample period 1977/78 to 2013/14. Growth in agricultural productivity was slow, but relatively steady throughout the period.

Combined together these two demand and supply factors lead to a fall in the average real price of agricultural produce. Figure 5.5 depicts a slight shift in demand (demand curve from D_1 to D_2). At the same time the supply curve moves substantially to the right (from S_1 to S_2) because of the increase in productivity in the sector. Combined together the result is a reduction in price from P_1 to P_2. This primary cause of declining farm incomes is one that has proved difficult to avoid. In fact, it would appear that any government assistance programme aimed at boosting agricultural incomes was futile in the longer term. Nonetheless it is possible that there exist some market failure/imperfection reasons why governments might bring about a more optimal allocation of resources in agriculture. We can now turn to some of the arguments that have been used to support agricultural assistance.

TABLE 5.1 Australian agricultural productivity growth, 1977/78 to 2013/14 (percentage, per annum)

	Outputs	Inputs	Productivity
All broad acre	0.1	−1.0	1.5
Cropping specialists	2.6	1.1	1.5
Sheep	−2.6	−2.9	0.3
Beef	1.1	−0.2	1.3
Sheep/beef	−2.1	−2.2	0.0
All agriculture	1.5	0.2	1.3

Source: Knopke et al. (1995); ABARE (2015, 2016).

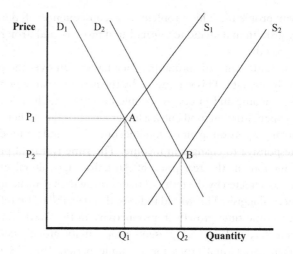

FIGURE 5.5 A graphic summary of the farm problem

Arguments for agricultural intervention

In the past there have been a number of reasons put forward for the need on the part of governments to assist the rural sector in Australia. Some of these are as follows:

- The first reason has been the considerable price and income variability that exists in agricultural markets. Typically, agricultural prices are far more volatile than prices for industrial goods. This is reflected in the substantial fluctuations in gross farm product in Australia, which is displayed in Figure 5.3. Unstable prices – it is argued – might create an added level of risk to the industry and therefore deter investment. In the past there have been a number of incidences in Australia of governments putting into place measures that have attempted to stabilise prices in order to address this problem.
- The second argument in favour of government intervention into agriculture is that farmers – because of their small size of operations and limited resources – may have had insufficient information about market conditions and scientific knowledge that would help them in the process of production. Both activities entail search costs that in many cases were just beyond the means of farmers.
- Third was the case of the possible existence of externalities that might have flowed from spending on research and development. If these externalities were significant then there would have been an incentive for each individual farmer to free-ride on the activities of others. If all attempted this, then spending on research and development would have fallen below the optimal level.
- A fourth argument is that farmers need to be compensated for the fact that they carried much of the cost of tariff protection that was granted to manufacturers.

- A fifth argument was a purely social one: that farmers often were underprivileged compared to those living in the cities, and price support schemes were a way to alleviate poverty in country areas.
- Another argument was that middlemen exercised market power over the farmers and therefore underpaid them for their produce. This was probably more likely in the distant past when markets were more fragmented; however, recent arguments by dairy farmers that supermarket chains have a degree of buyer power is a contemporary example of the argument.
- A final argument is that a single desk seller of the farmers' produce with compulsory acquisition powers might be able to exploit market power on behalf of farmers in international markets and raise national income in the process.

Some of these arguments are based on the notion of market failure, some on the notion of market imperfections and finally some on purely distributional grounds. The possible existence of research and development externalities is a simple case of a possible market failure. Arguments based on the supposed market power of a monopoly single desk seller or monopsony power on the part of produce purchases indicate examples of market imperfections.

All of these arguments were used at one time or another to justify government intervention, and a number of government agencies were established with the responsibility of tackling one or another of these problems. The establishment of the CSIRO, for instance, during the 1920s was in part a case of the government trying to conduct scientific research on behalf of farmers who had neither the resources to conduct such research nor the ability to capture all of the benefits that followed from any expenditure they made on this form of investment. State government departments of agriculture have conducted or financed scientific research as well as provided farmers with market information, information on technological advances, and a range of other extension services. By far the most extensive government intervention, however, was the attempt by a number of government bodies and quasi-government bodies to raise and stabilise prices for farmers through the operation of statutory marketing authorities (Gropp et al. 2000).

Instruments of assistance

In order to boost the prices and incomes of farmers, government agencies have used a number of different methods. On the whole these can be categorised into four different types: subsidy, stabilisation schemes, demand boosting and supply restraint.

The first method was to provide direct government subsidies to farmers. These subsidies might have been paid to subsidise inputs (such as the superphosphate bounty) or alternatively have been subsidies paid on production. The dairy and cotton industries were the major beneficiaries of the latter type of subsidy. Dairy farmers received an Australian Government subsidy on production between 1942 and 1975. Cotton growers received a subsidy for an even longer period

(1922 to 1971). In both cases the subsidy was justified as being a means of expanding smallholdings, the cotton subsidy for ex-servicemen after the First World War and the dairy subsidy for ex-servicemen after the Second World War (Sieper 1982; Piggott 1992). Both would have had the impact of increasing supply and therefore lowering prices, which meant that generally other means of government intervention were used in conjunction with the subsidy to boost farm incomes.

The second form of price and income support came in the form of buffer stock and buffer fund schemes. In Australia the most well known of these was the buffer stock scheme operated by the Australian Wool Corporation between 1971 and 1991. The basic purpose of a buffer stock scheme is to stabilise prices rather than to raise them. Figure 5.6 illustrates how this sort of scheme operates. Let us assume that the aim is to stabilise the price of a product around the price P and that the available supply is level X. If demand were low (demand curve D_1), then there would be a tendency for the price to fall towards P_1. The role of the buffer stock agency would be to enter the market, purchase the product, stockpile it and increase demand so that the price is raised back up towards the target rate. If demand were high (D_2) then the tendency would be for the price to rise to P_2. In this circumstance the buffer stock agency would sell produce from the stockpile it built up when demand was low, which would have the effect of lowering prices. A buffer fund scheme operates in a similar fashion except that it 'stockpiles' a levy paid by farmers when prices are high and then pays it back to farmers when prices are low.

The danger with this type of scheme is that a buffer stock agency might set a target rate that is too high. If this occurs and the buffer stock agency tries to maintain

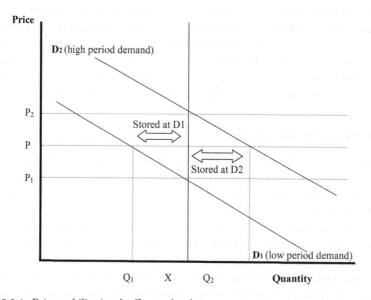

FIGURE 5.6 Price stabilisation buffer stock schemes

the price in a low-demand period, it might simply run out of money attempting to purchase and stockpile produce. This in fact occurred to the Australian Wool Corporation in 1991 when it attempted to maintain the price of wool at above $800 a bale (Haszler et al. 1996).

The third way that governments may attempt to raise prices for farmers is to attempt to boost demand for their produce. Often farmers have been compelled to pay levies on their produce to pay for advertising, marketing and product promotion. Governments have often assisted these marketing efforts as well by contributing money. If successful, these efforts should lead to an increase in demand (shown in Figure 5.7 by a shift in the demand curve from D_1 to D_2). This would have the effect of increasing the quantity demand for the produce as well as increasing the price. Some studies have shown that in some circumstances this can be a successful strategy for farmers (Australian Wool Corporation–Bureau of Agricultural Economics 1987).

The final method is to attempt to raise prices by reducing the supply of the produce. This method can take a number of different forms. The most straightforward instrument of this method is import tariffs and quotas, which reduce the supply by cutting back on imports. At the national level the first import tariff was placed on sugar imports in 1903. Further import tariffs and quotas were applied to the import of hops, bananas, tobacco, maize, nuts, onions and potatoes during the 1920s. One interesting aspect of this list of agricultural products is that they were important crops in two of the smaller states: Tasmania and Queensland. This fact is suggestive that the private interest theory of government intervention may have been in operation at the time. Concentrated groups of farmers in the two states would have been able to successfully lobby state parliamentarians and the two state governments to put pressure on the Australian Government. Later import tariffs and quotas were placed on other imported produce as well.

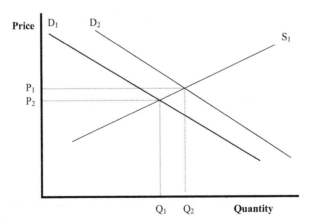

FIGURE 5.7 Increasing demand for agricultural produce with advertising

66 Economic policy

The other main supply control technique was to impose a 'two-price scheme'. Statutory marketing authorities, established by either the state or Australian governments, usually carried this out.[1] Farmers were compelled under law to sell their produce to these authorities, which then marketed the produce. These single desks, as they are known, would sell the produce in Australian markets at inflated prices and the surplus at lower prices overseas (hence the title: 'two-price'). Because of the market power that a single desk has in Australian markets the price elasticity of demand would be far more inelastic there than in international ones where overseas farmers competed. Figure 5.8 illustrates how this process operated for the dairy industry before 2000. Historically the state governments operated dairy marketing boards that purchased all of the liquid milk in each state and marketed it at inflated prices. Manufactured milk (butter, cheese, etc.) was then mainly sold overseas at prices determined by world market conditions. In terms of Figure 5.8, the demand curve Dd is shown to depict demand for domestic liquid milk. As the demand curve is relatively inelastic, price is set at a high level (Pd). In the overseas market the demand curve faced (Do) is more elastic, so price is set at a far lower level (Po). For this type of home price scheme to be successful, imports would need to be excluded in order to prevent overseas farmers free-riding off the scheme. In the case of the dairy industry, inflating the liquid milk price, which doesn't travel very well, and then selling cheese and butter overseas largely solved this problem.[2]

Now that we understand the main methods used and the main market failure/imperfection arguments it is possible to make an evaluation of whether these arguments warranted such government intervention. To make this judgement it is first useful to look at the background behind the introduction of these schemes.

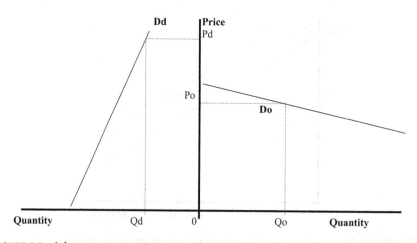

FIGURE 5.8 A home consumption price scheme

History

In Australia there were a variety of subsidy and tariff schemes that assisted agricultural production in key areas early in the twentieth century. The main device of government intervention, however, has been the operation of the statutory marketing authorities. These statutory marketing authorities generally were granted full acquisition powers, had the legal power to fix domestic prices (subject to the volume of imports and tariffs), and often raised levies from farmers in order to engage in research, development and promotional activities.

The main claim of the authorities was that they could exploit market power in international markets and that they helped to counterbalance the monopsony power of marketers.[3] The main way in which they supported the income of farmers, however, was through the raising of domestic prices at the expense of Australian consumers.

The authorities were first established by the state governments in the 1920s (see Table 5.2). This decade was a period of sagging agricultural prices and saw the rise in political influence of the Country Party (the predecessor of the National Party). Farmers first attempted cooperative voluntary schemes, but these generally collapsed because a significant number of farmers decided to operate outside of them and so undermined the power of these cooperatives to raise prices. It was only with the compulsory powers of the state and Australian governments that prices could be raised (Piggott 1990). As farmers pushed for price raising schemes, partially to compensate them for the higher cost of imported goods because of tariff protection and the higher cost of labour because of arbitration, this approach was often referred to as 'Protection all round'. There were reservations expressed about these schemes at the time. Edward Shann the Australian economist pointed out that:

> A government or board of control that seeks to fake the world's prices does so at the peril of the citizens and producers whom the faked prices mislead. It deranges and weakens its whole economy if it forces them to work with costs that the outer world is under no obligation to meet.
>
> *(Shann 1930, p. 447)*

TABLE 5.2 First agricultural statutory marketing authorities in each state

State	Data	Industry
Queensland	1920	Wheat
Western Australia	1922	Dairy
Tasmania	1924	Meat
Victoria	1925	Dried fruits
South Australia	1928	Dried fruits
New South Wales	1928	Rice
	1929	Honey

Source: Standing Committee on Agriculture (1980).

Despite these expressed concerns more statutory marketing authorities became established during the Second World War, and in the decades following the war they became the main means by which agricultural prices were established in Australia. Looking at some of the main Australian crops it is possible to see just how extensive this form of marketing control was.

1. Wheat. The Australian Wheat Corporation was established in 1939, the product of joint state and Australian government legislation. It operated a two-price scheme supported by an import tariff between 1939 and 1989. In 1989 its domestic monopoly was abolished, and since then it has had only acquisition powers for wheat that is exported. This export monopoly was abolished in 2008 (Table 5.3).
2. Dairy. The Australian Government operated a single desk export agency between 1925 and 2000. This body also raised a research/development/promotion levy. At the same time the state governments operated milk boards, which fixed domestic price and quotas for liquid milk between 1936 and 2000. In 2000 the whole industry was deregulated.
3. Wool. In the wool industry a research/development/promotion levy has been raised since 1936. A buffer stock scheme also operated in Australia between 1971 and 1991. No attempt has ever been made in the wool industry to operate a two-price scheme, mainly because most wool is exported.
4. Dried fruits. The Australian Government operated a single desk export board between 1925 and 1991. The state governments established domestic market boards in Victoria in 1925 and South Australia, New South Wales and Western Australia in 1928. The state boards were progressively phased out during the 1990s.
5. Sugar. Most of the sugar industry in Australia is located in Queensland. The Queensland Government has operated a single desk board from 1923. This scheme was phased out after 2007.
6. Meat. The Australian Government operated a single desk export board between 1925 and 1994. This board also raised a research/development/promotion levy during these years. The state governments operated meat boards in each state between 1936 and 1994 for domestic consumption.
7. Eggs. An Australian Government egg marketing export board operated between 1948 and 1989. State boards also operated at the same time to supply domestic consumption. The governments of New South Wales, South Australia and Queensland all abolished their boards in 1989, followed by the Government of Victoria in 1992.
8. Apples and pears. The Australian Government operated a single desk export board between 1938 and 1991.
9. Barley. A combined South Australian and Victorian single desk operated between 1939 and 2000. The Victoria market was deregulated in 2001. The domestic market was deregulated in South Australia in 1999, and export

monopoly in 2007. In New South Wales the Grains Board went into receivership in 2001, and in Western Australia and Queensland the Grainco and the Grain Pool were deregulated in 2008.

As can be seen from the examples, the interaction between state and Australian governments has complicated matters. Generally speaking, the model has been that the Australian Government operated the export desk and the various states operated acquisition boards for the domestic market. Only in the case of wheat were the Australian and state governments able to cooperate fully and establish a joint board that had full acquisition powers for both domestic and export markets.

In the late 1980s and early 1990s the Australian Government began to reduce its involvement in the statutory acquisition of agricultural produce. At the same time the Australian Government began to reduce tariffs on imports, which after all were essential to any two-price scheme that depended on inflated domestic market prices. By 1995 barley, cotton, fresh horticultural products, corn, wheat, wool, rice, meat and tobacco were all tariff free. By the end of the twentieth century citrus fruit, dairy produce, dried fruits, sugar and wine had also been added to the tariff free list.

At the state level the reduction in tariffs helped to unravel the various schemes. With imported produce potentially entering the country it became less possible to raise domestic prices, and so a number of the state boards were abolished. The statutory marketing authorities that tended to last the longest were the export grain boards and crops such as rice and sugar production, which are concentrated in a single state (New South Wales and Queensland respectively). The ones still surviving into the 2000s are listed in Table 5.3. In most of these cases even these have lost their compulsory acquisition powers. Through the 2000s payments were made to dairy, rice and sugar producers as transitional arrangements, but by the end of the decade only the dairy industry payments remained.

Assessment

After looking back over the history of the marketing bodies it is possible to make a judgement about whether government intervention and the operations of the statutory marketing authorities made any positive contribution to the wealth creation process at the national level.

To begin with there would seem to be more justification for government assistance for research and development expenditure at the production level compared to any other type of assistance. In the case of money spent on product development and promotional activities the danger of there being 'free riders' from producers in other countries is more likely. To some degree product developers, through the use of patents and licences for the products, can capture development innovations, and so there appears to be no justification for assistance at this level on the grounds that there are spillover effects. In the case of the wool levy there has in recent

TABLE 5.3 Marketing authorities/companies with single desk, Australia, 2000 to 2015

Australia	Single desk powers	Ownership
AWB Ltd	Wheat exports. Export monopoly ended in June 2008.	Publicly listed company with a portion of reserved shares for farmers. Sold to Canadian firm Agrium in 2011.
New South Wales		
NSW Grains Board	Malting barley in domestic market. Barley, oats, oilseed crops, grain sorghum exports.	Went into receivership in 2001.
Rice Marketing Board	NSW exports. Domestic market deregulated in 2006.	NSW government statutory marketing board.
South Australia		
ABB Grain Ltd	Barley exports. Export monopoly ended in 2007.	Publicly listed company with a portion of reserved shares for farmers. Sold in 2004.
Queensland		
Grainco	Barley exports. Export monopoly ended in 2008.	Publicly listed company owned by growers. Sold to GrainCorp in 2003.
Queensland Sugar Ltd	Queensland domestic seller and exporter of raw sugar. Monopoly ended 2007.	Company limited by guarantee, owned by growers and millers.
Western Australia		
Grain Pool Pty Ltd	Barley, canola and lupin exports. Monopoly ended 2008.	Owned by Cooperative Bulk Handling Ltd, which is in turn owned by growers.
Potato Marketing Corp.	Potatoes (deregulated in 2017)	Western Australian Government statutory marketing board.

years been a concentration of expenditure on innovation at the production level, with the former advertising and promotional spending being scrapped. This would appear to be recognition that the market failure characteristics are most likely at the level of scientific research into farming techniques.[4]

It would be difficult to claim that the two-price schemes were anything more than a device to redistribute income from consumers to producers – with resultant deadweight losses being created as with the case of tariffs on imported manufactured goods. No demonstrable market failure would appear to be involved, and these types of measures were in all likelihood simply the product of private interest groups' influence and therefore constitute a type of government failure.

Whether statutory marketing authorities could have taken advantage of imperfect markets is a little more problematic. Certainly there has been a range of studies that have attempted to establish that authorities have been able to extract monopoly rent from some markets.[5] On the whole it is unlikely that Australian producers could take advantage of any degree of market power given that in most cases Australian exporters make up such a small part of international markets. Use of this power in the past has been made more effectively by single desks in domestic markets, with significant costs to consumers. If there is scope for the marketing authorities to increase national income through the exploitation of their market power in international markets, then it could only very likely be the case in a very limited range of products in a very limited number of overseas markets for which Australia has some sort of advantage of proximity compared to other exporters. Certainly it is not an argument that justifies so extensive a range of marketing boards as existed in Australia's history.

Conclusion

The extensive government intervention into agricultural markets in Australia seems to be gradually becoming a thing of the past. With the possible exception of some research and development spillovers at the farm level and a weaker possibility that a very small number of statutory marketing authorities can take advantage of market power in some markets there appears to be little economic justification for government intervention on the scale of the past. On the whole the only result from the extensive intervention of the government into agricultural markets has been to transfer income from consumers and taxpayers to producers. This redistribution may have had some social justification but in economic terms would have led to the creation of some loss of allocative efficiency and creation of deadweight losses, which would have lowered overall national wealth. In the face of a continuing decline in the agricultural sector's terms of trade even these measures appear to have only slowed rather than turned around the decline in farm income. A growing realisation of this fact led to a gradual unwinding of the schemes during the 1980s. This took place in tandem with the decline in manufacturing tariffs, which saw reductions in agricultural tariffs as well.

One consequence of the unwinding of assistance to agriculture has been the growing interest on the part of agricultural lobby groups in the degree of competition that exists for other sectoral groups in Australia. As the level of assistance to agricultural groups declined, other forms of restrictions to competition in the economy began to appear less palatable to farmers. This trend combined with the interests of manufacturers, which also began to face stiffer levels of competition in the late 1980s as tariffs fell. Interest began to focus on the non-traded sector and the application of competition policy to all sectors of the Australian economy. This leads us to an analysis of the *Competition and Consumer Act* and the introduction of the National Competition Policy, which are the subjects of Chapters 7 and 8 respectively.

Notes

1 For an extensive account of statutory marketing authorities in Australia see Watson and Parish (1982); Industry Commission (1991); and Gropp et al. (2000).
2 An early attempt in the 1920s to inflate butter and cheese prices in Australia led to substantial imports from New Zealand. An import tariff on both products soon followed (Giblin 1928).
3 For a more extensive list see Gropp et al. (2000).
4 The Australian Government still raises levies on production and makes a contribution to a number of bodies that conduct agricultural research, development and promotion in such areas as wool, pork, wine grapes, dried fruit, sugar, horticulture, grains, dairy produce, cotton, meat, livestock and tobacco.
5 See for instance Meyers Strategy Group (1996) for barley; and the Sugar Industry Review Working Party (1996).

References

Australian Bureau of Agricultural and Resource Economics (ABARE) 2015, *Australian Commodities 2015*, ABARE, Canberra.
Australian Bureau of Agricultural and Resource Economics (ABARE) 2016, *Australian Farm Surveys 2015/16*, ABARE, Canberra.
Australian Bureau of Statistics (ABS) various issues, *Agriculture, Australia*, Cat. No. 7113.0, ABS, Canberra.
Australian Bureau of Statistics (ABS) various issues, *Australian National Accounts, National Income and Expenditure*, Cat. No. 5206.0, ABS, Canberra.
Australian Bureau of Statistics (ABS) various issues, *Value of Agricultural Commodities Produced, Australia*, Cat. No. 7503.0, ABS, Canberra.
Australian Wool Corporation–Bureau of Agricultural Economics 1987, *Returns from Wool Promotion in the United States: An AWC–BAE Analysis*, Occasional Paper No. 100, AGPS, Canberra.
Giblin, L.F. 1928, 'Some costs of marketing control', *Economic Record*, vol. 4, pp. 148–54.
Gropp, Lisa, Hallam, Tom and Manion, Vince 2000, *Single-Desk Marketing: Assessing the Economic Arguments*, Staff Research Paper, Productivity Commission, Melbourne.
Haszler, H.A., Edwards, G., Chisholm, A. and Hone, P. 1996, 'The wool debt: the wool stockpile and national interest: did the Garnaut Committee get it right?', *Economic Record*, vol. 72, pp. 260–71.
Industry Commission 1991, *Statutory Marketing Arrangements for Primary Products*, Report No. 10, March, Industry Commission, Canberra.
Knopke, P., Strappazzon, L. and Mullen, J. 1995, 'Productivity growth', *Australian Commodities*, vol. 2, no. 2, pp. 486–97.
Meyers Strategy Group 1996, *Economic Analysis of the Value of the Single Desk – Summary Report*, Meyers Strategy Group, Willoughby NSW.
Piggott, R. 1990, 'Agricultural marketing', in D.B. Williams (ed.), *Agriculture in the Australian Economy*, 3rd edn, Sydney University Press, Sydney, p. 240.

Piggott, R.H. 1992, 'Some old truths revisited', *Australian Journal of Resource and Agricultural Economics*, vol. 32, no. 2, pp. 117–40.

Shann, Edward 1930, *An Economic History of Australia*, Cambridge University Press, Cambridge.

Sieper, E. 1982, *Rationalizing Rustic Regulation*, Research Studies in Regulation No. 2, Centre for Independent Studies, St Leonards NSW.

Standing Committee on Agriculture 1980, *Statutory Marketing Authorities of Australia: A Compendium*, SCA Technical Report Series No. 9, CSIRO, Melbourne.

Sugar Industry Review Working Party 1996, *Sugar – Winning Globally*, DPIE, Brisbane.

Watson, A.S. and Parish, R.M. 1982, 'Marketing agricultural products', in D.B. Williams (ed.), *Agriculture in the Australian Economy*, 2nd edn, Sydney University Press, Sydney, pp. 223–39.

6

GOVERNMENT SUPPORT FOR RESEARCH AND DEVELOPMENT

Introduction

As markets became more open to competition because of the fall in tariffs and decline in support to farmers the government in Australia began to have a renewed look at the way in which it supported industrial development. One way in which governments decided to provide renewed assistance was in the form of the subsidy and granting of tax concessions on spending on research and development (R&D). Governments in Australia, at both the state and the national level, have a long history of involvement in the support of research that assists businesses. In Australia governments play an important role in supporting R&D by engaging in a range of activities. At the very basic level they do so by supporting the education and training of scientists and engineers and by funding high-value research that would not otherwise be undertaken by businesses, but is of assistance to businesses. They also contribute by funding research in universities and in other government research agencies. Not only does the Australian Government fund this sort of activity but state and territory governments also play an active role.

Before looking at this sort of assistance and seeing if it is economically rational, one must consider that spending on R&D is a type of investment by businesses that wish to gain from it a return. If government support of this spending is to enhance economic outcomes, however, it must have general characteristics that make it different from other types of investment. Part of the emphasis of this chapter will be to see if there is some degree of market failure or imperfection involved in the spending on R&D. Research and development is generally regarded as being:

> creative work undertaken on a systematic basis to increase the stock of knowledge including knowledge of man, culture and society, and the use of this stock of knowledge to devise new applications. Any activity classified

as research and experimental development is characterised by originality, should have investigation as a primary objective and should have the potential to produce results that are sufficiently general for humanity's stock of knowledge (theoretical and/or practical) to be recognisably increased.

(Australia, DEST 2005, p. 9)

In the business world R&D is undertaken with the intention that it will at some point provide the development of new applications even when there is no specific application apparent during the research phase. New product design and development is more often than not a crucial factor in the survival of a company and in the prosperity of a country over the longer term. In an industry that is fast changing, firms must continually revise their design and range of products. This is necessary because of continuous technology change and development as well as the impact of competitors on businesses' markets and the changing tastes of consumers. R&D, therefore, has a special role in enhancing the success of a company, and indeed a national economy as a whole.

R&D has a special economic significance apart from its conventional association with scientific and technological development. R&D investment generally reflects a government's or organization's willingness to forgo current operations or profit to improve future performance or returns, and its abilities to conduct research and development.

In general, R&D activities are conducted by specialised units or centres belonging to companies, universities and government agencies. In the context of business, R&D normally refers to future oriented, longer-term activities in science or technology, using similar techniques to scientific research without predetermined outcomes and with broad forecasts of commercial yield. In Australia most R&D is undertaken and self-financed by businesses themselves, although government agencies and universities are also important.

In this chapter we will look at the basis of this policy approach to see if there are any economic arguments for government support of R&D. The focus of this chapter will be on whether there were any substantial market failures or imperfections that may have justified government intervention of this sort.

R&D as an investment

The government has long had a role in the support of research into and the development of technology. Knowledge has both of the properties of a public good, so without some government intervention there will be underinvestment in research. The government encourages innovation by establishing intellectual property rights (through patents). Although patents thus allow innovators to appropriate some of the returns to their innovation, and thus provide incentives for the production of knowledge, they interfere with its efficient use. The patent system may impede innovation. The government also provides direct support for research, especially basic research, and indirect support through tax credits and the support of education – producing the scientists who are the critical input into research. Government programmes in support of technology are aimed at identifying areas in which there are large spillovers.

As R&D is a form of investment whereby businesses spend on R&D with the expectation of a future return, there needs to be some reason why this type of investment is different from other forms in terms of our previously defined market failures and imperfections.

In Australia, there have been two main rationales put forward for the public support of research and development. The first is that the public support of R&D gives assistance to the development of services provided by the public sector itself. This is particularly true in those areas of service provision where public delivery is most dominant (i.e. defence, health care, education, etc.). In this case the public sector is acting in a similar fashion to those businesses that spend on R&D. Public support in this case is just attempting to enhance the delivery of a set of services to the public.

The second rationale is that there are significant externalities or spillovers that flow from spending on research and development. It is possible in the case of spending on R&D that not all of the benefits of this spending are captured by the business undertaking it. This is especially true where the research conducted is of the most basic, fundamental type. If this is the case, there is an incentive for businesses to free-ride off the R&D activities of others and not to invest in R&D themselves.

The existence of these externalities on its own does not justify public funding or other types of support. Many investments that create externalities have sufficient private returns to provide sufficient incentives to investors. If that is the case, then the returns are sufficient to encourage investment. Indeed, most R&D expenditure in Australia is undertaken by companies that hope to realise sufficient gains from it to make the spending worthwhile. At the same time government can apply legal methods to enhance the ability of firms to reap the returns from their investments in R&D. One way that governments all around the world do this is to assign property rights to intellectual property through patents, trademarks and copyright. Even with these measures, however, it is difficult in some cases to capture all of the externalities through these types of measures.

It is because of these externalities that governments in Australia have been drawn into supporting R&D expenditure through subsidy and tax concessions. One additional problem, however, is that some of the externalities may flow overseas and not be capable of being captured by Australians. If the problem is that externalities are created and it is difficult for firms to capture then it is quite possible the same is true of government capturing, within the country, from government supported R&D. This means that public support of R&D, if it is to create the greatest value to the country, must be to those activities that generate substantial externalities but not to those where the externalities flow overseas. The identification of these types of R&D activities can be at times problematic, although not impossible.

In the case of R&D in agriculture, for instance, much effort is spent on solving problems faced by Australian farmers who face unique climatic and environmental conditions which mean that the externalities created are very regional in application. Nonetheless it is a problem that needs to be considered.

Origins

Governments in Australia have long had an interest in the promotion of research and development. At the state government level the agricultural departments of these governments first became interested in the funding and undertaking of research in farm related problems as far back as the 1890s. Farmers were regarded as simply not having the resources available to them to be able to engage successfully in this type of activity. Any individual farmer who did engage in this type of activity, if successful, would potentially create substantial advantages to many other farmers who might be able to free-ride off these efforts. Scientific research into farm related problems, therefore, has a long history in Australia, and the primary industry departments of the state governments are still actively engaged in this type of research.

After the federation of the colonies in 1901 the Australian Government also became involved when it established the precursor to CSIRO, the Advisory Council of Science and Industry, in 1916 at the initiative of Prime Minister Billy Hughes. In 1926 the *Science and Industry Research Act* established the Council for Scientific and Industrial Research Organisation (CSIRO) as a permanent body, and the agency has remained as one of the premier agencies of R&D in Australia to this day. Early in its existence, the CSIRO established divisions studying animal health and animal nutrition, but after the depression the CSIRO extended its activities into manufacturing. Other government agencies such as the Australian Nuclear Science and Technology Organisation and the Defence Science and Technology Organisation are also important government agencies engaged in R&D. In recent times governments have made funds available to industry groups like the automotive and clothing, footwear and textile industries to engage in R&D in response to falls in tariff protection. Generally, the sums made available have been worth far less to the industry than the protective tariffs were and have had sunset clauses attached to them, so making them transitional measures.

While the CSIRO was expanding its activities during the 1950s and 1960s Australian universities were becoming research based rather than just teaching institutions. Originally the universities in Australia were dependent on state government grants and had little capacity to engage in research. The Australian Government's first important involvement in supporting R&D in Australian universities occurred in the late 1940s when it created the mainly research focused Australian National University in Canberra. Its support was to spread to all universities in Australia during the 1950s. In 1957 the Murray Committee investigated the state of Australian universities on behalf of the Australian Government and found that they were overcrowded, short staffed, poorly housed and under-equipped.

Although demand for Australian university education had grown steadily in the mid- to late 1950s the state governments had found it difficult to raise the funds needed to support expansion of their universities. The Committee recommended that the Australian Government make a substantial contribution to funding so as to meet public demand. The Australian Government accepted the recommendations of the Murray Committee, and it was the intervention of the Australian Government in the form of capital grants to the states for higher education that led to the opening of many new universities in Australia during the 1960s. It also enabled the Australian universities to support a lot more scientific research in a number of fields, which has continued to the present day. Funding for higher education research accounts for a significant proportion of R&D spending in Australia (Productivity Commission 2007, p. xxix).

The third major type of government assistance to R&D comes in the form of tax concessions to business. Tax concessions were introduced in the mid-1980s and involved the granting of a 125 per cent concession on R&D expenditure. This tax concession is the largest single mechanism for government support of business R&D. It has an advantage over grant programmes in that it leaves firms with the flexibility to undertake the kinds of R&D suited to their own businesses rather than be dictated to by the wishes of government. One of its major limitations, however, is that it does not screen out R&D that businesses would have undertaken anyway. In fact, it is difficult to distinguish this from the R&D that it does encourage and would not have occurred in its absence. This type of approach was introduced during the 1980s, both because of the reduction in tariff protection that was occurring at the time and because it was felt that the R&D spending undertaken both by government agencies and by universities was not necessarily of the type demanded and used by businesses. By allowing businesses to make their own decisions about what type of R&D expenditure they wished to undertake it was felt that greater benefits would flow to the economy.

One final type of measure used by the government to promote research and development has been the compulsory levies that were mentioned in Chapter 5. Throughout the twentieth century both state governments and the Australian Government placed levies on farmers to raise money for spending on R&D. The compulsory nature of these levies was designed to overcome the free rider problem. Some of these levies still exist even though in most cases the single desk powers have been abolished.

Assessment

R&D expenditure in Australia is quite substantial. Gross domestic spending on R&D in Australia in 2012/13 was in total $26.0 billion (in current prices). This constituted around 2.2 per cent of gross domestic product. The trend has been for spending by Australia of R&D to rise (and as can be seen from Figure 6.2 the proportion of GDP devoted to R&D has doubled since the mid-1980s). Not all of this rise was brought about by the encouragement of government tax policies.

In addition, the growing complexity of modern Australian business and increased competition in Australian markets have helped to encourage Australian businesses to invest in R&D.

Although historically Australia spent less than most countries of the Organisation for Economic Co-operation and Development (OECD) on R&D, these days Australia is around average (see Figure 6.1). During the 1970s and early 1980s business R&D investment was very weak and Australia was regarded as being a country with a very low level of R&D expenditure. By the mid-2000s this situation had changed, and today Australia ranks in the middle of OECD countries in terms of R&D expenditure to GDP and active researchers to population. The country's contribution to scientific journals is solid, and patent numbers have been rising steadily.

Of this R&D spending figure just under 60 per cent was undertaken by private businesses, around one-quarter by the government and around 15 per cent by the universities (see Table 6.1). This proportion is slightly above the OECD average but by no means as high as that of countries like the United States, Japan or Germany.

R&D expenditure as a proportion of GDP has risen steadily since the mid-1980s, when it constituted only around 1.1 per cent of GDP (see Figure 6.2). This rise has been driven largely by a steady increase in business expenditure on R&D, which has risen at a much faster rate than government expenditure, which in turn has meant that the business proportion of R&D expenditure has risen from around one-third in the mid-1980s up to close to 60 per cent in the late 2000s. Direct government funding of research agencies has barely grown in real terms since the

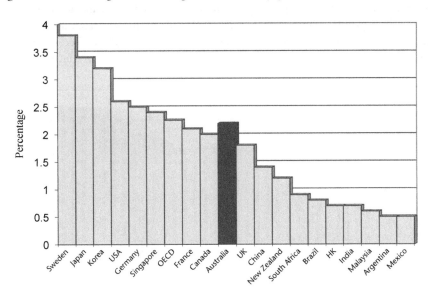

FIGURE 6.1 Proportion of GDP spent on research and development, various countries, 2014 (percentage)

Source: OECD (2014).

TABLE 6.1 Proportion of funding of R&D spending from various sources, various countries, 2010 (percentage)

	Business	Government	Higher education (government)	Higher education (funds)	Private non-profit
Australia	57.2	23.1	15.2	0.2	1.7
Canada	47.8	23.9	8.9	7.5	2.9
France	52.4	28.2	10.2	1.3	0.8
Germany	67.6	18.7	9.7	0.0	0.3
Japan	77.1	11.3	4.9	5.7	0.7
New Zealand	41.3	37.2	5.8	8.9	1.7
Singapore	58.3	36.4	0.0	0.9	0.0
Sweden	65.7	13.5	9.6	0.6	2.8
UK	45.2	22.9	9.0	1.3	4.6
USA	66.4	27.7	0.0	2.7	3.2

Source: OECD (2014).

mid-1980s compared with the strong growth in private sector spending. This has meant that there has been a shift in funding and spending on R&D in Australia over the longer term from government agencies to the private sector (see Figure 6.3).

Business R&D expenditure increased substantially between the mid-1980s and 2000s. The tax concession helped to lift R&D expenditure, but it was encouraged by a range of other factors as well. Competitive pressures on manufacturing and services industries as the economy was opened up to international competition helped to create additional incentives to business to invest in R&D. Initially business investment was concentrated on R&D spending in manufacturing, but gradually it switched more to the services sector. As business expenditure became a more important component of total R&D, this expenditure became more commercially focused and more skewed towards experimental development

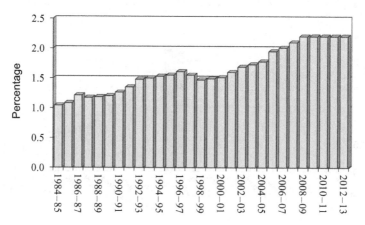

FIGURE 6.2 Proportion of GDP spent on R&D in Australia, 1984/85 to 2012/13 (percentage)

Source: ABS, Cat. No. 8112.0.

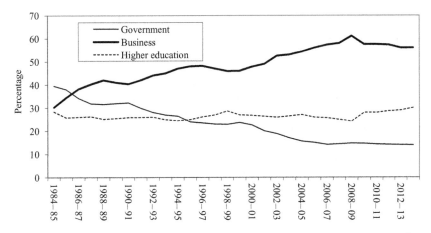

FIGURE 6.3 Proportion of gross expenditure on R&D by various sectors in Australia, 1984/85 to 2013/14 (percentage)

Source: ABS, Cat. No. 8112.0.

and applied research, which has assisted in Australian businesses becoming more internationally competitive.

The Productivity Commission conducted a review of the public support of science and innovation in Australia in the mid-2000s (Productivity Commission 2007; Shanks and Zheng 2006) and concluded that on balance the tax concessions and other support measures were advantageous to the Australian economy. It did, however, make some recommendations on improving the various measures. Given the basic problems involved in tracking and estimating the size and nature of externalities that flow from R&D it is unlikely that government policy will ever be settled on the issue of public support except, perhaps, to say that support in general is advantageous. One area that the Commission thought was particularly important was the education and training of scientists and other technical workers who could contribute to the R&D efforts of companies in Australia.

Conclusion

Although the support of R&D in Australia has for a long time been of interest to governments, over the past 20 years there has been a renewed interest in promoting this form of activity. With the phasing out of protective measures and the increase in competition in domestic markets from imports it was felt that Australian companies should be encouraged to undertake a greater effort in this field.

Since the mid-1980s the spending of Australian companies has increased steadily and brought Australia more into line with other OECD countries. The tax concession granted on R&D expenditure certainly encouraged this to occur but so too did the enhanced level of competition in Australian markets, which has pushed Australian companies to become more innovative.

References

Australia, Department of Education, Science and Training (DEST) 2005, *Definition and Methodological Notes – Statistics on Science and Innovation*, DEST, Canberra.

Australian Bureau of Statistics (ABS) various issues, *Research and Experimental Development: All Sector Summary*, Cat. No. 8112.0, ABS, Canberra.

Organisation for Economic Co-operation and Development (OECD) 2014, *OECD Science, Technology and Industry Outlook, 2014*, OECD, Paris.

Productivity Commission 2007, *Public Support for Science and Innovation: Research Report*, Productivity Commission, Melbourne.

Shanks, S. and Zheng, S. 2006, *Econometric Modelling of R&D and Australia's Productivity*, Productivity Commission Staff Working Paper, Productivity Commission, Canberra.

7
TRADE PRACTICES

Introduction

The lowering of tariff barriers to imports intensified the degree of competition faced by Australian manufacturers and farmers in the domestic market. This increase in competition did not however affect all of the Australian economy, as a great deal of economic activity does not directly compete with imports. The retail trades, the building industry, domestic transport industries and a number of other industries are non-traded goods in that they operate within the domestic economy and do not face competition from imported goods or services. At the same time as tariff barriers were lowered, domestic competition in non-traded goods was intensified by the application of laws that outlawed anti-competitive conduct.

In Australia, these competition laws are referred to as 'trade practices'. The *Trade Practices Act 1974* (replaced in 2010 by the *Competition and Consumer Act*) consisted of a set of laws that are primarily designed to promote competition and therefore economic efficiency. Competition enables markets to direct resources to the uses that will best satisfy consumers. Competition also puts pressure on companies to operate at close to levels of productive efficiency, and finally it allows for the entrance into markets of new companies that perhaps have innovation ideas and products. The purpose of the Act was to ensure that competition is fair, that there are no artificial barriers to entry into any business, that society's limited resources are effectively used and that consumers have available a wide range of goods at competitive prices.

By preserving the integrity of markets the Act made it less necessary for the government to arrogate to itself the function of deciding what gets produced, where and by whom. It makes it unnecessary for governments to set prices, allocate resources and generally intervene in business affairs.

The purpose of this chapter is to discuss the rationale behind the application today of the *Competition and Consumer Act* and its importance in creating a climate that promotes competition and therefore economic efficiency. It is not the intention to deal exhaustively with all the sections of the Act but to deal simply with a few of its more important sections. To begin with, the rationale behind the Act is examined. This is followed by a description of the Act's origins and structure, and finally some practical applications of the Act are given.

Markets

The notion that competitive individual behaviour promotes the public good is by no means a recent one and was expounded by Adam Smith as long ago as 1776. In the *Wealth of Nations*, he described rational man as minding his own business but at the same time being 'led by an invisible hand' to promote the larger interests of society. The view, therefore, is that if people are actively able to pursue their own personal interests they will maximise the wealth of any community. More modern economists have described it in this way: 'competition is superior not only because it is in most circumstances the most efficient method known but even more because it is the only method known by which our activities can be adjusted without coercive or arbitrary intervention of authority' (Hayek 1944).

Alexander Pope, however, described it more poetically as being a case where: 'God and nature link'd the general frame, and bade self-love and social be the same' (in Shenefield and Stelzer 2001, p. 5). In a competitive market economy, this process occurs where numerous sellers vie for customers and therefore must produce goods and services of sufficient quality and at acceptable prices or be driven out of business. This necessity forces them to be efficient: to buy inputs (labour, capital and materials) at the lowest possible price and to use them in such a way that production costs are kept at a minimum. Adam Smith, however, recognised that it was not merely private enterprise that was important but competitive private enterprise that was the source of growth and the wealth creation process. He understood the dangers of allowing private individuals to collude and thereby set prices at monopoly levels. 'People of the same trade seldom meet together, even for merriment and diversion, but the conversation ends in a conspiracy against the public, or in some contrivance to raise prices' (Smith 1776). Where competition fails, governments have three choices if they wish to reduce the scope of the extraction of monopoly rents by suppliers. They can regulate the firms concerned, take them over directly or restore competition through the enforcement of legislation that prohibits anti-competitive conduct.

In a small economy like Australia's the tendency toward anti-competitive conduct is probably more acute than in larger countries. In a small country if the government took no action it would probably lead to the creation of a collusive arrangement between the small number of producers in any industry and therefore the extraction of monopoly rents. If an oligopoly of a small number of firms can collude on price, then it can create the conditions of monopoly. Another tendency might be for a dominant firm to gradually force out of business its rivals and then create a monopoly, which can then take advantage of consumers.

Figure 7.1 illustrates the standard depiction of the problem associated with monopoly. A monopoly has the capacity to raise prices above the marginal cost of production by restricting output (in this case up to P_2). In doing so the monopoly maximises profit by transferring a portion of the possible consumer surplus to itself. In the process wealth is diminished because of the reduction in allocative efficiency. In other words, there are some consumers who would have been willing to pay a price that covers the marginal cost of production but are denied the opportunity to do so, as they are unwilling to pay the monopoly price (P_2) (Corones 1999).

The objective of the *Competition and Consumer Act* is to prevent oligopoly companies from acting in this fashion and dominant companies from attaining monopoly positions in markets. In most markets, the creation of perfect competition is probably not attainable or even desirable if there exist economies of scale. Workable competition is the general objective, with a reasonable number of firms actively competing with each other and thereby being responsive to the desires of consumers (Abelson 2012, chap. 14).

Competition laws like the *Trade Practices Act* and the *Competition and Consumer Act* have only been enforced in a meaningful way in Australia since the mid-1970s. They do however have a long history in the United States, and therefore when the Australian legislation was enacted it leaned heavily on the American example.

Origins

In the United States competition law is usually referred to as anti-trust law. This is because in the nineteenth century companies acting in collusion associated with each other under the ownership of trusts. The first anti-trust law was the Sherman Act, which was passed in 1890. The approach of the Americans was to list in

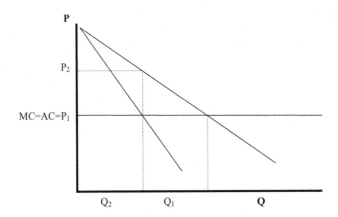

FIGURE 7.1 Monopoly solution

this Act, in broad terms, activities that the government wished to prohibit. The detail of the principles by which the law was to be applied was, however, left to the courts to interpret. The Sherman Act was passed at a time when there was mounting concern about the accelerating trend towards monopolisation in many American industries. Not only was it felt that there were economic gains to be had from maintaining a competitive structure but there was also a desire to limit the political power of large-scale, concentrated companies (Thorelli 1992).

Turning to the Sherman Act itself, section 1 prohibits contracts, combinations or conspiracies in restraint of trade. The most obvious instance of this was where companies fixed prices and market shares. The Clayton Act, which was passed in 1914, made it illegal to compel a supplier or customer to deal exclusively with a firm. The Clayton Act also made predatory pricing illegal. Predatory pricing is the practice of pricing below cost so as to drive out new entrants or bankrupt rivals in order to monopolise the market. The last innovation of the Clayton Act was that it prohibited mergers and acquisitions by companies if they 'substantially lessened competition' or 'tended to create a monopoly'. Together the main provisions of the Sherman and Clayton Acts have been copied in a variety of forms and have become the main provisions of competition laws in most countries – including Australia (Posner 2001; Shenefield and Stelzer 2001).

In the American case the main purpose of the anti-trust laws has been interpreted to be to prevent monopolistic behaviour, which reflects an economic objective designed to enhance consumer welfare by preventing practices that reduce competition. The proscription of cartels and various practices that are condemned if their effect is 'substantially to lessen competition, or tend to create a monopoly' would appear to reflect this concern with economic outcomes. Some have argued that the enhancement of consumer welfare should be the exclusive goal of the anti-trust laws (Bork 1978). Generally speaking, the promotion of competition and thereby efficiency has been the paramount objective of the American anti-trust laws, but from time to time there has also been a concern that there should be a diffusion of private power and maximum opportunities for individual enterprise (Shenefield and Stelzer 2001).

Australia's first experience of competition law came soon after the passing of the Sherman Act. In 1906 the Australian Parliament passed the *Australian Industries Preservation Act*. This Act was modelled on the Sherman Act and prohibited 'injurious combinations in restraint of trade in interstate and foreign commerce, and among foreign corporations or trading or financial corporations formed in Australia'. It was passed in Australia at a time when a number of quite public cartel arrangements in the coal and shipping industries were of concern to many. Soon after its passing important sections of the Act were declared invalid by the High Court (Sawer 1956). With no legal prohibition against the creation of price fixing cartels this form of arrangement became quite common. By the 1960s Australia had a very high incidence of cartels' anti-competitive agreements.

Australia's next attempt at the passing of competition law was not to occur until the 1960s. In 1965 the *Trade Practices Act* was passed. This Act dealt with agreements which restricted competition between firms supplying a market, covering for example market sharing, price fixing and exclusive dealing (Nieuwenhuysen 1976). This Act was rarely acted upon, and it is the *Trade Practices Act* of 1974 that was the main competition law in Australian history. As part of this legislation the Trade Practices Commission was established, with the job of monitoring restrictive trade practices and prosecuting outstanding cases in the courts. Private litigation is also still possible under the Act and – as in most countries with competition – law is the main way in which prosecutions are brought about.

Before 1995 not all parts of the legislation applied to the service sector or to firms that are not corporations (that is, small businesses, professional bodies and state enterprises). The legal responsibilities of the Australian Government are restricted to 'corporations law', so until 1995 businesses that were not incorporated were excluded from the Act. State government utilities were also exempt from the Act. Amendments to the Act in 1995 and supporting state government legislation extended the *Trade Practices Act* to all businesses. This approach was continued in the 2010 legislation.

Under the Act the Trade Practices Commission – and after 1995 its successor organization, the Australian Competition and Consumer Commission – can bring cases against companies that breach the Act to the Federal Court. The Trade Practices Commission was also given the right to authorise some practices if it was convinced they are in the public interest. The Trade Practices Commission – and now the Australian Competition and Consumer Commission – was also involved in giving administrative guidance on practices that are proposed. It can for instance assess applications for authorisation of practices that contravene the Act but are in the public interest. This 'prohibition with exemption' approach was modelled on Article 85 of the Treaty of Rome, which established the European Economic Community and is not a part of American anti-trust law.

The interested parties settle most trade practice cases out of court. Settlement often takes the form of agreements by the defendant to pay damages in order to avoid a trial. The damages are usually less than those claimed by the plaintiff. Also, the defendant might agree not to act in a particular fashion in the future. In recent times the Australian Competition and Consumer Commission has also been responsible for the enforcement of the consumer protection provisions of state legislation and the consumer protection provisions of the *Competition and Consumer Act* (Part V: False and misleading advertising, pyramid schemes, etc.).

That then is the general background to the nature of the Act. What is more interesting is its actual structure and the detail of some of the more important cases that have been brought.

Structure of the Competition and Consumer Act

The most important sections of the *Competition and Consumer Act* are contained in Part IV of the Act, which deals with restrictive trade practices.

Section 45 in Part IV of the Act deals with the case of collusion between firms. This section makes illegal horizontal anti-competitive agreements between firms on prices and market sharing as well as bid rigging and collective refusals to deal. The general economic rationale for making price fixing illegal is not that it leads to higher prices but that it restricts output, causing a deadweight loss without any offsetting gain to producers.

In practice collusion is probably not as common as might be expected. It is often undermined by the incentive to cheat on agreements. A reduction in costs by one company for instance might encourage it to attempt to undercut its rivals and break any agreement. A collapse in demand during a recession might encourage firms to regain sales by reducing prices. You will recall from the previous chapter that early attempts to establish agricultural prices through voluntary associations failed because of the tendency of a number of farmers to stay outside the associations.

Section 46 of the Act deals with the misuse of market power, or predatory pricing as it is also known. This is the practice of attempting to eliminate a competitor, prevent new entry or deter entry by pricing below cost, refusing to deal because of exclusionary arrangements, denying access to essential facilities, refusing to supply or refusing to allow reasonable access to spare parts, manuals and so on. For a prosecutor to win this sort of case it must show that the company has substantial market power and that it used that power for the purpose of eliminating a competitor. The degree of market power must be substantial, as otherwise it would not be possible for the 'predator' to monopolise the market. In these sorts of cases indicators of market power such as market share, barriers to entry, product differentiation, brand names, and extent of vertical integration are normally cited.

These cases can be very difficult to determine. Distinguishing between firms that are simply good at competing with their rivals, which is welfare enhancing to the economy, and those that are engaging in predatory pricing can be difficult. Often the lower prices of a dominant firm are simply a reflection of its greater level of efficiency. Acting to penalise a company through the use of the Act for its greater level of efficiency could be potentially damaging to the economy.

Section 47 of the Act deals with the vertical restraint known as exclusive dealing. This arises when a supplier imposes conditions for the supply of goods and services which restrict the freedom of the purchaser. The Australian Competition and Consumer Commission can authorise such actions if it regards them as giving specific and substantial benefits to the public and not leading to a lessening of competition. The other vertical restraint that is illegal is the practice of resale price maintenance (section 48). Under this provision a supplier cannot tell a retailer what price it wishes to on-sell a product at.

It was mentioned earlier that the Clayton Act had a provision that prohibited mergers and acquisitions that led to a substantial lessening of competition. The *Competition and Consumer Act* in section 50 has a similar provision. Mergers normally occur because of one of two reasons. Either the companies want to achieve greater economies of scale and therefore improve their efficiency levels or alternatively they wish to establish some degree of market power. Obviously, the former is a desirable outcome and the latter is not. Potential efficiency gains from a merger need to be traded off against the potential for monopoly pricing. Figure 7.2 displays the dilemma faced by the Australian Competition and Consumer Commission when it has judge whether a merger should occur. Imagine average costs to begin with are at ACo. If the market is competitive then price will be competed down towards the level Po. If the firms in the industry aim to merge, then it could lead to either a lowering of average unit costs – i.e. they could be lowered to AC_1 – or the creation of a monopoly that is able to extract monopoly rents by raising prices to P_2. Sometimes it is possible that both might occur.

Further provisions in the Act seek to protect consumers from false and misleading advertising. In terms of market theory, the justification for consumer protection is that it results in a more efficient allocation of resources. If consumers are deprived of full information about some goods and services, commodity bundles may be incorrectly ranked and therefore the consumer may not be able to maximise satisfaction from a given budget. Most state governments also have laws that seek to protect consumers from misleading and deceptive practices.

The *Competition and Consumer Act* establishes four organisations with a role in administering the Act. Part II establishes the Australian Competition and Consumer Commission, Part IIA establishes the National Competition Council, Part III establishes the Australian Competition Tribunal and Part IIIAA establishes the Australian Energy Regulator. The Australian Federal Court has the jurisdiction to determine private and public complaints made regarding contraventions of the Act. The Australian Competition and Consumer Commission, under the Act, also regulates certain industries by providing access to national infrastructure. The Australian Competition and Consumer Commission also has an educative role and seeks to educate both consumers and businesses as to their rights and responsibilities under the Act. The Australian Energy Regulator is a constituent but separate part of the Australian Competition and Consumer Commission and is responsible for economic energy regulation. It shares staff and premises with the

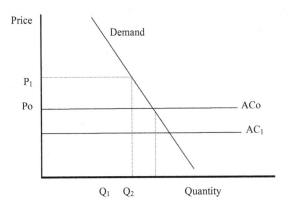

FIGURE 7.2 Benefits and costs of a merger

Australian Competition and Consumer Commission, but has a separate board, although at least one board member must also be a commissioner at the Australian Competition and Consumer Commission.

Given these main provisions of the Act let us now turn to a few recent applications of it.

Some results

Collusion (price fixing) (section 45A)

Trade Practices Commission v TNT Australia Pty Ltd, Mayne Nickless and Ansett Transport Industries (1995)

This was the largest and most complex case ever undertaken by the old Trade Practices Commission. The three major freight express companies listed above were found to have run a cartel from the 1970s to the early 1990s. Their conduct included: agreeing not to compete against one another in terms of prices; agreeing that, where one of the companies had an existing customer, other members of the cartel would not submit quotes to that customer or, if they did, it would be at a higher price; and agreeing in the event of a customer changing between cartel members that the new carrier would reimburse the old carrier. Alternatively, the new carrier would force a customer back by providing poor service (burning the customer). Mayne Nickless ended up having to pay $7.7 million in penalties and costs, TNT $5.175 million and Ansett $1.975 million. The penalties that could be imposed in these cases were increased after this case and today involve up to $10 million for a company and $500,000 for an individual manager.

Australian Competition and Consumer Commission v Roche Vitamins Australia, BASF Australia Ltd and Aventis Animal Nutrition Pty Ltd (2001)

On 1 March 2001, following proceedings instituted by the Australian Competition and Consumer Commission, the Federal Court imposed recommended penalties totalling $26 million against three animal vitamin suppliers for price fixing and market sharing in breach of the *Trade Practices Act*. Penalties were imposed against Roche Vitamins Australia ($15 million), BASF Australia Ltd ($7.5 million) and Aventis Animal Nutrition Pty Ltd ($3.5 million). The companies' conduct included operating a global anti-competitive agreement between their multinational parent corporations. The Australian Competition and Consumer Commission's investigation followed successful actions by overseas competition agencies. The Australian Competition and Consumer Commission and the Australian companies jointly recommended that the court impose penalties in the amounts set out above.

Australian Competition and Consumer Commission v Visy Group (2007)

On 2 November 2007, following proceedings instituted by the Australian Competition and Consumer Commission, the Federal Court imposed a $36 million fine on Richard Pratt and the Visy Group. Visy and Pratt were found guilty of price fixing in the packaging industry with Visy's rival company Amcor.

Predatory pricing (misuse of market power by a corporation with a substantial degree of monopoly power in a market) (section 46)

Australian Competition and Consumer Commission v Boral Ltd and Boral Masonry Ltd (formerly Boral Besser Masonry Ltd) (1999)

It was alleged that Boral Masonry reduced prices in Melbourne below its manufacturing costs and continued to do so to drive an efficient new independent entrant, C&M Bricks Pty Ltd, out of business. After the Federal Court held that Boral Masonry had not contravened section 46 the Australian Competition and Consumer Commission appealed to the Full Court of the Federal Court in November 1999. The Full Court unanimously held that Boral Masonry had contravened section 46 but dismissed the appeal against Boral Ltd. The Full Court found that Boral Masonry had a substantial degree of market power in concrete masonry products in Melbourne, that it had taken advantage of that power in pricing below manufacturing costs and that this had been done for the purpose of deterring new entrants and driving competitors out of the market.

Exclusive dealing (section 47)

Australian Competition and Consumer Commission v Health Partners Inc. (1997)

Health Partners Inc. is a health fund that gave notice terminating a pharmacy which participated in the fund's scheme to provide discounts to members because the pharmacy had withdrawn from a particular buying group. The company was found to have breached section 47 even though the termination notice was withdrawn.

Mergers (section 50)

Commonwealth Bank of Australia/Colonial Ltd

On 26 May 2000, the Australian Competition and Consumer Commission decided it would not oppose the proposed acquisition of Colonial Ltd by the

Commonwealth Bank of Australia subject to undertakings. The Australian Competition and Consumer Commission concluded that, in the product categories of retail insurance, retail investment and retirement savings, wholesale funds management and large corporate banking, the proposed acquisition was unlikely to lessen competition to any significant degree. The Australian Competition and Consumer Commission did however seek the divestiture of the combined company of Colonial's holdings in the Trust Bank of Tasmania on the grounds that it would significantly reduce competition in deposit/term products in Tasmania, where the Commonwealth Bank already had a significant market share.

Australian Competition and Consumer Commission v Pioneer International Ltd (1996)

Penalties totalling $4.8 million were imposed in relation to acquisitions in the south-east of Queensland for the production and supply of concrete masonry blocks, which had the effect of removing the third largest producer from the market and led to increased prices. The respondent gave undertakings to inform the Australian Competition and Consumer Commission if it intended to acquire any competitors in the market in the future.

Conclusion

The purpose of the *Competition and Consumer Act* in Australia is to promote competition in markets, which it is hoped will improve efficiency. Australia has been far less influenced by the notion that diffusion of economic and therefore social power is a good thing in itself, as has been the case in the United States of America.

Not only is the Act important for the prosecutions that are carried out but probably more importantly it helps to deter anti-competitive conduct and to help create a culture where price fixing and market sharing are not encouraged. Before the 1970s these sorts of conduct were quite common. In some ways, the *Competition and Consumer Act* is a reinforcement of the lower-tariff regime that has been implemented since the 1980s. The two policies act together to create competitive conditions in the Australian market and prevent misallocations of resources that can occur because of abuses of market power. In doing so they attempt effectively to prevent market failures created by a lack of competition in markets.

It should be remembered, however, that the *Trade Practices Act* before 1995 did not apply to large sections of the Australian economy. Government businesses, the professions and small businesses were all exempt. As large sections of the economy were opened up to competition in the late 1980s and early 1990s attention began to focus on those sectors of the economy that were exempt from the Act. This then is the subject of the following chapter, where we look at the development of the National Competition Policy.

References

Abelson, Peter 2012, *Public Economics: Principles and Practice*, McGraw-Hill, Sydney.
Bork, Robert H. 1978, *The Antitrust Paradox*, Free Press, New York.
Corones, S.G. 1999, *Competition Law in Australia*, LBC Information Services, Sydney.
Hayek, F.A. 1944, *The Road to Serfdom*, Routledge, London.
Nieuwenhuysen, J.P. (ed.) 1976, *Australian Trade Practice: Readings*, Croom Helm, London.
Posner, Richard 2001, *Antitrust Law*, 2nd edn, University of Chicago Press, Chicago IL.
Sawer, Geoffrey 1956, *Australian Federal Politics and Law 1901–1929*, Melbourne University Press, Carlton VIC.
Shenefield, John H. and Stelzer, Irwin 2001, *The Anti-Trust Laws: A Primer*, 4th edn, AEI, Washington DC.
Smith, Adam 1776, *An Inquiry into the Nature and Causes of the Wealth of Nations*, W. Strahan and T. Cadell, London.
Thorelli, H.B. 1992, *The Federal Anti-Trust Policy Origination of an American Tradition*, Johns Hopkins Press, Baltimore MD.

8
NATIONAL COMPETITION POLICY

Introduction

As mentioned previously competition policy really only began in Australia in 1974 with the passing of the *Trade Practices Act* by the Australian Government. This Act proscribed anti-competitive conduct but was restricted in its scope and did not apply to government owned businesses (most of which were owned by state governments), unincorporated businesses and the professions (e.g. lawyers, doctors and pharmacists), and in areas where Australian or state government legislation restricted competition (for example such things as postal services and milk).

These exemptions from the *Trade Practices Act* came to an end in 1995 when the Competition Principles Agreement came into force. The agreement was a joint agreement between the Australian, state and territory governments to pass supporting legislation that opened up all areas of the economy to competition. One noteworthy aspect of the agreement was that it opened up many of the government owned businesses to intensified competition. This meant that there had to be constructed a complex approach to dealing with government facilities that were monopoly businesses. A further aspect was that there is now provision for all government regulation that impedes competition to be periodically reviewed to determine if it is in the public interest.

The purpose of this chapter is to look at the nature of the National Competition Policy and its implications for the Australian economy. In particular, the implications in terms of the review process that has been put into place to judge whether government regulation that impedes competition is in the public interest will be examined.

Background

During the 1980s competition in Australian markets was increased by the lowering of tariff and quota barriers to import competition and the deregulation of the banking sector. This increase in competition in the private sector led to a questioning of the barriers to competition that existed with government owned business enterprises, many of which were important providers to business of factor inputs (i.e. telecommunications, energy, post and transport). The lack of competition in this sector meant that the level of efficiency was lower than industry best practice and prices were higher than they needed to be.

Concern was further heightened by the collapse in the terms of trade after 1984/85 and the slowdown of productivity growth from the 1970s onwards. Figure 8.1 illustrates the Australian terms of trade over a 20-year period. As can be seen from Figure 8.1 the terms of trade dipped downwards sharply in the mid- to late 1980s. At the same time the decade of the 1980s was one of slow productivity growth, which weakened the position of Australian exporters and competitors of importers.

The decision on the part of the Australian Government and state governments was to further extend competition to all sectors of the economy so as to put increased pressure on industries to improve levels of efficiency.

In economies there is perceived to be a relationship between the structure (concentration, barriers to entry), conduct (innovativeness, pricing, cost levels) and performance of companies. Thus, many buyers and sellers and low barriers to entry were assumed to promote competitive rivalry, which in turn tended to keep prices down, eliminate excess profits and promote economic efficiency and technological progress. A competitive market structure with low barriers to entry, therefore, will lead to economic conduct that involves low costs and prices, innovation and a tendency toward economic efficiency and solid productivity growth.

Productivity is simply the amount of output per unit of input achieved by a firm, industry or country. This may be per unit of a particular factor of production,

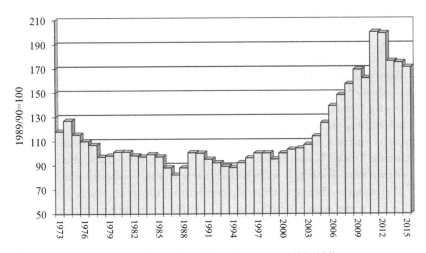

FIGURE 8.1 Terms of trade, Australia, 1973 to 2015 (1989/90=100)

Source: ABS, Cat. No. 5302.0.

for example labour employed, or total factor productivity, which entails the aggregating of the different factor inputs (land, labour and capital). Outputs and inputs are generally aggregated by weighting them according to the prices of the various outputs and inputs. Productivity growth is then the ratio of the output index to the input index. Productivity can be increased by longer hours of work, economies of scale, improved technology, improved skill, better management of resources and fuller use of capacity.

The stagnating performance of the Australian economy in the 1970s was attributed by many economists to the protection from competition of large sectors of the economy. It was felt protected businesses had little incentive to reduce costs and prices, produce new innovative products and use resources as efficiently as possible.

Reform process

The concern about the contribution made by the government owned businesses led in the late 1980s to a re-evaluation of their structure and ownership. The Industries Assistance Commission investigated the pricing and productivity levels of government owned business enterprises during the late 1980s, and this activity was continued into the 1990s by the Industries Commission and the Bureau of Industry Economics (Industries Assistance Commission 1989; Industry Commission 1991b, 1998; BIE 1992a, 1992b, 1995).

These reviews found that in many instances government businesses added considerably to costs and prices by overstaffing and excessive capital investment. Considerable cross-subsidisation of classes of customers also occurred, which distorted investment decisions.

Initially all of the state and territory governments embarked on their respective reform agendas separately. The process towards reform to competition was restricted by the divided responsibilities between the Australian and state governments, and eventually it was decided to take a joint approach.

In 1992 the Council of Australian Governments (comprising the state, territory and Australian governments) commissioned Professor Fred Hilmer to chair an independent committee of inquiry into a national competition policy. The report proposed a number of changes. Its general approach, however, was to regard the heightening of the degree of competition in Australian markets as the best approach (Australia, Independent Committee of Inquiry into Competition Policy in Australia 1993). '[Competition policy] is not about the pursuit of competition for its own sake. Rather, it seeks to facilitate effective competition in the interests of economic efficiency while accommodating situations where competition does not achieve economic efficiency or conflicts with other social objectives' (Australia, Independent Committee of Inquiry into Competition Policy in Australia 1993). Subsequently the Australian and state governments agreed to the Competition Principles Agreement in April 1995, and legislation was enacted in each state and territory and at the national level to carry out the recommendations of the Hilmer Report. All jurisdictions agreed that the principles should also apply to local governments.

Competition Principles Agreement 1995

The agreement between the Australian and state governments had several aspects to it.

- First, it included a broadening of the anti-competitive provisions of the *Trade Practices Act* to include professions, services and government enterprises (state government and Australian Government owned). Any firm seeking exemptions to the Act had to be subjected to a public interest test. This change meant that virtually all businesses were brought under the Act.
- All regulatory restrictions were to be periodically reviewed based on whether they were in the 'public interest', and these were linked to competition payments from the Australian Government. The benefits of the restrictions to the community as a whole had to outweigh the costs, and the restrictions had to be necessary to attain the benefits.
- A national access regime was put in place to enable competing businesses to use nationally significant infrastructure (like airports, electricity wires, gas pipelines and railway lines). Where there were elements that had natural monopoly characteristics (either private or public), these became the subject of price regulation in order to promote greater access to the 'bottleneck' facility and thereby promote competition in related markets. Chapter 9 takes up this aspect of the National Competition Policy in more detail.
- Under the agreement the governments agreed to establish independent price review bodies for natural monopoly elements. These were to set prices at levels that represented an efficient resource allocation. Chapter 10 will look at the issue of price regulation and the various methods that have been applied. If a state government did not do this, then there was scope for the Australian Government to take over this responsibility.
- Competitive neutrality was introduced so that privately owned businesses could compete with those owned by the government on an equal footing.
- There was general agreement on structural separation of regulatory and business functions in government run business.
- Three bodies were established: a competition enforcer (the Australian Competition and Consumer Commission), a policy adviser (the National Competition Council) and a tribunal of appeal (the Australian Competition Tribunal). The Australian Competition and Consumer Commission took over the role of the Trade Practices Commission as well as regulatory responsibilities in gas/electricity transmission and telecommunications and airports

price regulation. The role of the National Competition Council is to assess the government's progress on implementing competition reforms and to make recommendations to the Australian Government's Treasurer as to the level of competition payments, as well as to tender advice on the design and coverage of the access rules under the National Competition Policy.

One of the most important aspects of the National Competition Policy is that it changed the regulatory focus in Australia away from what interest groups demand and toward what is in the public interest. The National Competition Policy provides strict limitations on what governments can do to restrict competition and creates an environment for freer access to facilities owned by government owned enterprises. In many ways, it establishes competition and efficiency as the norms against which public policy is judged.

The purpose of the policy was never to enforce privatisation of government owned businesses, but it does make it considerably more difficult for them to operate profitably. By exposing them to competition it encourages them to operate more efficiently, but it also places greater risks on their operation.

The impact of the National Competition Policy has been very far reaching in its implications. Today the continual assessment of government regulation to determine if it is in the public interest puts pressure on governments not to act in the interest of private groups as well as opens up government regulation to a great deal more transparency and accountability. Assessing the impact on the Australian economy is a little more difficult, as the performance of the Australian economy is influenced by a range of factors. Nonetheless there has been an improvement in the performance of the Australian economy in terms of productivity growth through the 1990s, a part of which must be attributed to the application of the National Competition Policy.

From Table 8.1 it can be seen that the 1990s were a decade of considerable improvement in growth of productivity in Australia. Increasing the level of

TABLE 8.1 Average total factor productivity (multi-factor productivity) growth, Australia, 1964/65 to 2009/10 (percentage, per annum)

	Gross domestic product growth	Multi-factor productivity growth
1964/65 to 1968/69	5.68	1.2
1968/69 to 1973/74	5.40	1.5
1973/74 to 1981/82	2.98	1.0
1981/82 to 1984/85	3.06	0.8
1984/85 to 1988/89	4.22	0.4
1988/89 to 1993/94	2.35	0.7
1993/94 to 1999/2000	4.30	1.8
2000/01 to 2009/10	3.20	0.7

Source: ABS, Cat. Nos 5234.0, 5204.0.

Note: GDP is growth in constant dollar GDP; multi-factor productivity is for the non-farm market sector.

competition was important to improving Australia's productivity performance because it sharpened incentives for businesses to be more productive.

In the years 1988/89 to 1993/94 there is evidence of relatively strong productivity growth in agriculture, mining and manufacturing. This was in response to the reduction in tariffs and agricultural support schemes. Strong performers later include communications, electricity, gas and water. This took place in response to the reform of the largely government owned microeconomic reform process.

This growth in productivity meant that the average standard of living grew throughout the 1990s at a rate higher than previously. Table 8.2 gives data for the growth in real GDP per capita over the period 1950 to 2010. It also gives figures for a number of other countries as well as the OECD average. One of the interesting aspects of the figures is that Australian growth in real GDP per capita was below the OECD average in the 1950s, 1960s, 1970s and 1980s. This trend was reversed during the 1990s. During the 1990s the standard of living in Australia rose relative to the other members of the OECD for the first time since the Second World War. Part of this was probably due to the improvements associated with the application of the National Competition Policy.

The implications of the National Competition Policy are very widespread and it would be difficult to cover all aspects of it in a single chapter. Aspects of the policy are covered in the next two chapters, particularly where it comes to the issues of government owned businesses, regulation of monopoly facilities and national access regimes. As these aspects of the policy are covered in the following chapters it would seem more appropriate to present an example here of the application of a different aspect of the National Competition Policy. One industry that was extensively reviewed under the framework of the National Competition Policy was the dairy industry. By the end of the 1990s the industry had been entirely deregulated. Looking at how this took place is instructive.

TABLE 8.2 Growth in real GDP per capita, various countries, 1950 to 2010 (percentage, per annum)

	1950–73	*1973–90*	*1990–2001*	*2002–2010*
United States	2.42	1.94	2.04	1.22
Japan	7.75	2.92	1.05	1.64
Canada	2.70	1.84	1.16	1.05
New Zealand	1.71	0.59	1.40	1.26
Germany	4.59	1.57	1.19	1.76
United Kingdom	2.41	1.83	1.87	1.98
Sweden	3.02	1.59	1.35	1.90
Switzerland	3.03	1.01	0.33	1.26
Australia	2.31	1.70	2.53	1.63
OECD total	3.57	2.02	1.51	1.53

Source: Crafts (2002).

Example of reform

Prior to 2000 the Australian dairy industry was the subject of a complex structure of Australian and state government regulation. Over the course of the years of reform, effective levels of protection were progressively reduced (see Table 8.3).

The state government milk boards maintained liquid milk prices above the equivalent prices for milk for manufacturing purposes (for cheese, butter, etc.) through the framework of regulation. The state boards, with defined regional monopolies, were authorised to purchase milk and sell at prices fixed for both producers and consumers and thereby also controlled distributors' gross margins. The boards were empowered to fix prices, determine vendors' areas, license suppliers, distributors and vendors, and enforce minimum health and safety standards. Interstate trade in liquid milk was restricted under agreements between the various state marketing boards.

Throughout the 1980s, state government involvement in the processing, vending and retailing sectors was diminished. Victoria, South Australia, Western Australian and Tasmania abolished controls on most aspects of milk distribution and pricing beyond the farm gate, while New South Wales and Queensland finally followed suit on 1 July and 31 December 1998 respectively.

At the Australian Government level, under the Kerin Plan (1986 to 1992) a national levy of approximately 2 cents per litre on all milk produced on Australian dairy farms was used to provide an export payment for all Australian dairy product exports. Under the Kerin Plan, the returns dairy farmers received for their manufacturing milk were directly related to the ability of the company they supplied to maximise its returns. An Industry Commission inquiry in 1991 prompted a further set of arrangements (Industry Commission 1991a). This was the so-called Crean Plan (1992 to 1995), which continued the levy on all milk production, which was used to subsidise exports of dairy products, but on a gradually scaled down level.

Under the Competition Principles Agreement, reviews were held of each state's regulatory arrangements. The review committees in New South Wales, Queensland and Western Australia all contained government and industry representatives. In each case a majority of representatives on these committees supported

TABLE 8.3 Effective rates of assistance to the Australian dairy industry, 1970/71 to 1999/2000 (percentage)

	1970/71	1975/76	1980/81	1985/86	1990/91	1995/96	1999/2000
Milk production	156	90	40	159	70	62	73
Manufacturing milk	145	23	16	80	47	19	19
Liquid milk	176	>250	97	>250	123	>200	>200
Total agriculture	28	8	8	10	15	12	6
Manufacturing	36	28	23	20	14	8	4

Source: Productivity Commission (2015).

the maintenance of the regulatory arrangements. In each of these states the result was that the government passed legislation that continued these arrangements for a further five years, after which they would be again reviewed.

In the Victorian case the Centre of International Economics (CIE) was commissioned by the state government to undertake a review of Victoria's *Dairy Industry Act 1992*. Unlike the reviews in most other states, the Victorian review was undertaken by a private economic research agency on behalf of the Department of Natural Resources and Environment. The 'arm's length' review body was supported by the National Competition Council, which had been critical of multidisciplinary review committees where membership of those committees included industry representatives. The CIE review advocated deregulation of the industry and with the support of the United Dairy farmers of Victoria – the peak industry body in that state – the Victorian Government announced its intention to deregulate the industry. The South Australian and Tasmanian review committees also supported deregulation of the industry.

The Australian Government supported the move toward deregulation, and on the recommendation of the Australian Dairy Industry Council agreed to assist dairy farmers to make the transition to a deregulated environment, when state governments and the dairy industry went ahead with market deregulation on 1 July 2000. The Australian Government's package consisted of a $1.8 billion structural adjustment package for the dairy industry, funded through a levy of 11 cents on each litre of milk.

Reform of the dairy industry at the Australian and Victorian Government level after National Competition Policy initiated reviews led to the deregulation of the industry. After the deregulation occurred there was an initial reduction in retail and farm gate prices for milk. This reduction in prices was accompanied by the exit of many farmers from the industry, as well as a rebalancing of farm gate prices across the states (Victoria prices rising, New South Wales and Queensland ones falling). Twelve months after deregulation retail and farm gate prices began to recover (ACCC 2001; Productivity Commission 2015).

Conclusion

The introduction of the National Competition Policy in the mid-1990s meant that the principle that all business captivity should be subject to the greatest level of competition possible was accepted. Areas of economic activity that previously had been exempted from the policy were progressively opened up to competition, and the Australian economy experienced a burst in productivity growth (Parham 2002). The policy itself made no judgement about whether governments should own and operate businesses, but there were implications for the operation of such businesses as the policy was implemented. By putting competitive pressure on government owned businesses and raising the risk of operating them, the policy did in effect encourage the process of privatisation. The trend toward privatisation in Australia did, however, pre-date the formulation of the National Competition Policy, and it is to this area of public policy that we turn in Chapter 9.

References

Australia, Independent Committee of Inquiry into Competition Policy in Australia 1993, *National Competition Policy*, AGPS, Canberra (Hilmer Report).

Australian Bureau of Statistics (ABS) various issues, *Australian National Income Accounts*, Cat. Nos 5234.0, 5204.0, ABS, Belconnen ACT.

Australian Bureau of Statistics (ABS) various issues, *Balance of Payments*, Cat. No. 5302.0, ABS, Belconnen ACT.

Australian Competition and Consumer Commission (ACCC) 2001, *Impact of Farmgate Deregulation on the Australian Milk Industry*, ACCC, Melbourne.

Bureau of Industry Economics (BIE) 1992a, *International Performance Indicators – Electricity*, BIE Research Report, BIE, Canberra.

Bureau of Industry Economics (BIE) 1992b, *International Performance Indicators – Rail Freight*, BIE Research Report, BIE, Canberra.

Bureau of Industry Economics (BIE) 1995, *International Benchmarking – Overview 1995*, BIE Research Report, BIE, Canberra.

Crafts, N. 2002, *Britain's Relative Economic Performance 1870–1999*, Institute of Economic Affairs, London.

Industries Assistance Commission 1989, *Government (Non-Tax Charges)*, AGPS, Canberra.

Industry Commission 1991a, *Australian Dairy Industry*, Report No. 14, Industry Commission Inquiry Report, AGPS, Belconnen ACT.

Industry Commission 1991b, *Energy Generation and Distribution*, Report No. 11, Industry Commission Inquiry Report, AGPS, Belconnen ACT.

Industry Commission 1998, *Government Trading Enterprises Performance Indicators 1992–93 to 1996–97*, AGPS, Belconnen ACT.

Parham, Dean 2002, 'Productivity growth in Australia: are we enjoying a miracle?', Melbourne Institute and The Australian 2002 Economic and Social Outlook Conference, Towards Opportunity and Prosperity, Melbourne.

Productivity Commission 2015, *Trade and Assistance Review 2014–15*, Productivity Commission, Belconnen ACT.

9
GOVERNMENT BUSINESS ENTERPRISES AND PRIVATISATION

Introduction

Another long-standing aspect of Australian economic development was the prevalence of government owned business enterprises. Australian national and state governments in the past have operated a range of different business enterprises. These enterprises were mainly of such things as energy (gas and electricity), transport (railways, aviation, ports and public transport), finance (insurance and banks) and communications (post and telecommunications), but have also included betting agencies, printers, and defence manufacturers.[1] The reform process began in the 1970s, but debate over the status of the government business enterprises intensified in the 1980s after the success of the privatisation programme in the United Kingdom in the early to mid-1980s (Pollitt 1999). The Australian Government began moves to privatise the government owned airlines and Commonwealth Bank late in the 1980s amid a great deal of controversy about whether this was a desirable act or not. At the state level privatisation took place to varying degrees across the states. By the end of the 1990s a significant amount of government owned assets had changed to private ownership, but even today there are still in Australia a significant number of government owned business enterprises.

The purpose of this chapter is to examine the reason why Australia had such a large number of government business enterprises in the first place. Further study will then be undertaken as to the difficulties associated with the operation of these enterprises and finally the privatisation programme in Australia discussed.

Government business enterprises

A government business enterprise is a government owned firm which attempts to cover the bulk of its expenses by sales of goods and services to the public.

Therefore there is a clear distinction between a government business enterprise and general government bodies such as the providers of education, health care, social welfare and so on. The former tries to break even, while the latter generate very little revenue compared to the cost of the services they provide (Jones 1994).

Australia has a long tradition of managing key sectors of the economy through government owned enterprises. In the past, service government firms have operated seaports, airports, telecommunications facilities, postal offices, rail transport, electricity supply, gas supply, and water and sewerage. Before the privatisation process got under way in Australia the government business enterprises made up a significant part of the Australian economy. In 1989/90 Australian government business enterprises' output accounted for 7 per cent of gross domestic product ($25,845 million of $366,878 million), 9 per cent of total employment and 14 per cent of gross fixed capital expenditure ($13,029 million of $89,484 million). This proportion was relatively large by OECD standards. The size and scope of the government business enterprises had fallen dramatically by the end of the 1990s. By 2000/01 government business enterprises' gross fixed capital expenditure had fallen to 7.6 per cent of the total ($10,460 million of $137,196), and outlays as a proportion of gross domestic product had fallen to 2.3 per cent ($15,116 million of $641,553 million) (ABS 2017). By 2011/12 the output of government owned enterprises had fallen to only 1.3 per cent of GDP, and their gross fixed capital expenditure had fallen to only 1.8 per cent of the total (ABS 2017). Altogether the proceeds of privatisation in Australia since 1987 have amounted to around $194 billion in constant dollar terms ($2000) (Abbott and Cohen 2014). A list of all the government business enterprises sold is provided in Table 9.1.

TABLE 9.1 Privatisations of government owned enterprises in Australia, 1987 to 2017

Agency	Year		Sale value $m	Sale type	Industry
Belconnen Mall Shopping Complex	1987	Aust	87	Trade sale	Other
Williamstown Naval Dockyard	1987	Aust	102	Trade sale	Manufacturing
Commonwealth Accommodation and Catering Services	1988	Aust	15	Trade sale	Housing
Defence Service House Corporation loan portfolio	1988	Aust	1515	Trade sale	Housing
AMDEL	1989	Aust	1	Trade sale	Other
Australian Industry Development Corporation – 1	1990	Aust	25	Public float	Financial
Australian Industry Development Corporation – 2	1997	Aust	200	Trade sale	Financial
NSW Investment Corporation	1990	NSW	60	Trade sale	Financial
Australian Defence Force Home Loan Franchise	1991	Aust	42	Trade sale	Financial

Commonwealth Housing Loan Assistance Scheme (in the ACT)	1991	Aust	47	Trade sale	Financial
AUSSAT	1991	Aust	504	Trade sale	Communications
State Bank of Victoria	1991	VIC	1300	Trade sale	Financial
Commonwealth Bank – 1	1991	Aust	1311	Public float	Financial
Commonwealth Bank – 2	1993	Aust	1686	Public float	Financial
Commonwealth Bank – 3	1996	Aust	3390	Public float	Financial
Commonwealth Bank – 4	1997	Aust	1779	Public float	Financial
Loy Yang B power station – 1	1992	VIC	544	Trade sale	Electricity
Loy Yang B power station – 2	1997	VIC	1150	Trade sale	Electricity
Portland Smelter Unit Trust	1992	VIC	171	Trade sale	Manufacturing
Australian Airlines	1992	Aust	400	Trade sale	Aviation
Government Insurance Office	1992	NSW	1260	Public float	Financial
State Insurance Office	1992	VIC	125	Trade sale	Financial
Qantas – 1	1993	Aust	665	Trade sale	Aviation
Qantas – 2	1995	Aust	1450	Public float	Aviation
Snowy Mountains Engineering Corporation	1993	Aust	1.6	Trade sale	Electricity
Heatane Gas	1993	VIC	130	Trade sale	Gas
State Insurance Office	1993	TAS	42	Trade sale	Financial
NSW Grain Corporation	1993	NSW	96	Trade sale	Other
SAGASCO	1993	SA	417	Trade sale	Gas
State Government Insurance Office	1993	WA	165	Float	Financial
Sydney Fish Market	1994	NSW	5	Trade sale	Other
SA Finance Trust	1994	SA	8	Trade sale	Financial
Veterinary Laboratories	1994	VIC	2	Trade Sale	Other
Gladstone Power Station	1994	QLD	750	Trade sale	Electricity
Enterprises Investments	1994	SA	38	Trade sale	Financial
Austrust Trustees	1994	SA	44	Trade sale	Other
State Bank of NSW	1994	NSW	250	Trade sale	Financial
Moomba–Sydney pipeline	1994	Aust	534	Trade sale	Gas
Commonwealth Serum Laboratories	1994	Aust	299	Public float	Other
Grain Elevators Board	1994	VIC	52	Trade sale	Other
BASS	1994	VIC	3	Trade sale	Other
Pipelines Authority of South Australia	1994	SA	304	Trade sale	Gas
VicRoads Equipment Supply Division	1995	VIC	60	Trade sale	Other
Tabcorp	1995	VIC	609	Public float	Gambling
Port of Geelong	1995	VIC	51	Trade sale	Transport
United Energy	1995	VIC	1553	Trade sale	Electricity
GFE Resources	1995	VIC	56	Trade sale	Other
Solaris Power	1995	VIC	950	Trade sale	Electricity
Powercor	1995	VIC	2150	Trade sale	Electricity

(continued)

TABLE 9.1 *(continued)*

Agency	Year		Sale value $m	Sale type	Industry
Eastern Energy	1995	VIC	2080	Trade sale	Electricity
Citipower	1995	VIC	1575	Trade sale	Electricity
State Printing Division	1995	WA		Trade sale	Other
Island Seaway	1995	SA	3	Trade sale	Transport
Aerospace Technologies of Australia	1995	Aust	40	Trade sale	Manufacturing
Port of Portland	1995	VIC	30	Trade sale	Transport
State Government Insurance Office	1995	SA	175	Trade sale	Financial
Bank West	1995	WA	900	Trade sale	Financial
Commonwealth Funds Management	1996	Aust	63	Trade sale	Financial
Radio 5AA	1996	SA	8	Trade sale	Communications
Sign Services	1996	SA	0.3	Trade sale	Other
State Chemistry Laboratory	1996	SA	0.05	Trade sale	Other
State Clothing	1996	SA	2	Trade sale	Other
Yallourn Energy	1996	VIC	2428	Trade sale	Electricity
Hazelwood/Energy Brix	1996	VIC	2400	Trade sale	Electricity
State Bank of SA	1996	SA	720	Trade sale	Financial
Axiom Funds Management	1996	NSW	240	Trade sale	Financial
Forwood Products (Timber)	1995	SA	123	Trade sale	Other
Loy Yang A	1996	VIC	4746	Trade sale	Electricity
Healthcare Linen	1997	WA	14	Trade sale	Other
Samcor	1997	SA	8	Trade sale	Other
Port Bulk Handling Services	1997	SA	17	Trade sale	Transport
Suncorp–Queensland Industry Development Group	1997	QLD	698	Trade sale	Financial
Suncorp–Metway	1997	QLD	610	Public float	Financial
Powernet	1997	VIC	2555	Trade sale	Electricity
Brisbane Airport	1997	Aust	1387	Trade sale	Aviation
Melbourne Airport	1997	Aust	1307	Trade sale	Aviation
Perth Airport	1997	Aust	643	Trade sale	Aviation
Australian National Railways	1997	Aust	95	Trade sale	Transport
Avalon Airport Geelong	1997	Aust	1.5	Trade sale	Aviation
DASFLEET and other DAS business units	1997	Aust	437	Trade sale	Transport
Housing Loan Insurance Corporation	1997	Aust	108	Trade sale	Financial
State Gas Pipeline	1997	QLD	163	Trade sale	Gas
Southern Hydro	1997	VIC	391	Trade sale	Electricity
Telstra – 1	1997	Aust	14330	Public float	Communications
Telstra – 2	1999	Aust	16000	Public float	Communications
Telstra – 3	2006	Aust	15400	Public float	Communications
Victorian Plantations Corporation	1998	VIC	550	Trade sale	Other
Adelaide and Parafield airports	1998	Aust	362	Trade sale	Aviation

Darwin, Tennant Creek and Alice Springs airports	1998	Aust	110	Trade sale	Aviation
Australian Multimedia Enterprises	1998	Aust	43	Trade sale	Communications
ANL	1998	Aust	31	Trade sale	Transport
Totalizer Agency Board	1998	NSW	1000	Public float	Gambling
Canberra Airport	1998	Aust	65	Trade sale	Aviation
Coolangatta Airport	1998	Aust	106	Trade sale	Aviation
Launceston Airport	1998	Aust	18	Trade sale	Aviation
Townsville and Mount Isa airports	1998	Aust	16	Trade sale	Aviation
Moorabbin Airport	1998	Aust	8	Trade sale	Aviation
Jandakot Airport	1998	Aust	7	Trade sale	Aviation
Archerfield Airport	1998	Aust	3	Trade sale	Aviation
Dampier–Bunbury gas pipeline	1998	WA	2303	Trade sale	Gas
Auscript	1998	Aust	1.1	Trade sale	Other
Aluvic	1998	VIC	502	Trade sale	Manufacturing
Australian National Line	1998	Aust	21	Trade sale	Transport
National Transmission Network	1999	Aust	650	Trade sale	Electricity
Ecogen	1999	VIC	360	Trade sale	Electricity
Queensland TAB	1999	QLD	268	Trade sale	Gambling
V/Line Freight	1999	VIC	194	Trade sale	Transport
Gascor	1999	VIC	29	Trade sale	Gas
ETSA Transmission	1999	SA	3500	Trade sale	Electricity
Westar/Kinetik	1999	VIC	1630	Trade sale	Gas
Milinet/Ikon	1999	VIC	1970	Trade sale	Gas
Gasnet	1999	VIC	1025	Trade sale	Gas
ADI	1999	Aust	347	Trade sale	Manufacturing
Removals Australia	2000	Aust	14	Trade sale	Other
Northern Territory TAB	2000	Aust	8	Trade sale	Gambling
Broadcast Australia	2000	Aust	650	Trade sale	Communications
Torrens Island Power Station	2000	SA	295	Trade sale	Electricity
Alinta Gas	2000	WA	971	Public float	Gas
ElectraNet	2000	SA	938	Trade sale	Electricity
Essendon Airport	2001	Aust	22	Trade sale	Aviation
South Australian Totalizer Agency Board	2002	Aust	44	Trade sale	Gambling
National Rail Corporation and Freight Corporation	2002	Aust	1050	Trade sale	Transport
Sydney Airport	2002	Aust	5588	Trade sale	Aviation
Bankstown, Camden and Hoxton Park airports	2003	Aust	211	Trade sale	Aviation
Government Printing Service	2005	NSW	5	Trade sale	Other
DirectLink	2006	NSW	170	Trade sale	Electricity
Allgas Energy	2006	QLD	535	Trade sale	Gas
Sun Retail	2006	QLD	1200	Trade sale	Electricity
Sun Gas	2006	QLD	75	Trade sale	Gas
Powerdirect	2007	QLD	1200	Trade sale	Electricity
Hobart Airport	2007	Aust	350	Trade sale	Aviation

(continued)

TABLE 9.1 *(continued)*

Agency	Year		Sale value $m	Sale type	Industry
ComLand	2007	Aust	165	Trade sale	Other
NSW Lotteries	2010	NSW	850	Trade sale	Gambling
Country Energy – gas network	2010	NSW	109	Trade sale	Gas
QR National	2010	QLD	6222	Public float	Transport
WSN Environmental Solutions	2010	NSW	108	Trade sale	Other
EnergyAustralia	2011	NSW	2035	Trade sale	Electricity
Integral Energy and Country Energy – retail electricity	2011	NSW	3250	Trade sale	Electricity
South Australian Lotteries Commission	2012	SA	427	Trade sale	Gambling
TOTE Tasmania	2012	TAS	103	Trade sale	Gambling
Sydney desalination plant	2012	NSW	2072	Trade sale	Other
Delta Electricity power stations	2013	NSW	475	Trade sale	Electricity
Port Kembla and Port Botany	2013	NSW	5070	Trade sale	Transport
Macquarie Generation	2014	NSW	1505	Trade sale	Electricity
Port of Newcastle	2014	NSW	1750	Trade sale	Transport
Green State Power	2014	NSW	72	Trade sale	Electricity
Colongra Power Station	2014	NSW	233	Trade sale	Electricity
M7 rental payments	2015	NSW	174	Trade sale	Other
Transgrid	2015	NSW	10273	Trade sale	Electricity
Vales Point Power Station	2015	NSW	21	Trade sale	Electricity
Kooragang Island Advanced Water Treatment	2015	NSW	36	Trade sale	Water
Brown Mountain Hydro Power Station and Cochrane Dam	2016	NSW	4.5	Trade sale	Electricity
Ausgrid	2016	NSW	16	Lease	Electricity
Construction Services Group, NSW Public Works	2016	NSW	−0.8	Trade sale	Other
Pillar Superannuation Administration	2016	NSW	35	Trade sale	Financial services
Titles and Registry Business of Land and Property	2017	NSW	2.6	Lease	Other
Endeavour Energy	2017	NSW	7624	Lease	Electricity

Source: Reserve Bank of Australia (1997); Hodge (2003); *Mayne Report* (2010); Abbott and Cohen (2014).

Prior to the 1990s many of these enterprises were given monopoly status through legislation, which protected them against competition. Generally, this occurred to protect the value of the assets of the firms and employment levels, or in order to protect the cross-subsidisation that was built into pricing. Examples of this include rail services, telecommunications, post and electricity. The major exception was that of the state banks and the Commonwealth Bank, which all had to compete with private banks. Given the scale of government business enterprises in Australia it is important to understand why such a state of affairs came about in the first instance.

Why government business enterprises?

Generally speaking, the motivation for government ownership of business enterprises tends to be either ideological or economic, with the latter predominating in the Australian case. The following lists some of the economic reasons for the high level of government ownership in Australia (Boehm 1956; Butlin et al. 1982; Abelson 2012):

- Capital/expertise market failure. The underdevelopment of capital markets late in the nineteenth and early in the twentieth century made it difficult for private entrepreneurs to raise sufficient capital to establish some businesses. Often there were also associated skill shortages. This may have been true in the case of the railways and water and sewerage. Given the more highly developed nature of Australian capital markets today and the general integration of the Australian economy into the global economy this reason today would appear to have no validity.
- Natural monopoly. It has been felt that some utilities possessed 'natural monopoly' characteristics. Government ownership, it was felt, would ensure that those consumers were not exploited. This may have been a factor in the electricity and gas supply industries.
- Cross-subsidies. Governments sometimes took over monopoly businesses in order to effect a redistribution of income through pricing (e.g. postal services, which cross-subsidise country consumers from city ones) or to raise revenue for the government (e.g. gambling such as off-course betting).
- Non-contractable quality. One final justification has been that government enterprises might be able to maintain quality standards and internalise positive externalities (e.g. water and sewage). Generally speaking, governments can achieve the provision of a particular service by contracting out provision to more efficient private operators (e.g. road construction, garbage disposal, etc.). There are however instances where it might be possible that some quality aspects of the product are 'non-contractable'. There may be incentives for private contractors to reduce costs even if it comes at the expense of the non-contractable quality aspects. This reason is more valid for such things as the incorruptibility of police officers, the patriotism of soldiers or possibly the purity of water supplies.

In ideological terms, traditional socialist thought advocated that the means of production, distribution and exchange should be vested in state ownership to maximise the welfare of the population. Some examples of more ideological approaches in Australia include the establishment of the Commonwealth Bank and Qantas (now both privatised). These examples did however include some aspects of the rationale listed above (in the case of the airlines to cross-subsidise transport in the less populated states and in the case of the Commonwealth Bank to reduce the market power of the private banks). Despite these isolated examples, Australia has never had a government that was strongly committed to the nationalising of private businesses such as the post-war Labour Government in Britain or Mitterrand's first government in France.

Limitations of government business enterprises

Historically in Australia the performance of government enterprises has not been particularly impressive. Sheltered from market disciplines the government business enterprises in Australia tended to be relatively inefficient and unresponsive to consumer demands. They were the subject of poor levels of productivity, low rates of return, and overstaffing while at the same time demanding large amounts of government funded investments (Butlin et al. 1982; Industry Commission 1991). Although it was the lack of competition to the government business enterprises that was identified as the main factor that caused the low levels of efficiency the issue of ownership was also important. In the case of government business enterprises there is no easy mechanism by which ownership can be transferred. The significance of non-transferability is that the manager of a government enterprise has considerably more discretion in pursuing his/her own self-interest than a private sector manager. A government manager might use that discretion to pay higher wages and to implement simpler pricing structures than a private sector manager to make his/her work environment less conflict ridden. The lack of capital market disciplines can also be important. In the government sector the sanctions provided by the possibility of takeovers and the risks of insolvency are absent. There may be no significant group that has the incentive to monitor the performance of a government business enterprise, as is the case with private companies with significant holders of stock. Finally, government owned firms might be faced with a range of objectives, which are often contradictory. These contradictions might help to give managers further discretion to pursue their own self-interest.

This last difficulty is really an example of the 'principal–agent problem'. The principal–agent problem is simply that one person (say person A, the owner) might not be able to get person B (a manager) to act for A's benefit rather than follow self-interest. This is also a concern with many private companies where managers act in their own interests rather than in the interests of shareholders. It is a particularly strong concern in the operation of government business enterprises where managers act in the interests of themselves or a private interest group rather than their owners (i.e. the government or public) (Stiglitz 2001).

The politics of government ownership have also led to the underperformance of government owned enterprises. Governments have often used their control of state firms and other assets as a means of channelling benefits to political supporters (or potential supporters) through excessive employment levels, the provision of services below cost or investment in projects of dubious viability. Government firms, therefore, might be inefficient not just because their managers have weak incentives but because of the government's deliberate policy to transfer resources to supporters.

In Australia governments have long been conscious of the problems associated with owning government business enterprises. In fact, one of the earliest attempts to depoliticise and make more efficient the operation of a government business enterprise took place in the 1880s when the Victorian Railways Department was converted into a Railways Commission, with a board of directors and under the operational direction of a general manager. Despite early attempts such as these to improve the efficiency of government business enterprises it was only in the 1970s that a concerted effort began to find ways to improve the performance of the government business enterprises.

Attempts to improve performance: departments, commissions and corporations

Originally government enterprises were embodied in government departments, headed by a minister who sat in the parliament, and they usually carried out industry regulatory functions as well (e.g. the Postmaster-General's Department, railways departments, etc.). Government departments had advantages over firms at service delivery in that they had state powers over such things as land acquisition and planning; they had government guarantees on borrowing, didn't pay tax, and could integrate planning, regulation and operation functions.

Their disadvantages included political interference in their operations; they operated under restrictive employment regimes and were often committed to a variety of often conflicting objectives. The increasing strain of funding their loss making activities during the 1970s and 1980s pushed reform of the government departments. There also arose a growing awareness that taxpayers were being asked to subsidise public sector inefficiency.

In the reform process the first stage has usually been to specify more clearly the goals of an enterprise, stripping away non-commercial features and developing incentives for management consistent with those goals. This usually involved the establishment of statutory authorities to carry out the defined functions. Examples of this process include the establishment of the Australian Postal Commission and Telecommunications Commission in 1975 out of the old Australian Government Postmaster-General's Department (Abbott 2000). As mentioned previously this model has a long history in Australia, and from time to time the merits and disadvantages of this type of arrangement have been discussed.

Gradually a process of corporatisation has occurred that has involved most government owned enterprises in Australia. This has generally meant establishing them as legal entities, and putting them under the control of a board and a CEO responsible to that board. Financial targets generally are made explicit, and technical, safety and other regulatory functions have been taken away from them, leaving them as purely commercial operations. This separation of regulatory functions from business operations did not always occur when separate commissions were created. The Victorian Government's State Electricity Commission for instance had many electricity safety functions as well as its responsibilities in generating and delivering electricity.

The step beyond corporatisation is to transfer outright ownership from the government to the private sector (privatisation). This process might mean that the industry will still be the subject of rigorous government regulation, but commercial risks and responsibilities are transferred to private owners. It is quite possible in these circumstances that the regulatory intervention on the part of the government can become more explicit and transparent. For instance, if the government wishes to impose environmental or social welfare obligations on privatised companies it would do so through legislation rather than through the discrete direction of public sector managers of government business enterprises. Social obligations, such as the subsidisation of lower-income consumers, might be paid for directly to private firms from the government's budget rather than financed through hard to identify cross-subsidies.

There is, therefore, some limited evidence that governments, on average, are less efficient than private enterprises in providing comparable services (in the Australian case see Abbott and Cohen 2014). There are important exceptions, though, suggesting that government enterprises are not necessarily less efficient than their private counterparts.

Government enterprises differ from private enterprises in several respects: whereas private enterprises maximise profits, government enterprises may pursue other objectives; government enterprises often face soft budget constraints and limited competition; and they face additional constraints, in personnel policy (pay and firing), procurement and budgeting. Although there may be good reasons for these restrictions, they nonetheless interfere with economic efficiency. These differences lead to differences in individual incentives. Bureaucrats often try to maximise the size of their organization and to avoid risk. At the same time, public organizations share with private firms the principal–agent problem, the problem of ensuring that their employees act in the interests of the organization, or more broadly that managers and workers in firms act in ways that are congruent with the interests of shareholders and that public servants act in ways that are congruent with the interests of citizens.

It is also worth remembering that there do exist several organizational forms that lie between conventional public agencies and private corporations, including government corporations and performance based organizations. They may be able to achieve many of the efficiency benefits of private organizations and at the same time pursue public interests more effectively than purely private firms subject to regulations. Much of the debate in the future will be about the extent of utilization of these organizational forms and whether private firms should enter areas that were previously thought of as core government functions, such as prisons and social services. A hybrid public–private partnership model has emerged as a way to take advantage of the relative strengths of government and business while mitigating their respective weaknesses.

Privatisation in Australia

The privatisation of government owned assets became very common during the 1990s in Australia. At the national level the major examples include the sale of the Commonwealth Bank, Qantas, the major airports and Australian National Railways, and the partial sale of Telstra. At the state government level privatisation has varied across the states. In the most extreme case in Victoria the State Bank, SIO, SEC and Gas and Fuel, V/Line Freight, public transport (buses, trams and rail) and some ports were sold. In that state only water companies and some ports are left in government hands. At the other extreme is Western Australia, where there are still substantial business assets under government ownership, including rail, electricity, ports and an investment company. In Table 9.2 there is a list of the main government owned businesses left in Australia in 2016. Table 9.1 provides a list of the major businesses that have been privatised. The major areas of

TABLE 9.2 Government business enterprises in Australia, 2016

Jurisdiction	Company name	Industry
Australia	Australia Post	Post
	Australian Rail Track Corporation	Rail track
	Australian Energy Market Operator	Electricity and gas
	Airservices Australia	Aviation
	Medibank Private	Insurance
	NBN Co	Communications
	Snowy Hydro	Electricity generation
NSW	Hunter Water	Water
	Sydney Water Corporation	Water
	Sydney Catchment Authority	Water
	State Water	Water
	Sydney Port Corporation[a]	Port
	Essential Energy	Electricity distribution
	Country Infrastructure Authority	Rail track
	RailCorp	Rail track
	State Transit Authority of NSW	Public transport
VIC	Melbourne Water	Water
	Yarra Valley Water	Water
	South East Water	Water
	City West Water	Water
	Barwon Water	Water
	Central Highlands Water	Water
	Coliban Water	Water
	East Gippsland Water	Water
	Gippsland Water	Water
	Goulburn Valley Water	Water
	GWM Water	Water
	Lower Murray Water	Water
	North East Water	Water
	South Gippsland Water	Water
	Wannon Water	Water
	Westernport Water	Water

(continued)

TABLE 9.2 *(continued)*

Jurisdiction	Company name	Industry
	Goulburn–Murray Water	Water
	Lower Murray Water Rural	Water
	Southern Rural Water	Water
	Port of Melbourne Corporation	Port
	Victorian Regional Channels Authority	Port
	VicTrack	Rail track
QLD	Sun Water	Water
	SEQwater	Water
	Gladstone Area Water Board	Water
	Mount Isa Water Board	Water
	Energex	Electricity distribution
	Ergon Energy	Electricity distribution
	Powerlink	Electricity transmission
	CS Energy	Electricity generation
	Stanwell Corporation	Electricity generation
	Ports North	Port
	Port of Townsville Ltd	Port
	North Queensland Bulk Ports Corporation	Port
	Gladstone Port Corporation	Port
	Queensland Rail	Rail track
	Queensland Urban Utilities	Water
	Translink Transit Authority, Department of Transport and Main Roads	Public transport
SA	Department of Planning, Transport and Infrastructure (Office of the Rail Commissioner)	Public transport
	SA Water[a]	Water infrastructure
WA	Water Authority of WA	Water
	Busselton Water Board	Water
	AqWest – Bunbury Water Board	Water
	Western Power	Electricity transmission and distribution
	Horizon Power	Electricity transmission and distribution
	Synergy	Electricity retail and generation
	Public Transport Authority	Public transport
	Fremantle Ports	Port
	Broome Port Authority	Port
	Bunbury Port Authority	Port
	Dampier Port Authority	Port
	Esperance Port Authority	Port
	Geraldton Port Authority	Port
	Port Hedland Port Authority	Port
	Albany Port Authority	Port

Government business enterprises

TAS	TasWater	Water
	Aurora Energy	Electricity distribution
	Transend Networks	Electricity transmission
	Hydro Tasmania	Electricity generation
	TasPorts	Port
	TasRail	Rail
	Metro Tasmania	Public transport
NT	Power and Water Corporation	Electricity and water
	Darwin Port Corporation	Port
ACT	ACTEW	Water

Note: [a] In 2013 the New South Wales Government leased the Port Kembla and Sydney port assets to a private consortium. The two port corporations still exist as asset owners, similar to SA Water, which owns but leases the water assets in that state, and the Port of Brisbane, which is operated by a private company. The Newcastle Port Corporation was privatised in a similar fashion in May 2014.

continued government ownership are postal services, water supply, ports and in some states electricity, public transport and rail. On the whole governments have entirely divested themselves of banks and insurance companies, natural gas supply companies, airlines, shipping and major airports.

The breakdown of the sales is by no means uniform, by state, by industry or over time. Figure 9.1 shows when the asset sales occurred in Australia. As can be seen, the period when most occurred was the 1990s. From Figure 9.2 it can be seen that the bulk of the funds raised by the privatisation process was by

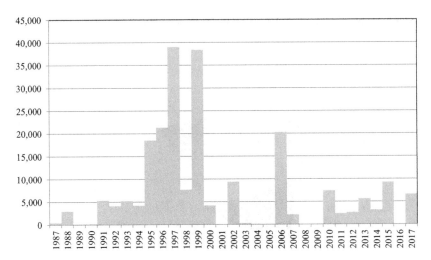

FIGURE 9.1 Annual value of privatisations in Australia, 1987 to 2017 (constant $2000)

Source: Abbott and Cohen (2014).

the Victorian and Australian governments. In terms of the industry areas, energy (electricity and gas), telecommunications and financial institutions are where the bulk of these funds were raised (Figure 9.3).

The motivation on the part of the various governments to sell assets has been partially to improve the performance of these industries, partially to avoid the risk involved in owning commercial assets and partially to use the proceeds from the sales to reduce government debt and allow greater freedom on the part of governments to spend on social expenditure (i.e. education, welfare, health) or to reduce taxation levels.

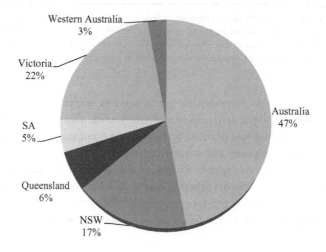

FIGURE 9.2 Jurisdiction of privatisations in Australia, 1988 to 2017 (percentage)

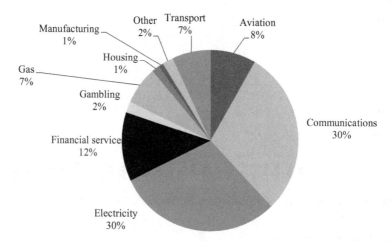

FIGURE 9.3 Privatisations in Australia by industry type, 1988 to 2017 (percentage)

In some cases, privatisation took place in a competitive context (Qantas, Commonwealth Bank), whilst in others there were concerns that privatised monopolies could exploit their market power, which meant that the formal development of economic regulation of pricing became necessary. In the case of the privatisation of government owned monopolies this meant that a tension arose between the aims of government in trying to regulate the prices of monopolies on the one hand and increase the proceeds of sales on the other. Regulating prices down meant that returns and the value of the assets would be reduced. This in turn would reduce the sale prices of the assets. Governments interested in privatising monopolies had to make a trade-off between lower prices for consumers and greater asset sale prices and subsequently greater levels of government services, lower debt and lower taxes.

The following list provides more detail on the privatisation process around Australia during the 1990s. As well as the raw sums involved it also gives the value of government debt for each jurisdiction to indicate the relationship between the privatisation process and the retirement of public debt.

- Australian Government:
    o $45 billion for half-sale of Telstra during 1997 and 2006;
    o $7.2 billion for the Commonwealth Bank in 1993 and 1996;
    o $4 billion for the airports, not including Sydney Airports Corporation; and
    o $2 billion for rail, shipping and Qantas in 1992 and 1995.

    The sale process was around $106 billion ($2000) and left the Australian Government's debt at relatively low levels – 7 per cent of GDP, compared to an average of around 50 per cent in Europe and the USA and over 100 per cent in Japan.

- Victoria:
    o $21.4 billion for electricity assets between 1993 and 1999;
    o $6.5 billion for natural gas assets;
    o $1.6 billion for public transport in 1999;
    o $675 million for the TAB and
    o extra amounts for ports, and a share of the aluminium smelter and plantations.

    The sale proceeds of around $48 million ($2000) meant that state debt was reduced from 26.7 per cent of gross state product to 3.1 per cent in June 2000.

- New South Wales: $12.9 billion ($2000) from financial, electricity and gaming business; state debt is now 8 per cent of gross state product.
- Queensland: $13.4 billion ($2000) from various assets; Queensland has no state debt, a product mainly of the high level of mining royalties in the state rather than from the proceeds of privatisation.

- South Australia: $10.3 billion ($2000) mainly from the sale of electricity assets in 1999; state debt in South Australia was largely eliminated.
- Western Australia: $6.5 billion mainly from the State Insurance Office and Bank West; state debt in Western Australia is now around 6.5 per cent of gross state product (Moran 2000).

The privatisation of Australian business enterprises did not take place in isolation from the rest of the world. From the early 1980s onwards the Thatcher Government in Britain undertook an extensive privatisation programme. This was copied in several countries around the world, including Australia. Figures 9.4 and 9.5 show a comparison of government ownership of key industries in the United States, Britain, Australia, New Zealand and Singapore in both 1983 and 2017. As can be seen the privatisation of assets was quite extensive across a range of countries and a range of industries.

Privatisation outcomes

Financial services

For the financial services sector, the starting point for microeconomic reform was the deregulation of the financial markets in the early 1980s. In terms of privatisation the national government owned Commonwealth Bank and the state government

	USA	UK	Australia	NZ	Singapore
Postal services	Yes	Yes	Yes	Yes	Yes
Telecommunications	No	Yes	Yes	Yes	Yes
Electricity supply	Part	Yes	Yes	Yes	Yes
Gas supply	No	Yes	Yes	Yes	Yes
Airports	Part	Yes	Yes	Yes	Yes
Airlines	No	Part	Part	Yes	Part
Rail	Part	Yes	Yes	Yes	Yes
Ports	Part	Yes	Yes	Yes	Yes
Coal mining	No	Yes	No	Yes	N/A
Steel manufacture	No	Yes	No	Yes	N/A
Banking	No	No	Part	Part	Part
Water supply	Part	Yes	Yes	Yes	Yes

FIGURE 9.4 Government ownership in various countries, 1983

	USA	UK	Australia	NZ	Singapore
Postal services	Yes	No	Yes	Yes	No
Telecommunications	No	No	No	No	Part
Electricity supply	Part	No	Part	Part	Part
Gas supply	No	No	No	No	Yes
Airports	Yes	No	No	Part	Yes
Airlines	No	No	No	Part	Part
Rail	Part	Part	Part	Part	Yes
Ports	Part	Part	Part	Part	Yes
Coal mining	No	No	No	No	N/A
Steel manufacture	No	No	No	No	N/A
Banking	No	No	No	No	Part
Water supply	Part	No	Yes	Yes	Yes

FIGURE 9.5 Government ownership in various countries, 2017

owned banks were all sold in the early 1990s, as were the state government owned insurance companies. The performance of banks is generally indicated by financial analysts and others using financial performance indicators such as the profitability of these organisations in terms of assets or equity invested. Using financial ratios often means making use of unreliable accounting data, which may not give a true indication of the firms' financial performance in terms of profits or costs (Berger and Humphrey 1992). In addition, several researchers have attempted to evaluate the efficiency performance of the industry since deregulation. These studies include those by Sathye (2002), Otchere and Chan (2003), Neal (2004), Sturm and Williams (2004), Kirkwood and Nahm (2006), Avkiran (2007), Wu (2007) and Abbott and Wu (2012) on the banks, Esho and Sharpe (1995, 1996) on the building societies and Worthington (1999, 2004) on the credit unions. The privatisation process took place amongst the banks rather than building societies and credit unions, which therefore means that the research on the latter two is not relevant to this survey.

What is shown in the studies on the banking sector is that the productivity of the banks did improve over time, but not at a constant rate. The most important gains from productivity occurred not immediately after deregulation in the 1980s, but much later in the strong growth periods of the mid-1990s and 2000s. The recessionary periods of the early 1990s and late 2000s were also periods when productivity growth tended to slow down. The studies by Sathye (2002), Otchere and Chan (2003), Neal (2004), Sturm and Williams (2004), Avkiran (2007), Wu (2007) and Abbott and Wu (2012) all broadly support this conclusion.

The problem, however, is discerning what degree of the improvement can be attributed to privatisation, rather than deregulation, enhanced competition and technological change. Did, for instance, the privatisation of the Commonwealth Bank (and the state banks) contribute at all to the steady improvement in productivity over time? The work on productivity by Avkiran (2007), Wu (2007) and Abbott and Wu (2012) does suggest that the privatisation process had some influence. In the 1980s, before privatisation, the Commonwealth Bank appears to have had a lower profit rate, higher operating expenses and a lower level of productivity than the three major private banks. Sathye (2002) found that the productivity growth of the Commonwealth Bank was strong in the period after privatisation. The work by Otchere and Chan (2003) also found that after full privatisation the cost efficiency of the Commonwealth Bank improved and its profitability rose.[2]

In the 1990s, therefore, there appears to be no significant difference in terms of productivity between the four major banks (including the privatised Commonwealth Bank). Neal (2004) and Sturm and Williams (2004) also found that the larger banks performed better in terms of productivity improvements than the smaller regional banks. As the privatisation process involved the incorporation of the relatively small regional state banks into larger national ones this may have helped to boost productivity. This evidence is hardly conclusive, however, and it seems far safer to say that it was deregulation, competition and technological change that were the major drivers of efficiency gains rather than privatisation.

In the case of the insurance industry there were even fewer studies undertaken on the impact of privatisation. For the insurance industry, most major studies of productivity have been of the health insurance sector (see for instance CRA International 2006; Carrington et al. 2011). One study was undertaken by Eling and Luhnen (2010) of an international sample of life and non-life insurance companies (including Australia) between 2002 and 2006 and found that Australia was around average in terms of efficiency. In this study, no attempt was made to show any relationship between ownership and efficiency, and not much can be inferred about the impact of privatisation on the insurance industry.

Another study, by Casey and Dollery (1996), looked at the privatisation of the New South Wales Government owned GIO Australia, the largest of the general government owned insurance companies. GIO Australia was privatised in 1992 through a public float. The researchers regarded the privatisation as 'successful' and cite its growth in business, revenue, assets, profits, share price and lowered costs and charges as evidence of this success. In terms of the industry these researchers felt the privatisation had less of an impact given the larger size of other private companies already operating in the market (i.e. AMP and NRMA).

The evidence in the case of the financial services industry is far from conclusive but it does seem the level of productivity of the industry is higher in recent times than it was at the time of deregulation. Increased levels of competition in markets would seem to be the main cause of this along with advances in technology. At the same time the conversion and merger of the government owned banks and insurance companies into private ones do seem to have made some contribution to rising levels of efficiency. That said, it is also clear that the impact of competition in driving efficiency gains was more important than that of ownership.

Aviation

A few studies have been undertaken that provide some impressions of the impact of privatisation of the aviation sector. One of the most well-known studies, internationally was the work by Davies (1971, 1977) comparing Australia's two domestic airlines, TAA (government owned) and Ansett (privately owned), in the 1970s. Davies studied their productive efficiency using partial productivity indexes over the period 1958–74 and found the privately owned airlines to be consistently superior in terms of passengers, freight carried and revenue earned per passenger. In the post-1990 era few studies have been undertaken of the aviation industry even though the nature of the industry has changed considerably. Forsyth (2001) analysed the change in total factor productivity (TFP) in the Australian domestic aviation industry between 1982 and 1999. TAA's name was changed to Australian Airlines and then merged with the government owned international carrier Qantas. Qantas was privatised in stages in 1993 and 1995. According to Forsyth productivity growth was strong after deregulation and air fares fell. Although Forsyth did not comment on how much this resulted from the privatisation of Qantas given its large presence in the domestic market, both before and after deregulation, a large part of the improved productivity of the industry in the 1990s must have come from improvements to this company. Finally, Small (2002), in looking at the workforce implications of the privatisation of Qantas, found that staff levels were reduced.

The major Australian airports were privatised after 1996. Unlike the banks or airlines in most cities in Australia they were monopolies. There have only been a few studies of the change in productivity and efficiency of Australian airports over the past 20 years. The main ones are by Hooper and Hensher (1998), Abbott and Wu (2002), the Tourism and Transport Forum Australia (2007) and Assaf (2010). The work by Hooper and Hensher was the first to attempt to calculate TFP indexes for Australian airports, but took place prior to the privatisation process. It found a rise in productivity during the period of corporatisation (1986–1998), as did the work by Abbott and Wu, who looked at the same period as well as the early years of privatisation using a DEA Malmquist approach. The Tourism and Transport Forum Australia commissioned URS Australia to undertake a report of the impact of airport privatisation in Australia. Its report in 2007 of eight major airports in Australia found that privatisation had led to an improvement in operational efficiency (in terms of average revenue and employee costs per work load unit), an increase in capital expenditure and increases in traffic diversity and non-aeronautical revenue. The work by Assaf (2010) also looked explicitly at the privatisation period and used a Bayesian panel stochastic frontier model of the 13 main Australian airports between 2002 and 2007. The paper found that during this period the Australian airports had significantly increased their levels of cost efficiency and largely attributed this to privatisation and the use of a light handed approach to price regulation. It also highlighted the heavy levels of investment undertaken by the private owners of the airports, especially at the more congested ones like Sydney Airport.

Owing to the ready availability of data on Australian airports collected by the Australian Competition and Consumer Commission, Australian airports have often been included in larger studies internationally undertaken for years in the 2000s. Of these Oum et al. (2003), Lin and Hong (2006) and Assaf and Gillen (2012) found that ownership was not important in influencing efficiency. Instead factors like the type of economic regulation, size and hub characteristics were more important. The studies by Oum et al. (2006, 2008) and Serebrisky (2012) found that private airports were more efficient, but in each case other factors were important as well. In these cases, it should be borne in mind that the Australian airports made up only a very small part of the sample and so not too much should be read into the results concerning Australian conditions. Efficiency seems to be affected strongly by the impact of size, hub characteristics and regulation in any case.

Some other studies highlighted some problems with privatisation. Forsyth (2008) pointed out some of the complaints of the airlines, as did Thomas (2010). More specifically O'Donnell et al. (2011), in looking at Sydney Airport, found that gains in efficiency had come at the expense of airlines' and other airport customers in the form of higher charges. Employees at the airport had also suffered from the loss of jobs and outsourcing. A Sydney Airport employee, Schuster (2009), writing on the issue of pricing on the other hand, wrote more positively on the light handed approach to pricing regulation. Finally, Freestone et al. (2006) detailed changes that had occurred to local and regional planning that resulted because of the privatisation of the airports and the attempts by owners to make more intensive use of airport property.

Despite the lack of research on the productivity of Australian airports there does seem to be evidence that the privatisation of the major airports has increased their levels of productivity. This is despite there being less competition in this market compared to many others and there being a relatively light handed approach to regulation. It is also noteworthy that considerable improvements in efficiency were made prior to privatisation through the corporatisation of the airports.

Telecommunications

The privatisation of the telecommunications company Telstra was the largest undertaken. The privatisation of Telstra has attracted a lot of attention from researchers; however, the tendency has not been to try to determine the level of productivity and efficiency change of the process but to focus on a range of other issues such as the financial costs and benefits to the government of Telstra's privatisation. In the case of telecommunications, estimating efficiency changes over time has been considerably more difficult than it has been for the financial sector and for the airports. This is because over the last 20 years there has been very considerable change in the industry in terms both of degrees of competition and of technological advances.

Distinguishing between changes brought on by privatisation and by increased levels of competition is always difficult. In the case of telecommunications, it is made more difficult by the change in composition of the industry's output with the explosion in the use of mobile phones, the internet and broadband. These reasons would justify why researchers have tended to shy away from trying to explicitly determine changes in levels of productivity in the industry.

In terms of the studies of the productivity of the telecommunications industry the Bureau of Industry benchmarked Telstra against companies overseas and found that the Australian industry performed 'reasonably well' in terms of efficiency and prices, and had improved greatly in the early 1990s. The Bureau reports found that telecommunications prices in Australia tended to be high for business and national trunk users but better for mobiles and international calls. In terms of productivity, labour productivity was found to be lower than in many other jurisdictions (multi-factor productivity also). This was before the privatisation of Telstra and in the early years of competition. This was followed by work by the Productivity Commission (1999). The Productivity Commission found things somewhat improved, with local and long-distance call charges falling and overall charges average by world standards. Later international benchmarking studies by the OECD (2008) came to similar conclusions in the late 2000s.

Following the work by the Bureau and Productivity Commission, Rushdi (2000) analysed the TFP of Telstra in the period 1980 to 1997. In doing so he found that the performance of Telstra greatly improved after the introduction of competition. The work by the Bureau and Rushdi, however, was of the industry when Telstra was still in government ownership, and so although it is possible to attribute the gains in productivity to increased levels of competition it is not possible to attribute this to privatisation. Tsai et al. (2006) benchmarked 39 international companies, including Telstra, in the years 1997 to 2004, a period in which Telstra had been partially privatised. The authors ranked Telstra highly in their sample (fourth of 39), a higher ranking than the Bureau had given Telstra. Although it is possibly the impact of competition that encouraged Telstra to move to such a relatively high standing, the part-privatisation may also have contributed. In addition, staff levels at Telstra were reduced (Barton 2002a). In all, the efficiency of the telecommunications market in Australia seems to have improved by the late 2000s (i.e. during the period of privatisation and after), although this might easily be attributed to the introduction of competition into the telecommunications market in the 1990s rather than privatisation. Given the nature of the research, just how much the privatisation of Telstra led to improvements in productivity and efficiency would be better considered an unproved question.

Electricity and gas

In the case of operational efficiency, the levels in the industry were found to have improved greatly by several researchers between the mid-1980s and the late 1990s. Abbott (2006), in looking at the state based electricity supply industries over the longer term, found that between 1986 and 1999 TFP rose substantially in the industry across all jurisdictions. This was so even in those states where government ownership was maintained, such as New South Wales and Queensland. The state in the study with the slowest growth in productivity was Western Australia, which remained outside of the National Electricity Market. Growth in productivity was seen as being driven by reductions in staff numbers, outsourcing and the greater use of generation and transmission capacity after earlier periods of overbuilding. A later study by Agham (2011) which also concentrated on the state based industries came to similar conclusions, and this study found strong growth in efficiency in the period 1986 to 1997. Growth in productivity was found to have tapered off somewhat between 1997 and 2002. Agham's study found strong growth again in the states of government ownership that were in the national market (i.e. New South Wales and Queensland) but not in Western Australia, which lay outside of the national market. A Productivity Commission report (2012) also found strong growth in productivity at the national level between the mid-1980s and mid-1990s but stagnation in productivity growth and even a fall after the mid-1990s. This stagnation it attributed to an increase in capital expenditure needed to accommodate growth in summer peak demand and the undergrounding of cabling and to meet a backlog of investment demands. These studies implied that competition has been the main driver of efficiency gains rather than ownership.

Studies of the productivity within electricity distribution (as opposed to electricity supply overall) include work by the Essential Services Commission and Pacific Economics Group (2006), Pacific Economics Group (2008), Lawrence (2009a, 2009b) and Mountain and Littlechild (2010). Although not all of these studies were especially concerned with the issue of government versus private ownership they do have some implications for the issue. The latter study in particular is important, as it compared the costs and allowed revenues of the government owned New South Wales distribution companies to the privately owned ones in Britain and Victoria. It found that revenues per customers were far higher in New South Wales than in Britain and significantly higher than in Victoria. It attributed this to an overinvestment in infrastructure, which was caused, in part, by government ownership. These findings were criticised in Australia, and a study commissioned by regulators by Wilson Cook & Co (2008) for the Australian Energy Regulators review and a study by Parsons Brinckerhoff (2009) found the government owned distribution companies in Australia at comparable levels of efficiency to the privatised companies. IPART (2010) estimated TFP for government owned generators, distributors and transmission in New South Wales and found that efficiency levels were comparable to those of 'peers'. An additional study by the Grattan Institute (2012) found that the government owned distribution networks had higher levels of capital expenditure than the privately owned ones and consequently higher costs.

There seems little doubt that the corporatisation and introduction of competition into the electricity industry has helped to boost efficiency levels in the electricity supply industry in Australia. What is less clear is the impact of the different types of ownership. Government owned electricity utilities in Queensland and New South Wales, where they have been exposed to significant competition, have raised their levels of productivity just as dramatically as they did in Victoria and South Australia. The privatised companies also seem to be experiencing the same degrees of productivity stagnation in more recent years as the government owned companies.

In terms of the distribution of the costs and benefits of the restructuring and privatisation a few studies have been undertaken. Chester (2007) in looking at the winners and losers identified investors, owners and creditors as being the major beneficiaries and employees as being the major losers. Abbott (2011) also identified the providers and receivers of public services as being major gainers in the form of increased employment levels of police, school teachers and nurses after the privatisation of Victoria's electricity and gas assets and subsequent reduction in state debt levels.

In the case of the gas supply industry, the extent of reform was less substantial. In Victoria, the government owned Gas and Fuel Corporation was split up into three distribution/retail businesses, and a separate transmission business, and the businesses privatised. In addition, pipeline investments were made that enabled improved linkages between markets with no or limited connectivity. There have been several studies of gas pipeline efficiency. These studies included a range of productivity measures. The papers included international benchmarking studies undertaken by the Bureau of Industry Economics (Australia, Bureau of Industry Economics 1994), IPART (1999) and Carrington (2002) and reports by Meyrick and Associates (2007) and the Pacific Economics Group (2008) that estimated TFP growth within the Victorian gas distribution industry. Lawrence (2009a, 2009b, 2010) examined TFP for gas distribution systems. Rushdi (1994) looked at a single company.

The Bureau of Industry Economics (Australia, Bureau of Industry Economics 1994) found that the Australian natural gas industry was performing relatively well in terms of operating efficiency, given its operating environment. Natural gas prices in Australia compared favourably with those of most countries. Within Australia, the government owned Gas and Fuel Corporation of Victoria had the lowest prices and performed relatively well in terms of labour, capital and overall technical efficiency. The State Energy Commission of Western Australia, although it had relatively high prices, was the best practice gas utility in Australia in terms of labour, capital and overall technical efficiency. Rushdi (1994) focused on TFP for the Gas and Fuel Corporation of Victoria (GFCV) for the period 1971 to 1989. The author found TFP growth for the GFCV was 8.5 per cent per year, with output growth at 12.4 per cent and input growth at 3.6 per cent.

The TFP results for gas distributors in Victoria that were estimated by Meyrick and Associates (2007, pp. 27–9) focused on the post-privatisation period (1998 to 2006). This period was characterised by strong TFP growth of 2.7 per cent per year, with output growth of 1.8 per cent, and a decline in input growth of 0.9 per cent a year. The explanation was that the high TFP growth rate was achieved in part by reducing operating and maintenance expenditure, which declined by 4.3 per cent a year. Another study which estimated TFP for the Victorian gas distribution industry for the years 1998 to 2007 was undertaken by the Pacific Economics Group (2008). The TFP growth rate was estimated at an average annual rate of 2.9 per cent, with output growth estimated at 1.1 per cent, and input growth falling by 1.8 per cent. While the average annual growth rates for output and input may be different between the two studies, it is important to note that, over the long term, outputs exceeded inputs and therefore productivity rose.

It would appear, therefore, that privatisation in the Victorian case was associated with a substantial increase in productivity. It should also be remembered, however, that Rushdi (1994) found that, prior to privatisation, growth in productivity in Victoria was strong and also that the Bureau of Industry Economics (Australia, Bureau of Industry Economics 1994) found the Victorian industry to be a reasonably good performer. In addition, Barton (2002b) found that employment levels at the GFCV were reduced, both in the lead-up period to privatisation and after.

Lawrence (2010) estimated TFP and partial factor productivity (PFP) in six individual gas distribution businesses over the period from the late 1990s to the late 2000s. He found that productivity among the businesses varied – some displayed steady growth while others experienced a more variable performance. For example, Envestra SA recorded strong annual average TFP growth of 1.5 per cent a year for the period 1999 to 2010, largely because of significant reductions in operating expenses. In contrast, over the same period, the TFP performance of Envestra Queensland was an average annual growth rate of −0.2 per cent. Carrington *et al.* (2002) attempted to measure the efficiency of the Australian gas distributors relative to each other and to distributors in the United States. A number of techniques were employed, including partial productivity measures and data envelopment analysis. The results for the Australian distributors were below those of the American ones on average, and their variance from one another was attributed partly to local conditions. As all of the distributors in the Australian sample by this stage were privatised it seems to imply that more is needed than simple privatisation to raise productivity levels to world's best practice.

In the case of the electricity and gas supply industries the introduction of competition seems to have been the main driver of efficiency gains. In each industry both privately and government owned companies have improved levels of efficiency since the early 1990s. Although it is probable that the privatisation of electricity and gas companies may have increased levels of efficiency the evidence on this is not conclusive.

Multi-industry studies

In addition to industry-specific studies, there are also a number of major multi-industry studies which have attempted to gauge the overall impact of the privatisations that have occurred since the 1980s. Most of the multi-industry studies were undertaken relatively soon after privatisation began to be common in Australia, and tended to focus on the effects of the process itself and on such things as the budgetary position of the government and the immediate distributional effects of the privatisation rather than on the long-term impact on efficiency.

Wettenhall (1999), Collyer et al. (2001, 2003), Considine (2001) and Walker and Walker (2001) all pointed out the costs of privatisation in terms of the transactions costs involved in the process. Walker and Walker in looking at a range of different privatisations pointed out several weaknesses in the process. Wettenhall in looking at the sale of the Government Insurance Office in New South Wales (GIO), the Commonwealth Serum Laboratory and TabCorp in Victoria also highlighted that new shareholders and senior managers were the main gainers from the process. Collyer et al. looked at the sale of nine government owned businesses and concentrated on identifying the immediate winners and losers from the process. The winners were identified as being politicians, senior managers, consultants, political parties and new owners. The losers were employees, local communities and customers.

Harris and Lye (2001) looked at the sale of nine government owned businesses and the impact on the net worth to the government, bearing in mind the potential in reducing debt and forgone interest payments and revenue streams. They concluded that there was a cost to underpricing of sales and the net impact could be negative, but in some cases where the government enterprise sold was inefficient the government may have realised a net gain. Toner (2003) and Aulich and Wettenhall (2005) detailed the impact of privatisation on levels of employment and training, both of which fell after privatisation. Overall the early, mainly multi-industry, studies indicate there were transactions costs associated with the sale of the assets, the costs fell disproportionately on some groups and the financial benefits to government in the long term depended on the scale of the sale prices. In terms of the efficiency performance of the privatised companies little was found, although Harris and Lye did identify some gains in efficiency. Early multi-industry studies were not conclusive about the impact on efficiency.

Case studies (post and airports)

Another way to look at the problem of operating government owned businesses and the process of privatisation is to take a couple of examples and follow them though. In this section two government business enterprises are observed: Australia Post and the Federal Airports Corporation (FAC). The former is still in government ownership and the latter was privatised in the late 1990s.

Postal services

Australia Post Limited is a sizeable organisation. In 2000/01, it employed 35,397 full- and part-time employees, processed 4.76 billion pieces of mail and earned revenues of almost $3.7 billion. For most of the twentieth century the postal service in Australia was run by a Cabinet level department known as the

Postmaster-General's Department, which also operated Australia's telephone service. In 1975 the department was separated into two autonomous commissions – the Australian Postal Commission being responsible for the country's postal service and the Australian Telecommunications Commission for the telephone system. In 1989 the Australian Postal Commission was corporatised and became Australia Post Limited under the *Australian Postal Corporation Act*. Under the Act Australia Post operates with a board and has commercial objectives as well as community service obligations (Abbott 2000).

The aim of both reorganisations of the postal service was to increase the commercial focus of the organisation, as well as encourage it to operate as 'efficiently and economically' as possible, while at the same time maintaining its community service obligations, primarily the universal service obligation (Australia Post 1990). Under the 1989 Act Australia Post is expected not only to cover its operating and capital expenses but also to pay taxes and to generate a reasonable return for the government.

Australia Post is an unusual organisation in that it combines several objectives. Australia Post is clearly a commercial undertaking with commercial objectives, but it also has no shareholders and is obliged to carry out a number of non-commercial obligations. It is a government owned monopoly but also competes for the provision of many services with private firms. As well as the standard letter delivery, it provides a parcel service, international mail, retail services, financial services and ancillary products. A large part of its revenue is still derived from services that are reserved to it under the *Australian Postal Corporation Act*. However, the bulk of its profit comes from non-reserved services. In 1997 about 35 per cent of Australia Post's operating profit was derived from reserved services (NCC 1998). The main products covered by the reserved service provisions include standard and large letters weighing up to 260 grams, for which the fee is up to four times the standard letter rate. Australia Post's community obligations include the obligation to deliver letters anywhere in Australia at a uniform rate. This obligation is currently funded out of the profits earned on the parts of its operations where letter delivery costs less than the uniform rate.

In terms of its operational performance the corporatisation of Australia Post would appear to have been a success. Since 1989 the real price of stamps has fallen and returns to the business have risen, a product of the higher levels of productivity achieved by the company (see Figure 9.6 and Table 9.3).

Airport services

The operation of Australia's major airports by a government department came under scrutiny in the early 1980s because of the non-commercial nature of many of the management decisions made in their operation. In the early 1980s Australia's airports were managed by the Australian Government's Department of Aviation, which, as well as operating the airports and air traffic control systems, was responsible for carrying out aviation policy, funding airport development and collecting airport fees. Airport projects had to compete for funds against all other

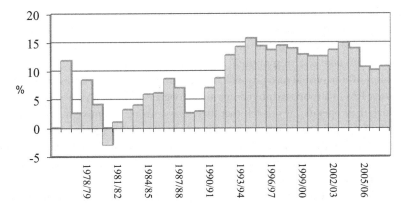

FIGURE 9.6 Australia Post earnings (before interest and tax)/total assets, 1976/77 to 2007/08 (percentage, per annum)

Source: Australia Post (various issues).

TABLE 9.3 Average total factor productivity (multi-factor productivity) growth, Australia Post and national averages, 1975/76 to 1998/99 (percentage, per annum)

	Australia Post			National MFP	
	Output	Input use	TFP	GDP growth	MFP
1975/76 to 1980/81	2.28	−0.60	2.98	2.15	1.54
1981/82 to 1987/88	3.85	1.50	2.40	3.60	1.39
1989/89 to 1998/99	4.35	−1.17	5.52	2.99	1.36
1975/76 to 1998/99	3.72	−0.31	4.03	3.20	1.46

Source: ABS, 1976–1999a, 1976–1999b; Abbott (2000).

Note: GDP is growth in constant dollar GDP. Multi-factor productivity is for the non-farm market sector.

government capital expenditure demands, which meant that airport infrastructure development tended to be influenced by political pressures rather than by the requirements of the aviation industry. Delays in government funding led to a deterioration of facilities and congestion at several of Australia's main airports. In response to these concerns the Hawke Labor Government, after coming to office, established the National Airports Authority Task Force in November 1983 to develop a detailed proposal on a National Airports Authority for the government's consideration (Eames 1998; Abbott and Wu 2002).

In response to the Task Force's report the Australian Government announced in August 1985 that the FAC would be established with responsibility for eight primary and nine secondary Australian airports. In announcing the proposed formation of the FAC the Minister for Aviation declared that it would be financially self-sufficient, commercially orientated and more responsive to the needs of airport users. The FAC began its operations on 1 January 1988, functioned with a board and commercial objectives, and was expected not only to cover its operating and capital expenses but also to pay taxes and generate a reasonable return for the government. At the same time the Civil Aviation Authority was established to take over responsibility for air traffic control, flight service, and the provision of non-visual navigational aids and fire and search and rescue services.

As the FAC's airports exhibited significant degrees of market power in the cities in which they operated it was felt that there was a strong incentive for the FAC to achieve its financial goals by abusing this power. The FAC's aeronautical charges were declared under the *Prices Surveillance Act 1983* on 5 April 1991 and were subject to prices surveillance by the Prices Surveillance Authority and subsequently the Australian Competition and Consumer Commission.

The FAC pursued a policy of attempting to keep a lid on employment levels in order to improve the productivity of airports as traffic grew (Eames 1998). In terms of technological change, improvements came in the form of the introduction of more advanced computer systems and air traffic systems that allowed for the accommodation of greater traffic flows through the airports. This process helped the airports to overcome their congestion problems and accommodate an expansion of output even without the construction of new and enlarged terminals and runways. The FAC carried out an extensive capital works programme throughout its life. To make up for the backlog of demands for expansion and improved services, which emerged under departmental control, the FAC greatly increased capital expenditure.

The FAC was, therefore, able to improve the performance of Australia's airports in terms of productivity over their performance under departmental control. The FAC was able to improve the labour productivity of the airports, carry out a substantial capital works programme and introduce technological advances that helped to improve traffic management and deal with growth in traffic.

The Keating Labor Government began preparations for the privatisation of the FAC in 1995. In doing so it decided to break up the FAC and sell the airports separately. This was justified on the grounds that although many of airports' activities are monopolistic in character there are some activities where competition can be promoted, such as aircraft maintenance and flight hubbing. By breaking up the FAC it was hoped that the airports would be subject to further market pressures that would encourage further efficiency improvements, which in turn would flow on as lower aeronautical charges.

After the election of the Howard Liberal/National Coalition Government in 1996 the Australian Government pressed ahead with privatisation. The Australian Government granted long-term leases at Brisbane, Melbourne and Perth airports in July 1997 and at Adelaide, Alice Springs, Canberra, Coolangatta, Darwin, Hobart, Launceston and Townsville airports in May 1998. The privatised airports were also made subject to a range of economic regulations put in place by the government in the lead-up to privatisation. Sydney Airport was privatised in 2002 after the Olympic Games were undertaken.

Again, the process of corporatisation appears to have been a success, at least in terms of improving the levels of labour productivity of the airports (see Table 9.4). It also meant an increase in private sector investment at the airports, which in turn allowed for the movement of greater volumes of passengers through the airports (see Figure 9.7). The privatisation process has only quite recently occurred, so it is

TABLE 9.4 Australian growth per annum of GDP, aviation passenger numbers, cargo and productivity indicators, 1940s to 2010s (percentage)

	GDP growth %	Passenger growth %	Cargo growth %	Labour productivity growth %	Capital productivity growth %	Total factor productivity growth %
1940s	3.1	28	68.9	–	–	–
1950s	4.4	5.3	8.0	1.5	0.7	1.2
1960s	5.5	9.4	5.2	7.4	6.2	6.6
1970s	3.4	8.1	5.3	4.0	8.6	6.2
1980s	3.4	5.3	4.7	6.8	1.7	4.1
1990s	3.3	6.5	6.3	6.7	−9.2	2.0
2000s	2.0	5.7	−2.8	4.9	−2.2	4.5
2010s	2.5	3.2	3.4	–	–	–

Source: GDP growth – ABS 2017. Passenger and cargo growth – Australia, Department of Civil Aviation (1939–1960, 1961–1966, 1967, 1968–1973); Australia, Department of Transport (1974–1981); Australia, Department of Aviation (1981–1987); Australia, Department of Infrastructure and Regional Development (2016). Productivity figures: 1940s to 1980s – labour productivity = passenger numbers/ number employed, capital productivity = passenger numbers/real value of fixed assets; 1990s – Abbott and Wu (2002), total factor productivity; 2000s – Assaf (2010).

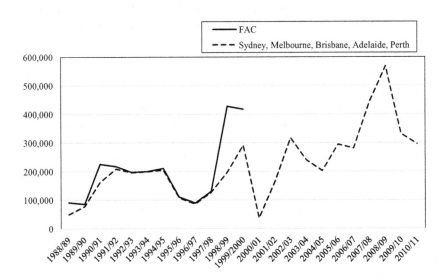

FIGURE 9.7 Capital expenditure on Australian airports by the FAC and major airports, 1988/89 to 2010/11 (constant 1988/89 prices)

Source: FAC (1988–1998); ACCC (1998–2011).

probably still too soon to judge the performance of the airports under this form of ownership, especially since airports tend to have a very long life.

Conclusion

Over the course of the 1990s the nature of government business enterprises in Australia has been largely transformed. In nearly all cases the operational efficiency of these enterprises has been improved, regulatory functions have been separated, which leaves the commercial functions more focused, and the opening up of the enterprises to competition has created additional incentives which create an ongoing spur to further improvements. These measures were largely undertaken because there was a perception that the government business enterprises were simply not performing as well as they could, subject as they were to bureaucratic failures and political pressures to cross-subsidise. Privatisation has also occurred particularly at the national level and in Victoria and South Australia. In some cases, the desire has been to raise even further the efficiency levels of the businesses, although it is probably true that reducing levels of risk and debt was a more important motivation.

One final result of the process of corporatisation and privatisation is that it has made government regulation more transparent. This does not necessarily mean that government regulatory responsibilities in such areas as employment, safety standards and welfare provision have become lighter; in some cases, they may have even been intensified. What it has meant is that regulatory activities have become more transparent, as they now must be formally applied by government to corporatised government firms or to privately owned companies. This is particularly true in the case of the pricing of monopoly facilities. Historically pricing decisions on things like electricity, telephone and water charges were made within government departments or commissions in consultation with political authorities. The process of corporatisation and privatisation has meant that a much more formal and transparent system of pricing regulation has had to be implemented. It is to this issue that we turn in Chapter 10.

In terms of efficiency improvements, some privatisations were a success (e.g. GIO Australia). In other cases, most of the improvements in efficiency took place after corporatisation rather than privatisation. In most cases the industries that were privatised did see improvements in productivity and efficiency; however, these improvements were likely due, in varying (and sometimes substantial) parts, to regulatory reform, increases in competition and technological change. The interaction of such factors and privatisation does complicate the issue of attributing causation for improvements in efficiency. What can be concluded in the context of Australian privatisations is as follows:

- Privatisation can lead to increases in efficiency. This is shown, for example, in the case of airports, where efficiency levels were raised when monopoly facilities were privatised.

- In a number of cases increased competition drove efficiency gains. This is clear in the case of electricity, where both private and government owned generation companies increased their levels of efficiency.
- In some cases, distinguishing between the gains from privatisation, regulatory reform and increased competition is very difficult. This is especially true where technological change has been rapid (e.g. in the case of Telstra).
- Where gains were achieved (from either privatisation or increased competition), generally the costs and benefits were disproportionately either borne or enjoyed by employees, consumers and shareholders.

Notes

1 Butlin et al. (1982). Not all of these types of enterprises are natural monopolies, but in most cases they were perceived as possessing some degree of market power. The government banks are examples of this.
2 From the mid-1980s on, the Commonwealth Bank undertook a major restructure of its bank branches, including those of the State Bank of Victoria after it took over that entity.

References

Abbott, Malcolm 2000, 'An economic evaluation of the Australian Postal Corporation Act', *Economic Papers*, vol. 19, no. 3, pp. 1–27.
Abbott, Malcolm 2006, 'The productivity and efficiency of the Australian electricity supply industry', *Energy Economics*, vol. 28, pp. 444–54.
Abbott, Malcolm 2011, 'The impact of energy asset privatisation on state government debt management and service provision in Victoria and New South Wales', *Australian Journal of Public Administration*, vol. 70, no. 1, pp. 94–104.
Abbott, Malcolm and Wu, Su 2002, 'Total factor productivity and efficiency of Australian airports', *Australian Economic Review*, vol. 35, no. 3, pp. 244–60.
Abbott, Malcolm and Cohen, Bruce 2014, 'Survey of the privatization of government owned enterprises since the 1980s', *Australian Economic Review*, vol. 47, no. 4, pp. 432–54.
Abelson, Peter 2012, *Public Economics: Principles and Practice*, McGraw-Hill, Sydney.
Agham, R.F. 2011, 'Dynamics of productivity change in the Australian electricity industry: assessing the impacts of electricity reform', *Energy Policy*, vol. 39, pp. 3281–95.
Assaf, A.G. 2010, 'The cost efficiency of Australian airports post privatisation: a Bayesian methodology', *Tourism Management*, vol. 33, pp. 267–73.
Assaf, A.G. and Gillen, D. 2012, 'Measuring the joint impact of governance form and economic regulation on airport efficiency', *European Journal of Operational Research*, vol. 220, pp. 187–98.
Aulich, C. and Wettenhall, R. 2005, *Howard's Second and Third Governments: Australian Commonwealth Administration*, UNSW Press, Sydney.
Australia, Bureau of Industry Economics 1994, *International Performance Indicators: Gas Supply*, AGPS, Canberra.
Australia, Department of Aviation 1981–1987, *Annual Report*, AGPS, Canberra.
Australia, Department of Civil Aviation 1939–1960, *Report on Civil Aviation in Australia and New Guinea*, Department of Civil Aviation, Melbourne.

Australia, Department of Civil Aviation 1961–1966, *Report by the Minister*, Department of Civil Aviation, Canberra.
Australia, Department of Civil Aviation 1967, *Civil Aviation Report*, Commonwealth Government Printer, Canberra.
Australia, Department of Civil Aviation 1968–1973, *Civil Aviation*, Commonwealth Government Printer, Canberra.
Australia, Department of Infrastructure and Regional Development 2016, *Aviation Statistics*, http://bitre.au/statistics/aviation/ (accessed 4 April 2016).
Australia, Department of Transport 1974–1981, *Australian Transport*, AGPS, Canberra.
Australia Post various issues, *Annual Report*, Australia Post, Melbourne.
Australia Post 1990, *Annual Report 1990*, Australia Post, Melbourne.
Australian Bureau of Statistics (ABS) 1976–1999a, *Australian National Accounts: Multifactor Productivity*, Cat. No. 5234.0, ABS, Belconnen ACT.
Australian Bureau of Statistics (ABS) 1976–1999b, *Australian System of National Accounts*, Cat. No. 5204.0, ABS, Belconnen ACT.
Australian Bureau of Statistics (ABS) 2017, *Australian National Accounts: National Income, Expenditure and Product*, Cat. No. 5206.0, ABS, Belconnen ACT.
Australian Competition and Consumer Commission (ACCC) 1998–2011, *Regulatory Report – Sydney; Regulatory Report – Melbourne; Regulatory Report – Brisbane; Regulatory Report – Perth; Regulatory Report – Phase II Airports; Price Monitoring and Financial Reporting – Price Monitored Airports*, ACCC, Melbourne.
Avkiran, N.K. 2007, 'Rising productivity of Australian trading banks under deregulation 1986–1995', *Journal of Economics and Finance*, vol. 24, no. 2, pp. 122–40.
Barton, R. 2002a, 'Internationalising telecommunications: Telstra', in P. Fairbrother, M. Paddon and J. Teicher (eds), *Privatisation, Globalisation and Labour: Studies from Australia*, Federation Press, Leichhardt, pp. 51–77.
Barton, R. 2002b, 'Privatisation by stealth: the Gas and Fuel Corporation of Victoria', in P. Fairbrother, M. Paddon and J.H. Teicher (eds), *Privatisation, Globalisation and Labour: Studies from Australia*, Federation Press, Leichhardt, pp. 131–57.
Berger, A.N. and Humphrey, D.B. 1992, *Megamergers in Banking and the Use of Cost Efficiency as an Antitrust Defence*, Finance and Economics Discussion Series No. 203, Board of Governors of Federal Reserve System, Washington DC.
Boehm, E.A. 1956, 'Ownership and control of the electricity supply industry in Australia', *Economic Record*, vol. 32, pp. 257–72.
Butlin, N.G., Barnard, A. and Pincus, J.J. 1982, *Government and Capitalism: Public and Private Choice in Twentieth Century Australia*, George Allen & Unwin, Sydney.
Carrington, R., Coelli, T. and Groom, E. 2002, 'International benchmarking for monopoly price regulation: the case of Australian gas distribution', *Journal of Regulatory Economics*, vol. 21, pp. 191–216.
Carrington, R., Coelli, T. and Prasada Rao, D.S. 2011, 'Australian private health insurance productivity growth: is there scope to limit premium increases?', *Economic Record*, vol. 87, March, pp. 125–39.
Casey, A. and Dollery, B. 1996, 'The privatisation of GIO Australia: success or failure?', *Australian Journal of Public Administration*, vol. 55, no. 3, pp. 18–25.
Chester, L. 2007, 'Who benefits from the restructuring of the Australian electricity sector?', *Journal of Economic Issues*, vol. 41, no. 4, pp. 981–1001.
Collyer, F., Wettenhall, R. and McMaster, J. 2001, *Case Studies in Australian Public Enterprise Disinvestment*, Public Institute of Management and Investment, University of the South Pacific, Suva.

Collyer, F., Wettenhall, R. and McMaster, J. 2003, 'The privatisation of public enterprises: Australian research findings', *Just Policy*, no. 31, pp. 1–23.

Considine, M. 2001, *Enterprising States: The Public Management of Welfare to Work*, Cambridge University Press, Cambridge.

CRA International 2006, *The Impact of the Privatisation of Medibank Private on Private Health Insurance Premiums*, Final Report, Prepared for the Department of Finance and Administration, CRA International, Kingston ACT.

Davies, D.G. 1971, 'The efficiency of public versus private firms: the case of Australia's two airlines', *Journal of Law and Economics*, vol. 14, pp. 149–65.

Davies, D.G. 1977, 'Property rights and economic efficiency: the Australian airlines revisited', *Journal of Law and Economics*, vol. 20, pp. 223–6.

Eames, Jim 1998, *Reshaping Australia's Aviation Landscape: The Federal Airports Corporation 1986–1998*, FAC, Sydney.

Eling, M. and Luhnen, M. 2010, 'Efficiency in the international insurance industry: a cross country comparison', *Journal of Banking and Finance*, vol. 34, pp. 1497–1509.

Esho, N. and Sharpe, I. 1995, 'Long-run estimates of technological change and scale economies in a dynamic framework: Australian permanent building societies, 1974–1990', *Journal of Banking and Finance*, vol. 19, pp. 1135–57.

Esho, N. and Sharpe, I. 1996, 'X-efficiency of Australian permanent building societies, 1974–1990', *Economic Record*, vol. 72, no. 218, pp. 246–59.

Essential Services Commission and Pacific Economics Group 2006, *Total Factor Productivity and the Australian Electricity Distribution Industry: Estimating a National Trend*, Essential Services Commission, Melbourne.

Federal Airports Corporation (FAC) 1988–19981, *Annual Report*, FAC, Sydney.

Forsyth, P. 2001, 'Total factor productivity in Australian domestic aviation', *Transport Policy*, vol. 8, pp. 201–7.

Forsyth, P. 2008, 'Airport policy in Australia and New Zealand: privatization, light handed regulation, and performance', in W. Clifford and Gines de Rus (eds), *Aviation Infrastructure Performance: A Study in Comparative Political Economy*, Brookings Institution Press, Washington DC, pp. 65–99.

Freestone, R., Williams, P. and Bowden, A. 2006, 'Fly buy cities: some planning aspects of airport privatisation in Australia', *Urban Policy and Research*, vol. 2, pp. 491–508.

Grattan Institute 2012, *Putting the Customer Back in Front: How to Make Electricity Cheaper*, Grattan Institute, Carlton VIC.

Harris, M. and Lye, J.N. 2001, 'The fiscal consequences of privatisation: Australian evidence on privatisation by public share float', *International Review of Applied Economics*, vol. 15, no. 3, pp. 305–21.

Hodge, G.A. 2003, 'Privatization: the Australian experience', in D. Parker and D. Saal (eds), *International Handbook on Privatization*, Edward Elgar, Cheltenham, pp. 161–86.

Hooper, P. and Hensher, D.A. 1998, *Measuring Total Factor Productivity: An Index Number Approach*, Working Paper No. ITS-WP-98-2, Institute of Transport Studies, University of Sydney, Sydney.

Independent Pricing and Regulatory Tribunal of New South Wales (IPART) 1999, *Benchmarking the Efficiency of Australian Gas Distributors*, Research Paper No. Gas 99–9, IPART, Sydney.

Independent Pricing and Regulatory Tribunal of New South Wales (IPART) 2010, *Review of the Productivity Performance of State Owned Corporations: Other Industries – Final Report*, July, IPART, Sydney.

Industry Commission 1991, *Energy Generation and Distribution*, AGPS, Canberra.

Jones, Ross (ed.) 1994, *Australian Microeconomic Policies*, Prentice Hall, Sydney.
Kirkwood, J. and Nahm, D. 2006, 'Australian banking efficiency and its relationship to stock returns', *Economic Papers*, vol. 82, no. 258, September, pp. 253–67.
Lawrence, D. 2009a, *Energy Network Total Factor Productivity Sensitivity Analysis*, Report prepared for Australian Energy Market Commission, 9 June, Economic Insights, Hawker ACT.
Lawrence, D. 2009b, *The Productivity Performance of Jemena Gas Networks' NSW Gas Distribution System*, Report prepared for Jemena Gas Networks (NSW), August, Economic Insights, Hawker ACT.
Lawrence, D. 2010, *The Productivity Performance of Envestra's South Australian and Queensland Gas Distribution Systems*, Report prepared for Envestra, September, Economic Insights, Hawker ACT.
Lin, L.C. and Hong, C.H. 2006, 'Operational performance evaluation of international major airports: an application of data envelopment analysis', *Journal of Air Transport Management*, vol. 12, no. 6, pp. 342–51.
Mayne Report 2010, 'The great privatisation list', 7 July, http://www.maynereport.com/.
Meyrick and Associates 2007, *The Total Factor Productivity Performance of Victoria's Gas Distribution Industry*, Report prepared for Envestra, Multinet and SP AusNet, 23 March, Meyrick and Associates, Canberra.
Moran, Alan 2000, 'Privatisation in Australia', *Privatisation International*, July.
Mountain, B. and Littlechild, S. 2010, 'Comparing electricity distribution network revenues and costs in New South Wales, Great Britain and Victoria', *Energy Policy*, vol. 38, pp. 5770–82.
National Competition Council (NCC) 1998, *Review of the Australian Postal Corporation Act*, 2 vols, NCC, Melbourne.
Neal, P. 2004, 'X-efficiency and productivity change in Australian banking', *Australian Economic Papers*, vol. 43, no. 2, pp. 174–91.
O'Donnell, M., Glennie, M., O'Keefe, P. and Kwon, S.H. 2011, 'Privatisation and "light handed" regulation: Sydney Airport', *Economic and Labour Relations Review*, vol. 22, no. 1, 65–80.
Organisation for Economic Co-operation and Development (OECD) 2008, *Communications Outlook 2008*, OECD, Paris.
Otchere, I. and Chan, J. 2003, 'Intra-industry effects of bank privatization: a clinical analysis of the privatization of the Commonwealth Bank of Australia', *Journal of Banking and Finance*, vol. 27, pp. 949–75.
Oum, T.H., Yu, C. and Fu, X. 2003, 'A comparative analysis of productivity performance on the world's major airports: summary report of the ARTS Global Airport Benchmarking Research Report 2002', *Journal of Air Transport Management*, vol. 9, pp. 285–97.
Oum, T.H., Adler, N. and Yu, C. 2006, 'Privatization, corporatization, ownership forms and their effects on the performance of the world's major airports', *Journal of Air Transport Management*, vol. 12, no. 3, pp. 109–21.
Oum, T.H., Yan, J. and Yu, C. 2008, 'Ownership forms matter for airport efficiency: a stochastic frontier investigation of worldwide airports', *Journal of Urban Economics*, vol. 64, pp. 422–35.
Pacific Economics Group 2008, *TFP Research for Victoria's Power Distribution Industry: 2007 Update*, Pacific Economics Group, Madison WI.
Parsons Brinckerhoff 2009, *Review of ETSA Utilities' Regulatory Proposal for the Period July 2010 to June 2015*, Parsons Brinckerhoff, Melbourne.
Pollitt, Michael G. 1999, 'A survey of the liberalisation of public enterprises in the UK since 1979', Unpublished mimeo, University of Cambridge, Cambridge.

Productivity Commission 1999, *International Benchmarking of Telecommunications, Prices and Price Changes*, Productivity Commission, Melbourne.
Productivity Commission 2012, *Productivity in Electricity, Gas and Water: Measurement and Interpretation*, Staff Working Paper, Productivity Commission, Melbourne.
Reserve Bank of Australia 1997, 'Privatisation in Australia', *Reserve Bank of Australia Bulletin*, December, pp. 7–16.
Rushdi, A. 1994, 'Productivity changes in the Gas and Fuel Corporation of Victoria', *Energy Economics*, vol. 16, pp. 36–45.
Rushdi, A.A. 2000, 'Total factor productivity measures for Telstra', *Telecommunications Policy*, vol. 24, pp. 143–54.
Sathye, M. 2002, 'Measuring productivity changes in Australian banking: an application of Malmquist indices', *Managerial Finance*, vol. 28, no. 9, pp. 48–59.
Schuster, D. 2009, 'Australia's approach to airport charges: the Sydney Airport experience', *Journal of Air Transport Management*, vol. 15, no. 3, pp. 121–6.
Serebrisky, T. 2012, *Airport Economics in Latin America and the Caribbean: Benchmarking, Regulation and Pricing*, World Bank, Washington DC.
Small, R. 2002, 'Entering the international aviation industry: privatisation of Qantas', in P. Fairbrother, M. Paddon and J. Teicher (eds), *Privatisation, Globalisation and Labour: Studies from Australia*, Federation Press, Leichhardt.
Stiglitz, Joseph, E. 2001, 'Information and the change in the paradigm in economics', *American Economic Review*, vol. 92, no. 3, pp. 460–501.
Sturm, J.E. and Williams, B. 2004, 'Foreign bank entry, deregulation and bank efficiency: lessons from the Australian experience', *Journal of Banking and Finance*, vol. 28, no. 7, pp. 1775–99.
Thomas, G. 2010, 'Pitfalls and promise: Australia's airport privatization gets mixed marks', *Air Transport World*, September, pp. 56–9.
Toner, P. 2003, 'Declining apprentice training rates: causes, consequences and solutions', Discussion Paper, Australian Expert Group in Industry Studies, University of Western Sydney, Sydney.
Tourism and Transport Forum Australia 2007, *Assessing the Impact of Airport Privatization*, URS Australia, Sydney.
Tsai, H.C., Chen, C.M. and Tzeng, G.H. 2006, 'The comparative productivity efficiency for global telecoms', *International Journal of Production Economics*, vol. 103, pp. 509–26.
Walker, R.G. and Walker, B.C. 2001, *Privatisation: Sell Off or Sell Out? The Australian Experience*, Australian Broadcasting Corporation, Sydney.
Wettenhall, R. 1999, 'Privatisation in Australia: how much and what impact', *Asian Review of Public Administration*, vol. 10, pp. 144–58.
Wilson Cook & Co 2008, *Review of Proposed Expenditure of ACT & NSW Electricity DNSPs*, Volume 1: *Main Report, Final*, October, Wilson Cook & Co, Sydney.
Worthington, A.C. 1999, 'Malmquist indices of productivity change in Australian financial services', *Journal of International Financial Markets, Institutions and Money*, vol. 9, no. 3, pp. 303–20.
Worthington, A.C. 2004, 'Determinants of merger and acquisition activity in Australian cooperative deposit-taking institutions', *Journal of Business Research*, vol. 57, no. 1, pp. 47–57.
Wu, S. 2007, 'Efficiency and productivity analysis of the Australian banking sector under deregulation', PhD thesis, University of Melbourne, Melbourne.

10
ENERGY POLICY

Introduction

Before taking up the issue of the pricing of monopolies it is useful to look at the restructuring of the electricity and gas industries in Australia, which to a large degree made the formal regulation of utility pricing necessary. The restructuring of the Australian electricity and gas industries during the 1990s and 2000s was one of the largest reforms undertaken and led to the dismantling of industry structures that had existed in Australia since the 1920s.

Reform of the electricity industry took place all round the world during the 1990s and 2000s. The process of reform in Australia was influenced by developments in the United Kingdom, the United States and New Zealand. In each country, the reform process generally involved the break-up of vertically integrated monopoly companies (either government or privately owned) into separate entities associated with the various distinct sections of the industry (generation, transmission, distribution and retail) and competition being introduced into some of these sections (Pollitt 1997; Steiner 2001). After electricity is generated it is sent through high-voltage transmission lines to the regions in which it is to be consumed. Before it is consumed it is transformed into a lower voltage and then sent through a distribution network to final customers. The retailing of electricity involves the sale of electricity to final customers and involves the negotiation of supplies of power from generators on behalf of customers, metering, billing and marketing. In most countries – including Australia – all these sectors have historically been bundled together within a single entity. Reform has been undertaken in most countries on the assumption that the generation and retail segments of the industry are potentially competitive. By introducing competition into these segments, it is hoped that it will raise the general level of efficiency of these segments (Borenstein 2000, 2001; Borenstein and Bushnell 2000).

In the case of the natural gas supply industry a similar process occurred. This involved the separation of the natural monopoly element of the industry – distribution and transmission – and the opening up as far as possible of the other elements to competition. In addition, regulatory functions concerning pricing and safety were separated from the companies and given to newly established regulatory agencies.

The purpose of this chapter, therefore, is to present an explanation of the motivation for and result of the reform and restructuring process that took place in the Australian electricity and gas industries during the 1990s and 2000s. This involved not just a restructuring of the industry but also in many cases the large-scale privatisation of government owned electricity and gas assets.

Electricity and gas markets

To begin with one should look at the breakdown of primary energy use in Australia. From Table 10.1 it can be seen that the most important energy sources are from oil, coal and natural gas. Overall fuel consumption has tended to rise over the longer term (see Figure 10.1), but this has tended to be fairly stable since around 2008.

Oil is important in the transport industry, and both coal and natural gas are important in the generation of electricity. Natural gas is also used for cooking and heating. Over the past 20 years there has been some change in the mix of fuel sources, with natural gas and renewables becoming more important and coal and oil declining as a share of total fuels (see Figure 10.2). In the case of electricity generation (Table 10.2) coal is still the most important fuel used (around 70 per cent), with natural gas being important as well. Renewables have increased in importance since the 1990s but are still far less important.

Turning more specifically to the electricity and gas industries the basic concern of governments was that, under the old model of vertical integration, the electricity industry was divorced from market disciplines. This traditional structure involved government owned, vertically integrated companies (combining generation, transmission and distribution), with there being no separation of commercial

TABLE 10.1 Primary energy in Australia, consumption by fuel, 2015 (MTOE)

	Million tonnes oil equivalent (MTOE)	*%*
Oil	46.2	35.2
Natural gas	30.9	23.5
Coal	46.6	35.5
Hydro	3.1	2.4
Renewables	4.5	3.4
Total	131.4	100.0

Source: BP (2015a).

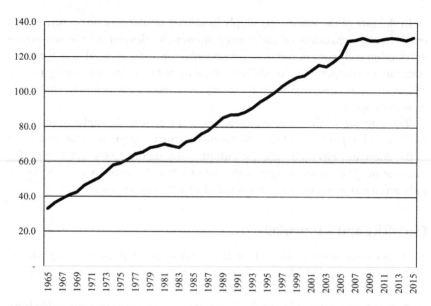

FIGURE 10.1 Primary energy consumption, Australia, 1965 to 2015 (MTOE)

Source: BP (2015a).

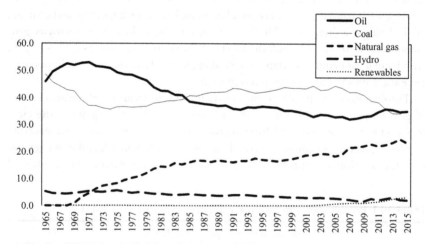

FIGURE 10.2 Fuel shares of primary energy consumption, Australia, 1965 to 2015 (percentage)

Source: BP (2015a).

functions from policy and regulation (i.e. safety, etc.). In Australia, each state had a separate, vertically integrated company, and there was no competition.

TABLE 10.2 Principal electricity generation by fuel type, Australia, 1994, 2015 (GWh)

	2015		1994	
	GWh	%	GWh	%
Hydro	17,748	8.3	16,296	9.8
Biofuels	43	0.0	0	0.0
Coal	151,321	70.5	137,898	82.9
Coal seam methane	7,766	3.6	0	0.0
Natural gas	27,376	12.8	11,636	7.0
Oil	122	0.1	579	0.3
Solar	22	0.0	0	0.0
Wind	10,237	4.8	4	0.0
Total	214,635	100.0	166,413	100.0

Source: BP (2015b).

The lack of market disciplines meant that there were weak incentives for the authorities to prevent overinvestment in generator and transmission facilities and overstaffing of their operations. This in turn led to excessive prices for electricity. In the late 1980s and early 1990s several studies of the Australian electricity industry found that it was operating below best practice levels (see for instance ESAA 1994; BIE 1996). As electricity is an important input good in the process of production of all other goods and services any inefficiencies would be passed on to the whole of the economy.

The emphasis of reform, therefore, was on the introduction of competition and therefore separation of the industry (vertically and horizontally). Potential competition was introduced into the generation and retail sectors of the industry and the natural monopoly elements confined to distribution and transmission. Wholesale markets were established in each state and linked into a national market. The Victorian market was the first and opened in 1994. New South Wales followed in 1996, and the two were linked together in 1998 (National Electricity Market). Queensland and South Australia were added at the same time, and Tasmania was added in 2005. In addition, regulation was separated (environmental, safety and pricing).

The general approach to economic reform in Australia during the 1980s had been to increase the level of competition in Australian markets. The reform process in electricity in the 1990s was to extend this approach to the electricity industry as well. By fostering competition where it was possible, it was hoped that it would promote a more flexible and cost efficient industry with the ultimate objective of delivering lower electricity prices than were likely under a vertically integrated regulated monopoly (Industry Commission 1991). At the national level this approach made no commitment to encouraging state owned or privately owned facilities. The main theme was to introduce competition, which would apply to both privately owned and state owned assets. Privatisation would be pursued on a state by state basis and so therefore has not been a consistent national policy in the electricity industry.

TABLE 10.3 Approximate breakdown of electricity tariffs, Australia (percentage)

Generation costs	45–50%
Transmission costs	10–15%
Distribution costs	30–35%
Retail costs	5–10%
	100%

Source: Approximations based on ORG (2001).

In the electricity industry – as previously mentioned – it is perceived that generation and retail of electricity are potentially competitive. From Table 10.3 it can be seen that these two segments combined make up over one-half of the total cost of generating electricity. By injecting competition into these two segments it is hoped that average cost will be reduced through the achievement of higher levels of technical and allocative efficiency. This still leaves the transmission and distribution elements as monopoly providers. To ensure that competing generation and retail companies are treated fairly an access regime needs to be created that gives these companies access to these essential facilities at prices that do not embody monopoly rent. The distribution and transmission elements because of their central and essential nature can potentially impede competition in the generation and retail markets by restricting access or by offering it at excessive prices.

Similar problems of access and monopoly pricing exist in the natural gas supply industry. Despite the vertical separation of natural gas production from transmission and distribution, historically there was little scope for competition in the natural gas supply industry before the reform process was undertaken. The long distances between the capital city markets meant that traditionally each capital city was supplied from a single source. This further meant that transmission of gas was also provided on a monopoly basis. Finally, distribution and retail were bundled together so that any potential competition in retail was not realised. The process of reform has been undertaken with the idea of isolating the monopoly elements and then providing regulated access to these essential facilities. In this way, it is hoped that both gas supply and retail will become competitive. This has proved more difficult than in the case of electricity because of the restricted number of supply sources in Australia, but it is hoped that by giving access to the transmission and distribution elements new exploration and developments, as well as the construction of new transmission pipelines, will create a more competitive market for natural gas.

Electricity reform process

At the beginning of the 1990s the electricity industry in each state of Australia consisted of a single vertically integrated state government owned authority or a collection of state government owned authorities. These bodies were also responsible for regulation of the industry in such areas as electrical safety.

Under these arrangements investment in new generation was largely the responsibility of state governments and their electricity authorities. Electricity prices were set by the state governments, and were designed to cover the industry's costs plus any return required by them as owners. Often politically motivated cross-subsidies were built into price structures. The six main electricity supply companies for the six states were respectively: the Electricity Commission of New South Wales, the State Electricity Commission of Victoria, the Queensland Electricity Commission, the Electricity Trust of South Australia, the State Energy Commission of Western Australia (which included gas as well as electricity) and the Hydro-Electric Commission of Tasmania. Except for the states of New South Wales and Queensland each company operated a vertically integrated operation including generation, transmission and distribution of electricity. In New South Wales and Queensland distribution was carried out by a series of local power boards. In addition, the Australian Government operated the Snowy Mountains Hydro-Electric Authority purely as a generation company (owned jointly by the Australian, New South Wales and Victorian governments). In some states like South Australia and Victoria the electricity authorities were also responsible for the extraction of fuel sources. In all states, the predominant government electricity authority had industry regulation responsibilities as well.

In July 1991 the Council of Australian Governments agreed to reforms intended to introduce competition into the electricity industry. The key reforms involved industry restructuring – in particular the separation of generation, transmission, distribution and regulatory functions – and the formation of a national electricity market in the southern and eastern states. In April 1995, these reforms were reaffirmed and extended under the National Competition Policy.

The reforms followed an investigation by the Industry Commission. In the process it reported that:

> Concern has been expressed that the electricity and gas industries have not been functioning efficiently. It has been asserted that there is little incentive for efficiency. Virtually all of the electricity supply industry and significant parts of the gas industry are publicly owned and immune from commercial disciplines such as insolvency and the threat of takeover. Competition within each industry is negligible. Unlike many other domestic industries, there is no direct competition from overseas suppliers. To a large degree, the cost of any inefficiencies is borne by users and by taxpayers generally rather than by the electricity or gas industries.
>
> *(Industry Commission 1991, vol. II, p. 2)*

Its response was to recommend that there should be an:

> Increase competition in the electricity supply industry by, first, notionally separating (ie ring fencing) activities . . . and, second, fully separating activities as soon as possible. . . . This would require government action in

particular to: separate ownership of generation, transmission and distribution functions; break up existing publicly owned generating capacity to form a number of independent generating bodies; form a public body to acquire and operate all transmission assets ... create multiple distribution franchises in states where currently they do not exist; require all transmission and distribution bodies to provide open access.

(Industry Commission 1991, vol. I, p. 24)

Victoria led the way in the implementation of the electricity reform process. Initially that state's integrated company was disaggregated into three interim operating businesses (generation, transmission and distribution/retail). Subsequently distribution/retail was divided into five companies with separate franchise areas, and generation was broken up into seven separate generation companies. In the years 1995 to 1997 the separate generation, distribution/retail and transmission companies were privatised (Figure 10.3). In New South Wales three competing generation entities were established, as well as an independent transmission business, and six new distribution/retail companies (later reduced to four) were created from the consolidation of 25 distribution boards in December 1995. These entities remained in government ownership into the 2010s. In Queensland, Tasmania and South Australia a similar process was subsequently undertaken with the creation of separate entities responsible for generation, transmission and distribution functions. In the South Australian case the electricity assets were privatised.

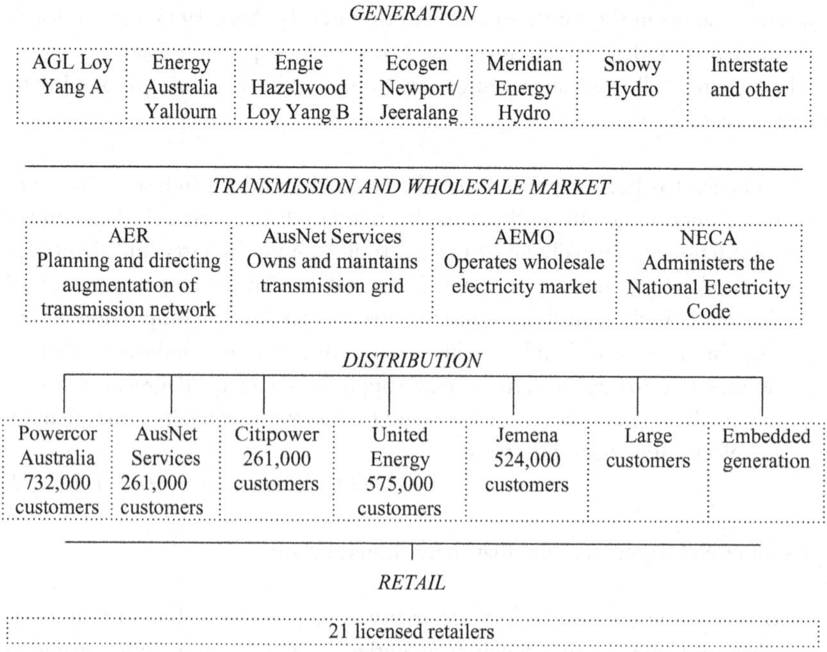

GENERATION

AGL Loy Yang A	Energy Australia Yallourn	Engie Hazelwood Loy Yang B	Ecogen Newport/ Jeeralang	Meridian Energy Hydro	Snowy Hydro	Interstate and other

TRANSMISSION AND WHOLESALE MARKET

AER Planning and directing augmentation of transmission network	AusNet Services Owns and maintains transmission grid	AEMO Operates wholesale electricity market	NECA Administers the National Electricity Code

DISTRIBUTION

Powercor Australia 732,000 customers	AusNet Services 261,000 customers	Citipower 261,000 customers	United Energy 575,000 customers	Jemena 524,000 customers	Large customers	Embedded generation

RETAIL

21 licensed retailers

FIGURE 10.3 Victorian electricity industry structure, 30 June 2016

A competitive wholesale market was introduced in Victoria in October 1994 with electricity trade through a 'pool' arrangement managed by the Victorian Power Exchange. A similar market began operating in New South Wales in the following year, and harmonisation of the two markets occurred in May 1997. The National Electricity Market (NEM) began its operations in December 1998. The NEM is a wholesale market for the supply and purchase of electricity combined with a regime of open access for transmission and distribution in the participating jurisdictions of Victoria, New South Wales, Queensland, the ACT and South Australia. Two companies, the National Electricity Code Administrator Limited (NECA) and the National Electricity Market Management Company Limited (NEMMCO), were formed in 1996 to implement the NEM. NECA supervised, administered and enforced the industry code of conduct, and NEMMCO managed the wholesale electricity market in accordance with the code (NEMMCO 2001).

Today the Australian Energy Market Operator (which replaced NEMMCO) operates the NEM. The NEM is an energy-only gross pool with mandatory participation. Generators sell all their electricity through the market, which matches supply to demand instantaneously. From the generators' offers, the market determines the combination of generation to meet demand in the most cost efficient way. AEMO then issues dispatch instructions to these generators. The market determines a spot price every half-hour for each of the five regions. AEMO settles the financial transactions for electricity traded based on these spot prices. Generators and retailers often protect themselves from movements in the spot price by entering into hedge contracts.

The NEM plays the role of balancing demand and supply and of allocating supplies from competing generators in the short run and provides economic signals for the entry of new suppliers in the long run. Generators bid electricity into a common 'pool', and distribution/retail companies or independent retailers purchase from the pool and on-sell it to final consumers. To smooth out fluctuations in the spot market prices, distributors or retailers enter into financial hedging contracts with generator companies. Competition in this segment of the market is important, as generation makes up the most significant portion of the cost of supplying electricity (approximately 45–50 per cent; Table 10.3).

In most countries. the final stage of electricity market reform has been the introduction of competition into the retail end of the industry. This stage of reform, although less important in terms of its relative size (5–10 per cent of total costs; Table 10.3), is the one that is most noticed by the bulk of a country's consumers. Retail competition involves giving access to transmission and distribution networks to retail companies that operate independently of the distribution companies. With the separation of generation, transmission and distribution, generator companies initially supply distribution companies on behalf of final customers. Retail competition means that consumers can choose from a variety of retailers, which purchase electricity on behalf of consumers and pay charges for the use of transmission and distribution networks to deliver it to them. If distribution is separated before retail competition into a variety of zones supplied by companies with exclusive rights to distribution and retail (as was the case in Queensland, New South Wales and Victoria) then retail competition when it begins might involve the entry of the incumbent distribution companies into retail in zones besides their own. It might also involve the entry of entirely new retailers. In some cases, such as in New Zealand, the government can even mandate the separation of retail from distribution so that distributors act only as 'wires' companies and do not on-sell electricity to final consumers.

Whether it is the distribution companies that conduct the retail function or independent retailers that do so, it must be stressed that electricity supplied to final consumers comes from a common pool. Distributor–retailers cannot purchase electricity directly from specific generators. Electricity flows follow physical laws rather than contractual arrangements. The contracts that distributor–retailers enter into with generators to supply electricity are purely financial hedging contracts, the retailers having to purchase electricity from the common pool. Retailers, therefore, have no control over the reliability of the electricity supply. Instead retailers provide consumers with the additional services of meter reading, billing, risk management and so on.

The demand and prices that were created in these markets helped to send better signals to the markets. Figures 10.4, 10.5 and 10.6 display how prices change over time. In South Australia and Victoria, for instance, electricity demand tends to peak in the summer months (as it does in most Australian states), which means that the composition of fuel use changes over time. Figure 10.6 shows that over the course of a day electricity demand changes as well, as do wholesale electricity prices. Demand and supply are matched by the system operator, and wholesale prices fluctuate to bring this about. At the retail level consumers purchase electricity from energy retailers.

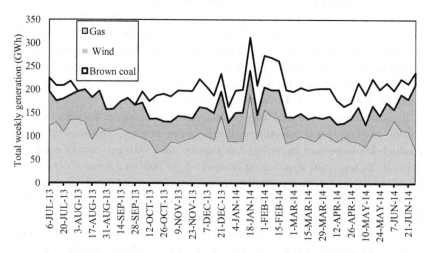

FIGURE 10.4 South Australia: weekly generation by fuel type, 2013/14 (GWh)

Source: ESAA (various issues).

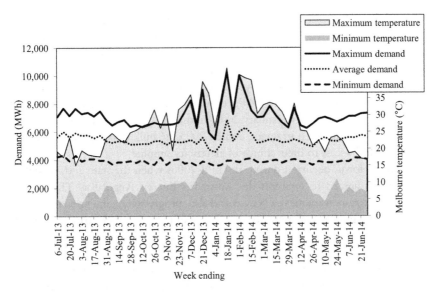

FIGURE 10.5 Victoria: system demand, 2013/14 (MWh)

In the Australian case retail competition was introduced in the different states in a series of stages. Initially only a small number of large consumers in Australia could exercise consumer choice. In Victoria, for instance, retail competition for large consumers with an annual consumption of 40 GWh or more began in December 1994. Other customers were obliged to purchase electricity from one of the five distribution/retail companies depending upon where they were situated.

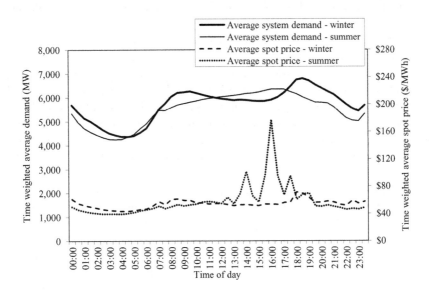

FIGURE 10.6 Victoria: system demand and spot prices (MW)

Consumers in the competitive section of the market in contrast could purchase electricity from any retailer, which in turn purchased electricity from the wholesale market. This competitive market became gradually larger in succeeding years. From July 1995 consumers of 4 GWh per annum or more were made competitive. Consumers of 750 MWh or more were made competitive in July 1996, consumers of 160 MWh per annum in July 1998, consumers of 40 MWh in January 2001 and finally all other consumers in January 2002. In the rest of the country retail competition was also introduced in stages, and by 2003 the bulk of Australia's electricity consumers had access to their choice of electricity supplier.

Further reforms occurred during the mid-2000s when the state and Australian governments agreed to establish the Australian Energy Regulator. This agency took over the responsibilities of NECA and also, progressively, the price regulatory powers of the state governments on regulation of the gas and electricity networks and powers of the Australian Competition and Consumer Commission on transmission network regulation. The purpose behind these reforms was to create more general uniformity of regulation in energy markets across the various jurisdictions.

Although horizontal and vertical separation was carried out in all states the issue of the privatisation of government owned enterprises in the industry was not so universal. In Victoria, the industry was broken up and privatised (raising $A19.3 billion in the process). This also occurred in South Australia ($A4.7 billion). State ownership remained in New South Wales, Queensland, Tasmania and Western Australia, although later privatisation occurred in New South Wales and Queensland ($A14.5 billion and $A3.2 billion respectively), mainly of the generation and retail segments of the industry.

As well as the creation of corporatised and privatised electricity companies there was a separation of regulatory functions. This involved the creation of economic regulators to regulate pricing (see the various agencies listed in Table 10.4) and safety regulators (see Table 10.5). In the case of price regulation of access to the natural monopoly elements this issue is discussed in Chapter 11. In the case of safety regulation separate safety regulators were established and took over such things as the licensing of electricians and electrical contractors. They also set and enforced standards in the production and sale of appliances, enforced codes of conduct in wiring and undertook safety promotional campaigns. These measures appear to have been reasonably effective, as the number of fatalities in Australia since the reforms took place have tended to fall (see Figure 10.7). It should be

TABLE 10.4 Economic regulator in each jurisdiction in Australia, 2016

Jurisdiction	Name	Areas of responsibility
Australia	Australian Energy Regulator – ACCC	Electricity and gas distribution/transmission. Telecommunications, airports, post.
New South Wales	IPART	Water, sewerage, train/bus/ferry charges, rail access, electricity and gas retail, local government rates.

Victoria	Essential Services Commission	Water, sewerage, port charges, rail access, electricity and gas retail.
Queensland	Queensland Competition Authority	Water, sewerage, rail access, electricity and gas retail, local government rates.
South Australia	Essential Services Commission	Water, sewerage, port charges, rail access, electricity and gas retail.
Western Australia	Economic Regulation Authority	Water, sewerage, rail access, electricity and gas retail/distribution/transmission.
Tasmania	Office of the Tasmanian Economic Regulator	Water, sewerage, electricity and gas retail.
ACT	ICRC	Water, sewerage, electricity and gas retail.
Northern Territory	Utilities Commission	Water, sewerage, electricity and gas retail/distribution/transmission.

TABLE 10.5 Safety regulator in the electricity industry in each jurisdiction in Australia, 2016

	Main safety agency
VIC	Energy Safe Victoria
QLD	Electricity Safety Office – Department of Justice and Attorney-General
SA	Office of the Technical Regulator – Department of Transport, Energy and Infrastructure
WA	Energy Safety WA – Department of Consumer and Employment Protection
TAS	Workplace Standards Tasmania – Department of Justice
ACT	ACT Planning and Land Authority
NT	NT Worksafe – Department of Employment, Education and Training

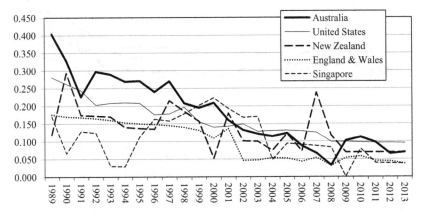

FIGURE 10.7 Fatalities from electrical accidents, various countries, 1989 to 2013 (number per 100,000 people)

Source: Singapore, RBD (various issues); United Kingdom, ONS (various issues); United States, CPSC (various issues); ABS (2013); AIHW (2013); New Zealand MOH (2013).

noted, however, that this decline has taken place in several countries at the same time and is at least partially due to the improvements in technology and quality of electrical appliances.

Benefits and problems with the reform process

The perceived benefit of the reform process, in its entirety, is that competition will drive improvements in efficiency, which in turn will lead to reductions in real prices. A variety of studies have found that the reform process has led to large increases in the industry's level of productivity (Productivity Commission 1999; BCA 2000; Access Economics 2001) and reductions in the real price of electricity (Figure 10.8). So far, most of these gains have come from the restructuring of the generator sector and the competition created by the operation of the wholesale market and have been enjoyed by large users of electricity rather than by residential consumers. The prices fell mostly in the years straight after the reforms took place as employment levels and costs were reduced (see Figure 10.9) and reserve margins of capacity fell (see Figure 10.10). Since around 2000, however, prices have tended to rise, as additional capital expenditure was undertaken in the industry and had to be recovered by investors (see Figures 10.8 and 10.11).

Several difficulties have been associated with the whole process. First, there have been concerns expressed that some generator companies possess market power so that they are able to take advantage of consumers (ABARE 2002). Second, the

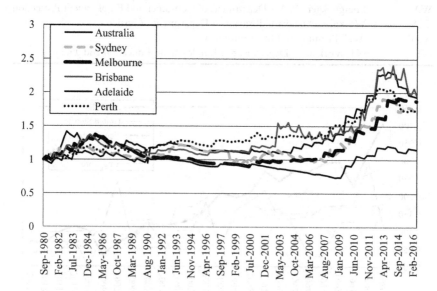

FIGURE 10.8 Index of real retail electricity prices, Australia and cities, September 1980 to February 2016 (September 1980=1.0)

Source: ESAA (various issues).

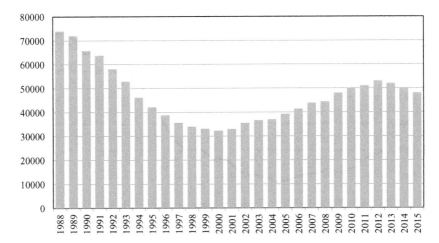

FIGURE 10.9 Australian electricity supply industry: numbers employed, 1988 to 2015

Source: ABS, Cat. Nos 8155.0, 8226.0.

determination of the pricing of the monopoly elements (distribution and transmission) has attracted controversy. Many fears have been expressed that investment in new capacity to meet rising demand will be inadequate. Finally, there were high costs and delays associated with the introduction of retail competition. There have also been some social distress and high unemployment in some regions owing to the reductions in employment in the industry.

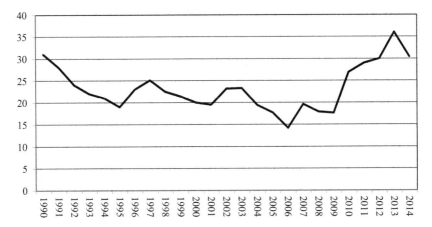

FIGURE 10.10 Australian average reserve plant margin, 1990 to 2014 (percentage)

Source: ESAA (various issues).

Note: Reserve plant margin equals (installed capacity−system peak demand)/system peak demand.

152 Economic policy

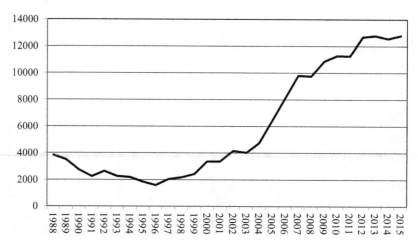

FIGURE 10.11 Australian net capital investment in electricity supply, 1988 to 2015 ($A million)

Source: Australian Bureau of Statistics, Cat. Nos 8155.0, 8226.0.

Nonetheless the process has seen a considerable rise in the industry's level of operational efficiency in all states regardless of whether assets have been privatised or not. Overinvestment and overstaffing have been reduced, and market signals encourage new investment (especially in peaking plant). The states that have privatised assets have been able to reduce state debt and use the proceeds to expand other government services. New combined retail services (gas and electricity) have been introduced, and system reliability levels have tended to be improved (see Figure 10.12).

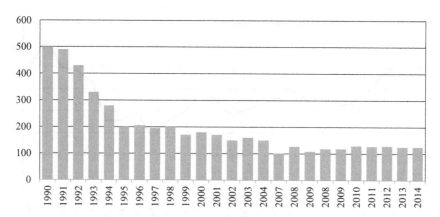

FIGURE 10.12 System reliability, Victoria, 1990 to 2014 (average number of minutes lost per customer)

Source: ESAA (various issues).

Note: CAIDI = average customer outage time (customer minutes interrupted/total number of customer interruptions).

Gas market reform

The natural gas industry has been reformed along similar lines to the electricity industry. The supply of natural gas involves a number of separate stages. After extraction, natural gas is treated and then transported in high-pressure transmission pipelines to the 'city gate'. It is then distributed in low-pressure pipelines to final consumers. In most of the Australian states before 1991 there was no effective competition at any stage of this process. The natural gas industry in each of the Australian states emerged with a structure based on a single source of supply, a single transmission company and a single distributor/retailer. At the production end the natural gas industry in Australia began in the 1960s when the reserves of the Cooper and Gippsland basins were developed. Gas production from the Cooper Basin began in 1969 and was sold into the markets of Adelaide, Brisbane and Sydney. Gippsland gas was made available for sale in Victoria from 1970. Perth was supplied from the Perth Basin from 1971, and the gas reserves of the Carnarvon Basin began supplying Perth in 1985. These reserves were developed by private companies, BHP/Esso for the Bass Strait, Santos for the Cooper and Woodside/North West Shelf Gas for the Carnarvon Basin reserves.

Natural gas industry reforms were similar to those of the electricity industry, although to begin with there was more separation and private ownership in the case of natural gas. The natural gas transmission and distribution networks, however, were developed by a combination of government owned authorities and private companies. Petroleum companies were important in natural gas extraction and treatment. The natural gas industry, therefore, was vertically separated, and private ownership was prominent in a number of states. For instance, as previously mentioned, the extraction of natural gas in each state was developed by private companies separately from the transmission and distribution of gas. Private ownership also occurred in some states in gas distribution/retail. In New South Wales and the ACT, for instance, a private company undertook the distribution/retail of natural gas, although the Australian Government owned Pipeline Authority controlled the transmission pipeline from the Cooper Basin to Sydney. A similar situation existed – and still exists – in Brisbane, where two privately owned companies carry out distribution. In some states mixed public–private utilities existed; for example about 28 and 21 per cent respectively of the issued shares of the Gas and Fuel Corporation of Victoria and the holding company of the South Australia Gas Company, SAGASCO Holdings, were privately owned, with the remainder government owned.

Reform of the Australian natural gas market began after the release of the Australian Government's Industry Commission report in 1991 entitled *Energy Generation and Distribution*. In response to this report the December 1992 meeting of the Council of Australian Governments (COAG) agreed in principle to open up the Australian gas supply industry to greater competition. In February 1994 COAG agreed to reforms to remove impediments to 'free and fair' trade in natural gas. The underlying objective was to develop a nationally integrated and competitive industry in which consumers could contract directly with a gas producer of their choice, and separately with a pipeline operator for gas haulage. To achieve this COAG agreed that specific reforms would be introduced, including the introduction of a uniform framework for access to gas transmission pipelines, the reform of gas franchise arrangements, the corporatisation of government owned utilities, and the implementation of structural separation or ring-fencing of vertically integrated transmission and distribution activities. In addition, investment was encouraged in the transmission pipelines that linked up the various markets and helped to create a national integrated industry.

As well as the introduction of these reforms the level of government ownership and operation of transmission and distribution infrastructure has been reduced. The Australian Government sold the Cooper Basin to Sydney Pipeline in June 1994; the South Australian Government sold its majority holdings in SAGASCO Holdings Limited in October 1993 and in June 1995 its control of the Cooper Basin to Adelaide Pipeline. The Victorian Government began restructuring the Gas and Fuel Corporation of Victoria in 1994. At first it was separated into two legally corporatised entities responsible for transmission and distribution/retail respectively. Later the distribution/retail company was horizontally separated into three companies, which were privatised, along with the transmission company. In Western Australia, the gas operations of the State Energy Commission were separated into a stand-alone gas company, AlintaGas, in 1995. AlintaGas transmission and distribution businesses were privatised in 1998–99. Today government owned gas networks are limited to two small municipal owned networks in Queensland (Roma and Dalby) and southern New South Wales (Country Energy). In Victoria assets were broken up and sold for $A6.5 billion, the Western Australian assets for $3.3 billion, the Queensland assets for $773 million and the South Australian assets for $721 million.

As the structure of the industry was changed during the 1990s the nature of economic regulation of the gas industry was also reformed. In particular, efforts were made to introduce more formal regulatory arrangements into the previously state owned utilities. Economic regulation was standardised across both state owned and private companies, and greater focus was given to the economic regulation of the elements of gas supply that possess natural monopoly characteristics. As gas distribution and transmission networks reap economies of scale that make duplication costly, third-party access arrangements to these facilities have been developed. By 2000 all state governments had passed legislation governing conditions of access to gas network facilities including pricing arrangements. By this date vertical separation of gas transmission, distribution and retail had occurred. In each state retail competition is being progressively introduced. The general emphasis in this reform process, therefore, has been to introduce competition into the natural gas supply industry, both for private and for government owned companies. Privatisation of government assets has occurred. However, the general emphasis of COAG was not to promote privatisation per se rather than competition.

As in the case of electricity, natural gas wholesale markets were established. In Australia, the Victorian Declared Wholesale Gas Market commenced in 1999 to manage and balance flows across the state of Victoria's transmission system. Today it is operated by the Australian Energy Market Operator. The Government of Victoria pursued the privatization, separation and opening up of the gas industry the most rigorously of all Australian states; hence, it was in this state that a wholesale market for gas was first introduced. This market, along with the three other short-term trading markets, provides wholesale gas spot markets for participants to manage contractual imbalances and facilitate secondary trading and demand-side response from end-users. The Adelaide, Sydney and Brisbane markets are also operated by the Australian Energy Market Operator and function as hubs connecting transmission pipelines and distribution networks, commencing at the Sydney and Adelaide hubs in 2010, and the Brisbane hub in 2011. The purpose of these markets is to complement long-term gas contracts and provide an option for making up short-run supply and demand shortfalls. However, they only currently trade insignificant gas volumes and may have only a limited relevance to the price of the long-term gas contracts that dominate Australian markets (Australia, Department of Industry, Bureau of Resources and Energy Economics 2013).

Historically, the Australian gas market was isolated from other countries; but since the early 2000s it has become increasingly integrated with the rest of the world via the export of LNG. Domestically long distances between gas sources and urban centres have meant that local conditions have varied across the country. The building of gas transmission lines in the 1990s and 2000s has meant that the local markets have become more integrated, and market prices across the country have converged. Open access was introduced in Australia during the 1990s and 2000s (along with a national access code for gas), as part of a national agreement, and retail competition to all consumers was progressively introduced.

In terms of regulation, there has also been a degree of convergence in Australia. Originally, regulation was undertaken in a similar fashion to regulation in Canada and the United States, with a national regulator undertaking the regulation of transmission services, and state regulators undertaking the regulation of final gas prices and distribution transport. In the early 2000s, the Australian Energy Regulator was established and became the sole regulator of pipeline services, introducing an integrated approach not only to market development but also to regulation (with the notable exceptions of Western Australia and the Northern Territory, which have separate systems). The development of both long- and short-term markets for gas in Australia has facilitated greater integration of the gas industry both within Australia and with other countries.

Renewables

To reduce emissions from the generation of electricity various governments in Australia have undertaken measures to promote the use of renewable energy. Renewable electricity has undergone substantial growth in Australia since 2000, especially in the last few years. In 2015 renewables made up 5.8 per cent of Australia's total energy sources (2.4 per cent from hydro and 3.4 per cent from other renewables; Table 10.1). It is estimated that Australia produced 28,050 gigawatt hours (GWh) of renewable electricity (or equivalent) over the year 2014/15, representing 13.1 per cent of the total production in Australia (see Table 10.2). By way of comparison, in 2006, approximately 9,500 GWh of electricity came from renewable sources, representing less than 4 per cent of nationally generated electricity. Of all renewable electrical sources in 2014/15, hydroelectricity represented 63 per cent and wind 36 per cent. Biomass and geothermal sources also made contributions (ESAA 2016). In addition, bioenergy solar PV and solar hot water heating made significant contributions.

As is the case in many other countries, development of renewable electricity in Australia has been encouraged by government energy policy implemented in response to concerns about climate change. A key policy that has been in place since 2001 to encourage large-scale renewable energy development is a mandatory renewable energy target, which in 2010 was increased to 41,000 gigawatt-hours of renewable generation from power stations. This was subsequently reduced to 33,000 gigawatt-hours by the Abbott Government. Alongside this there is the Small-Scale Renewable Energy Scheme, an uncapped scheme to support rooftop solar power and solar hot water, and several state schemes providing feed-in tariffs to encourage photovoltaics. In 2012, these policies were supplemented by a carbon price and a $10 billion fund to finance renewable energy projects, although these initiatives were later withdrawn by the government.

Of the renewables industry the two major hydro schemes include the Snowy Mountains Scheme, constructed between 1949 and 1974, consisting of 16 major dams and seven major power stations, and having a total generating capacity of 3,800 MW. In addition, Hydro Tasmania operates 30 power stations and 50 dams, and has a total generating capacity of 2,600 MW.

The most important change in the renewables industry in Australia has come from the opening of wind farms. Around one-half of the installed capacity is in South Australia. In 2013/14, South Australia wind generation accounted for 35 per cent of the state's total principal generation (see Figure 10.4). Australia has also developed world leading solar thermal technologies, but with only very low levels of actual use. Domestic solar water heating is the most common solar thermal technology.

There are a number of government policies in place in Australia that influence the development of renewable energy. A key policy encouraging the development of renewable energy in Australia includes Mandatory Renewable Energy Target (MRET) schemes at both Commonwealth and state levels. In 2001, the Howard Government introduced an MRET of 9,500 GWh of new renewable energy generation by 2010. This target has since been revised, with the Gillard Government introducing in January 2011 an expanded target of 45,000 GWh of additional renewable energy between 2001 and 2020 (later reduced to 33,000). Several states have also implemented their own renewable energy targets independent of the Commonwealth.

In 2012, the Gillard Government implemented a carbon price of $23 per tonne to be paid by 300 liable entities representing the highest business emitters in Australia. The carbon pricing legislation was repealed by the Abbott led

Australian Government on 17 July 2014. The Australian Government announced the creation of the new $10 billion Clean Energy Finance Corporation, which commenced in July 2013. Feed-in tariffs have also been used on a state by state basis in Australia to encourage investment in renewable energy by providing above commercial rates for electricity generated from sources such as rooftop photovoltaic panels or wind turbines. The schemes in place focus on residential-scale infrastructure by having limits that effectively exclude larger-scale developments such as wind farms. Feed-in tariff schemes in Australia started at a premium, but have mechanisms by which the price paid for electricity decreases over time to be equivalent to or below the commercial rate. Many of these schemes have now ceased, but this growth has continued. Finally, the increase in electricity prices that has occurred since 2000 has also encouraged greater investment in renewables.

Conclusion

The basic aim of the restructuring of the electricity and gas industries during the 1990s has been to extend the level of competition from the rest of the economy to these industries. In doing so the aim has been to encourage a higher level of efficiency in the industry, which in turn should lead to lower prices for energy.

So far most of the gain has been enjoyed by larger businesses, which saw real prices fall throughout most of the 1990s. This occurred because there was a significant increase in the level of technical efficiency brought about by the lowering of staff levels and the fuller utilisation of capacity. At the same time, there have been allocative efficiency gains made, as well as, increasingly, a concentration of new investment in the industry in the construction of plant that provides electricity at peak periods rather than base load plant. As most of the new growth in demand for electricity is at peak demand times this is an appropriate and better use of resources.

Even though it has been perceived that electricity generation, natural gas extraction and treatment, and retail of energy are potentially competitive segments of the two industries this cannot necessarily be said about the distribution and transmission elements. As in many cases the wire and pipe segments of the two industries are monopolies this has meant that they are still subject to regulation. Imposing economic regulation on monopoly firms is a complicated process and has the potential to bring about many costs as well as benefits. A number of approaches to this type of intervention have arisen, and it is to this topic that we turn in Chapter 11.

References

Access Economics 2001, *Impact on Victoria of the Privatisation of the State's Electricity and Gas Assets*, Report Prepared for TXU Australia, Access Economics, Canberra.

Australia, Department of Industry, Bureau of Resources and Energy Economics 2013, *Eastern Australian Domestic Gas Market Study*, Department of Industry, Canberra.

Australian Bureau of Agricultural and Resource Economics (ABARE) 2002, *Competition in the Australian National Electricity Market*, ABARE Current Issues, January, ABARE, Canberra.

Australian Bureau of Statistics (ABS) various issues, *Australian Industry*, Cat. No. 8155.0, ABS, Canberra.
Australian Bureau of Statistics (ABS) various issues, *Electricity, Gas, Water and Waste Services Australia*, Cat. No. 8226.0, ABS, Canberra.
Australian Bureau of Statistics (ABS) 2013, *Causes of Death, Australia*, Cat. No. 3303.0, ABS, Canberra.
Australian Institute of Health and Welfare (AIHW) 2013, *General Record of Incidence of Mortality Books: Accidents Caused by an Electric Current*, ICD10 W85–W87, AIHW, Canberra.
Borenstein, Severin 2000, 'Understanding competitive pricing and market power in wholesale electricity markets', *Electricity Journal*, vol. 13, July, pp. 49–57.
Borenstein, Severin 2001, *The Trouble with Electricity Markets (and Some Solutions)*, University of California Energy Institute POWER Working Paper No. PWP-081, University of California Energy Institute, Berkeley.
Borenstein, Severin and Bushnell, James 2000, 'Electricity restructuring: deregulation or regulation?', *Regulation*, vol. 23, no. 2, pp. 46–52.
BP 2015a, *BP Statistical Review of World Energy*, BP, London.
BP 2015b, *BP Energy Outlook 2035*, BP, London.
Bureau of Industry Economics (BIE) 1996, *Electricity 1996: International Benchmarking*, Research Report No. 96/16, BIE, Canberra.
Business Council of Australia (BCA) 2000, *Australia's Energy Reform: An Incomplete Journey*, Report prepared for BCA by Rod Sims, Port Jackson Partners, Sydney.
Electricity Supply Association of Australia (ESAA) various issues, *Electricity Australia: The Electricity Supply Industry in Australia*, ESAA, Melbourne.
Electricity Supply Association of Australia (ESAA) 1994, *International Performance Measurement for the Australian Electricity Supply Industry 1990–1991*, ESAA, Melbourne.
Energy Supply Association of Australia (ESAA) 2016, *Electricity Gas Australia 2016*, ESAA, Melbourne.
Industry Commission 1991, *Energy Generation and Distribution*, Report No. 11, 3 vols, 17 May, AGPS, Canberra.
NEMMCO 2001, *An Introduction to the National Electricity Market*, www.nemmco.com.au, NEMMCO, Sydney.
New Zealand Ministry of Health (MOH) 2013, *Deaths Due to Accident Caused by Electric Current*, ICD-9 code E925, ICD-10 code W85–W87, MOH, Wellington.
Office of the Regulator-General (ORG) 2001, *Approach to Benchmarking Electricity Retail Costs*, ORG, Melbourne.
Pollitt, M. 1997, 'The impact of liberalization on the performance of the electricity supply industry: an international survey', *Journal of Energy Literature*, vol. 3, no. 2, pp. 3–31.
Productivity Commission 1999, *Update of Productivity Estimates*, Productivity Commission, Melbourne.
Singapore, Registrar-General of Births and Deaths (RBD) various issues, *Report on Registration of Births and Deaths*, RBD, Singapore.
Steiner, Faye 2001, *Regulation, Industry Structure and Performance in the Electricity Supply Industry*, OECD Economics Department Working Paper No. 238, OECD, Paris.
United Kingdom, Office for National Statistics (ONS) various issues, *Mortality Statistics: Review of the Registrar General on Deaths by Cause, Sex and Age in England and Wales*, ONS, London.
United States, Consumer Product Safety Commission (CPSC) various issues, *Electrocutions Associated with Consumer Products*, CPSC, Washington DC.

11
UTILITY REGULATION IN AUSTRALIA

Introduction

The privatisation of government business enterprises and the identification of elements of parts of industries as being monopoly providers meant that during the 1990s there developed in Australia a concern that price regulation of these utilities be implemented in a way that enhanced efficiency. Price regulation in Australia was by no means new, it having been used in a range of industries ever since the First World War (Butlin et al. 1982). Price regulation of utilities such as electricity, gas, telecommunications and rail however had, generally speaking, not been used before the 1990s because these had been under government ownership and therefore pricing was determined as part of the political process.

The tendency during the 1990s was to deregulate markets and let the forces of demand and supply determine prices, but there was a range of industries – or rather elements within these industries – that were identified as being 'natural monopolies'. If these natural monopolies – such as the electricity and gas distribution described in the previous chapter – are not going to be sufficiently the subject of competition, which restrains market power, then government regulation of pricing becomes necessary.

A series of government agencies were established in the 1990s to undertake this price regulation. At the national level the Australian Competition and Consumer Commission (ACCC) has responsibility for the regulation of postal charges, airport charges, telecommunications, access to interstate rail track, natural gas transmission and electricity transmission. At the state level organisations such as the Queensland Competition Agency, New South Wales IPART and Victorian Government's Essential Services Commission had responsibility for the regulation of gas and electricity distribution, seaport charges and access to intrastate rail. The changes that occurred in the mid-2000s meant that regulation of the transmission and distribution elements of electricity and gas passed to the newly established Australian Energy Regulator (for a list of economic regulators in Australia see Table 11.1).

The purpose of this chapter is to look at the various approaches a government can take to utility price regulation. There are considerable problems when it comes to determining the prices at which regulated utilities should price. If prices are set too low then there will be an underinvestment in the industry, which will ultimately damage consumers. On the other hand, if prices are set too high, then the utility will be able to reap monopoly profits at the expense of the consumers. Determining prices, therefore, has become a complex and controversial process.

TABLE 11.1 Regulatory agencies in Australia, 2016

Jurisdiction	Name	Areas of responsibility
Australia	Australian Energy Regulator, ACCC	Electricity and gas distribution and transmission.
	ACCC	Telecommunications, airport monitoring and post.
New South Wales	IPART	Water and sewerage, train/bus/ferry charges, rail access, electricity and gas retail, local government rates.
Victoria	Essential Services Commission	Water and sewerage, port charges, rail access, electricity and gas retail.
Queensland	Queensland Competition Authority	Water and sewerage, rail access, electricity and gas retail, local government rates.
South Australia	Essential Services Commission	Water and sewerage, port charges, rail access, electricity and gas retail.
Western Australia	Economic Regulation Authority	Water and sewerage, rail access, electricity and gas retail/distribution/transmission.
Tasmania	Office of the Tasmanian Economic Regulator	Water and sewerage, electricity and gas retail.
Australian Capital Territory	Independent Competition and Regulatory Commission	Water and sewerage, electricity and gas retail.
Northern Territory	Utilities Commission	Water and sewerage, electricity and gas retail/distribution/transmission.

Source: NERA Economic Consulting (2014); Abbott et al. (2016).

Natural monopolies

In some cases, the provision of a good or service is by a monopoly. A firm that is the only seller of a product or service having no close substitutes is said to be a monopoly. Standard economic arguments as put forward in earlier chapters suggest that monopolies are inefficient forms of industrial organisation. However, in restricted circumstances, where large capital costs inhibit facility duplication, economic theory supports monopoly as the best form of market organisation.

Generally, there are two types of monopolies: legal and natural. A legal monopoly is one where the firm is protected from competition by some sort of legal restraint, for instance the ownership of a patent or government licence. Australia Post for example is a monopoly because of the legal restraint on the delivery of standard size letter mail: its so-called reserved service. A natural monopoly on the other hand is the market situation where unit costs are minimised by having a single firm produce a good or service. The industry is therefore subject to increasing returns to scale up to the size of the market. In this case the long-run marginal costs decline as output increases. If the entire demand within a relevant market can be satisfied at lowest cost by one firm rather than two or more the market is a natural monopoly (Posner 1999). Examples of natural monopolies are the electricity and gas distribution network providers that were discussed in Chapter 10. With these industries monopoly provision is desirable but runs the risk of the firm exploiting its market power. The problem is, therefore, how society can enjoy the benefits of least cost production, which requires single firm production, while at the same time avoiding monopoly pricing.

If the government wishes to avoid the costs associated with monopoly pricing, then it has three alternatives to utility provision. The first was discussed in Chapter 9, that is the operation of government owned enterprises. The second is to contract out the service and use competitive bidding for the contract to inject efficiency enhancing competition into the industry. The third is to allow a private provider to operate, but to regulate it, so as to restrain the potential for it to abuse its position of monopoly power. Generally, the approach used now in Australia is to open up to competition all elements of an industry where competition is possible. For those segments left, such as gas and electricity distribution, airports and the local loop of the telecommunications industry, price regulation is imposed. This applies both to privatised utilities and to the corporatized government owned utilities.

To better understand the costs of monopoly provision the standard monopoly diagram is provided (Figure 11.1). The level of output Qc depicts the point of output where the marginal cost curve cuts the demand curve. Under very competitive conditions the tendency is for prices to be competed down to the level of price Pc and for quantities sold and produced to Qc. A monopoly can avoid this process and maximise profit by raising the price level above the marginal cost. If there are substantial barriers to entry and no close substitutes, then consumers will be forced to pay this higher price. In Figure 11.1, there is a square segment that depicts the consumer surplus that is transferred to the producer. There are also two triangular areas that depict the deadweight losses to the economy. This deadweight loss is referred to as the social cost of monopoly.

The social cost of monopoly involves higher prices and the exclusion of a group of potential customers to whom the utility of the product exceeds its cost of manufacture. The monopoly price therefore prevents the economic system from meeting wants that could be met perfectly well. Customers are led to substitute costlier or less desirable products (allocative inefficiency).

There are two additional costs of monopoly to society. These are the costs associated with rent seeking behaviour – that is obtaining and maintaining a monopoly position – and the welfare losses that rent seeking imposes on third parties, principally competitors and potential competitors that seek to oppose it. In addition, monopoly producers are not necessarily compelled to produce at the level of the lowest possible average total costs (productive inefficiency). The marginal cost curve that appears in Figure 11.1, therefore, might not be the one that indicates the best possible level of efficiency. Finally, it is possible that dynamic efficiency might be impaired because of the lack of incentive for the natural monopoly to innovate.

One caveat here that should be remembered is that the firm might have the desire to generate super-profits. That is, although it is not the subject of competition it still does have the incentive to minimise costs because this would increase the amount of monopoly profits and additional consumer surplus that it can extract.

One of the characteristics of the reform process over the last ten years in Australia has been to identify the natural monopoly components of industries and then allow access to them by competitors at regulated prices. In some cases, this has involved legal separation of the monopoly elements into separate corporate

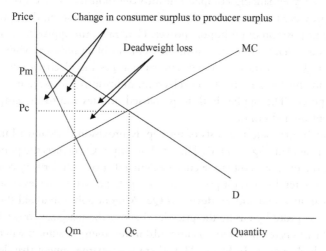

FIGURE 11.1 Restriction in output to boost prices

entities. In the rail industry for instance the Australian Government now owns a rail track company known as the Australian Rail Track Corporation, which owns and leases interstate rail track but operates no actual trains and instead sells access at regulated prices. In other cases, firms are made to 'ring-fence' the monopoly elements into separate accounting entities so that access to these facilities can be regulated. An example of this is Queensland Rail, which operates a rail track division within its corporate structure that competitors can seek access to.

The role of the regulator

One approach to monopoly provision is for the government to subject the monopoly firm to economic regulation. Economic regulation typically refers to government imposed restrictions on firm decisions over price, quantity and entry and exit. The proper role of the government as regulator here is that of a substitute for competitive markets where those forces are weak or absent. The regulator's task is to determine the rules of behaviour that the regulated firm could have been expected to follow if it operated free of regulation in a market with fully effective competitive forces, and then to constrain the regulated firm to behave as if it were operating in such a market (Baumol and Sidak 1994).

In a perfectly competitive market, firms that can operate with the lowest costs will carry out production. This is consistent with economic efficiency in that it maximises the general welfare of producers and consumers; that is it maximises consumer and producer surplus.

Under these conditions firms will make a zero economic profit (normal profit), that is including earnings sufficient to pay interest to those that have lent funds to the firms and returns to equity holders that are consistent with the prevailing level of interest payments, after adjusting for differences in the risk of debt and equity. Competition limits earnings to the cost of capital (normal profit).

In Figure 11.2 the various prices that might be regulated to are provided. In this case the firm is a natural monopoly, as the average cost curve is downward sloping all the way along its length. That is the larger the firm, the lower its average unit costs, which means it can outcompete any smaller rivals and force them out of business. This monopoly would profit-maximise at the point Pm. The role of the regulator would be to determine where the average cost curve cuts the demand curve and attempt to set prices at this level. The approaches used to determine this price are varied and by no means perfect. They include the light handed approach, rate of return regulation, CPI-X price caps and efficient cost of service.

Light handed approach

This approach is one that has not been extensively used in any country except New Zealand (Bollard and Pickford 1995). It was devised in that country because of the aversion to the more prescriptive forms of price regulation that were used there during the 1970s. This approach involves a number of main aspects:

164 Economic policy

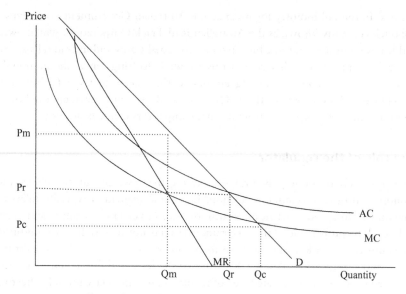

FIGURE 11.2 Regulating the price of a natural monopoly

- The first is that the company is the subject of the country's main competition legislation (i.e. anti-trust in the United States, the *Trade Practices Act* in Australia and the *Commerce Act 1986* in New Zealand). In particular, the company is the subject of the provision in the relevant legislation that makes illegal the abuse of monopoly power, predatory pricing and the attempt to create or enforce a monopoly.
- The firm is compelled to provide access to natural monopoly facilities on reasonable terms or risk breaching the competition law.
- The company is compelled to disclose information on the operations of the natural monopoly components, information that would be of use in any prosecution under the legislation.
- There is a mandated elimination of statutory barriers to entry as well as separation and ring-fencing of monopoly elements of the industries.

This approach depends upon a country having well-developed and effective competition law in place. It is an approach worth considering and is one that is very useful when there is a degree of uncertainty about whether a firm has monopoly power or not or if the government has limited resources available to it and possibly a lack of expertise at regulating prices. In these circumstances, it can be applied and then if significant abuse of market power is detected the government can either prosecute the company under the competition law of the country or alternatively seek to have heavier handed price regulation imposed.

This approach has not been used explicitly in Australia. In the case of the privatised airports this approach was implicitly used from 2002 onwards in that the government after that date simply monitored prices, costs and profits of the major airports with the threat of possible heavier handed regulation after a period of observation. Presumably the published information on the airports could become the basis of a prosecution under the *Competition and Consumer Act* if an airport user felt it was being unfairly exploited.

Rate of return regulation

The second approach that can be used is known as the 'rate of return' approach. Rate of return has been traditionally used in the United States, where privately owned utilities are common (Kahn 1970–71; Priest 1993; Viscusi *et al.* 2001). In that country, its use dates back to the late nineteenth century, and it has been also used extensively to regulate privately owned utility pricing in Japan, Hong Kong and Canada. It was used for a long period in Queensland and New South Wales between the 1920s and 1980s to regulate the private gas supply companies in those two states.

Rather than attempting to regulate prices directly, the rate of return approach allows a monopolist to set its own prices subject to a regulatory constraint based on production costs. Rate of return requires the regulator to set a maximum rate of return for the monopoly. The underlying idea is that the company's revenues must just equal its costs (including the cost of capital), so that economic profit is zero.

The allowed revenue is calculated as follows:

Allowed revenue = expenses + r(RB)

Where r is the allowed rate of return and RB is the rate base (the value of the assets of the company)

As an example, imagine that the total value of capital stock of a company is $10 million (rate base). Furthermore, its operating expenses are $5 million and the government regulated allowed rate of return 10 per cent. The total revenue allowed would be $6 million.

Allowed revenue = $5m + $1m = $6m

There are problems involved in determining what are the legitimate costs of the enterprise (including the cost of capital, i.e. the allowed rate of return). Also, there are problems in determining the value of the rate base.

If an unconstrained monopoly earns more than this regulated level, then it must lower prices and profits or alternatively expand its rate base. The former is preferable but the latter possible; this is known as the Averch–Johnson effect. The Averch–Johnson effect is simply the case where firms are given the incentive to substitute capital for other inputs so as to add to the rate base and therefore boost allowed revenue. It was the possibility of the Averch–Johnson effect that encouraged people to attempt to determine another approach to utility pricing.

One example was the case of the Australian gas transmission case in 1998. This case involved allowing a 7.75 per cent rate of return on an asset base of $363 million, which equals an allowed revenue of $28.1 million.

CPI–X

The problems associated with rate of return led to the development of 'CPI–X' price cap regulation. Price cap regulation was pioneered in the United Kingdom during the early 1980s and was associated with the privatisation of monopolies like British Telecom and British Gas (Pollitt 1999). Under this approach prices are set for a defined period, for example five years. The price caps are automatically adjusted for inflation plus an 'X value'. The X value is the expected productivity improvement above that of the economy.

The advantages of its use are that it is simple to apply, it is not based on accounting valuations of costs or asset bases, and it creates incentives for businesses to improve efficiency. As an example, in Australia the privatised airports were regulated under this approach between 1997 and 2002. The X values for three of the airports were Melbourne 4.0, Brisbane 4.5 and Perth 5.5 per cent. This meant that prices could be increased at Melbourne for instance by the value of the CPI (say 2 per cent per annum) minus 4 per cent (an overall reduction of 2 per cent). If the airport could reduce its average costs by more than the 4 per cent, then it would obviously make an increased profit. There is therefore an inbuilt incentive under this approach to increase the level of efficiency (ACCC 1997a). Another example is the case of the January 2003 New Zealand electricity transmission, in this case CPI – 3 per cent in 2003 to 2008. This meant that as inflation was 2 per cent there were 1 per cent price reductions each year.

The difficulty in using this approach is with the calculation of the appropriate level of the X value. If an X value that is too high is chosen, then the company will not make any money and underinvestment will probably eventuate. If the X value is too low, then the company will be able to make monopoly profits.

Efficient cost of service

In Australia, the most common approach used has been the efficient cost of service approach. Under this approach business can set prices at levels that cover the costs of provision (including the cost of capital) of an efficient supplier. In a perfectly contestable market, competitive behaviour is imposed upon the incumbent firm by the threat of entry by efficient producers. Thus, the highest price or price combination that the incumbent can select is one that is just insufficient to attract the entry of new firms. This implies that a regulator should base its price determinations on estimates of the cost of efficient delivery rather than the actual costs of the incumbent.

It is important to note that the pertinent costs are not those incurred by the regulated firm but rather the cost that would be incurred by the entry of a hypothetical efficient entrant. The Australian Competition and Consumer Commission uses this approach in its price regulation of telecommunications facilities. This approach is known as total service long-run incremental costs (TSLRIC), which are the incremental or additional costs the firm incurs in the long term in providing the service, assuming all its other production activities remain unchanged (ACCC 1997b). TSLRIC is the forward looking incremental cost of supplying the whole service when the other activities of the firm remain unchanged. It includes the costs an efficient firm would incur in providing the service, or alternatively the costs that would be avoided if the service were not provided. The costs that are included in TSLRIC include operating costs, common costs and capital costs.

Operating costs are the ongoing operational costs of providing the service, including the labour and materials costs that are causally related to the provision of the service. Common costs are the costs incurred in the provision of a group of services. These costs are incurred if any one of the services within the sub-group are produced and are not avoided, unless the production of all the services ceases. Such common costs often arise when different services use the same network element. For example, the costs of (non-usage based) maintenance of the local loop are common to the provision of local and long-distance calls.

Telecommunications is highly capital intensive. Capital costs therefore constitute a significant proportion of total costs. The cost of capital is the opportunity cost of the debt and equity funds to finance the operations of the firm. A cost of capital that exceeds the return in the market earned by investments of similar risk encourages overinvestment. On the other hand, a cost of capital below the normal commercial return will prevent providers from gaining a legitimate return on their investments and discourages future investment, which is not in the long-term interests of consumers.

The cost of capital is usually calculated as the weighted average cost of capital (WACC). In the WACC, the cost of debt financing for a firm is separated from equity financing. Debt financing costs can be measured directly by the current effective interest rate on the various debts held by the firm. The starting point for estimating the cost is the risk free rate of return (for example the return on ten-year government bonds). The cost of equity may be adjusted above the risk free rate if investment in the asset subjects the investor to risk. In determining the value of the asset base, replacement costs are generally used. Replacement cost is the present-day cost of replacing the asset with another asset that provides the same service potential. This need not be the same asset, but rather the asset that hypothetically is the best (least cost) option under current technology.

As common costs are not directly attributable to the production of any one service, the allocation of these costs across services is somewhat arbitrary. One approach is to use fully distributed costs. This involves measuring the directly attributable costs (directly attributable costs exclude common costs) of each service within the group and allocating the common costs based on each service's proportion of the total directly attributable costs.

Another approach is to allow price discrimination between various bounds. Price discrimination is not only the profit maximising strategy for a monopoly; it might also be the only way in which an efficient allocation of resources can be achieved. Utility monopolies often have very large capital and sunk costs and subsequently very low marginal or incremental costs. Charging everyone the same price that recovers an average of the sunk costs might deter some customers from using the facility. Therefore, the allocation of resources would not be optimal.

An example of how price discrimination improves efficiency in this fashion is as follows. Imagine a designated rail line is built for a coal mine. Imagine as well that the stand-alone costs of operating the rail line for the mine are $10 million (fixed costs $8 million and marginal costs $2 million). If a second mine is opened then the fully distributed cost approach would mean that a fixed cost charge of $4 million would be attributed to the new mine plus a marginal cost of $2 million. If the new mine is unable or unwilling to pay this and therefore does not operate then the fully distributed costs approach leads to an inefficient allocation of resources. One alternative would be to attribute a smaller proportion of the fixed costs, i.e. between $0 and $4 million, plus charge the attributable costs, i.e. $2 million. As long as prices cover the marginal costs of providing the service then the rail line operator benefits (Posner 1999). This approach to pricing is usually referred to as Ramsay pricing. Basically, what it entails is charging prices inverse to demand elasticities. That is if the demand elasticity of consumers is low (inelastic) then a high price is charged and vice versa.

In regulating, a popular approach, therefore, is to operate floor and ceiling levels, which are in turn based upon costs. Under the competitive market standard for regulation, marginal costs and average incremental costs are the figures pertinent for the floor and stand-alone costs for the ceiling.

- Average incremental costs: the difference in the firm's total costs with and without the good being supplied, divided by the output of the good; the cost per unit of output that is added to a firm's total costs as a result of its supply of the current outlay of the good. It includes any fixed cost that must be incurred on behalf of that product alone.
- Stand-alone costs: the cost that would be incurred by an efficient entrant to the industry if it were to decide to produce only some specified set of commodities.

By setting these floors and ceilings the firm is unable to exploit its monopoly power but would still have the discretion to price lower to consumers that have a low willingness to purchase the product or high propensity to switch to something else. As examples, most of the state based intrastate rail pricing regimes have floor and ceiling price controls in place.

The problem with the efficient cost of service approach is that it does entail a considerable amount of information on the part of the regulator. The regulator has to be able to determine what an efficient provider's costs would be, which is often by no means clear.

In the case of the water supply industry there are several examples of the cost of service approach being used in Australia. Table 11.2 provides detail on the forms of regulation used to determine water prices in the regulated industry. Although most water companies are still government owned in Australia, they are the subject of price regulation for the various state and territory economic regulators. Table 11.3 provides detail on the regulation of other, non-water, government owned utilities in Australia. In most cases a starting price level is determined using a cost of service approach, including a calculation of an asset base valuation. A variety of accounting asset valuation techniques are used. Prices are then allowed to change over a five-year period along the lines of a CPI−X price path. Prices are then reviewed again. Other non-water government utilities are treated in a similar fashion if they have some natural monopoly component. What is true of

TABLE 11.2 Regulatory approaches, Australian water industry, 2014

	Form of regulation	*Financial reporting**	*Regulated capital base*	*Regulated depreciation*
New South Wales	Cost of service building block approach	Historical cost and fair value	Deprival value/ line in the sand + roll-forward	Straight line method
Victoria	Cost of service building block approach	Fair value	Deprival value/ line in the sand + roll-forward	Straight line method
Queensland	Cost of service building block approach	Fair value	DORC + roll-forward	Straight line method
South Australia	Cost of service building block approach	Fair value	Fair value + roll-forward	Straight line method
Western Australia	Cost of service building block approach	Historical cost and fair value	Deprival value + roll-forward	Straight line method
Tasmania	Cost of service building block approach	Historical cost and fair value	DORC + roll-forward	Straight line method
Australian Capital Territory	Cost of service building block approach	Historical cost and fair value	Deprival value/ line in the sand + roll-forward	Straight line method
Northern Territory	Price cap	Historical cost and fair value	NA	NA

Source: NERA Economic Consulting (2014); Abbott *et al.* (2016).

Note: *Sydney Water, Melbourne Water, SEQ Water, SA Water, Water Corporation of WA, Southern Water (Tasmania), ACTEW (ACT), Power and Water Corporation (NT).

government owned electricity transmission and distribution networks is also true of the privately owned ones, which are price regulated in a similar fashion.

- Combined approach (rate of return and CPI−X). In Australia the most common approach has been the efficient cost of service approach. Businesses can set prices that cover the costs of provision (including the cost of capital) of an efficient supplier.
- In most cases a starting price level is determined using a cost of service approach. Prices are then allowed to change over a five-year period along the lines of a CPI−X price path. Prices are then reviewed again.
- The combined approach is commonly used for distribution and transmission in Australia.

Table 11.4 provides an example of the cost of service approach. In this case the example of the supply of electricity in the Australian Capital Territory is provided.

TABLE 11.3 Non-water, government owned regulated businesses in Australia, 2016

Company	Industry	Jurisdiction and regulator	Valuation in regulation
Australia Post	Post	ACCC	Fair value
Australian Energy Market Operator	Electricity	AER	DORC
ARTC	Rail	ACCC	DORC
VicTrack	Rail	ESC (Victoria)	
NBNCo	Communications	ACCC	Actual costs
Queensland Rail (Aurizon Networks from 2013)	Rail	QCA (Queensland)	DORC
Office of the Rail Commissioner	Rail	ESCSA (South Australia)	DORC
RailCorp	Rail	IPART (NSW)	DORC
Country Rail Infrastructure Authority	Rail	IPART (NSW)	DORC
Transgrid	Electricity transmission	IPART (NSW)	DORC
Powerlink	Electricity transmission	QCA (Queensland)	DORC
Transend	Electricity transmission	OTER (Tasmania)	DORC
Western Power	Electricity transmission distribution	ERA (Western Australia)	Deprival value
Power and Water	Electricity lines	UC (Northern Territory)	Deprival value then DORC
AusGrid	Electricity distribution	IPART (NSW)	DORC
Endeavour Energy	Electricity distribution	IPART (NSW)	DORC

Essential Energy	Electricity distribution	IPART (NSW)	DORC
Energex	Electricity distribution	QCA (Queensland)	DORC
Ergon Energy	Electricity distribution	QCA (Queensland)	DORC
Aurora	Electricity distribution	OTER (Tasmania)	DORC
ActewAGL	Electricity distribution	ICRC (ACT)	DORC

Source: NERA Economic Consulting (2014); Abbott et al. (2016).

TABLE 11.4 ActewAGL revenue and tariff models, 2009 to 2014

Building block components	2009/10	2010/11	2011/12	2012/13	2013/14
Return on capital	52.6		61.1	65.0	68.2
Return of capital	15.2		18.8	20.5	22.3
Operations and maintenance	62.3		75.0	82.1	86.9
Benchmark tax liability	4.7		5.7	5.4	5.6
Total	134.8		160.6	173.0	183.0
Regulated asset base	650.4		739.5	775.9	809.4
Weighted average cost of capital	8.79	8.79	8.79	8.79	8.79

Performance monitoring

If any of the above methods of price regulation are imposed then it may also be necessary to establish a performance monitoring regime. If a company is the subject of price regulation, then one strategy is simply to reduce expenditure on service quality. If expenses decline, then profits will be enhanced. Most regulatory regimes therefore have some component of either performance monitoring or performance regulation. This may take the form of simply making observations about whether service quality is being maintained while reserving the right to take remedial action if necessary. Alternatively, a firm might be finally penalised if standards deteriorate or even be allowed to raise additional revenue through price rises if it meets present improvements in standards.

Conclusion

The changes that occurred to the basic utilities in Australia during the 1990s meant that a considerable amount of work had to be put into the construction of pricing regulations for these industries, especially those possessing natural monopoly characteristics. Competition was introduced as far as possible. However, in some cases some aspects of the various industries are deemed to still possess natural monopoly characteristics. Amongst these are the major airports, the telecommunications local loop, access to rail track, gas pipelines and electricity lines. Because of Australia's federal nature of governance, which includes a national and state governments, separate bodies have been established to deal with intrastate and interstate pricing problems. This has meant that there are now state agencies and a national agency with responsibilities in this area.

Choosing the appropriate pricing approach can be controversial, but the more likely it is that competition can emerge and become effective then the more light handed the pricing approach should be. The efficient cost of service approach for instance should be used for those monopoly facilities that very clearly have natural monopoly characteristics (for instance the case of electricity distribution). Where the degree of monopoly power is more open to debate – such as is the case with airports and rail – more light handed approaches are probably more appropriate. Whichever approach is used the results will be controversial because the sums of money involved and potential damage that can be inflicted on an industry by ill-conceived regulation can be substantial. The risk, therefore, of government failures being heaped on top of the market failure of natural monopoly is a real risk and one that will be argued about for many years to come.

References

Abbott, M., Tan-Kantor, A. and Raar, J. 2016, *Asset Valuation of Government Business Enterprises: A Re-evaluation of Pricing Issues*, CPA Australia, Melbourne.

Australian Competition and Consumer Commission (ACCC) 1997a, *Administration of Airport Price Cap Arrangements*, ACCC, Melbourne.

Australian Competition and Consumer Commission (ACCC) 1997b, *Access Pricing Principles – Telecommunications: A Guide*, ACCC, Melbourne.

Baumol, William J. and Sidak, Gregory 1994, *Toward Competition in Local Telephony*, MIT Press, Cambridge MA.

Bollard, Alan E. and Pickford, Michael 1995, 'New Zealand's "light-handed" approach to utility regulation', *Agenda*, vol. 2, no. 4, pp. 411–22.

Butlin, N.G., Barnard, A. and Pincus, J.J. 1982, *Government and Capitalism: Public and Private Choice in Twentieth Century Australia*, George Allen & Unwin, Sydney.

Kahn, Alfred E. 1970–71, *The Economics of Regulation: Principles and Institutions*, 2 vols, John Wiley & Sons, New York.

NERA Economic Consulting 2014, *Regulatory Asset Valuation and Pricing: A Report to the Essential Services Commission*, NERA, Sydney.

Pollitt, Michael G. 1999, 'A survey of the liberalisation of public enterprises in the UK since 1979', *Unpublished mimeo*, University of Cambridge, Cambridge.

Posner, Richard A. 1999, *Natural Monopoly and Its Regulation*, 30th anniversary edn, Cato Institute, Washington DC.

Priest, George L. 1993, 'The origins of utility regulation and the theories of regulation debate', *Journal of Law and Economics*, vol. 36, pp. 289–323.

Viscusi, W. Kip, Vernon, John M. and Harrington, Joseph E., Jr 2001, *Economics of Regulation and Antitrust*, 3rd edn, MIT Press, Cambridge MA.

12

INFRASTRUCTURE

Introduction

In the past Australian governments spent considerable amounts on infrastructure, in such things as rail, roads, telecommunications, seaports and airports. Indeed, at the beginning of the twentieth century government fixed capital expenditure was on roughly the same scale as private spending and constituted around 7 per cent of GDP (Butlin *et al*. 1982; see also Table 12.1; Abelson 2012, chap. 19). At first this proportion of GDP rose as governments in Australia spent more on such things as

TABLE 12.1 Gross domestic product and gross fixed capital formation in Australia, 1900 to 2015

	GDP $m	GFCF $m	GFCF/GDP %	GFCF public/GDP %	GFCF private %
1900	419	56	13.4	6.9	6.4
1910	623	80	12.8	6.4	6.4
1920	1,253	206	16.4	8.5	8.0
1930	1,566	239	15.3	9.0	6.3
1940	1,980	288	14.5	5.9	8.7
1950	5,099	1,064	20.9	8.2	12.6
1960	13,718	3,405	24.8	8.8	16.0
1970	29,894	7,903	26.4	9.2	17.3
1980	134,315	35,555	26.5	7.2	19.3
1990	404,086	111,976	27.7	6.6	21.2
2000	660,728	171,978	26.0	4.4	21.6
2010	1,296,707	359,677	27.7	6.2	21.5
2015	1,609,992	427,395	26.5	4.4	22.1

Source: Maddock and McLean (1987).

rail track, roads and urban development projects but after the 1930s it declined, as road transport replaced the railways and other forms of private capital formation became more important.

During the 1980s and 1990s public sector capital expenditure again fell as a proportion of GDP as parts of the private sector were privatised. The transfer of much of the electricity, gas and airports sector was important in this regard. Despite this decline both the Australian and the state governments still spend considerable amounts on infrastructure projects. Indeed, during the 2000s public sector capital spending grew from 4 to 6 per cent of GDP, largely because of the considerable spending on infrastructure to support expansion of the mining industry in Western Australia and Queensland, and to construct water and sewerage assets during a period of drought.

Since the Global Financial Crisis in 2008 and tightening government budgets, the growth of spending on public infrastructure projects has slowed up somewhat, and today public sector capital expenditure is at about 4 per cent of GDP. This is considerably less than in the peak years of the 1920s and 1950s, but is still a considerable sum, in 2005 being around $71 billion. The purpose of this chapter, therefore, is to provide a brief overview of the question of public spending on infrastructure. Related to the issue of spending on public infrastructure is the issue of the application of public planning laws. Local and state governments in Australia as well as spending money on infrastructure are responsible for regulating land use, which can have important implications for the way in which infrastructure spending is conducted.

Background

The term 'infrastructure' refers to the structures, systems and facilities serving a country, city or area, including the services and facilities necessary for an economy to function (Sullivan and Sheffrin 2003, p. 474). It typically includes such things as roads, tunnels, bridges, water supply, sewerage, electricity grids, telecommunications and other facilities, and can be defined as: 'the physical components of interrelated systems providing commodities and services essential to enable, sustain or enhance societal living conditions' (Fulmer 2009).

Infrastructure may be owned and managed by governments or by private companies. In the Australian case, historically most infrastructure was government owned, but in recent years many facilities such as airports, seaports and electricity and gas networks have been privatised.

Despite the privatisation of large numbers of government owned enterprises in Australia, governments are still responsible for large-scale capital investment projects. Many of these projects are generally referred to as 'infrastructure' projects. Government owned infrastructure may be paid for from taxes or tolls, whereas private infrastructure is generally paid for by metered user fees. Major investment projects are generally financed by the issuance of long-term bonds.

The issue of financing can seem clear for private owners of infrastructure (such as toll freeways). However, it is possible that they may receive government subsidies to carry out their projects, and some government owners of infrastructure such as electricity grids receive most (if not all) of their revenue from charges to customers rather than from tax revenue.

In recent years several governments have experimented with public–private partnerships, where a government contracts with a private party to build and operate a facility. In doing so the public sector gets a facility built with (hopefully) higher levels of private sector expertise and efficiency and does so without incurring any borrowing costs (although often it has an alternative liability in the form of a requirement to pay the private company).

Infrastructure process

In undertaking infrastructure projects the government needs to go through a fairly straightforward process. First, the government needs to identify what the specific need is and what the source of demand for the government programme is. The second part of the process is to identify what market failure exists (if it exists) and ascertain whether what is at issue is a concern for (the consequences of) the distribution of income or the provision of a merit good. A market failure is important, because if it does not exist then it is likely that the private sector will respond to the demand for the facility and invest in it. At this stage, it is necessary to identify what private sector investment responses there are, and what barriers there are that are preventing this investment.

After the need and market failure are identified then the possible alternative programmes that address the perceived problems can be considered. In ascertaining and evaluating the impacts of alternative programmes, paying attention to the importance of particular design features is essential.

In the process, at this stage it is necessary to identify the efficiency consequences of possible alternative programmes. Once the efficiency questions have been addressed then it is important to see what the distributional consequences of alternative programmes are, as well as any trade-offs between equity and efficiency considerations. Finally, it is possible to see to what extent alternative programmes achieve public policy objectives and how the political process affects the design and implementation of the public programme. At the heart of this process is the necessity to undertake a vigorous cost–benefit analysis of the proposed project to understand what the impacts of it will be.

Although the benefits of public infrastructure programmes are potentially great they also can create considerable costs, including external costs, which can be quite substantial. In the Australian case one example of this has been in the water sector. High levels of salinity in Victoria, for instance, have in part been caused by past government failures in water sector administration. Water allocation rules encouraged the overuse of underpriced water at the margin, which in turn led to water table rises in some irrigation districts. While investment in storage capacity and associated infrastructure was provided, insufficient attention was given to the effective removal of saline drainage water (Harris 2007). To ensure that these types of mistakes are not repeated cost–benefit analysis that takes into account all of the costs of projects needs to be undertaken.

Cost–benefit analysis

Cost–benefit analysis provides a systematic set of procedures by which a firm or government can assess whether to undertake a project or programme and, when there is a choice among mutually exclusive projects or programmes, which one to undertake.

Private cost–benefit analysis entails determining the consequences (inputs and outputs) associated with a project, evaluating these using market prices to calculate the net profit in each year, and finally discounting profits in future years to calculate the present discounted value of profits.

Social cost–benefit analysis involves the same procedures as private cost–benefit analysis, except that a broader range of consequences is considered, and the prices at which inputs and outputs are evaluated may not be market prices, either because the inputs and outputs are not marketed (so market prices do not exist) or because market prices do not accurately reflect marginal social costs and benefits, owing to a market failure.

When the government makes available a good or service that was not previously available (e.g. constructs a bridge across a river), the value of the project is measured by the consumer surplus it generates; this is the area under the (compensated) demand curve.

The government must make inferences (based on market data or observed behaviour) concerning the valuation of non-marketed consequences, such as lives and time saved or impacts on the environment.

The rate of discount used by the government to evaluate projects may differ from that used by private firms.

To evaluate risky projects, the certainty equivalent of the benefits and costs needs to be calculated. Distributional considerations may be introduced into evaluations, either by weighting the benefits accruing to different groups differently or by assessing the impact of the project on some measure of inequality. It is also important to undertake post-expenditure evaluation to assess and improve government performance.

In recent years the mining industry has required considerable amounts of infrastructure spending because of the remote location of much of it. Although the private mining companies provide a substantial amount of this, the state governments also make considerable investments in transport and energy infrastructure.

Figure 12.1 shows a simple economic model which illustrates how such infrastructure services should be priced and under what conditions investments in additional infrastructure should be undertaken (Abelson 1989).

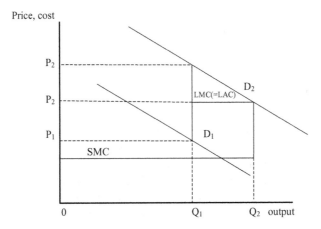

FIGURE 12.1 A model showing the short-run price and long-run price and investment decisions for infrastructure

In Figure 12.1, the short-run marginal cost curve (SMC) reflects the costs of operating the infrastructure, whereas the long-run marginal cost curve (LMC) reflects the cost of making additions to infrastructure capacity. If the initial capacity is at output Q_1, the short-run cost curve becomes vertical at this output. If demand was at D_1, price (=SMC) of P_1 would be required to cover the costs of rationing available supply. If demand was at D_2, putting price equal to SMC would give P_2, which is greater than the level of LMC. Now there is an incentive for the infrastructure provider to invest in additional capacity capable of producing Q_2. In the final equilibrium, with capacity at Q_2 optimally matched to demand, the price P_3 is charged (=SMC = LMC).

If infrastructure prices do not reflect the SMC of rationing available supply, existing facilities will be inefficiently used. At some point additions to the infrastructure capacity will be indicated, with optimal additions achieved by putting price equal to long-run marginal costs. If price is less than the LMC then the provider of infrastructure is subsidising the infrastructure user. This has happened in several cases in Australia in the past with state governments providing infrastructure at pricing below cost. Prices of infrastructure should reflect the costs of establishing and operating these facilities at efficient levels, including a return on capital.

Unfortunately, much of the debate around infrastructure pricing in the past in Australia has centred on welfare concerns rather than efficiency. Keeping infrastructure prices low, however, or not letting them increase in times of peak demand represents a poor way to transfer income to the less well off. It tends to distribute the greatest gains to those who make most use of the underpriced infrastructure, who may not necessarily be the worst off. Good policy comes from aligning policy objectives with the instruments best placed to influence the relevant outcomes. Infrastructure pricing can only influence welfare outcomes a little.

Infrastructure pricing, however, is fundamental to the supply of and demand for infrastructure. It can also have a profound effect on the use of infrastructure, which is the key driver of its efficient use.

Case study

There are numerous examples that could be used to illustrate the general problems of accessing the economic viability of infrastructure projects. One example is that of the Geelong Ring Road in Victoria, which runs for 27 kilometres, bypassing the city of Geelong from the Princes Freeway at Corio and rejoining the Princes Highway on the other side of Geelong at Waurn Ponds. The freeway was built in sections, with sections one and two being officially opened on 14 December 2008, section three on 14 June 2009 and section four (an additional section beyond Waurn Ponds) in January 2013.

Plans to build a ring road around Geelong date back to March 1969, when a report was released by the then Geelong Regional Planning Authority on the issue. Later in the mid-1970s the Geelong Regional Planning Authority sponsored the Geelong Transportation Plan, which canvassed several options, including the construction of a Geelong bypass (Begg 1990). Despite this early interest, the considerable cost involved and controversy over the various possible routes of the road meant that it was delayed for a number of years, leading to considerable traffic congestion in central Geelong.

In 2001 the Victorian Government initiated a project to investigate options for a Geelong bypass. It involved a steering committee, technical committee and community consultation committee. Although the ring road is not a pure public good it does have considerable externalities. In terms of whether it is exclusive, users could be compelled to pay tolls, so it does not have the characteristic of being non-excludable, and, although at low levels of use it could be said to be non-rival, during periods of traffic congestion users of it would rival each other. The freeway saves fuel and travel time for commuters and freight transporters. However, these users could be made to pay through tolls. In terms of whether it is rival, the externalities that exist are both external costs and benefits. The benefits flow from the reduced congestion of drivers using roads in central Geelong, who would endure less traffic congestion. Industrial undertakings located close to the new freeway would also see their properties rise in value. The external costs came in the form of the environmental impact of the construction of the freeway. Some opponents of the construction of the Geelong Ring Road feared that the inclusion of the road in the local Geelong roads ecosystem would have adversely affected the environmental conditions in the Geelong area.

The substantial size of the positive externalities gives some justification for public funding, although it would also have been economically rational for the users to make some contribution through tolls. The Victorian Government, however, decided not to go down this route but instead fully funded the construction (with Australian Government help).

Construction on the Geelong Ring Road began in early 2006, with a total of $384 million from the Victorian and Australian governments being committed initially to fund the first three sections of the project. A further $128 million was later committed for the construction of stage four. Although the freeway was funded by a combination of state and Australian government funding, the design and construction contracts went to private companies. The contract for section one was awarded to Abigroup Contractors in November 2005 for $134.8 million (Victoria, Minister for Public Transport 2008). Section two was delivered via two separate design and construction contracts (Cut and Fill Pty Ltd for $31.7 million, while FRH (now Fulton Hogan) won the $15.5 million contract for the Moorabool River bridges). The $108.3 million design and construction contract for section three was awarded to Abigroup Contractors (Victoria, Premier 2007). The design and construction contract for section four was awarded to Fulton Hogan.

Land use planning

Related to the investment in infrastructure by governments in Australia is the use of statutory planning laws and regulations to influence land use. Statutory planning, otherwise known as town planning, development control or development management, is the part of the planning process that is concerned with the regulation and management of changes to land use and development. These measures can have a great political dimension.

In Australia ownership of property provides the owner with the right to use the property in particular ways, and others with the duty to let the owner exercise the right. Governments, however, can affect the way that people use their land through a variety of legal measures. These measures can be locationally generic or locationally specific. In the former case these involve actions such as the application of building ordinances, such as minimum ceiling heights, fire regulations, heat insulation requirements, connections to clean water and adequate sewerage, and so on. These types of measure prohibit particular behaviour. Measures can also include those that try to create incentives to act in a particular way. These measures might include subsidies, fines and so on.

In the process prohibitions and incentives act to correct for perceived market deficiencies in meeting collective and private interest roles. In the case of property use there are two main types of market failures. The first is of externality, where the use of property can infringe on the rights of others. The other is the case of monopoly, where some plots of land have a location that is both unique or very scarce and desired. An example is a plot of land required to complete a road link or round off a new shopping centre.

Land use planning attempts to correct for these market failures and takes the form of market regulation. If the market has undesirable outcomes, a government agency intervenes in the market with measures based on public law. The difficulty for the government agency is that it can have trouble obtaining the necessary information to be able to correct the failures and might also act in response to pressures from special interest groups. Land use policy can mean that substantial redistribution effects are created. There are also substantial trade-offs in the use of these regulations, as they can considerably increase the cost of constructing buildings and by restricting or delaying land use greatly increase prices for land.

The main measures used include planning permission or developmental approval, which is the approval needed for construction or expansion (including significant renovation) in some jurisdictions. It is usually given in the form of a building permit (or construction permit). Generally, the new construction must be inspected during construction and after completion to ensure compliance with national, regional and local building codes. Planning is also dependent on the site's zone. In Australia the criteria for planning permission are a part of urban planning and construction law, and are usually managed by town planners employed by local governments. Land use planning often leads to land use regulation, which typically encompasses zoning. Zoning regulates the types of activities that can be accommodated on a given piece of land, as well as the amount of space devoted to those activities, and the ways that buildings may be situated.

In the Australian case the country is one of the most highly urbanised societies in the world, and continued population growth in Australian cities will place increasing pressure on land use and infrastructure. Land use policy will therefore continue to be important in the future. Authority is usually delegated by state governments to local governments, including counties and cities. It is these local governments that most frequently exercise police power in land use planning matters. The legal framework for land use zoning in Australia is established by states and territories, and hence each state or territory has different zoning rules (see Table 12.2). Land use zones are generally defined at local government level, and are most often called planning schemes. In reality, however, in all cases the state governments have an absolute ability to overrule the local decision making. There are administrative appeal processes such as those to challenge decisions.

Urban planning in Australia has evolved since early British colonial settlement, and has been heavily influenced by contemporary planning movements in

TABLE 12.2 Planning framework at the state and territory level in Australia, 2017

State/territory	Planning framework	Land use regulation
ACT	Territory Plan 2008	Land use policy
NT	Planning Act	Planning scheme
NSW	Environmental Planning and Assessment Act 1979	Local environmental plan (LEP)
QLD	Sustainable Planning Act 2009	Planning scheme
SA	Development Act 1993	Development plan
TAS	Land Use Planning and Approvals Act 1993	Planning scheme
VIC	Planning and Environment Act 1987	Planning scheme
WA	Planning and Development Act 2005	Planning scheme

Britain, the United States of America and Western Europe. The first examples of town planning in Australia occurred during the early phases of the colonial era, where critical decisions locked in 'path dependency' for the future form of cities. Typically this involved colonial governors undertaking surveying for land grants and subdivisions, and making executive decisions on the location and construction of roads, rail transport, water supply and other basic infrastructure to support early penal and military settlements.

Australian cities and urban centres, particularly capital cities, experienced significant growth after the Second World War, which was largely driven by a combination of rapid economic expansion, high birth rates and unparalleled levels of immigration, particularly from Western Europe and, from the 1970s, South-East Asia. Furthermore, increasing ownership of the motor car, combined with cheap fuel, resulted in an explosion in the urban form of many Australian urban centres. Australia's long period of post-war economic growth resulted in federal and state governments developing metropolitan plans in an attempt to address some of the negative aspects associated with urban growth. Typically, many capital cities engaged in creating metropolitan-wide spatial plans to guide development over long periods of up to 20 years or more. Particular focus was given to land release on the rural/urban fringe establishing a hierarchy of urban centres, the construction of new public housing estates and a preference towards building car based infrastructure (such as new highways, etc.).

Australia's federal system of governance, the nationwide Australian Government, the six states and two territories have their own urban planning laws and procedures, resulting in separate systems of planning and land use management, including separate administrative departments that oversee and regulate planning and land use activities. The Australian Government is increasingly playing a role in the urban planning process in Australia, mainly through the regulation of development in areas that are of national environmental significance or through actual development activities on federal land.

Conclusion

Past Australian governments spent considerable amounts on infrastructure, on such things as rail, roads, telecommunications, seaports and airports. During the 1980s and 1990s public sector capital expenditure fell as a proportion of GDP as parts of the private sector were privatised. Despite this decline both the Australian and state governments still spend considerable amounts on infrastructure projects. Today public sector capital expenditure is at about 4 per cent of GDP. This is considerably less than in the peak years of the 1920s and 1950s, but is still a considerable sum. Although there is potential to improve economic efficiency through the judicious spending on public infrastructure projects, Australia has a long history of wasting money on capital projects that were motivated more by political considerations.

The purpose of this chapter, therefore, has been to provide a brief overview of the question of public spending on infrastructure. Related to this issue of spending on public infrastructure is the issue of the application of public planning laws; therefore an account has also been given of the way local and state governments apply their land use planning and zoning laws.

References

Abelson, Peter 1989, 'An introduction to pricing, output and investment decisions by government business enterprises', *Economic Papers*, vol. 8, no. 3, pp. 20–6.

Abelson, Peter 2012, *Public Economics: Principles and Practice*, McGraw-Hill, Sydney.

Begg, P. 1990, *Geelong: The First 150 Years*, Globe Press, Geelong.

Butlin, N.G., Barnard, A. and Pincus, J.J. 1982, *Government and Capitalism: Public and Private Choice in Twentieth Century Australia*, George Allen & Unwin, Sydney.

Fulmer, J. 2009, 'What in the world is infrastructure?', *PEI Infrastructure Investor*, July/August, pp. 30–2.

Harris, E. 2007, 'Historical regulation of Victoria's water sector: a case of government failure?', *Australian Journal of Agricultural and Resource Economics*, vol. 51, pp. 343–52.

Maddock, R. and McLean, I.W. 1987, *The Australian Economy in the Long Run*, Cambridge University Press, Cambridge.

Sullivan, A. and Sheffrin, S. 2003, *Economics*, Prentice Hall, New York.

Victoria, Minister for Public Transport (2008), 'Geelong bypass section 2 officially launched', Media release, 27 September, Victoria, Minister for Public Transport, Melbourne.

Victoria, Premier 2007, 'Green light for the next stage of Geelong Ring Road', 14 September, Victoria, Premier, Melbourne.

13

LABOUR MARKET INTERVENTION

Introduction

Australia has a long history of government intervention into the functioning of labour markets. Labour market intervention refers to specific government regulations aimed at the labour market. These regulations might be restrictions on wage rates (award minimums, etc.) or alternatively restrictions on employment conditions such as payroll taxes, leave entitlements, occupational health and safety regulations, dismissal restrictions and so on. One aspect of labour market intervention is wages policy. This policy is concerned with the broad determination of wages either through government intervention such as the establishment of legally enforced minimum wages or through the determinations of such bodies as in the past the Australian Industrial Relations Commission and today the Fair Work Commission. The cost of labour includes not just wages and salaries but also paid leave, leave loading, compulsory superannuation and compulsory training. In the Australian case these constitute around 30 per cent of total labour costs to employers. Government intervention can have an impact on these aspects of labour costs as well as the level of wages.

As Australian governments have a long history of intervening in labour markets it is important to understand the justification for this intervention and its impact. Since the reduction of tariffs on imports and agricultural support began, pressure has been applied to bring about the 'deregulation' of the labour market. To some degree this has occurred. The motivation for this deregulation is like that of the other markets of factors of production. Labour – just as much as for instance electricity and gas – is an important input in the production process. If manufacturers and farmers are to face intensified overseas competition, then the view is that these businesses should also purchase their inputs from competitive domestic markets. This has been thought to apply not just to services like transport, telecommunications and energy but also to labour.

184 Economic policy

The purpose of this chapter is to look at some of the economics of labour markets and gauge the degree to which labour markets have been altered by government intervention. To begin with, the general background to intervention is presented, as well as some of the possible market failures or imperfections that might justify intervention. Finally, an evaluation of the impact of labour market reform is undertaken, as well as a discussion of the impact on immigration provided.

Labour economics

In a competitive labour input market (with many buyers and many sellers) the demand for the input is derived from the marginal revenue product, the product of the firm's marginal revenue and the marginal product of the input (Norris 1996). This represents the general worth of an employee to the firm. In a competitive market firms will hire workers to the point at which the marginal revenue product of labour is equal to the wage rate (plus other costs of employing labour). This is reflected then in the demand for labour, which is a derived demand from the goods and services produced by the firm. The demand and supply for labour can be depicted in a conventional demand and supply diagram with the price of labour simply being set at the equilibrium. This is presented in Figure 13.1.

Any growth in labour productivity will raise the marginal revenue product of labour and therefore demand for it. The supply of labour is determined by demographic factors such as population growth (natural and immigration), the participation rate and the age structure of the population. In any individual industry, the number of people determines the supply of labour with appropriate skills for employment in that industry.

Any attempt by the government to maintain the price of labour (which includes any non-wage costs of employing incurred by the employer) above the

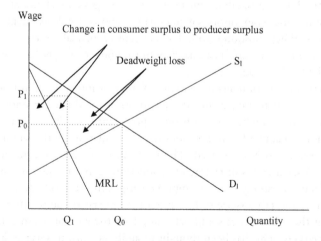

FIGURE 13.1 Monopoly power of sellers of labour

equilibrium price will reduce demand for labour and help to boost unemployment. Any mandatory minimum wages that raise the price of labour above the equilibrium price, for instance, will not only raise wages for some employees but also affect the demand for labour. The costs of such an intervention will fall heavily on low-skilled workers by raising the real wage above the marginal revenue product, which would discourage employment of them.

Likewise, the efforts of a trade union to increase labour costs above the equilibrium in any particular segment of the labour market will lead to increased unemployment in that industry.

Finally, depending on the precise nature of the markets in question the costs of any mandatory regulations will fall in some proportion on workers – through fewer jobs – and on consumers through higher prices for goods and services.

The diagram in Figure 13.1 can be used to depict these regulatory interventions. In this case the market equilibrium of the labour market is where the demand for labour curve crosses the supply of labour curve. At this point the equilibrium price and quantity are set at P_0 and Q_0 respectively. If labour costs are kept above the equilibrium (say at P_1) then the labour supply will exceed that of the labour demand (the difference between Q_0 and Q_1). This surplus labour will constitute the unemployed in the economy.

It should also be borne in mind that immigration policy can impact on labour markets. In this case not only the scale of immigration is important at increasing the labour supply but also the composition of the skills brought by migrants.

In terms of unemployment, this is caused by the market for labour not clearing, that is the supply of labour being greater than its demand. Economists usually refer to three types of unemployment:

1. frictional (caused by people moving between jobs);
2. structural (caused by a mismatch between the skills and location or labour and the jobs available);
3. cyclical (caused by a lack of demand for labour in times of cyclical business downturns, i.e. during recessions).

Labour market regulation can contribute to the second type and would therefore be regarded as a type of government failure. This is, however, an additional explanation of structural unemployment known as the efficiency wage hypothesis.

This hypothesis argues that wages, at least in some markets, form in a way that is not market clearing. Specifically, it points to the incentive for managers to pay their employees more than the market clearing wage to increase their productivity or efficiency, or reduce costs associated with turnover, in industries where the costs of replacing labour are high. This increased labour productivity and/or decreased costs pay for the higher wages. Because workers are paid more than the equilibrium wage, there may be unemployment. Efficiency wages therefore offer a market failure explanation of unemployment – in contrast to theories which emphasise government intervention. However, efficiency wages do not necessarily imply unemployment, but only uncleared markets and job rationing in those markets. There may be full employment in the economy, and yet efficiency wages may prevail in some occupations.

Labour market interventions

In the past, several possible sources of market imperfections or failures have been cited as justification for the intervention by governments into labour markets in Australia. To begin with, labour market intervention undertaken by the government has been justified on the grounds that employers possess some form of monopsony power over their employees. That is, it has been argued that these companies can use their market power as large-scale consumers of labour to force wage levels downwards.

A second possible justification is that there may be considerable information imperfections. If employees or employers lack knowledge about conditions in the labour market, then labour demand and supply levels might create an equilibrium that does not reflect an optimal use of resources. This too, then, might constitute justification for some form of government intervention.

Finally, it might be argued that industrial harmony has a pure public good characteristic. Industrial disputes between employers and employees can obviously affect non-participants in an industry in certain circumstances. In the energy and transportation industries, for instance, a great number of industries would be adversely impacted by any industrial disruption. This would mean that institutions such as industrial tribunals that effectively resolve industrial disputes act as a means of promoting the public interest.

Henry Bourne Higgins, the first judge of the Australian Conciliation and Arbitration Court, expressed the point early in the twentieth century in this way: 'Reason is to displace force; the might of the state is to enforce peace between industrial combatants as well as between other combatants; and all in the interests of the public.' Further he stated: 'By stopping work employees cause inconveniences and loss to the public, as well as intense suffering in their own families' (Higgins 2001). This view as expressed by Higgins was one that incorporates a perception that industrial harmony is a quasi-public good, that is that industrial disputes adversely affect third parties not directly involved in the dispute. If government intervention can operate to reduce industrial disputation, then a public good is created. This of course does assume that the government is effective at improving industrial relations and by its actions does not make them worse.

Arbitration and awards

The Australian Government's original labour market intervention came in the form of the establishment of a quasi-legal wage setting system, institutionalised for a long time in the Australian Industrial Relations Commission and state tribunals (today in the Fair Work Commission). This type of legally enforced arbitration of industrial disputes is unusual in most countries, where either collective bargaining arrangements or free market contracts are more common.

The Australian arbitration system was originally designed to solve industrial disputes between employers and unions, but gradually it established a complex institutional structure of fixed wages and conditions. As the union structure in Australia was occupation based rather than industry based, so-called awards that established minimum wages and conditions tended to be set on an occupational basis; that is, workers with a given job description were covered by centrally determined wages and conditions. To some degree, therefore, the arbitration system was a product of Australia's substantial union movement. This today is still large but falling in numbers. Figure 13.2 presents the size of the unionised workforce as a percentage of the total workforce. As can be seen this figure has been falling since the mid-1980s, and today is heavily concentrated amongst public sector workers.

At the same time that union membership has declined there has been a growth in the use of new forms of labour market regulation in the form of protective laws on subjects such as health, safety, superannuation, hiring and firing, leave entitlements, discrimination and disability.

The trade unions and industrial tribunals have a long history in Australia (McIntyre 1989). State tribunals were first established in the late nineteenth century. The Australian constitution gives the Australian Government powers to make laws with respect to 'conciliation and arbitration for the prevention and settlement of industrial disputes extending beyond the limits of any one State'. This does not give the Australian Government the power to legislate directly to control wages and conditions. It does, however, allow the Australian Government to establish courts and tribunals that can settle disputes that cross state borders at the national level.

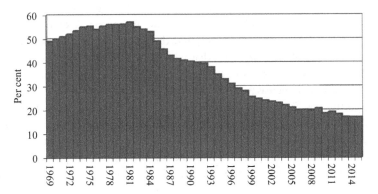

FIGURE 13.2 Trade union membership as a percentage of all employees, Australia, 1969 to 2015 (percentage)

Source: ABS, Cat. Nos 6202.0, 6204.0.

Legislation that applied to industrial relations was first passed at the national level in 1904. Under the *Conciliation and Arbitration Act 1904* the Commonwealth Court of Conciliation and Arbitration was established. The Court exercised judicial and arbitral powers. The Court could create new rights and obligations for employers and employees by making awards prescribing terms and conditions of employment. By the late 1920s more than 50 per cent of all wage changes were effected by Australian Government awards.

The influence of the Court was enhanced by the development of the notion of the 'basic wage'. This was originally a needs based minimum wage necessary to support what was thought to be an average sized family (two adults and three children). A second level was then built into all awards known as a margin for skill. In settling disputes the Court would take the basic wage and then add a mark-up depending on the level of skill. By changing the level of basic wage the Court changed the wages of all workers.

Over the course of its life the Court juggled with the conflicting problems associated with granting wage rises on social grounds (because of rising prices) and the economic considerations related to the capacity of industry to pay these levels. In its early years, the chief concern of the Court was maintenance of real earnings. Over the period 1922 to 1953 adjustments to the basic wage were generally based on price movements. This even involved a 10 per cent cut during the depression when prices fell considerably.

In 1953 there was an abandonment of automatic quarterly adjustments, and the Court reverted to trying to judge the capacity of industry to pay. This approach was maintained until 1961.

In 1956 the Court was reconstituted as two distinct bodies: the Commonwealth Industrial Court (judicial powers) and the Commonwealth Conciliation and Arbitration Commission (arbitral). Throughout the 1960s the tribunals attempted to balance the conflicting views of the determination of the basic wage (cost of living versus the capacity of companies to pay). By the late 1960s and early 1970s many wage increases took place outside of the arbitration system. During this period, there was a shortage of labour, and the direct negotiation of unions and employers brought about wage rates that were above the award rates of pay.

In April 1975 wage indexation was reintroduced, that is adjustments directly associated with price increases. These adjustments were based on CPI movements, plus opportunities for increases based on improved national productivity. This established formal wage fixing principles to govern the operation of the wages system. It was designed to support a centralised system of wage fixation through indexation in response to the high inflation of the 1970s. In 1976 partial indexation was introduced as an anti-inflation measure. Indexation, in turn, was abandoned in 1981, after which occurred a wages blow-out. In response, the government imposed a wages freeze (1982–83).

When the Hawke Labor Government came to office in 1983 it established the 'Incomes Accord', and this survived in various forms up until the Labor Party lost office in 1996. The Incomes Accord was an agreement between trade unions, business and government to moderate wage demands in return for a moderation of price increases and the maintenance of the social wage (wages plus welfare benefits). The Incomes Accord meant that there was an implicit acceptance that excessive wage increases contributed to higher levels of inflation and unemployment.

Even with the Incomes Accord in place from March 1987 onwards the wages system became gradually more decentralised. The *Industrial Relations Act 1988* amended industrial relations legislation, which was further changed by the *Workplace Relations and Other Legislation Amendment Act 1996*. The changes in 1988 created a two-tiered structure. This incorporated basic cost of living increases plus links to productivity gains (ability to pay). At the time, the Incomes Accord was criticised as being insufficiently flexible, so that it did not reflect the capacity of individual firms to pay.

Partial labour market reform took place in 1993 and then again in 1996. From 1996 onwards the Liberal/National Party Coalition Government introduced enterprise agreements, which covered only employees within a single enterprise (Preston 1991). In 2006 the Howard Government introduced 'Work Choices', which created the Fair Pay Commission to set the minimum wage rate for employees and to replace the Australian Industrial Relations Commission. Amongst the provisions was a provision that the dismissal regulations did not apply to small businesses. Most of the provisions of the 2006 legislation were repealed in 2009 by the Rudd Government under the *Fair Work Act*. This legislation reintroduced the award system, but streamlined it from over 4,000 to only 122. Ten minimum conditions of work were also enacted, including regulations concerning the dismissal of employees. The Fair Work Commission, which replaced the Fair Pay Commission, has functions that include the setting and varying of industrial awards, minimum wage fixation, dispute resolution, the approval of enterprise agreements, and handling claims for unfair dismissal.

Evaluation

Figures 13.3, 13.4 and 13.5 provide data on conditions in the labour market. In Australia labour market outcomes appeared to have worsened during the 1970s. In particular unemployment levels rose (Figure 13.3), the total number of working days lost was high (Figure 13.4), and real unit labour costs rose above growth rates in productivity (Figure 13.5). At this time, if the figures in Figure 13.4 are any indication, it would appear hard to argue that the industrial tribunals created any pure public good in the form of industrial harmony. It was this worsening of conditions that prompted policy makers to search for new solutions.

The Incomes Accord appears to have had some success. After 1983 the number of working days lost per annum declined, unemployment levels fell and real wages moved back in line with productivity growth rates. Although the Incomes Accord was not the only factor it probably made a solid contribution to this improvement.

190 Economic policy

After a recession in the early 1990s – when unemployment rose to alarming levels – the labour market outcomes began to improve again. The number of working days lost fell to levels not seen since the early 1950s, and unemployment levels fell to pre-recession levels.

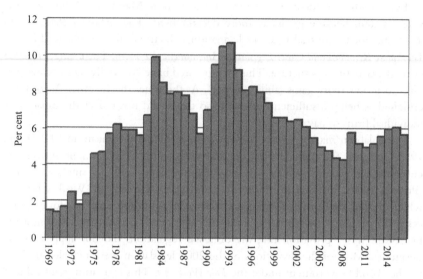

FIGURE 13.3 Unemployment rate in Australia, 1969 to 2016 (percentage)

Source: ABS, Cat. Nos 6202.0, 6204.0.

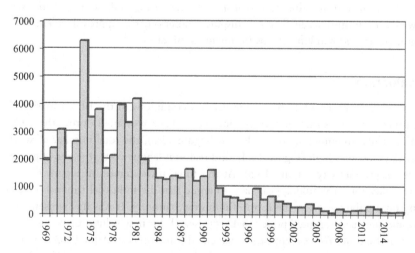

FIGURE 13.4 Total working days lost in industrial disputes, Australia, 1969 to 2016 ('000 days)

Source: ABS, Cat. Nos 6202.0, 6204.0, 6321.0.

FIGURE 13.5 Real unit labour costs and labour productivity, Australia, 1972 to 2015 (1972=1.0)

Source: ABS, Cat. Nos 5260.0, 6302.0.

The success or failure of the enterprise bargaining structure is yet to be tested fully. Since its widespread introduction in Australia during the mid-1990s the economy has experienced neither high inflation nor deep recession. The industrial systems in place during the 1970s and 1980s struggled to adapt to the stresses of the high inflation of the 1970s and recession of the early 1980s and early 1990s. Although it is expected that the present wage determination system would prove more flexible and able to adapt to worsening economic conditions it has not had a chance to prove that to be the case.

Workplace health and safety

Another form of labour market regulation is that of workplace health and safety. Levels of these are affected by three sets of influences: the market, direct regulation by government agencies and the safety incentives created through workers' compensation. In each case safety is promoted by creating financial pay-offs for firms to invest in workplace characteristics that will improve worker safety. These incentives arise because improved safety leads to reduced wage premiums for risk, lower regulatory penalties for non-compliance and reduced workers' compensation premiums.

In Australia, the principal direct regulatory mechanism is state based legislation in the form of occupational health and safety Acts, which involve penalties for breaches but also workers' compensation insurance schemes. The premiums paid by firms are generally related to the degree to which they avoid accidents in the workplace.

Compensating wage differential theory

The fundamental market approach to worker safety was first sketched as long ago as 1776 when Adam Smith observed that workers will demand a compensating wage differential for jobs that are perceived to be risky or otherwise unpleasant. These differentials create an incentive for firms to promote safety, since doing so will lower their wage bill. In particular, wage costs are augmented by reduced turnover costs and workers' compensation premium levels, both of which provide incentives for safety improvements by the firm. The firm in providing greater levels of safety, however, will incur additional marginal (incremental) costs that increase as the level of safety becomes greater. The two critical assumptions, however, are that workers are aware of the risk (which might not always be the case) and that they would rather be healthy than not. If workers do not perceive the risks, then workers will not demand additional compensation.

Inadequacies in the market

It is generally accepted that employees do have some perception of the degrees of risk, but the degree of risk will not be uniform across all classes of risk. As a rough generalisation, external risks are better understood by employees than long-term health risks. The latter can involve low-probability risks that often don't have clear cut indicators of exposure to risk. If workers were to have full knowledge of the risks, then there would be no need for government regulation. Even if employees have accurate perceptions of risk one cannot be confident that the decision ultimately made by employees will be ideal.

In assessing the results of the various occupational health and safety provisions implemented in Australia it is difficult to determine their effectiveness. Over the longer term there has been a trend towards safety improvements because of the greater wealth of Australian society and the increased demand for safety that Australians have placed on their social institutions. Technological improvements have also had the effect of making many appliances and equipment safer in their use. Figure 13.6 provides data on the number of electrical fatalities in Australia over the longer term (both in the home and at work). From the figure, it can be seen that the number declines from the mid-1960s, a result of safety appliances being used, safety equipment being used in industry and safer standards being imposed by regulators. Distinguishing between the effects can be difficult.

Migration

The Australian Government has used migration policy to influence the level of skills available to the Australian economy, as well as the overall size of the Australian population and economy. Migration has an important influence on Australian society and the economy affecting the size, composition and geographic location of the population and workforce. Today around one-half of Australia's population

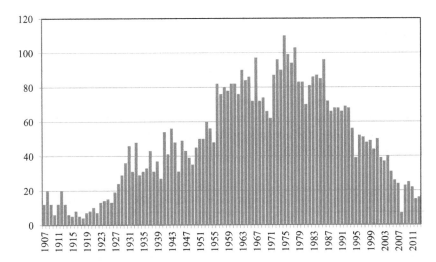

FIGURE 13.6 Number of deaths from electrical accidents, Australia, 1907 to 2013

Source: ABS, Cat. No. 3303.0; AIHW (2013).

growth is from migration. This immigration, therefore, increases the total labour supply in the economy and demand for goods and services.

In terms of migration policy, several features of Australia's policy have changed over the longer term. The first is that the countries of origin of immigrants to Australia have become more diverse over time. During the 1950s and 1960s large proportions of immigrants were from the United Kingdom, Ireland and Europe. From the 1970s onwards the origins of migrants have become more diverse.

The second way in which policy has changed is that in recent years the emphasis of Australia's migration programme has been on skills and increased numbers of temporary migrants. Immigration can address skill shortages without the costs of training the domestic workforce. Positive effects from additional skilled migrants arise from higher participation rates, slightly higher hours worked per worker, and the upskilling of the workforce. In addition, immigration can help to create greater economies of scale as the population rises (Foster 1996; Garnaut 2002; Corden 2003; Withers 2003). The diversity of immigrants can lead to a reallocation of economic activity between the various sectors of the economy (Weil 2005). Immigrants through their links to and knowledge of international markets might facilitate access to those markets.

However, migration can also dampen the labour market price signals that encourage investment in training by domestic businesses and individuals. Some of the economy-wide consequences are capital dilution and a decline in the terms of trade. Capital dilution means that there is less capital per person and therefore a lower level of average productivity (Borjas 1995). It also reduces the ratio of natural resources per capita, which can mean lower productivity.

194 Economic policy

The degree of economic effects of migration depends on the demographic and labour market differences between migrants and the Australian-born population. The impact is mitigated by the fact that the annual flow of migrants is small relative to the stock of workers and population. In many respects migrants are not very different in relevant respects from the Australian-born population, and over time the differences become smaller. These effects have meant that Australia's immigration policy has tended to concentrate on more skilled immigrants rather than family reunion (today most are either spouses or children of immigrants) or refugee programmes (see Table 13.1).

TABLE 13.1 Migrants by class of visa to Australia, 1988/89, 1998/99, 2008/09, 2014/15

	Permanent					Temporary	Skill/permanent %
	Family	Skill	Special	Humanitarian	Total	457 visa	
1988/89	72,700	51,200	800	11,309	136,009		37.6
1998/99	32,038	35,000	890	11,356	79,284	29,230	44.1
2008/09	56,366	114,777	175	13,507	184,825	10,1280	62.1
2014/15	61,085	127,774	238	13,756	202,853	96,084	63.0

Source: Phillips and Klapdor (2010); Australia, Department of Immigration and Border Protection (2017).

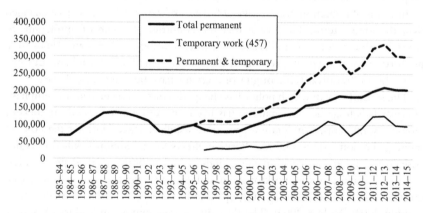

FIGURE 13.7 Migrant visas issued by the Australian Government, 1983/84 to 2014/15

Source: Phillips and Klapdor (2010); Australia, Department of Immigration and Border Protection (2017).

Conclusion

Australia has a long history of government intervention into the functioning of labour markets. In recent years the trend has been toward the encouragement of more enterprise based agreements on wages and conditions rather than industry or professional based agreements. The purpose of this process has been to enable firms to respond more quickly to changing economic conditions and adapt work conditions according to their own circumstances.

The labour market system during the 1970s and 1980s proved to be unable to deal very well with the conditions of high inflation and recession, although it should be noted that the implementation of the Incomes Accord during the 1980s did contribute to the lowering of inflation and unemployment in that decade.

Enterprise bargaining is designed to enable companies to adapt work conditions to their own circumstances, and it remains to be seen if this new system can deal adequately with the circumstances of high inflation or recession.

Finally, labour market intervention by government does not only take place through the determination of wages and conditions by industrial tribunals. Over the years both the Australian and state governments have recognised an important role for themselves in providing higher education and vocational education and training services. It is to this form of intervention that we turn in Chapter 14.

References

Australia, Department of Immigration and Border Protection 2017, *Migration Programme Statistics*, https://www.border.gov.au/about/reports-publications/research-statistics/statistics/live-in-australia/migration-programme.

Australian Bureau of Statistics (ABS) various issues, *Average Weekly Earnings, Australia*, Cat. No. 6302.0, quarterly, ABS, Canberra.

Australian Bureau of Statistics (ABS) various issues, *Causes of Death, Australia*, Cat. No. 3303.0, ABS, Canberra.

Australian Bureau of Statistics (ABS) various issues, *Estimates of Industry Multifactor Productivity*, Cat. No. 5260.0, annual, ABS, Canberra.

Australian Bureau of Statistics (ABS) various issues, *Industrial Disputes, Australia*, Cat. No. 6321.0, monthly, ABS, Canberra.

Australian Bureau of Statistics (ABS) various issues, *Labour Force: Australia*, Cat. No. 6202.0, monthly, ABS, Canberra.

Australian Bureau of Statistics (ABS) various issues, *Labour Statistics, Australia*, Cat. No. 6204.0, ABS, Canberra.

Australian Institute of Health and Welfare (AIHW) 2013, *General Record of Incidence of Mortality Books: Accidents Caused by an Electric Current*, ICD10 W85–W87, AIHW, Canberra.

Borjas, G.J. 1995, 'The economic benefits from immigration', *Journal of Economic Perspectives*, vol. 9, no. 2, pp. 3–22.

Corden, W.M. 2003, '40 million Aussies? *The immigration debate revisited*', Inaugural Richard Snape Lecture, 30 October, Productivity Commission, Melbourne.

Foster, W. 1996, *Immigration and the Australian Economy*, Prepared for the Department of Immigration and Multicultural Affairs, AGPS, Canberra.

Garnaut, R. 2002, 'Immigration: who wins and who loses', *Migration: Benefiting Australia*, Conference Proceedings, Sydney, 7–8 May, Department of Immigration and Multicultural and Indigenous Affairs, Sydney, pp. 131–64.

Higgins, Henry Bourne 2001, 'Industrial arbitration: HB Higgins, President of the Commonwealth Court of Conciliation and Arbitration, 1907–1921', *Australian Bulletin of Labour*, vol. 27, no. 3, pp. 177–91.

McIntyre, Stuart 1989, *The Labour Experiment*, McPhee Gribble, Melbourne.

Norris, K. 1996, *The Economics of Australian Labour Markets*, 4th edn, Longman Cheshire, Melbourne.

Phillips, J. and Klapdor, M. 2010, *Migration to Australia since Federation: A Guide to the Statistics*, Australia, Parliament, Parliamentary Library, Canberra.

Preston, Alison 2001, 'The changing Australian labour market: developments during the last decade', *Australian Bulletin of Labour*, vol. 27, no. 3, pp. 153–76.

Weil, D.N. 2005, *Economic Growth*, Addison-Wesley, Boston MA.

Withers, G. 2003, 'Core issues in immigration economics and policy', *Economic Papers*, vol. 22, no. 1, pp. 13–23.

14
TRAINING AND EDUCATION MARKETS

Introduction

Since the 1970s there has been a degree of dissatisfaction expressed about the performance of labour markets in several countries. In most Western countries, the 1970s were a decade where unemployment levels began to rise, and labour markets were effectively stabilised at a level of disequilibrium with labour supply exceeding labour demand. Economically this meant that there was a considerable waste of an important resource. There was in Australia a significant increase in the level of unemployment throughout the 1970s. This rise in unemployment was accompanied by a slowdown in growth of productivity. This rise in unemployment and productivity growth slowdown brought about two main policy responses in various countries.

The first involved attempting to make labour markets more flexible and adaptive to changing circumstances. This approach was looked at in Chapter 13 and assumes that the disequilibrium in the labour market was caused by the rigidities created by either government intervention or abuses by trade unions. It therefore could be said to regard the high level of unemployment as being a result of government failure. In freeing up labour markets this approach might allow for the creation of additional jobs even if it might lead to a fall in the real incomes of the least skilled as the government regulations or union prohibitions were removed or reformed.

The second policy approach was to place more emphasis on upgrading the skills of the labour force. It has been argued that a better-educated workforce will produce more jobs at higher pay. Education and training enhance labour productivity by increasing skill levels and therefore raising the marginal revenue product of labour compared to the real wage. This increases demand for labour and therefore employment levels. This approach assumes that there are some general characteristics of the labour market that lead to an insufficient level of investment in training and education of the workforce. If this were so, then the cause of unemployment would be attributed to some form of market failure.

In Australia policy makers have been sensitive to both suggestions. That is, the move toward enterprise bargaining has been implemented to remove restrictions that prevent the marginal revenue product of labour from equalling the real wage and to enable the labour market to clear. Second, the Australian and state governments have invested heavily in vocational education and training (VET) and higher education.

The effect of labour market rigidities was considered in Chapter 13. The purpose of this chapter is to examine the reason why government might decide to invest in education and training. In particular, the possible economic gains from doing so will be examined. The way in which the Australian Government has structured its assistance to education and training will also be examined.

Human capital

In the past, governments in Australia have not only invested in the economy's physical capital (infrastructure) such as roads, ports, electricity wires and gas pipelines, but have also invested in the education and training of Australia's human resources, i.e. its human capital. The Australian Government has attempted to raise the quality of the labour force by extending subsidies to students and businesses, expanding the number of places in tertiary education and encouraging on the job training. This has resulted in the quality of the Australian workforce – as indicated by the years of education and training – increasing markedly over the past 20 years.

This notion that education and training can enhance the productivity of labour is not a new one. Adam Smith in 1776 surmised 'that a man educated at much expense and time to tasks that require dexterity and skill may be compared to an expensive machine that adds more to earnings than the cost of operating it' (Smith 1776, book I, chap. X, part I). Alfred Marshall and Benjamin Franklin stated something similar: 'The most valuable of all capital is that invested in human beings' (Marshall 1890, book VI, chap. IV). 'An investment in knowledge pays the best interest' (Franklin 1758). This idea that investment in education and training can raise the productivity of the workforce and generate returns to investors has been embodied into economics in the form of human capital theory. This theory assumes that investment in human resources is similar to that in physical capital, in that costs are incurred in the process in the expectation that future economic gains will be made. Human capital orthodoxy views expenditure on education and training, whether it is by an individual, a business or a government, as an investment (Mincer 1958; Schultz 1961; Becker 1964). As with any investment there must be a rate of return. This rate of return manifests itself in the form of higher incomes for those individuals who invest in education for themselves and higher productivity and growth for the businesses and nations that do so.

From the individual's point of view, the cost of investing includes not just the cost of education fees and so on but also the income forgone by studying full time and staying out of employment.

Education has been seen to enhance the productivity of workers by imparting the basic skills and knowledge of the three Rs, by providing highly vocational skills and techniques, and by encouraging appropriate values, desirable work habits, agility of mind and the ability to solve problems. Not only will the productivity of labour be enhanced by education and training but also it may lead to the better use of other inputs and the introduction of new technology. A variant to this argument is that education teaches people how to perform well in the workforce by teaching them how to obey orders, follow directions, work in teams, be punctual and work to achieve long-term goals. A wide variety of studies have been undertaken on the link between investment in human capital and growth rates. The OECD in its studies of the link between growth in per capita output and variety of input factors found that there was a significant relationship between growth in output and investment in human capital (Table 14.1). According to the figures in Table 14.1 this relationship is by no means a uniform one across nations, and is not the only factor that promotes growth, but was found to be both consistent across all OECD countries and a significant contributor to the growth process.

Support for human capital theory is by no means universal. Generally human capital theory views the higher average earnings that more highly educated and trained people get as evidence of their higher productivity and returns from investment. Criticism of human capital theory is generally based on what is known as the 'screening hypothesis' (Arrow 1973; Blaug 1985). According to this hypothesis, although there is a correlation between the average level of formal education

TABLE 14.1 Decomposition of changes in annual average growth rates of GDP per capita, 1980s to 1990s

	Percentage change in output per capita growth rate	Contribution from					
		Investment share	Human capital	Population growth	Variability of inflation	Size of government	Trade exposure
Australia	0.80	−0.16	0.17	0.46	0.05	0.03	0.57
Canada	−0.60	0.24	0.19	−0.10	0.01	−0.02	0.60
France	0.04	0.01	0.35	0.27	0.23	−0.02	0.42
Ireland	1.21	−0.17	0.54	−0.75	0.35	0.13	0.46
Netherlands	0.97	−0.04	0.43	0.32	0.07	0.10	0.25
New Zealand	−0.26	0.33	0.21	−0.47	0.68	0.06	0.44
Spain	−0.64	−0.19	0.42	−0.05	−0.20	0.02	0.33
Sweden	−0.64	−0.19	0.42	−0.05	−0.20	0.02	0.33
UK	0.01	0.08	0.44	0.05	–	0.03	0.25
USA	−0.19	0.19	0.07	−0.06	0.13	0.07	0.65

Source: OECD (2015).

people have and average level of income they receive this does not necessarily signify that the education creates the extra income earning capacity directly if the formal qualifications are being used as a 'screening' device. It is possible that employers pay higher wages and salaries to holders of higher qualifications because they expect these people to be of higher intelligence and diligence than those without them. That is, the formal education process acts as an indicator of intelligence rather than a creator of abilities (Maglen 1995).

There is some substance to this hypothesis, but it can quite easily be taken too far. It would be difficult to argue that people who had invested in their education as doctors, dentists, engineers, accountants and so on were just doing so to pass a screening test. Clearly employers of these people are very interested in the skills they have obtained though their education. Investment in some (at least) education and training increases the productive level of the workforce and helps to contribute to a higher level of output.

Even if it can be shown that investment in education and training leads to an increase in the productive capacity of an economy this does not necessarily justify government intervention. As private investment in human capital creates private returns then it would be expected that this would create incentives for individuals to invest in education. If higher levels of education lead eventually to higher incomes for a person then there is an incentive for them to pay for it. If a firm benefits from its workforce being more highly educated, then there is an incentive for it to invest in the human capital of its workers. To justify government assistance there needs to be a demonstrable market failure that leads to sub-optimal levels of investment in human capital. In other words, there needs to be a social return on investment that exceeds that of the individual returns, perhaps because of the external benefits that flow from investment in education and training from individuals and firms to other people. This then returns us to the question of whether there are market failures or externalities in the education market (Quiggin 1999).

Education and training benefits

The view, therefore, is that education and training raise individual, and with it national, productivity. From this it is argued that without substantial support from governments the market would fail to allocate resources in either an efficient or an equitable manner; therefore, it is argued that additional expenditure is required by governments at the higher education and VET levels.

There are a variety of justifications besides distributional ones that have been used to explain the market failures that might arise in education and training markets. These are listed as follows:

- Consumer ignorance (merit good). A merit good is one that is good for consumers but which they might not be inclined to consume. An example of this might be the use of seat belts in motor cars, which clearly are of benefit to consumers but which consumers might be disinclined to use. Education at the primary school level might be considered to be a merit good, as children would not be in an informed position to make choices about it. Although most parents are willing to undertake spending on behalf of their children, some are not. Related to this are notions of risk. Investments in education can be risky, as people never really know what the total gains will be. Many people would be reluctant to invest in education simply because the cost would be risky. A rationale for public expenditure on primary and secondary education is on the distributional grounds that a child's access to education should not be based on the choices made by its parents, or their ability to pay.

- Education as a natural monopoly. This is less likely in this day and age, and in towns and cities, but might be the case in isolated regions where duplicates of education facilities are uneconomic.
- Public good characteristics. A public good is one where people cannot be excluded from the benefits and is consumed collectively. Clearly this is not the case with the education of individuals who can be charged fees for the education and training and excluded from education institutions. Further, the marginal cost of educating an additional person is far from zero. This type of market failure might possibly be more relevant when it comes to investment in basic research and development, that is in 'pure' research where the benefits are difficult to retain by individuals or firms.
- Externalities. If positive spillovers are created by investment in education and training that are not captured in market prices, then there would be an underinvestment in education and training. It is often claimed that there are important externalities with having an educated citizenry, one of which is that people can participate in public affairs. In addition, people who work alongside those who are educated and skilled gain from their education. Finally, people with scarce skills are a key to technological progress, and typically innovators only capture a fraction of their own overall contribution to any increase they bring in productivity.

If governments perceive that one of these market failures exists, then it can intervene in education and training markets in a variety of ways. To begin with it can provide education and training through the operation of government owned schools, colleges, universities and training centres. Australia has a long history of this approach. Second, it can provide financial assistance through directly subsidising private providers or by directly providing assistance to students or trainees. Historically the main example of this approach in Australia has been the subsidisation of the private secondary school sector in Australia. Third, it can regulate the allocation of resources into education and training, say by imposing training levies on industry. All three of these approaches have been undertaken in the past in Australia.

Government intervention

Historically the main funders and operators of primary and secondary schools in Australia are the state governments, and in recent years there has been considerable discussion and debate about the quality of education at the primary and secondary school level. In addition, there has been considerable debate about the split in funding between government owned and privately owned schools. Much of this discussion is on equity and distributional grounds rather than related directly to economic policy.

In the case of economic policy much of the discussion has centred on the VET and higher education sectors. Although the state governments formally own the technical and further education (TAFE) colleges and universities, they are largely funded by the Australian Government. Under the system as it operates today the scope of tertiary education (VET plus higher education) is at a comparable level in Australia to that in other OECD countries in terms of expenditure and numbers of people with tertiary qualifications (Tables 14.2 and 14.3). There is in Australia, however, a higher dependence on private funding at both the secondary and the tertiary levels (Table 14.2) than in other OECD countries. At the vocational education and training level there is a similar balance of VET to university expenditure in Australia to the OECD average (Table 14.2). This means that the university sector is much greater in size that the VET sector in terms of qualifications of the workforce (Table 14.3). This state of affairs was a product of the substantial intervention on the part of the Australian Government into higher education expansion since the end of the Second World War.

In the late 1940s Australia's universities were modest institutions, and there was a single university in each state capital along with the newly established, research orientated Australian National University in Canberra. In addition, two university colleges were located in Canberra and Armidale in New South Wales.

TABLE 14.2 Expenditure (government and private) on tertiary education as a percentage of GDP (VET and university), 2012

	Government	*Private*	*Total*
Australia	0.9	0.7	1.6
Canada	1.5	1.0	2.5
France	1.3	0.2	1.5
Germany	1.2	0	1.2
Japan	0.5	1.0	1.5
Korea	0.8	1.5	2.3
New Zealand	1.2	0.7	1.9
Sweden	1.5	0.2	1.7
UK	1.2	0.6	1.8
USA	1.4	1.4	2.8
OECD *total*	*1.2*	*0.4*	*1.6*

Source: OECD (2015).

TABLE 14.3 Educational attainment of the workforce (25 to 64 years), 2014 (percentage)

	VET	University	Total
Australia	11	31	42
Canada	25	28	53
France	14	18	32
Germany	–	–	27
Japan	21	37	58
Korea	13	40	53
New Zealand	5	30	35
Sweden	10	28	38
UK	11	31	42
USA	11	34	45
OECD total	8	28	36

Source: OECD (2015).

The number of university students enrolled in Australian universities in 1949 at 31,753 was tiny compared to the numbers enrolled in higher education at the beginning of the twenty-first century: 726,418 in 2001 (Australia, Commonwealth Bureau of Census and Statistics 2001; Australia, DET 2001). Up until the Second World War the Australian Government made only a minor contribution to university funding in the form of assistance for some research. In 1942 the Australian Government introduced a scheme of financial assistance to students enrolled in faculties reserved as essential to war industries to overcome shortages of graduates, especially in science and engineering. This assistance was continued after the war when the universities became the recipient of funding under the Commonwealth Reconstruction Training Scheme, which assisted thousands of returned service personnel to enter tertiary institutions.

Late in the 1950s the Australian Government began to make a more substantial, permanent intervention into higher education policy. In 1957 the Murray Committee investigated the state of Australian universities on behalf of the Australian Government and recommended that the Australian Government make a substantial contribution to recurrent and capital funding of the universities (Australia 1957). The Australian Government accepted these recommendations, and the increased expenditure was used to establish several new universities in Australia during the 1960s (Harman and Smart 1982).

Because of the heavy financial burden placed on the Australian Government by the taking over of financial responsibility for the expansion of the universities a rethink of this process took place in the early 1960s. In particular, a 25-year experiment began in 1965 with the creation of the 'binary' higher education system of universities and colleges of advanced education. This system survived until the late 1980s, when the binary system was replaced with a Unified National System. One of the main justifications for the creation of the binary system in the 1960s was that it was hoped that it would enable the expansion of higher education in Australia without incurring the full costs that would have been incurred if universities had simply been expanded to meet demand.

The advanced education sector of Australian higher education developed from the mid-1960s on the basis of the recommendations made by the Committee on the Future of Tertiary Education in Australia to the Australian Universities Commission in 1964–65 (Australia, Committee on the Future of Tertiary Education in Australia 1964–65). The Committee advocated the establishment of colleges, which would concentrate on teaching at the higher education level rather than conduct research. Most of the colleges of advanced education that were established in the 1960s traced their origins to the development of teacher training and technical education. Before the intervention of the Australian Government in the early 1960s each state government developed a network of diploma courses concentrated in engineering, science and commerce, conducted in senior technical colleges as well as education department run teachers' colleges.

The main rationale for additional government support of tertiary education in the 1960s was that it was 'an essential condition for the growth of national production and the maintenance of Australia's place in the ranks of the technologically advanced nations' (Australia, Committee on the Future of Tertiary Education in Australia 1964–65, Vol. 1, p. 221). Furthermore, the Committee felt that: 'Education should be regarded as an investment which yields direct and significant economic benefits through increasing skills of the population and through accelerating technological progress. The Committee believes that economic growth in Australia is dependent upon a high and increasing level of education' (Australia, Committee on the Future of Tertiary Education in Australia 1964–65, Vol. 1, p. 221). This argument mirrors the strong case made by human capital theorists at the time that education contributed to economic growth and productivity and hence public policy should be aimed at raising the participation levels in higher education (Mincer 1958; Schultz 1961; Becker 1964).

Throughout the 1970s the cost of higher education funding became a concern to public policy makers. In terms of efficiency it was pointed out that, although it might be accepted that education contributes to economic growth, so too did many other activities and so what must be shown to justify subsidies to higher education was that more education contributes to growth at the margin more than expenditure on other activities such as health, housing, transport or public utilities. Worried about inflation, stagnating growth, higher unemployment and increasing claims on the public purse many Western governments became reluctant to finance additional funding of higher education expansion. In the early 1980s the universities and colleges faced a depressed level of funding owing to a period of recession. On 30 April 1981, the so-called 'Razor Gang' – an Australian Government committee formed to consider ways of reducing government expenditure – announced that 30 higher education institutions around Australia must arrange amalgamations if they were to continue to receive Australian Government funding.

By the mid-1980s the Hawke Labor Government had become keen to encourage expansion of the higher education system, but wanted to avoid putting too much of a financial burden on taxpayers. The response was the introduction of the Higher Education Contribution Scheme, where students have the option of paying a fee when they enrol (at a discount) or when their annual earnings reach the national average, at which point they pay through the taxation system.

The motivation for this expansion was the perceived need to boost higher education to promote economic efficiency and economic growth. In this there was a reflection again of the views expressed at the time of the Murray and Martin Committee investigations. The view was again expressed that a more highly educated population would help to create a workforce that was more skilled and adaptive to the changing needs of industry and commerce. The Australian Government's Green Paper on Higher Education (Australia, Department of Employment, Education and Training 1987), for instance, stated that expansion of higher education was necessary 'to achieve the educated workforce that is essential for Australia's economic growth'. The major structural change announced in the White Paper in 1988 (Australia, Department of Employment, Education and Training 1988) was the replacement of the binary system of higher education by the Unified National System, which was to be the focus of the government's support for growth and reform in higher education. Since the amalgamations have taken place there has been considerable confusion within higher education in Australia about whether economies of size have been achieved. This confusion has been enhanced by the changing role of the institutions themselves. Some studies, however, have found that the amalgamations have shown 'modest cost gains which are in general, due to scale effects' (Lloyd et al. 1993, p. 1089). The scope for cost gains however has been restricted by the need to operate multi-campus universities, which has involved some additional expense.

In terms of the funding of higher education institutions the Unified National System has seen several changes. Under the Unified National System institutions are funded triennially and on the basis determined by their respective educational profiles rather than by institutional title. Resources for research are granted on a competitive basis throughout the higher educational system according to institutional performance. A relative funding model has been developed to access institutions' relative funding position based on teaching and research activities. Funds are given according to disciplines, enrolments and level of study, and a component is given according to an institution's research output. In addition to the research component of operating grants there are government targeted research funds available on a competitive basis on the recommendation of the Australian Research Council.

Since the establishment of the Unified National System in the late 1980s several important changes have occurred. First, there has been a substantial expansion of student numbers in higher education. From an equivalent full-time student (EFTS) level of 354,235 in 1989 numbers rose to 588,204 in 2001 and 977,237 by 2014 (Table 14.4). Also, there occurred an expansion of government real expenditure on higher education over the same period from $3,583 million (in 2000 $) in 1989 to $4,281 million in 2001 and $7,416 million by 2014 (Table 14.4).

This growth in real expenditure, however, lagged behind growth of student numbers, GDP and the total level of government expenditure. This meant real expenditure per Australian student fell from a peak of $11,072 per Australian EFTS in 1995 to $8,645 in 2002.

There has, therefore, been a growing emphasis on the private funding of higher education expansion. From Table 14.5 it can be seen that higher education funding from private sources (fees and charges plus other) has risen from 12.7 per cent in 1986 to over 50 per cent by 2014. This reflects several changes – including the greater number of overseas student in Australian universities – but includes the view that higher education is at least partially a private good rather than a purely public one. As substantial amounts of government expenditure are still made on higher education the view that there is still a public good characteristic of higher education is one that holds some validity but not to the extent that higher education institutions should receive all of their funds from public sources.

TABLE 14.4 Government higher education expenditure in Australia, 1989 to 2014

	Australian students EFTS	Total students EFTS	Overseas students %	Real government expenditure 2000 $000	Real expenditure/ EFTS 2000 $
1989	335,667	354,235	5.9	3,582,817	10,820
1990	354,485	376,522	6.2	3,643,292	10,084
1991	396,279	422,563	6.2	3,798,305	9,586
1992	403,944	433,005	6.7	4,122,000	9,850
1993	412,866	441,085	6.4	4,239,734	10,162
1994	410,768	444,407	7.6	4,560,023	10,560
1995	423,560	462,087	8.3	4,738,121	11,072
1996	436,251	487,977	10.6	4,892,902	10,989
1997	453,848	514,727	11.8	4,726,358	10,276
1998	460,590	528,838	12.9	4,553,284	9,816
1999	466,192	544,143	14.3	4,377,750	9,409
2000	464,435	557,763	16.7	4,217,830	9,097
2001	478,140	588,204	18.7	4,280,810	8,967
2002	500,975	629,526	20.4	4,331,115	8,645
2003	502,621	649,875	22.7	4,452,048	8,858
2004	496,428	656,956	24.4	4,708,892	9,486
2005	494,510	664,659	25.6	5,092,590	10,297
2006	500,181	678,188	26.2	5,437,034	10,870
2007	529,016	725,892	27.1	5,587,530	10,562
2008	542,503	757,850	28.4	6,292,890	11,600
2009	574,084	813,049	29.4	6,449,775	11,235
2010	608,522	861,459	29.4	6,823,572	11,213
2011	627,673	879,981	28.7	7,089,489	11,295
2012	659,710	903,094	27.0	7,580,153	11,490
2013	693,310	937,661	26.1	7,414,518	10,694
2014	719,363	977,237	26.4	7,416,391	10,310

Source: Australia, Department of Education and Training (various issues).

TABLE 14.5 Australian higher education funding, 1939 to 2014 (percentage)

%	1939	1957	1964	1979	1986	1995	2001	2014
Australian Government	–	31.3	42.1	89.2	84.5	57.2	41.2	41.3
State governments	45.0	38.9	36.4	0.7	2.8	1.4	3.9	1.4
Fees and charges	31.8	13.0	9.6	2.0	5.1	23.7	38.1	42.6
Other	23.2	16.8	11.9	8.1	7.6	17.7	16.8	14.7

Source: Australia, Commonwealth Bureau of Census and Statistics (various issues).

Note: Fees and charges include HECS.

The private funding of higher education in Australia has mainly come about as a result of the government charging student fees for enrolment in government owned universities. There has been no attempt to direct government funds directly to students to use equally at private universities or overseas universities rather than Australian Government owned ones. Nor have government funds been directed to privately owned universities. To a substantial degree, therefore, the government owned universities are shielded from competition from private universities. They do have to compete for students and with each other and with overseas universities for overseas students. However, there is not competitive neutrality between themselves and private universities in Australia.

Conclusion

Human capital theory suggests that investment in education and training can improve the economic growth performance of a country. This on its own does not justify government support by increased expenditure on education and training unless there can be shown to be some significant market failure that creates the condition of underinvestment in this sector. Any government support of an industry necessarily comes at the expense of other activity (through either reduced government spending or higher taxes). If the supported industry doesn't overcome some substantial market failure then the net result will be an economic loss. In the case of support for education and training at the post-secondary school level the main justification for government support is that this sector creates substantial externalities that spill over to those individuals and firms that do not enjoy the benefit directly of the education. As individuals clearly benefit from their own education in terms of higher incomes it appears appropriate for them to make some contribution to their education, although it would be inappropriate on economic grounds to expect them to support the spillover effects that flow to others.

There is, however, a difficulty involved in determining just what the relative contributions of the individual and the government should be. Externalities are notoriously difficult to quantify. Debate therefore about the relative contribution that should be made on economic grounds will always prove to be controversial. The implementation of government programmes can also be the subject of government failures. The Building the Education Revolution programme, for instance, which was implemented by the Australian Government in the late 2000s, was criticised as being too rushed in implementation (political failure) and poorly implemented (bureaucratic failure). In the latter case a lack of expertise within the government department at running such a scheme was cited as a cause (Lewis et al. 2014). Nonetheless human capital theory and the theories of market failure do suggest that some contribution should be made by the government if an optimal economic outcome is to be achieved.

References

Arrow, Kenneth 1973, 'Higher education as a filter', *Journal of Public Economics*, vol. 2, pp. 193–216.
Australia 1957, *Report of the Australian Universities Commission on Australian Universities*, Government Printer, Canberra (Murray Report).
Australia, Committee on the Future of Tertiary Education in Australia 1964/65, *Tertiary Education in Australia: Report on the Future of Tertiary Education in Australia to the Australian Universities Commission*, 3 vols, Government Printer, Canberra (Martin Report).
Australia, Commonwealth Bureau of Census and Statistics various issues, *Official Yearbook of the Commonwealth of Australia*, Government Printer, Melbourne.
Australia, Department of Education and Training (DET) various issues, *Selected Higher Education Statistics*, DET, Canberra.
Australia, Department of Employment, Education and Training 1987, *The Challenge for Higher Education in Australia*, AGPS, Canberra.
Australia, Department of Employment, Education and Training 1988, *Higher Education: A Policy Statement*, AGPS, Canberra (Dawkins Report).
Becker, Gary 1964, *Human Capital: A Theoretical and Empirical Analysis with Special Reference to Education*, National Bureau of Economic Research, Columbia University Press, New York.
Blaug, M. 1985, 'Where are we now in the economics of education?', *Economics of Education Review*, vol. 4, no. 1, pp. 17–28.
Franklin, Benjamin 1758, *The Way to Wealth*, Applewood Books, Carlisle MA.
Harman, G. and Smart, D. 1982, *Federal Intervention in Australian Education*, Georgian House, Melbourne.
Lewis, Chris, Dollery, Brian and Kortt, Michael A. 2014, 'Building the education revolution: another case of Australian Government failure?', *International Journal of Public Administration*, vol. 37, pp. 299–307.
Lloyd, P., Morgan, M. and Williams, R. 1993, 'Amalgamations of universities: are there economies of size or scope?', *Applied Economics*, vol. 25, pp. 1081–92.
Maglen, L.R. 1995, 'The role of education and training in the economy', *Australian Economic Review*, 2nd Quarter, pp. 128–47.
Marshall, Alfred 1890, *Principles of Economics*, Macmillan, London.
Mincer, J. 1958, 'Investment in human capital and personal income distribution', *Journal of Political Economy*, vol. 66, pp. 281–302.
Organisation for Economic Co-operation and Development (OECD) 2015, *Education at a Glance 2015*, OECD, Paris.
Quiggin, John 1999, 'Human capital theory and education policy in Australia', *Australian Economic Review*, vol. 32, no. 2, pp. 130–44.
Schultz, T.W. 1961, 'Investment in human capital', *American Economic Review*, vol. 51, pp. 1–17.
Smith, Adam 1776, *An Inquiry into the Nature and Causes of the Wealth of Nations*, W. Strahan and T. Cadell, London.

PART III
Social policies, environment and taxation

PART III

15

SOCIAL POLICY AND THE WELFARE STATE IN AUSTRALIA

Introduction

All societies have made some provision for the poor and destitute. The manner in which the very poor are taken care of has, however, changed dramatically over time in many countries. This has been the case as much in Australia over the years. Modern governments have long taken responsibility for providing for the needy and providing social protection for the aged, the unemployed and the disabled. Indeed, in the last 50 years this has come to be viewed as the primary function of government by many.

This has meant that today a large part of what governments do in Australia is social policy, concerned not in the first instance with the production of wealth, but rather with the distribution of wealth. At the centre of social policy is the welfare state. The modern state is a welfare state in that it provides an extensive range of social services and income support to its citizens. This includes such things as unemployment benefits, youth and student allowances, sole parent benefits, health care, disability benefits, old age pensions and a range of other measures.

Social policy involves spending vast amounts of money either through direct transfer to recipients or through the provision of services. In some programmes income support measures are delivered through the tax system – either in the form of deductible expenses (which tend to favour those on the highest incomes) or in the form of tax credits, which are used in places such as Britain and the United States to subsidise those on low incomes. Social policy also covers non-monetary instruments.

If we measure the significance of an issue by the amount of money spent on it, then social policy must be judged as being the most important policy area of modern government. The 2015/16 Australian Government budget, for instance, devoted $152 billion to the 'social security and welfare' portfolio alone – by far the

212 Social policies, environment and taxation

largest proportion of the Australian Government's total spending of $432 billion (Australia, Treasury 2016 p. 5–7). In contrast health at $69 billion came a distant second, with defence at $26 billion and education at $32 billion. Figure 15.1 gives a breakdown of the major areas of Australian Government spending in Australia. As can be seen from the figure, around 40 per cent of the Australian Government's expenditure is on social security and welfare.

This large scale has not always been the case. In Australia, government support for welfare was at a rudimentary stage at the beginning of the twentieth century. The tendency was for this involvement in the economy to increase over time (in fits and starts), and it had effectively replaced the activities of the government business enterprises as the major public involvement in the economy by the middle years of the twentieth century. While it is now over a century since the first government welfare measures were introduced in Australia it was only in the 1960s and 1970s that these were consolidated and expanded such that they began to dominate government spending. It seems vital, therefore, to begin with a study of why and how this expansion has taken place.

History

In the 20 years before 1914 major shifts in the balance between private and public decisions in fields of behaviour formerly subject almost exclusively to private choices within and beyond the market laid the foundations of Australia's welfare state. For the greater part of the nineteenth century the private sector played the dominant role in Australian welfare services and assistance. Private, non-profit charities and religious groups provided a range of welfare institutions and services.

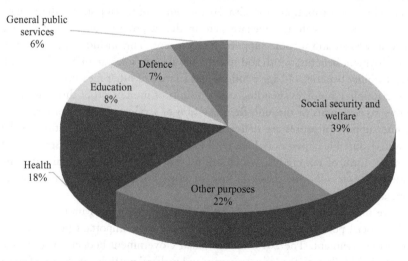

FIGURE 15.1 Australian Government expenditure by function, 2015/16 (percentage)

In the 1890s many of these charities were subsidised by public funds provided by the colonial, later state, governments. In the years after federation this dominance by private charity of social services began to decline in relative importance.

Constitutionally responsibility for social policy in Australia was originally left to the state governments as part of their residual powers. The main exception to this was the decision at federation to assign to the Australian Government a concurrent power to 'make laws for . . . invalid and old-age pensions', under section 51(xxiii) of the constitution. With the exception of military and old age pensions, therefore, social responsibilities were a state matter. This provision was made in the constitution just after the first government welfare measures were introduced.

Amongst the Australasian colonies the first measure was introduced in 1898 when New Zealand introduced a national old age and invalid pension scheme. This was soon followed by similar measures in Victoria and New South Wales. After federation in 1901 these initiatives were superseded by Australian Government legislation. This occurred in 1908 when the Government of Alfred Deakin passed the *Invalid and Old-Age Pension Act*. This Act established a system of pensions under the administration of a commissioner of pensions. Age pensions became payable at 65, or 60 in the case of the permanently incapacitated. The pension was made available to those who came under an income and asset test and was a non-contributory scheme funded out of general revenue. This welfare programme has largely survived until the present day in much of its original form.

The real significance of this legislation was that it was the first national expression of social welfare policy involving non-contributory benefits paid from public funds. This measure was the main one, which existed for the next 40 years, delivered by the Australian Government, although the state governments at this time undertook child endowment and unemployment relief schemes at different times as well as cash allowances to some deserted wives and widows. The other national measure introduced by the Australian Government was the *Maternity Allowances Act 1912*, which was an allowance payable to any woman, married or unmarried and regardless of her means and character, on the birth of her first child. It was also provided from general revenue, although unlike the pension was paid to all regardless of income.

There was little opposition to these measures, and the early focus on the plight of the aged was probably a result of the ageing of the Australian population that occurred in the last years of the nineteenth century. At this time, many of the gold rush generation were reaching old age, and a number did not have much in the way of family support. The support given to children was also a reflection of the view at the time that population growth was something that should be encouraged.

Before the First World War the ability of the Australian Government was constrained by its limited taxing powers. These were restricted to customs, excise and a land tax, although this changed during the First World War when a national income tax was introduced. Between the wars both the state and Australian governments levied income taxes, the state ones being superseded by the Australian Government one during the Second World War. After the end of the First World

War the main emphasis in the 1920s was on major initiatives in the field of the development of support programmes for returned servicemen. This had the effect of directing attention away from the poor and needy towards the needs of returned servicemen regardless of their economic background. Cash payments to persons and free medical and hospital attention became the central, enduring features of veterans' benefits. The *Australian Soldiers Repatriation Act 1917* established a Repatriation Commission empowered to make regulations for the granting of assistance and benefits to returned soldiers and to the widows and children of deceased soldiers. The Commission and state boards made recommendations and carried out the regulations.

The state governments continued to provide many forms of social assistance. However, the provision of massive unemployment schemes during the 1930s tended to change attitudes to this form of intervention. Periodically debates were conducted over whether contributory schemes should be introduced, and indeed one was established in 1938 by means of the *National Health and Pension Insurance Act 1938*, which provided for a system of compulsory insurance for all persons on the basis of contributions from consolidated revenue, from employers and from employees. Under this legislation a National Insurance Commission was created to administer the funds, pay for age and invalid pensions and disablement allowances and pay for medical and pharmaceutical benefits. The system however was not put into operation, and it was superseded by measures that were introduced during the Second World War.

During the Second World War a great shift and expansion took place. Welfare policy was also increasingly centralised, with the Australian Government taking over the income taxing powers of the states. This move was encouraged by the view held by many politicians and bureaucrats that there was a need to balance the sacrifices of the war years with the prospects of a better post-war world.

For most of the pre-Second World War years, public social security benefits (veterans' benefits apart) were designed with the express purpose of advantaging limited dependent groups outside the workforce (the aged, the young and the disabled). Workers were thought to be protected by the arbitration system, and at least until the depression of the 1930s unemployment was regarded as a temporary and infrequent hazard. Another major exception was the granting of assistance to mothers of children, which was granted to all and not on the basis of a means test.

During the Second World War the *Child Endowment Act* of 1941 and 1942 provided for a weekly payment to persons maintaining more than one child under the age of 16 in respect of each such child in excess of one maintained. There was no means test. This was followed by the *Widows Pension Act* of 1942 and 1943, which provided for payment of pensions to widows of any age maintaining one or more children, and widows aged 50 or over without children. The *Unemployment and Sickness Benefits Act 1944* established a system of payments for unemployed persons and those prevented from working because of illness. Assistance of varying forms for meeting hospital, pharmaceutical and medical expenses was also introduced. Low-income groups were assisted through the provision of low-rental housing and legal aid.

Constitutional amendment and taxation centralisation paved the way for social policy to become predominately a national rather than a state concern. In 1946 the constitution was amended, giving the Australian Government powers under section 51(xxiiiA) to: 'make laws for ... the provision of maternity allowances, widows' pensions, child endowment, unemployment, pharmaceutical, sickness and hospital benefits, medical and dental services ..., benefits to students and family allowances'.

Since then Australian social policy has been dominated by the Australian Government, while retaining significant state roles. Almost all social welfare funds come from the Australian Government, and today the core programmes of the Australian welfare state are operated by the Australian Government's Department of Social Services and Department of Human Services. The focal point for services delivery is the latter department's Centrelink.

The states also have their equivalent ministries running state based and joint programmes. The Specialist Homelessness Services, the Home and Community Care programme and the National Disability Insurance Scheme are funded and directed by the Australian Government but delivered by the states on the basis of bilateral intergovernmental agreements and specific purpose payments.

After Labor was defeated at the 1949 election further expansion of social policy was minimal and tended to be market conforming. The government did, however, relax the means test on property and income, making the old age pension more accessible. Between 1947 and 1970 those eligible for the means tested pension rose from 37 per cent to 60 per cent of the aged (Fenna 2004, p. 342). The other main change was in child support, where the system of tax rebates was replaced by tax deductions for dependent spouses and children, a benefit to single income families.

Policies from 1949 to 1966 tended to favour middle and upper income groups. However, after 1966 the conservative governments were gradually moved to consider the problems of the traditional needy groups and of those newly recognised. The share of government spending devoted to welfare rose from an average of a quarter in the second half of the 1930s to a third during the 1960s to half in the 1970s. The way in which these outlays were financed also changed. Early in the twentieth century the Australian Government's outlays were largely paid for from customs and excise duties (which made their impact fairly regressive). During the Second World War not only did social welfare payments get centralised but so too did taxation. Increasingly welfare measures were paid for by income taxes levied by the Australian Government, which made them more redistributive in impact.

Labor returned to power in 1972 with an ambitious social policy agenda. Prominent amongst the policies of the Whitlam Government were the abolition of means tests on old age pensions, the supporting mother's benefit, the introduction of Medibank and other schemes. The Fraser Government which was elected in 1975 maintained and extended some of these programmes but dismantled Medibank. The Hawke Government that followed from 1983 reintroduced a public health insurance scheme in the form of Medicare and introduced a system of compulsory occupational superannuation for the first time. Both schemes were universal in nature and in the latter case was one based on contributions. Through this period the proportion of the population receiving social benefits rose from 12 per cent in the early 1970s to 27 per cent by the early 1990s.

The introduction of occupational superannuation, first on an incremental basis and then on a more systematic one, was a major change, as was the introduction of Medicare. In 1992 the government legislated to make occupational superannuation compulsory. In addition, the government legislated for staged increases in the level of contributions. The superannuation consists of mandatory employer contributions to a private pension plan. The pension plans may be operated by employers, industry associations, financial service companies or even individuals themselves. The mandatory contribution rate was 9 per cent from 2002/03, and starting in 2013/14 it started to gradually increase, the target being 12 per cent by 2019/20.

In 2016 Australia's retirement income system had three components: a means tested age pension funded through general taxation revenue; a compulsory employer contribution to private superannuation savings and voluntary superannuation contributions and other private savings. Superannuation savings are encouraged through taxation concessions. The age pension is payable from age 65, and will be increased by six months every two years from 2017 until it reaches 67 in 2023. The minimum age for withdrawing superannuation benefits is currently 55, but this will increase gradually to 60 by 2025. By 2016 the Australian welfare system had become a comprehensive one, and incorporated several important characteristics.

Characteristics

Tables 15.1 and 15.2 provide a breakdown of the major components of social spending in Australia. Table 15.1 presents the spending as a proportion of GDP and includes all levels of government spending (Australian, state and local). It includes spending on health benefits as part of the social benefits category. In 2014 the total figure stood at 19 per cent of GDP, a figure that has been rising since the early 1980s (see Figure 15.2). Australia's level of social spending is not especially striking compared to other members of the OECD. Figure 15.3 provides a comparison of

TABLE 15.1 Australian social spending as a percentage of GDP, 2014

Pension	3.50
Unemployment	0.50
Family benefits	2.75
Social benefits (including health)	8.07
Incapacity	2.60
Labour markets	0.95
Other	0.63
Total	*19.0*

Source: OECD (2016).

Social policy and the welfare state **217**

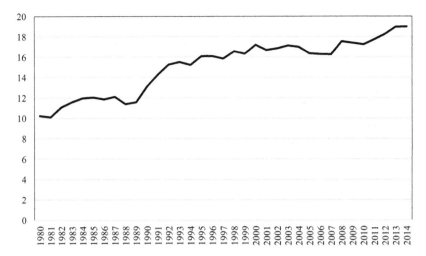

FIGURE 15.2 Australian social spending as a percentage of GDP, 1980 to 2014

Source: OECD (2016).

the OECD countries and, as can be seen, Australia at 19 per cent lies below the OECD average of 21.6 per cent.

Table 15.2 provides a breakdown of the Australian Government's social spending in the 2015/16 budget (not including health related payments). As can be seen from the figures, spending on the elderly and families with children still is the focus of the Australian welfare state, even after 100 years of operation.

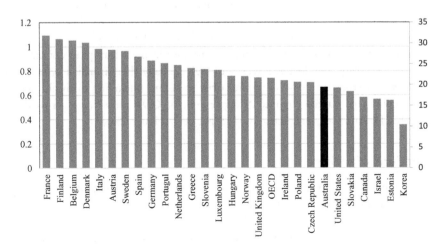

FIGURE 15.3 Social spending as a percentage of GDP, 2014

Source: OECD (2016).

TABLE 15.2 Summary of Australian Government expenses: social security and welfare, 2015/16 ($ million)

	$m
Aged	59,995
Veterans and dependants	6,619
People with disabilities	29,084
Families with children	38,889
Unemployed and sick	10,896
Other welfare programmes	1,508
Indigenous Australians	2,153
General administration	3,694
Total social security and welfare	*152,838*

Source: Australia, Treasury (2016).

Australia's welfare state focuses on spending on poverty alleviation and has four characteristics:

1. Age orientation. The welfare state caters in large part to the elderly, and around one-third of Australian Government transfers go to this group. Around 70 per cent of pension age Australians receive age pensions. The other major focus is spending on support for families with children.
2. Funded from general revenue. Unlike many schemes overseas, most programmes are funded from general tax revenue rather than earmarked from employee contributions or payroll taxes. A major exception to this has been the superannuation scheme that has operated since 1992.
3. Targeted. Also unlike the case in many overseas countries, welfare in Australia tends to be means or asset tested rather than universally provided. It is also paid at a flat rate to all recipients. There have been exceptions to this (i.e. child bonuses and veterans' benefits), but overall this has been mostly true.
4. Moderate commitment. Compared to the case in most European countries, social security spending is lower, although globally the Australian system is fairly generous. In 2014 all public social spending (including on health and employment training) ran at 21.6 per cent of GDP on average across the OECD. Australia's percentage was 19 per cent (Figure 15.3).

Functions of welfare

Social policy is by definition an action that alters market outcomes, often intended to compensate for some of the adverse consequences of markets on society. Because of this, approaches to social policy are often classified according to the degree to which they contradict the logic of the market. Policies that interfere only minimally with market forces or market outcomes are described as being market conforming.

In modern times, social policy is delivered as being targeted or universal. In the former case this has generally meant beneficiaries are the subject of means testing (demanding proof of poverty) and then allocating them the minimal levels of assistance. This means that benefits are only targeted at those on low incomes. An alternative was the institutional philosophy of welfare that sought to entrench collective provision as about locking all citizens into dependence on the state and to make it more universally popular. In Australia, the tendency has been for the former approach to prevail. In a number of European countries, the latter approach is more popular. This generally involves benefits on the basis of contributions, giving it a social insurance aspect and creating a principle of entitlement.

Figure 15.4 compares Australian spending on means tested programmes with spending by other OECD countries. Australia (like Britain and Canada) has a well-developed concentration on means tested programmes.

A large part of the debate over social policy has been a debate about what the functions of social policy should be. Chief among these purposes are typically said to be the following:

1. Protecting against risk. There is a wide agreement that society should draw on its collective strength to supply its members with support in times of need. This safety net function is by definition one of temporary assistance to see individuals through occasional periods. There is a view that a civilised society cannot allow individuals to starve or die as result of insufficient income or inadequate health care. This safety net adds to people's sense of security and well-being.

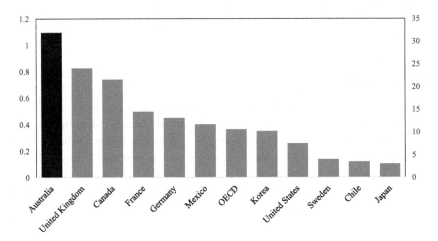

FIGURE 15.4 Percentage of public social expenditure on means tested programmes, various countries, 2007

Source: OECD (2016).

2. Reducing poverty. Social policy is also expected to provide an amelioration of the plight of the poorest in society. This involves some redistribution from the rest of society to its poorest.
3. Balancing life cycle needs. Social policy attempts to smooth out income highs and lows throughout the life of an individual. In principle, this redistributes income from one phase of an individual's life to another. Programmes aimed at children can also help to give them an opportunity to fulfil their long-term potential.
4. Reducing inequality. A more extreme view is that social policy should aim to carry out the first three functions, but also substantially redistribute a nation's income (with the help of a progressive tax system) from the wealthiest towards average income and below average income people.

Economic efficiency and social policy

It would seem that the main purpose of social policy, therefore, is not economic but rather to redistribute income in society or to provide a basic safety net for people. This has meant that economists have tended to analyse social policy in terms of the trade-offs that occur between the economic efficiency lost from social programmes with the greater equity gained.

In terms of economic efficiency social policy, like other forms of policy, can enhance efficiency if it overcomes some substantial market failure. Some economists have pointed out that there are some market failures that social spending programmes act to alleviate. Governments by providing social spending programmes effectively provide a form of insurance to people to assist them to overcome a number of risks. Private markets could potentially provide people with the ability to provide for an alleviation of these risks, but these markets face problems of adverse selection, moral hazard, high transaction costs and the creation of negative externalities.

Risk mitigation

Social policy protects against risk. The purpose of insurance is reducing risk; however, private markets are often not very good at some forms of risk mitigation. An important risk, for instance, of those facing saving for retirement is what the cost of living will be in 20 or 30 years' time, yet no private insurance policy addresses this risk. In addition, a number of risks come in the form of 'common shock', such as the impact of recessions, which affect many people at the same time. These risks tend to be hard to insure against.

Adverse selection and moral hazard

The insurance industry is also prone to the problems of adverse selection and moral hazard. Because individuals will be prone to purchase insurance the more they think they will need it, there is a pronounced tendency for only the worst risks to participate (adverse selection). In turn those who are insured tend to be prone to have greater incentives to undertake the activity insured against (moral hazard).

High transaction costs

Private insurance markets also tend to have high transaction costs, as companies spend a lot of time trying to identify the bad risks, which they will refuse to insure.

Spillovers

As a redistributive device, social policy can be seen as a way to help create greater social cohesion and to reduce negative externalities. Poverty and disadvantage create problems that while primarily affecting those directly involved might affect others as well (e.g. through crime rates).

Incentives

Just as there are market failures, public policy can also lead to the creation of government failures. In the case of social policy the greatest debates surrounding welfare programmes have focused on the set of incentives and equity issues. Do welfare programmes, for instance, discourage work? How can people most effectively be moved from welfare to work?

Like all government policy, social programmes do have an effect on the way markets function through their influence on people's incentives. They have an effect on the labour supply (most notably through their effect on early retirement) and capital formation (through their effects on savings). Changes in birth rates, life expectancy and labour force participation are affected by social programmes.

Some have argued that social security affects the supply of labour by encouraging early retirement, and that unemployment benefits increase the transitional time that people spend between jobs, as they use the benefits to help them to look for the most suitable employment available to them.

The provisions of social security reduced individuals' need to save for retirement. There is a concern that this leads to lower savings levels and therefore leads to a lower investment and growth of productivity. The main justification for making occupational superannuation compulsory in 1992 was that the more widespread use of the age pension was leading to a decline in savings rates in Australia.

Welfare programmes provide disincentives to work longer hours, as effectively there is a high marginal tax rate on working longer hours. Benefits with thresholds which suddenly disappear when income exceeds a particular level have especially adverse incentive effects near the cut-off level.

Poverty rate

In determining the effectiveness of social policy, a number of indicators are generally used. The first is the so-called poverty rate. The poverty rate is the fraction of the population whose income lies below a threshold that is intended to measure the minimal level required to maintain a subsistence living standard. The threshold clearly needs to be adjusted each year to reflect increasing prices. Typically, the poverty rate used in Australia is a figure based on a comparison to the median household income. Figure 15.5, for instance, provides the percentage of persons living with less than 50 per cent of the median equalised household income in 2010 for a range of OECD countries. One criticism of this form of indicator is that it is more an indicator of relative poverty than of absolute poverty. As can be seen from Figure 15.5, Australia has on average a less equal distribution of income than most OECD countries.

An additional measure is that of the Gini coefficient (sometimes expressed as a Gini ratio or a normalised Gini index). This is a measure of statistical dispersion intended to represent the income distribution of a nation's residents, and is the most commonly used measure of inequality. It was developed by the Italian statistician and sociologist Corrado Gini and published in 1912. A Gini coefficient of zero expresses perfect equality, where all values are the same (e.g. where everyone has the same income). A Gini coefficient of 1 (or 100 per cent) expresses maximal inequality among values (e.g. for a large number of people, where only one person has all the income or consumption and all the others have none, the Gini coefficient will be very nearly 1). The Gini coefficient is usually defined

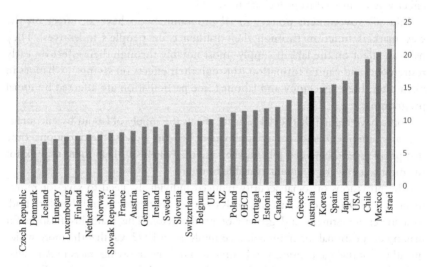

FIGURE 15.5 Percentage of persons living with less than 50 per cent of median equalised household income, 2010

Source: OECD (2016).

TABLE 15.3 Gini coefficient, after taxes and transfers, various countries, 1975, 1990, 2000, 2010

	1975	1990	2000	2010
Australia			0.317	0.336
Canada	0.304	0.287	0.318	0.324
France		0.290	0.287	0.293
Germany		0.256	0.264	0.295
Italy		0.297	0.343	0.337
Japan			0.337	0.329
Netherlands	0.263	0.292	0.292	0.294
New Zealand		0.318	0.339	0.330
South Korea				0.315
Sweden	0.212	0.209	0.243	0.259
Switzerland			0.279	0.303
UK	0.268	0.354	0.351	0.345
USA	0.316	0.348	0.357	0.378

Source: OECD (2016).

mathematically based on the Lorenz curve, which plots the proportion of the total income of the population (y axis) that is cumulatively earned by the bottom x per cent of the population.

Table 15.3 provides data comparing the Gini coefficient for Australia with those for a range of other OECD countries. The higher the coefficient the more unequal income in the country is. The Australian coefficient tends to be relatively high (although not the highest of the countries shown). Overall these figures in Table 15.3 and Figure 15.5 seem to indicate that the Australian welfare system has a less redistributive effect than systems elsewhere, supporting the view that the impact of the Australian system has mainly been to support the disadvantaged rather than to fundamentally change the distribution of income in Australia.

Conclusion

In this chapter, the way in which governments in Australia redistribute wealth has been examined. At the centre of this social policy is the welfare state. The modern state is a welfare state in that it provides an extensive range of social services and income support to its citizens. This includes such things as unemployment benefits, youth and student allowances, sole parent benefits, health care, disability benefits, old age pensions and a range of other measures. Social policy involves spending vast amounts of money either through direct transfer to recipients or through the provision of services.

If we measure the significance of an issue by the amount of money spent on it, then social policy must be judged as being the most important policy area of modern government, and around 40 per cent of the Australian Government's expenditure is on social security and welfare. To understand modern Australian economic policy, therefore, it seems vital to understand the impact that this expenditure has on economic performance.

References

Australian Council of Social Service (ACOSS) 2014, *Poverty in Australia*, ACOSS, Strawberry Hills NSW.

Fenna, A. 2004, *Australian Public Policy*, 2nd edn, Pearson Longman, Frenchs Forest NSW.

Organisation for Economic Co-operation and Development (OECD) 2016, *Social Expenditure Database*, www.oecd.org.

16
HEALTH CARE

Introduction

Included in the social policy area is health care provision. In modern times health care provision is one of the major forms of government intervention and policy making. Governments may be involved in the health care system in a variety of ways, directly paying for health care, subsidising individual purchases of health care and health insurance, providing health care services, financing and conducting research, preventing the spread of communicable diseases and regulating drugs and medical devices. In addition, tax concessions are given to encourage the take-up of private insurance. In Australia, the government is involved in each of these areas, but to a lesser degree than in some countries, such as Britain, where the major health care delivery system is run by the government. Public health services are provided by all levels of government: local, state, territory and Australian. Private sector health service providers include private hospitals, medical practitioners and pharmacies. Primary health care is delivered in a variety of settings, including general practices, community health centres and allied services, as well as within the community, and may incorporate activities such as public health promotion and prevention. Primary health care accounts for almost as much health spending as hospital services (36 per cent compared to 38 per cent in 2014). Secondary care is medical care provided by a specialist or facility upon referral by a primary care physician. In Australia hospital services are provided by both public and private hospitals. In 2011/12 there were 1,345 hospitals in Australia (AIHW 2013).

Figure 15.1 in the previous chapter showed that expenditure on the health care sector makes up 18 per cent of the Australian Government's total expenditure. At the state level government expenditure is also important given that the state governments are the main owners and operators of the public hospitals in Australia. Overall health care in Australia is provided by both private and government institutions.

Medicare, administered by the Australian Government, is the publicly funded universal health care system, which was instituted in 1984. The Medicare scheme covers subsidies for out of hospital medical treatment, the payment of benefits or rebates for professional health services listed on the Medicare benefits schedule, subsidization of the costs of a wide range of prescription medicines under the Pharmaceutical Benefits Scheme and funding for free universal access to public hospital treatment. It coexists with a private health system. According to the Private Health Insurance Administration Council at June 2013, 10.8 million Australians (47 per cent of the population) had some form of private health cover and 12.7 million (55 per cent) had some form of general treatment cover (PHIAC 2013).

Medicare is funded partly by a 2 per cent Medicare levy (with exceptions for low-income earners), with the balance being provided by government from general revenue. An additional levy of 1 per cent is imposed on high-income earners without private health insurance. As well as Medicare, there is a separate Pharmaceutical Benefits Scheme also funded by the Australian Government which considerably subsidises a range of prescription medications. At the 2011 Australian Census there were 70,200 medical practitioners (including doctors and specialist medical practitioners) and 257,200 nurses recorded as currently working in Australia. Australia's health expenditure to GDP ratio (9.4 per cent) in 2014 was below that of the average of the OECD countries at 12.1 per cent (Table 16.1). In addition, government expenditure on health care is about 67 per cent of the total expenditure on health care, which is below the OECD average of 75 per cent.

TABLE 16.1 Health expenditure as a percentage of GDP, and public health expenditure as a percentage of health expenditure, various countries, 2014

	Health expenditure as a percentage of GDP	Public health expenditure as a percentage of health expenditure	Public health expenditure as a percentage of government expenditure
Australia	9.4	67.0	17.1
Canada	10.4	0.9	17.0
Chile	7.8	49.5	15.6
Denmark	10.8	84.8	16.8
France	11.5	78.2	16.0
Germany	11.3	77.0	18.0
Italy	9.2	75.6	13.7
Japan	10.2	83.6	17.9
Korea	7.4	54.1	12.3
New Zealand	11.0	82.3	23.4
Sweden	11.9	84.0	19.0
United Kingdom	9.1	83.1	15.1
United States	17.1	48.3	18.7
OECD	12.1	75.0	16.6

Source: World Bank (various issues).

Private health insurance funds private health and is provided by a number of private health insurance organisations, called health funds. The largest health fund, with a 30 per cent market share, is Medibank. Although government owned, the fund has operated as a government business enterprise since 2009, operating as a fully commercialised business paying tax and dividends under the same regulatory regime as for all other registered private health funds. Highly regulated regarding the premiums it can set, the fund was designed to put pressure on other health funds to keep premiums at a reasonable level. Some private health insurers are 'for profit' enterprises, and some are non-profit organisations. The Australian Government has introduced several incentives to encourage adults to take out private hospital insurance.

Although decisions about health are difficult, resource allocation (choices among alternative uses of funds) must be made. Choices must be made on a range of issues, including the degree to which governments support health care and the form this support will take. Economic analysis may be useful in making such decisions in a systematic and consistent way. Like areas such as education, health services raise questions of public and private choice with respect to redistribution and welfare on the one hand and human capital on the other. Governments have also sought to influence the quality of Australia's human capital through spending on education and health services. Investment in human capital is analogous to investment in physical capital in that costs are incurred in the expectation of a stream of economic gains in the future in terms of productivity improvements. Before the 1940s government investment in physical capital greatly exceeded that of human capital, although since then the increase in spending on health and education has meant that relatively human capital investment is now more important.

Three separate and somewhat conflicting concerns about health care systems exist: excessive costs, insurance coverage and the fiscal strains that providing health care imposes on governments. Besides expenditure on high-profile and popular schemes such as Medicare there is also government expenditure on public hospitals, medical research, teaching in universities, and public health. Altogether these constitute an especially heavy financial burden on the government. Rising health costs put a strain on government budgets, pushing up government expenditure on schemes such as Medicare.

This growth in costs of the various schemes is due to a variety of factors, especially an increase in the elderly population, greater quantities of services being used by the aged, and health care prices that are rising at a higher level than the inflation rate. With the ageing of the population, advances in technology and rises in income it might be natural for Australia to increase its expenditure on medicine. Expenditure growth will also be driven by the increased prevalence of chronic conditions, diseases and risk factors. Given the heavy burden of expenditure on the government, and the prospect that this will continue to rise as Australia's population ages, there is a need for improvement in both the efficiency and the effectiveness of Australia's health care sector.

Background

The Australian health system consists of a complex network of governance and funding mechanisms that support policy, legislation, regulation and funding aspects of delivering medical services. The system has the joint responsibility of all levels of government, with the planning and delivery of services being shared between government and non-government sectors. Health providers include medical practitioners, nurses, allied and other health professionals, hospitals, clinics and government and non-government agencies. According to the World Health Organization, a health system is 'all the activities whose primary purpose is to promote, restore and/or maintain health' (WHO 2013).

Health services in the decade before federation were basically provided through the market. When people needed it, those who could afford it were treated in their home. About one-fifth of people in the 1890s were members of a friendly society which provided insurance and the services of associated doctors and pharmacists. Hospitals, on the other hand, existed essentially to provide services to the very poor, and most were established by religious and charitable organisations or by groups of philanthropic subscribers. Many also received government subsidies. There were some profit making, private hospitals which charged fees, but these were rare and only used by the wealthy.

The role of hospitals changed in the early decades of the twentieth century, and by the 1930s had become major centre points in the health care of the whole community. Medical developments meant that hospital treatment became more common, and it became increasingly possible to undertake treatments in hospitals which were impossible in people's homes. This meant that hospitals admitted a widening range of people from different income groups, and the spending of the state governments on hospitals became an important part of state budgets. It also meant that a professional bureaucracy specialised in health care was created, both in hospitals and in government departments.

Before the First World War most hospitals were run either by the state governments or by charitable concerns, but in the 1920s the Australian Government established repatriation hospitals to cater for the medical needs of returned servicemen. There were also important developments and extensions in public and private provision for child and infant welfare, in the form of baby health centres, pre- and post-natal health education services, day care centres, infant care facilities and medical and dental inspections of school children during the 1920s and 1930s.

Campaigns against major outbreaks of specific infectious diseases as well as long-term programmes to eradicate them were organised and financed by governments. The main thrust of the health care industry, however, was in the increased provision and use of hospital accommodation, largely financed by state governments. In the case of the hospitals, patients were expected to make financial contributions to their treatment in public hospitals (although increasing numbers had private insurance), although it was based on their ability to pay.

Before the Second World War government policy, with the exception of repatriation services, was undertaken by the state governments. In the late 1940s the Labor Government did attempt to establish a national health service similar to the one established in Britain at the time. However, it met considerable opposition from doctors, and significant parts of the legislation passed to establish it were declared unconstitutional by the High Court. The constitutional amendments in 1946, however, did allow for the Australian Government to have powers to provide 'pharmaceutical, sickness and hospital benefits, medical and dental services'. The increased taxation powers of the Australian Government also meant that, increasingly, the state governments were dependent on grants from the Australian Government to pay for the operation of their hospitals. This basic division of responsibilities between the states and the Australian Government has remained to the present day, with the states owning and operating the public hospitals, and the Australian Government making grants to states to run them (from 1945 onwards) and benefits to individuals.

After 1949 the Australian Government concentrated on identifying specific 'needy' groups such as veterans, the aged, invalids and widow pensioners for full public support. For the rest, the government provided subsidised private insurance, a publicly guided use of the market. Throughout the period the Australian Government continued to provide repatriation hospital services without charge to patients and to support its territorial public hospitals. It also provided grants to the states for the operation of their hospitals (Butlin *et al.* 1982).

In 1974 the Whitlam Government established Medibank, which commenced on 1 July 1975 after the passing of the Medibank legislation by a joint sitting of Parliament on 7 August 1974. The goal of Medibank was to provide universal coverage, financed from a taxpayer levy (instead it was financed from general revenue). The hospital side of Medibank involved free treatment for public patients in public hospitals, and subsidies to private hospitals to enable them to reduce their fees. Benefits for public hospitals were provided through hospital agreements with state governments, under which the Australian Government made grants equal to 50 per cent of net operating public hospital costs. After the Whitlam Government's dismissal in 1975 the Medibank scheme was dismantled in stages, although after the election of the Hawke Government in 1983 a new universal health scheme was created. Medicare, as it is known, came into operation on 1 February 1984, following the passage in September 1983 of the *Health Legislation Amendment Act 1983*, including amendments to the *Health Insurance Act 1973*, the *National Health Act 1953* and the *Health Insurance Commission Act 1973*.

Funding for Medicare was to be 'offset' by a Medicare levy, originally set at 1 per cent of taxable income, later raised to 1.5 per cent and still later to 2 per cent. Otherwise it is similar in operation to the original Medibank. Medicare provides financial assistance to eligible people who incur medical expenses in respect of professional services rendered by eligible qualified medical practitioners, participating optometrists, eligible dentists and eligible allied health workers. Medicare benefits are paid based on 85 per cent of the Medicare schedule fee. Medicare also provides free in-hospital services in public hospitals for patients who choose to be treated as public patients. Under the Medicare arrangements, public patients in public hospitals are not charged for their medical services or hospital accommodation costs. Funding for services to these patients is shared between the Australian Government and state and territory governments under Australian health care agreements. Some dental services, including cleft lip and palate services, also attract Medicare benefits. For private patients in hospital Medicare will cover 75 per cent of the schedule fee.

Structure of government intervention

In 2016 the bulk of Australian Government expenditure was on medical services, grants to states, benefits and pharmaceutical benefits (Table 16.2). The medical services and benefits sub-function, which primarily consists of Medicare and private health insurance rebate expenses, is 43 per cent of total estimated expenditures. Growth in Medicare expenses is the major driver of growth in this category and is expected to continue as Australia's population ages. The contribution of the Australian Government to the running of the states' hospitals is included in the category of assistance to the states for public hospitals.

There are four broad areas of health spending: hospitals, primary health care, other recurrent expenditure and capital expenditure. In 2011/12, the largest component of health spending was for hospital services ($53.5 billion, or 38.2 per cent of total health expenditure), delivered by both public and private providers. The second largest component of health spending was for primary health care services ($50.6 billion, or 36.1 per cent of total health expenditure). Primary health care includes a range of front-line health services delivered in the community, such as GP services, dental services and other health practitioner services. Almost 70 per cent of total health expenditure is funded by government, with the Australian Government contributing 42 per cent and state and territory governments 27 per cent. The remaining amount was paid by patients, private health insurers and accident compensation schemes.

TABLE 16.2 Summary of health expenditures, Australian Government, 2015/16 ($ million)

	2015/16 $m
Medical services and benefits	29,025
Pharmaceutical benefits and services	11,022
Assistance to the states for public hospitals	17,196
Hospital services	1,755
Health services	6,322
General administration	3,106
Aboriginal and Torres Strait Islander health	746
Total health	69,172

Source: Australia, Treasury (2016).

Health expenditure in Australia is at a similar level to that of many other OECD countries (Table 16.1). The government share of health expenditure in Australia is average as well (two-thirds). The government pays around two-thirds of all health care expenditures, with insurance payments and out of pocket expenses making up the rest. The tendency has been for health care expenditure as a proportion of GDP to rise, a trend that dates back to the 1960s (see Figure 16.1). This is a trend that is expected to continue as the Australian population ages.

The changes in the early 1980s with the introduction of Medicare saw the proportion of health care expenditure coming from government sources rise to over 70 per cent (Figure 16.2). This level has stabilised at around 65 to 68 per cent, and most governments have undertaken measures over the years to keep the public sector proportion below 70 per cent. Part of the difficulty in controlling government expenditure has been the increase in the cost of medical treatments. As medical technology has advanced the increasing complexity of medical treatments has seen costs rise. This has meant that the health care CPI has been consistently above that of the overall CPI since the 1980s (see Figure 16.3).

Overall coordination of the public health system is the responsibility of all Australian health ministers – Commonwealth, state and territory ministers. Managing the individual health systems is the responsibility of the relevant health ministers and health departments in each jurisdiction.

State and territory governments license or register private hospitals, and each state or territory has legislation relevant to the operation of public hospitals. State and territory governments are also largely responsible for health relevant industry regulations such as for the sale and supply of alcohol and tobacco products. The Australian Government's regulatory roles include overseeing the safety and quality of pharmaceutical and therapeutic goods and appliances, managing international

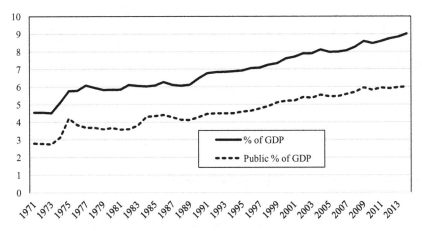

FIGURE 16.1 Expenditure on health as a percentage of GDP, Australia, 1971 to 2014

Source: World Bank (various issues).

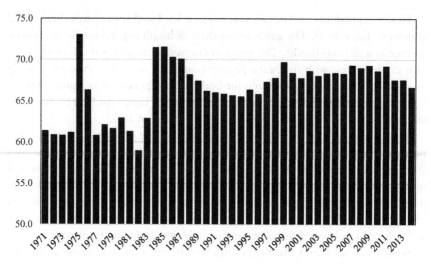

FIGURE 16.2 Public proportion of health expenditure, Australia, 1971 to 2014 (percentage)

Source: World Bank (various issues).

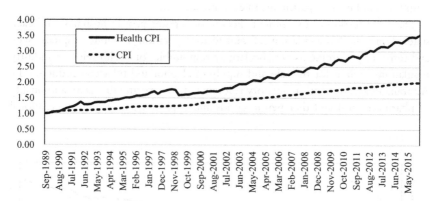

FIGURE 16.3 Health care costs and the CPI, 1989 to 2015 (September 1989=1.00)

Source: ABS (2017).

quarantine arrangements, ensuring an adequate and safe supply of blood products, and regulating the private health insurance industry (AIHW 2010).

The health care sector and government

Government involvement in the health care sector is widespread around the world and can be traced back to a number of possible market failures. 'That risk and uncertainty are, in fact, significant elements in medical care hardly needs argument. I will hold that virtually all of the special features of this industry, in fact, stem from the prevalence of uncertainty' (Arrow 1963, p. 942). The health care market in Australia has a number of failures and imperfections, some of which have led to government intervention. The first two of these are imperfect information and limited competition. The other two relate to the large role played by non-profit institutions and the insurance industry in the health care sector.

It is worth also recognizing that, even if there were no market imperfections in the sector, there might be justification for government intervention for distributional reasons. Certainly, the provision of greater levels of health care through government funding has often in Australia been justified on the grounds of distributional equity.

Imperfect information

When consumers go to a doctor in large part they are buying the doctor's knowledge and/or information. As a patient, the consumer must rely on the doctor's judgement as to what medicine is required or whether an operation or other procedure is advisable. Because they lack medical expertise, patients generally cannot effectively assess and evaluate their doctor's advice. They may not even be able to tell whether a doctor is qualified. This explains why government has long taken a role in licensing doctors and regulating the drugs they can administer to their patients, and the activities of hospitals (Arrow 1963).

These information problems are far more severe than those faced by consumers in other markets. In the case of repeat purchases, like groceries, consumers either can judge the quality of the products themselves or come to rely on a grocery store. Typically, however, individuals do not make repeat purchases of medical goods or procedures.

Insurance companies that pay on behalf of patients also encounter information problems relating to doctors and patients. Like patients they must rely largely on doctors to determine what procedures are necessary and useful. Imperfect information about patients creates problems in the market for insurance.

Limited competition

Imperfect information decreases the effectiveness of competition. A firm selling a standard commodity knows that it can attract new customers by lowering prices. Customers can easily ascertain where they are getting the best value. In contrast potential patients, when seeing a doctor, may regard a lower price as being an indicator of a lower level of service and expertise, as the low price is an indicator of low demand for that doctor's services. By the same token the heterogeneity of medical services makes price and quality comparisons difficult and thus inhibits the effective dissemination of information.

The practices of the medical profession may compound the limitations of competition, such as the practice of not advertising. Given, however, the potentially large variations in quality, simply knowing about price is of limited value to patients trying to make choices.

In addition, it is possible that in small communities there are only a limited number of medical practitioners. Also, there may be limited competition between hospitals. In the event of an emergency an individual is seldom able to make choices among hospitals. Even if the choice is made an individual is not likely to make the choice, but his or her doctor.

Absence of profit motive

Another important difference between medical markets and standard competitive markets is the large role of not for profit organizations in the provision of health care. For a long time, not for profit hospitals vastly outnumbered for profit hospitals. Such institutions do not view their objectives as simply minimizing the cost of delivery or maximising profits. For profit hospitals also have problems in the health sector in that quality is hard to evaluate, and profits might be maximised at the expense of quality.

Incentive problems encountered with both non-profit and for profit institutions arise in large measure from imperfect information. If patients could easily judge the quality of what they purchased, then they could make better decisions and providers would be under more pressure to achieve both high quality and efficiency.

Role of insurance

Individuals are risk averse, which is why they buy insurance. In doing so they face some of the problems of moral hazard and adverse selection.

The possibility is that insurance increases the likelihood that whatever is insured becomes more likely. With insurance, therefore, there is a tendency to create incentives to behave in a less healthy fashion. As only a small fraction of health care costs is paid directly by patients this helps to create incentives to seek over-servicing. The tax system might also be designed to encourage excessive consumption of health care services. This is what is known as the moral hazard problem in health care insurance.

In the case of adverse selection there is a tendency for those least likely to need insurance not to seek it and for those who most need it to do so. This can mean that the costs for the most at risk are very high, and lead to a disinclination on the part of insurers to insure them. This concern for the lack of coverage of certain high-risk groups has formed one of the strongest motivations for expansion of the government's role in health care, and in particular the creation in many countries of universal health benefit systems (Stiglitz and Rosengard 2015).

Pharmaceuticals

One part of the health care industry in Australia that is especially the subject of policy decisions on the part of the government is the pharmaceutical industry.

The pharmaceutical industry (including biological therapies and vaccines) is heavily regulated and yet has no intrinsic natural monopoly characteristics. Indeed, it is a fairly competitive industry from research through to selling. Market power is generally temporary in this industry and is derived from public policy in the form of government granted patents on individual products. The industry is also a leading high-tech industry and has a high proportion of its costs derived from investment in research and development.

Despite the industry having no natural monopoly characteristics, its development has been accompanied by the development of an extensive range of government regulations and subsidies for drugs produced. The market failure rationale for intervention instead rests on imperfect information. Often consumers don't have knowledge of the drugs they consume and often don't directly make decisions on the purchases, but instead rely on doctors, who write prescriptions for them and are often the target of pharmaceutical marketing. This leads to consumers being relatively price insensitive, a situation that is reinforced if the drugs are vital for one's health and if the cost is covered by insurance.

In terms of industry concentration previously the chemistry of drug discovery favoured larger firms. However, more recently drug discovery has shifted to biology, with comparative advantages for smaller firms. Small firms often specialise in discovery research, sometimes forming alliances with larger companies. There is some evidence of economies of scale and scope in the sales and marketing of products. However, market power is limited. The market is generally contestable as well, with potential new entrants being large.

The regulatory issues in the industry, therefore, arise from several other factors that characterise this field. First, there is a lack of immediate observability regarding the product efficacy and safety, which are critical to patient health. This leads to regulation of market access by the requirements to have a product licence. A second key feature is the importance of patents in allowing companies to earn a return on research and development. The product is often easy to replicate, although this is less true of biological than of chemical products. Extensive clinical trials, however, need to be undertaken in order to get approval and licensing. Another important factor is the nature of health care provision, with third-party payers providing insurance cover, giving rise to moral hazard and leading to economic regulation of industry prices and profits. Heavily insured consumers are price insensitive. Producers can, therefore, charge higher prices than in the absence of insurance. Price regulation and other reimbursement controls are a response of government payers to this interaction of insurance and patents.

In terms of the development of new products in the industry governments also play a more direct role. Universities typically undertake research, with public funding of blue skies research. This leads to scientific publications that are public goods. Biopharmaceutical companies directly and indirectly invest in this process, through grants and research collaboration. Companies also undertake basic research, and the public sector undertakes translational research and the patenting of compounds.

Companies continue research and development after product launch, and additional clinical trials may identify longer-term outcomes. All this means that the industry is characterised by high research and development costs.

The main regulatory issue concerns the optimal mix of agency regulation and tort liability. There is a strong argument that structuring and interpreting clinical trials to ensure safety standards is a public good best delivered by an expert regulatory agency. The possibly asymmetric nature of information makes it difficult for doctors and patients to make accurate evaluations of efficacy prior to use.

In Australia, new products are regulated by a national government agency. The Australian Drug Evaluation Committee (ADEC) was a committee that provided independent scientific advice to the Australian Government regarding therapeutic drugs. The committee was originally formed in 1963 and more recently authorised under the *Therapeutic Goods Act 1989* as part of the Therapeutic Goods Administration (TGA). In 2010, the ADEC was replaced by the Advisory Committee on Prescription Medicines (ACPM). The ADEC provided advice to the Minister for Health and Ageing and the Secretary of the Department of Health on:

- the quality, risk–benefit, effectiveness and accessibility of drugs referred to ADEC for evaluation;
- medical and scientific evaluations of applications for registration of new drugs.

The Therapeutic Goods Administration is the regulatory body for therapeutic goods (including medicines, medical devices, gene technology and blood products) in Australia. It is a division of the Australian Department of Health and is responsible for conducting assessment and monitoring activities to ensure that therapeutic goods available in Australia are of an acceptable standard and that access to therapeutic advances is timely. The availability of drugs and poisons is regulated by scheduling under individual state legislation, but is generally under the guidance of the national Standard for the Uniform Scheduling of Drugs and Poisons (SUSDP).

In addition to support for basic research and regulation of new drugs the Australian Government acts to subsidise the consumption of drugs mainly for distributional reasons. Medicare subsidises a wide range of prescription pharmaceuticals under the Pharmaceutical Benefits Scheme (PBS). Under the PBS, Australians pay only part of the cost of most prescription medicines bought at pharmacies. The rest of the cost is covered by the PBS. The amount paid by the patient varies, up to a maximum of $36.10 for general patients and $5.90 for those with a concession card (Australia, Department of Health 2013). If a medicine is not listed under the PBS schedule, the consumer must pay the full price, as it is a private prescription. However, pharmaceuticals provided in public hospitals are generally provided to public patients free of charge, with the cost covered by state and territory governments. The existence of these schemes raises issues of how to control pharmaceutical expenditures given that the subsidisation helps to boost demand. In Australia, there is a process of review of the cost effectiveness of all new drugs as a condition of reimbursement under the PBS.

Conclusion

Health care provision is included in the social policy area. In modern times health care provision is one of the major forms of government intervention and policy making. Governments may be involved in the health care system in a variety of ways: directly paying for health care, subsidising individual purchases of health care and health insurance, providing health care services, financing and conducting research, preventing the spread of communicable diseases and regulating drugs and medical devices. In addition, tax concessions are given to encourage the take-up of private insurance.

Public health services are provided by all levels of government: local, state, territory and Australian. Private sector health service providers include private hospitals, medical practitioners and pharmacies. Government expenditure on health care is about 67 per cent of the total expenditure on health care. Although decisions about health are difficult, resource allocation (choices among alternative uses of funds) must be made. Choices must be made on a range of issues, including the degree to which governments support health care and the nature this support will take. Like areas such as education, health services raise questions of public and private choice with respect to redistribution and welfare on the one hand and human capital on the other. Governments have also sought to influence the quality of Australia's human capital through spending on education and health services. Investment in human capital is analogous to investment in physical capital in that costs are incurred in the expectation of a stream of economic gains in the future in terms of productivity improvements. Given the heavy burden of expenditure on the government, and the prospect that this will continue to rise as Australia's population ages, there is a need for improvement in both the efficiency and the effectiveness of Australia's health care sector.

References

Arrow, K. 1963, 'Uncertainty and the welfare economics of health care', *American Economic Review*, vol. 53, no. 5, pp. 941–73.

Australia, Department of Health 2013, *Schedule of Pharmaceutical Benefits*, Department of Health, Canberra.

Australia, Treasury 2016, *Budget Papers, 2016/17, Budget Paper No. 1: Budget Strategy and Outlook*, Treasury, Canberra.

Australian Bureau of Statistics (ABS) 2017, *Consumer Price Index, Australia*, Cat. No. 6401.0, ABS, Belconnen ACT.

Australian Institute of Health and Welfare (AIHW) 2010, *Australia's Health 2010*, Cat. No. AUS 122, AIHW, Canberra.

Australian Institute of Health and Welfare (AIHW) 2013, *Australia's Hospitals 2011–12: At a Glance*, Health Services Series No. 49, Cat. No. HSE 133, AIHW, Canberra.

Butlin, N.G., Barnard, A. and Pincus, J.J. 1982, *Government and Capitalism: Public and Private Choice in Twentieth Century Australia*, George Allen & Unwin, Sydney.

Private Health Insurance Administration Council (PHIAC) 2013, *Membership and Coverage June 2013*, PHIAC, Canberra.

Stiglitz, J.E. and Rosengard, J. 2015, *Economics of the Public Sector*, 4th edn, W.W. Norton, New York.

World Bank various issues, *World Development Indicators*, World Bank, Washington DC.

World Health Organization (WHO) 2013, *Health Systems Strengthening Glossary*, WHO, Geneva.

17
REVENUE RAISING AND TAX POLICY

Introduction

Given the large scale of the modern welfare state and the involvement of governments in financing the health care sector in Australia, one of the most important ongoing policy concerns is that of revenue raising. How the government raises money brings into sharp focus several issues of equity and efficiency. What is the fairest way to distribute the burden of taxation? What is economically and administratively the most efficient way to raise revenue? These two aspects, equity and efficiency, are often at odds with each other, and in many circumstances there is a trade-off between them. Given the burden of taxes it is not surprising that designing tax systems has always been a subject of considerable controversy.

In the past few decades, reform of tax systems has been a consistent area of policy debate in most countries, including Australia. In the Australian case tax policy has been an area of major political controversy and looks likely to remain so for a number of years into the future. This debate will continue around efforts to achieve an optimal tax structure that balances the gains from additional redistribution of income through taxation and welfare spending with the costs in terms of loss in efficiency.

Tax systems and principles

Governments around the world use varying mixes of tax methods to raise the revenue they need, and we can assess these mixes against standards of 'good tax design'. To decide on what constitutes good tax design we need to decide on who should carry the burden of it and decide which types of activities it is most appropriate to tax. Broadly speaking there are three possible bases for taxation: income, expenditure and capital or wealth. Imposts on one's income are generally referred to as direct taxes, on the basis that they are levied directly on the person paying it.

Imposts on one's expenditure are normally referred to as indirect taxes, on the basis that they are often levied on transactions, with the burden being passed on to the person who directly pays it to the government. Taxes on capital or wealth are regarded as being forms of direct taxation.

The Australian tax system is dominated by the Australian Government, a reality that has existed since the High Court's ruling in the Uniform Tax Case 1942. The Australian Government controls around 80 per cent of the tax revenue raised in Australia, which makes it the main player in the formulation of tax policy, and contributes considerably with its influence in a range of other policy areas. The states do, however, impose a range of taxes, including motor vehicle charges, stamp duties, gambling taxes, property taxes and payroll taxes.

Income is taxed in Australia solely by the Australian Government, which levies personal income tax on individuals, corporate income tax on businesses and capital gains tax. Expenditure (or consumption) is taxed in Australia first and foremost by the goods and services tax (GST), but also comes in the form of various state government charges and of the alcohol, tobacco and fuel excises that were previously levied by the states but now are levied by the Australian Government. In the past consumption was also taxed quite significantly by the Australian Government in the form of customs tariffs on imports (some of these still exist but in recent years tariff levels have been considerably reduced). Wealth was taxed by the Australian and state governments up until the 1970s in the form of inheritance taxes (also known as probate taxes), which were then abolished. Taxes on capital gains from assets have been levied by the Australian Government since the mid-1980s, and local governments levy property taxes, both being forms of wealth tax (for a list of major Australian Government legislative tax changes see Table 17.1).

Figure 17.1 provides a breakdown of the various sources of tax revenue raised by the Australian Government in 2015/16. Income and corporate income taxes are still the major source of revenue, making up around two-thirds of revenue raised. Most other taxes are small by comparison, although in recent years the GST has risen in importance (see Figure 17.2). At the same time customs and excise taxes have been declining in importance. Table 17.2 gives a comparison of the Australian tax breakdown with that of other OECD countries. As can be seen from the table Australia still seems to have a higher than average tax take from personal income compared to other countries.

The major change to the Australian tax system in the last 20 years was the introduction of the GST and its replacement of many of the wholesale taxes that then existed. The GST is a type of value added tax (VAT), which involves a tax on the value added at each stage of production, that is the difference between the value of the sales and the value of purchased (non-labour) inputs. Other major changes were made in the mid-1980s with the introduction of taxes on capital gains and fringe benefits and in more recent years with the introduction of the mineral resources rent tax and carbon emissions tax (both of which were subsequently abolished). All of these changes involved considerable political dispute and controversy before being implemented.

Revenue raising and tax policy **241**

TABLE 17.1 Major legislative changes to tax at the Australian Government level

Legislation	Notes
Customs Tariff Act 1902	Customs tariffs.
Excise Act 1901	Excise duties.
Estate Duty Act 1914	Probate taxes, abolished 1979.
Land Tax Act 1910	Land tax, abolished 1952.
Income Tax Assessment Act 1915	Income tax, including taxes on company profits.
Entertainments Act 1916	Wartime measure, abolished 1933.
War-Time Profits Act 1917	Wartime measure, abolished 1950.
Sales Tax Assessment Act 1930	Wholesale taxes, repealed 2006.
Pay-Roll Tax Assessment Act 1941	Tax powers passed to the states in 1971.
Uniform tax legislation 1942	Gave sole power over income taxes to the Australian Government.
Income Tax Assessment (Capital Gains) Act 1986	Capital gains tax.
Fringe Benefits Tax Act 1986	Fringe benefits tax.
Petroleum Resource Rent Tax Assessment Act 1987	Resource rental tax on petroleum and natural gas.
A New Tax System (Goods and Services Tax) Act 1999	GST.
Minerals Resource Rent Tax Act 2012	Abolished 2014.
Clean Energy Act 2011	Abolished 2014.

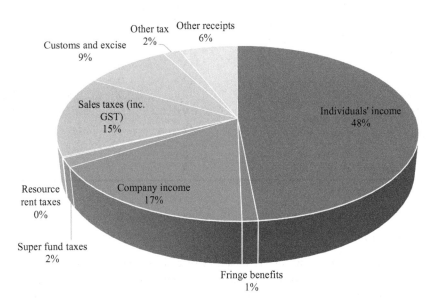

FIGURE 17.1 Sources of Australian Government revenue, 2015/16 (percentage)

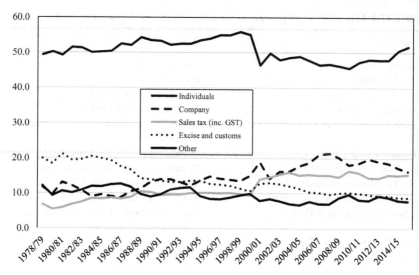

FIGURE 17.2 Sources of Australian Government revenue, 1978/79 to 2014/15 (percentage)

Source: Australia, Treasury (2016).

TABLE 17.2 Government revenue, OECD countries, 2013 (percentage)

	Personal income %	Corporate taxes %	Social security %	Payroll %	Property %	GST %
Australia	39.2	4.9	0.0	1.4	2.6	7.8
Canada	36.6	3.0	4.8	0.6	3.2	7.4
France	18.6	2.5	16.7	1.6	3.8	10.8
Germany	26.1	1.8	13.4	0.0	0.9	10.2
Italy	26.6	3.2	13.1	0.0	2.7	11.5
Japan	19.2	4.0	12.4	0.0	2.7	5.3
Korea	15.3	3.4	6.4	0.1	2.5	7.5
New Zealand	38.0	4.4	0.0	0.0	1.9	12.0
Sweden	28.4	2.6	10.0	4.6	1.1	12.2
UK	27.7	2.5	6.2	0.0	4.0	10.9
USA	38.7	2.1	6.1	0.0	2.9	4.4
OECD average	24.4	2.9	9.1	0.4	1.9	11.0

Source: OECD (2016).

Tax principles

In terms of devising a mix of tax measures several principles become apparent. These principles revolve around the issues of equity and efficiency. In terms of equity, the central concern is that of 'vertical equity', or equity between people on different economic levels. However, it is also the case that a good tax system should have 'horizontal equity'. That is, identical individuals should pay identical taxes. The principle of vertical equity says that those who are most able to pay, or who have a higher welfare, should pay higher taxes. Income is the most commonly used measure of either ability to pay or economic welfare, but it is a flawed measure. Some argue that consumption provides a better basis, and others prefer to rely on the wealth of an individual. Taxing lifetime consumption is equivalent to taxing lifetime income, and both are widely viewed as superior to basing taxes on annual income. Tough questions are posed by what adjustments should be considered – for instance for differences in health, marital status or the number of dependent children.

Income tax has been the mainstay of government revenue raising since the Second World War. Generally, it has incorporated a graduated tax scale whereby people on higher incomes pay tax at higher rates. This gives it a strong component of vertical equity that is absent from excise taxes or customs duties. The degree of redistribution involved in this approach depends on the degree of progressivity built into the system and the degree to which that progressivity is maintained over time. Calculations in the past have found that the Australian tax system has had the effect of redistributing income; a study conducted in the late 1990s found that it effected a 12 per cent redistribution of income and this was complemented on the expenditure side by a social welfare system that added another 22 per cent of redistribution (Saunders 2001, p. 190).

Graduated income taxes may promote equity, but are they efficient? It is possible that higher taxes provide disincentives to people to work harder and to invest. The main concerns of efficiency are that the system should operate with as few administrative costs as possible and operate in such a way as not to create too many distortions to economic behaviour. Pareto efficient tax structures are those such that, given the tools and information available to the government, no one can be made better off without someone else being made worse off. Income taxes can also create incentives for people to engage in tax minimisation and evasion schemes. These disincentives and the resources wasted in tax minimisation or evasion schemes lead to slower economic growth. The increased reliance on consumption taxes in recent years has been a response both to these disincentives and to tax raising problems.

Another way to look at the issue of equity and efficiency is to break them up into five basic properties of good tax design.

1. Economic efficiency. The tax system should not interfere with the efficient allocation of resources. A persistent concern is the extent to which the tax system discourages savings, work and investment, and distorts other decisions relating to consumption and production. All taxes affect behaviour, and some distortions encourage an individual to attempt to avoid paying them. Tax distortions arise when behaviour is altered in an attempt to avoid or reduce taxes. Except for lump sum taxes, all taxes create such distortions. Taxes affect decisions in all markets, including labour supply and savings decisions, and have

impacts on financial and organization structures. Taxes on the future returns of an asset are typically capitalised in the value of the asset at the time the taxes are announced.
2. Administrative simplicity. The system should be easy and relatively inexpensive to administer. The system should be devised so as to make compliance easy and voluntary.
3. Flexibility. The system should be able to respond easily to changing economic circumstances.
4. Political transparency. The system should be designed so that individuals can ascertain what they are paying and evaluate how accurately the system reflects their preferences.
5. Fairness. The system ought to be fair in its relative treatment of different individuals. The tax system should also be 'corruption proof'.

Tax as a policy instrument

Efficiency and equity issues also arise in the microeconomic role of tax policy. Tax policy may be directed primarily by revenue raising needs. However, it can also serve as an instrument for other policy goals. Taxes can, for instance, be imposed or removed, raised or lowered, to influence the behaviour of people. High levels of taxation may be imposed to discourage undesirable but persistent activities, for example taxes on cigarettes and alcohol. Recent attempts in Australia to place taxes on carbon emissions are also designed to deter activity that is potentially environmentally damaging. Taxes that reduce the negative externalities of pollution can be efficiency enhancing. In addition, in the past Australian governments have used customs duties, not only to raise revenue, but at times to promote domestic manufacturing growth by deterring people from buying imports.

Alternatively taxes may be imposed at concessional levels to encourage desirable activities. Examples include the dependent child deductions offered to individuals and concessional tax rates applied to superannuation. Tax concessions are also granted to business on investment in research and development. These 'tax expenditures' as they are known can be important instruments of economic policy. Certainly, as was explained in Chapter 6, tax concessions on investment in research and development have been an important government policy since the mid-1980s.

History of tax in Australia

The nineteenth century

Over the course of Australia's history, the balance between direct and indirect taxes, and between higher- and lower-income earners, has undergone significant changes. Established in the late eighteenth century and early nineteenth century, Australia's colonies operated as separate economies and political units up until federation in 1901. Government revenue needs in these years were mainly met through an expansion in the range of indirect taxes levied. In Sydney at the end of the eighteenth century colonial authorities raised small amounts of revenue through wharfage fees, port entry and exit fees and duties on alcohol. From 1813 customs duties were also levied on a range of major export commodities. The main attraction of using customs duties (on imports and exports) was that they could be easily collected at the few ports then existing. Levying customs on necessities also ensured a steady flow of revenue, and colonial authorities realised from very early on the revenue benefits of placing excises on the production and import of alcohol.

Early customs and excise duties on goods such as tobacco and alcohol were not only intended to raise revenue, but also introduced as 'sin taxes', for example in response to concern over the level of alcohol consumption in the colonies. By 1840, customs duties had been extended beyond luxury goods to essential items such as tea, sugar, flour, meal, rice, grain and pulses (see Mills 1925). The narrow base and the high consumption of these goods by poorer households, relative to their income, meant that the tax system at the time could be regarded as being fairly regressive in impact.

Each of the separate colonies also introduced several taxes on services. These included: liquor retailing fees; auction licence fees; stamp duties; probate fees (service charges for the issue of probate and letters of administration by public legal clerks and judges); and stock taxes. After the gold rushes began in 1851 governments raised revenue from gold licensing. However, these were to trigger a revolt by Victorian miners – the Eureka Stockade. The primary reason for revolt was the high level at which the licence fees were set, but also the lack of public spending on the gold fields and lack of link to the amounts gold miners earned from their efforts. Gold licence fees were subsequently replaced with a gold export tax and a much reduced miner's right, which were easier to collect and more equitable (see Smith 1993). Another significant early contributor to colonial government revenue was fees on grants of land and leases. New South Wales in particular relied heavily on revenue from land sales and rent. In the years leading up to federation, the main political divide in Australia centred on colonial attitudes towards tariff protection. The colonies of South Australia and Victoria were strongly protectionist, relying heavily on customs duties and tariffs, whereas New South Wales declared itself a free trade colony.

Federation and after

At the end of the nineteenth century each of the six Australian colonies had distinct tax systems, which were mostly reliant on customs and excise duties and, in some states, land sales and taxes. The design of these tax systems was largely driven by administrative concerns rather than principles of equity or efficiency. This emphasis was partly because it was administratively easier to impose these forms of taxation in an era when the machinery of government was not especially sophisticated. This approach to taxation could be regarded as 'regressive' in impact, in that taxes were often set in absolute values and so fell as a proportion of higher-income earners' income. Customs duties were also designed in the case of some of the colonies to act as trade barriers between the colonies and with countries overseas. One of the significant results of federation in 1901 was the removal of all duties on goods traded between Australian states.

The reliance on customs and excise duties also meant that the level of government spending was relatively small. At the time of federation Australia's tax to GDP ratio was around only 5 per cent. This ratio remained reasonably constant until the introduction in 1915 of the Australian Government's income tax, which was used to fund Australia's war effort. At this time, however, Australia was evolving from a frontier and migrant settlement to a modern economy with growing urban and rural populations, rising wealth, and demands for a greater role for government. Social and demographic changes were to lead to corresponding changes in taxation to pay for these demands to be met. Formerly dependent on hidden and regressive indirect taxes such as customs and excise duties, late in the nineteenth century the colonies began to introduce direct, progressive taxes on land and income. The rate of change to the tax bases varied between the colonies according to their stage of development. At the same time one of the main challenges of federation was the creation of a two-tier system of government that centralised control of some functions while allowing each state sufficient autonomy to meet the social preferences of its constituency. The Australian constitution allocated most of the expenditure responsibilities to the states.

As part of federation the states gave up customs and excise duties to secure interstate free trade and ensure adequate protection for Australian industry (Groenewegen 1985). Uniform federal tariff and excise duties were introduced in 1901. They largely applied to the goods that had been taxed by the former colonies – tobacco products, beer and spirits, and some basic food and clothing. As the Australian Government's revenue needs were limited, it was expected that revenue from customs and excise duty would be sufficient. Indeed, as customs and excise duties were by far the greatest source of taxation revenue at the time, the states were left with a shortfall of funding. To resolve this fiscal imbalance, the constitution provided for a revenue sharing arrangement for the first ten years following federation. The Australian Government retained one-quarter of customs and excise duty revenue, with the remainder distributed to the states along with any revenue that was surplus to Australian Government needs. It was not long after federation that fiscal inequality between the states led to federal funding in support of fiscal equalisation. In 1910/11, Western Australia requested fiscal assistance to compensate for the loss of tariffs, which had been its primary revenue source. In 1911/12, Tasmania also became a recipient of Australian Government grants, and South Australia became a recipient in the 1920s.

In addition to customs and excise duties the major form of tax used was land taxes. Land taxes were first introduced by state administrations in the late nineteenth century after a long period of debate and blocking of such taxes by parliaments dominated by wealthy landowners. Land taxes were also introduced at the national level in 1910 as a form of wealth tax and as a means to break up large tracts of underutilised land and to pay for the first Australian Government aged and maternity benefit payments. In most states land was taxed at progressive rates, based on unimproved value, while the Australian Government's land tax was introduced as a flat rate tax. As a form of wealth tax, land taxes became less effective over time as the productivity base of the economy diversified from being mostly agrarian at the beginning of the twentieth century, and wealth was held in more diverse forms. Land taxes were also unpopular, and in 1952 land taxes were abolished at the national level, but still operate at the state and local level.

As the states lost their access to customs and excise duties a number turned to the use of income taxes, each with its own definition of assessable income and different rates applying to differing categories of income. During the First World War income taxes were introduced at the national level on the wealthy, to help pay for the increased expenditure on armaments. The Australian Government rates were low and cut in at a high income threshold, minimising double taxation. Following the war, the Australian Government continued to impose income tax, meaning that two tiers of government were sharing, and competing for revenue from, a common taxation base.

In addition, the Australian Government introduced probate duties at this time on the wealthy as well. Estate taxes were first introduced in the form of probate duties (a tax on property passing by will) charged by courts in the early part of the nineteenth century in New South Wales. By 1901 estate taxes had been adopted by all of the colonies. In general, estate duties were relatively low cost to administer and, when introduced, were more readily accepted than a wealth tax levied throughout a taxpayer's life. Gift duties aimed to ensure that estate duties were not circumvented. At the end of the war these taxes (income and probate) were retained and mainly used to pay for the increased welfare payments that were being made (increased repatriation costs as well).

The onset of the 1930s Great Depression had a significant impact on the (then) Australian Government's ability to raise revenue, particularly through customs duties. In addition to falling revenues, the government's debt servicing costs had increased significantly as the result of a large spending programme in the late 1920s. Faced with a large budget shortfall, the government introduced the wholesale sales tax in 1930. Raising indirect taxes was favoured because the incidence was disguised, making the tax more politically palatable. It was also argued at the time that such taxes had a smaller impact on labour supply decisions than income taxes. The tax was levied at a rate of 2.5 per cent, but within a year the rate had been increased to 6 per cent, and by 1940 the rate had been further increased and a multiple rate structure introduced. The tax was levied on many classes of consumables, but provided preferential treatment for food, primary produce and some primary industry inputs (Smith 1999).

Between the two world wars, government expenditure and tax revenues grew significantly, and by the beginning of the Second World War Australia's tax take was over 11 per cent of GDP. This process was enabled by growth in the use of the income, probate and wholesale taxes.

The Second World War

The Australian Government increased its income taxation in the early years of the Second World War to meet the costs of the war effort. Between 1938/39 and 1941/42, Australian Government income tax revenue grew from 16 per cent to 44 per cent of total Australian Government revenue. With reliance on income taxation rising at both the Australian and the state government levels, differences in state income taxes led to concern about the inequitable tax burdens between taxpayers in different states. In 1942 the Australian Government introduced legislation that increased the Australian Government income tax rates to raise more revenue. The legislation provided for reimbursement grants to the states provided that they ceased to levy their own income taxes. The uniform taxation arrangements were initially only meant to apply for the duration of the Second World War and one year thereafter. At the end of the war, the states sought to regain their income taxing powers but were unsuccessful. This move was upheld in favour of the Australian Government by the High Court in 1942 after a challenge to it by four of the state governments. The pay as you earn (PAYE) method of skimming the tax due directly off wages at the source was also introduced at this time to reduce administrative costs. The PAYE system was more convenient for taxpayers, created a more even flow of revenue for government and improved compliance, as evasion was more difficult with income taxed at source (Groenewegen 1985). Payroll taxes were also introduced at this time, and there was a downward extension of the income tax as the Australian Government became more involved in providing welfare and health care expenditures. This system was fairly 'progressive' in that the rate at which the income taxes were levied increased with income. Between 1945 and 1970 government outlays on welfare were largely paid for by direct taxes on personal and corporate incomes (Mathews and Grewal 1997).

By the end of the Second World War, taxation revenue had grown to over 22 per cent of GDP. The further increase in taxation largely reflected Australia's involvement in the war and the introduction of government support programmes, such as the widows' pension in 1942 and unemployment relief in 1944. Tax revenues tended to fall in the middle of the twentieth century, and by 1963/64 the tax take was around 18 per cent of GDP. It then increased significantly between 1973 and 1975, largely because of increased funding for social programmes. There has since been a modest rise in Australia's tax take, similar to the experience of many other OECD countries.

Developments in Australian Government taxation can be broadly classified into two periods. Up until the 1970s, the focus of significant changes to the tax system was on expanding the revenue base to fund expenditure programmes. Since the 1980s, increased attention has been paid to reforming the tax system to improve equity and efficiency and, more recently, to reducing tax system complexity.

Tax reform

By the late 1960s and into the early 1970s, the state and Australian governments were coming under increasing pressure to amend or remove estate duties. As estate duties had not been adjusted since the 1940s, individuals with relatively modest levels of wealth were becoming subject to them. At the same time, more wealthy individuals were seen to be avoiding the tax through effective estate planning (Groenewegen 1985). With the increasing impost on smaller estates, estate duties became costlier to administer. Rural producers and small business owners also objected to the taxes on the basis that they impeded business succession. By the 1970s pressure for estate duty concessions had gradually reduced the tax base. In the end, state tax competition led to the abrupt demise of estate duties. After Queensland dispensed with its tax in 1977, there was concern in other states about emigration of residents and capital, and the potential impact of the tax on electoral outcomes (Pedrick 1981). The Australian Government also abolished its estate and gift duties in 1979. By 1984 all estate duties, both state and Australian government, had been removed.

At the same time the states' tax base was supplemented in 1971 when the then Australian Government ceded control of payroll taxes to the states. State payroll taxes are now levied at rates ranging between 4.75 per cent and 6.85 per cent. Tax competition between states and lobbying by individual employers and employer groups for exemptions have reduced the payroll tax base to less than half of the comprehensive labour income tax base (Freebairn 2005; Abelson 2012).

A growing concern about the equity of the taxation system led to the establishment of the Taxation Review Committee in the early 1970s (Asprey *et al.* 1975). A key theme of the Asprey Report was the need to broaden the tax base to improve equity and efficiency. In 1985, the Draft White Paper recommended a broadening of the tax base through the adoption of a broad based consumption tax, the introduction of a capital gains tax and comprehensive taxation of fringe benefits (Australia 1985).

The inflation of the 1970s also encouraged a shift towards reform because of the incidence of 'bracket creep'. This was the situation where prices and nominal wages both rose, pushing wage earners up into higher tax brackets without increasing their levels of real income. A combination of tax evasion/avoidance and bracket creep helped to create political pressure for tax reform.

The recommendations relating to capital gains and fringe benefits taxation were adopted following the Draft White Paper, but there was insufficient support for the implementation of a broad based consumption tax at that time. In the late 1980s there were also fundamental changes to the taxation of corporate income. When income tax was first introduced in 1915, companies were taxed on their profits after deduction of dividends (that is only on retained profits). Where dividends were paid out of accumulated profits, shareholders were entitled to a rebate of tax at the lesser of the company tax rate and their personal rate to compensate for tax already paid. In 1940, with additional revenue needed to fund Australia's involvement in the Second World War, the rebate of tax on dividends received by individual shareholders and non-resident companies was removed. The company tax rate was increased, and an undistributed profits tax was imposed on public companies. The removal of the rebate was not intended to remain a permanent feature of the system but remained in place well past the end of the war (Australia, Treasury 1974). From 1940 to 1986, Australia maintained this classical company taxation system, under which profits were taxed at the company rate and at personal rates when distributed. In 1987, Australia introduced an imputation system. Prior to this there had long been calls from business to remove what was seen as double taxation under the two-tier system. The classical system resulted in both equity and efficiency problems (Australia 1985). For example, it provided a disincentive to incorporate, distorted corporate financing decisions by providing a bias towards debt and, combined with the absence of a capital gains tax, provided an incentive for companies to retain profits.

From its introduction in 1915, the income tax base had been gradually broadened. In the post-war period, income tax base broadening was limited until the implementation of some of the recommendations included in the 1985 Draft White Paper (Australia 1985). In 1985 a capital gains tax was introduced, and in 1986 the fringe benefits tax was introduced. The primary motivation behind these base broadening measures was to address gaps in the income tax base, which had led to growth in tax avoidance and evasion activity. In 1999 the removal of accelerated depreciation and a range of other base broadening measures were introduced as part of a broad programme of business tax reform.

Prior to 1985, Australia had no general tax on capital gains, with most capital gains excluded from the income tax base. Of the capital gains taxes that were in operation, the most important was that applying to gains from property held for less than one year, which was introduced in the early 1970s. The Draft White Paper and tax academics also argued for taxing capital gains to improve economic efficiency and reduce tax avoidance. In particular, it was argued that the lack of a capital gains tax distorted investment towards assets providing returns in the form of capital gains rather than income streams, and provided an incentive to convert income into capital gains. It was also argued that, combined with the classical taxation of dividends (discussed above), the lack of a capital gains tax created incentives for companies to retain profits, potentially resulting in less efficient investment choices from an economy-wide perspective. The capital gains tax arrangements introduced in 1985 applied to realised gains and losses on assets acquired after 19 September 1985.

Fringe benefits (indirect, non-cash benefits provided to employees in addition to wages or salary) have been legally taxable in Australia since the inception of the Australian Government income tax. Because of difficulties in determining the value of fringe benefits and for a range of other administrative and related reasons, in practice there was an almost universal non-inclusion of most fringe benefits in assessable income by employees (Australia 1985). In recognition of the growing trend of remunerating employees with non-cash business benefits (particularly for those employees on higher incomes), the explicit taxation of fringe benefits was proposed in the Draft White Paper (Australia 1985). Fringe benefits tax was subsequently introduced in 1986.

Prior to 1983, the taxation levied on end benefits from superannuation funds depended on whether they were paid out as a lump sum or an annuity. Lump sum benefits were taxed very concessionally, with only 5 per cent of the lump sum included in assessable income and taxed at marginal rates. In contrast, annuities were taxed at marginal rates (with an exemption for contributions made from post-tax monies). Reforms to the taxation of superannuation benefits were introduced in 1983 to address concerns that individuals whose remuneration package included superannuation contributions were accessing lower effective marginal tax rates than those individuals who received their remuneration exclusively as salary and wages. The taxation on lump sum payments was raised to 15 per cent for amounts below a specified threshold, with amounts above this threshold taxed at 30 per cent. Contributions and earnings remained untaxed, and the taxation of annuities was largely unchanged. The reforms were applied to service after 1 July 1983, while the pre-1983 arrangements were 'grandfathered'. Further revisions to the taxation of superannuation benefits were announced in 1988, when the government imposed a 15 per cent tax rate on both contributions and earnings. To compensate for these changes, the government reduced the tax rate on the taxed element of lump sum superannuation benefits. The rate was reduced from 15 per cent to zero (provided the benefit was preserved until age 55) for amounts up to the low rate threshold. Amounts above this threshold were taxed at the reduced rate of 15 per cent. While annuities remained taxed at marginal rates, the government introduced a 15 per cent rebate when benefits were paid to the individual. The Superannuation Guarantee (SG), introduced in 1992, provides for a percentage of an eligible employee's remuneration to be directed into a superannuation fund by means of a compulsory employer contribution. The SG rate was phased up from 3 per cent to 9 per cent between 1992 and 2002.

Despite these changes the greatest controversy revolved around the replacement of wholesale taxes with a GST. Wholesale taxes were neither efficient nor simple. The narrow base and differential rate structure created distortions to production and consumption decisions in favour of low taxed or untaxed goods or services. The cascading of wholesale taxes through the production chain reduced economic efficiency and export competitiveness by increasing the cost of production in Australia. The arbitrary range of wholesale tax rates and exemptions imposed significant costs in terms of complexity and compliance. In addition, over time the base declined as a proportion of consumption, with an increasing share of consumption expenditure directed towards services. By 1995, the share of private consumption subject to wholesale taxes had fallen to 22 per cent (Groenewegen 1983).

A broad based consumption tax was proposed in the findings of the Asprey Committee (Asprey et al. 1975). However, the introduction of a broad based consumption tax in Australia proved difficult, with unsuccessful attempts to introduce such a tax in 1985 and in 1993. In July 2000, the Australian Government finally introduced a goods and services tax, based on the value added tax model, as part of a broader package of taxation reform. The GST replaced the wholesale taxes and a range of inefficient state taxes, in conjunction with reforms to federal financial relations. Revenue from the GST is paid to the states and territories, providing them with a stable and growing source of revenue and removing their reliance on general assistance grants from the Australian Government. The introduction of the GST was also accompanied by significant changes to personal income taxes and social security payments. This part of the package included significant reductions in personal income taxes and large increases in government payments to families, pensioners and low-income earners. Adjustments were also made to excise taxes and some specific indirect taxes to adjust for the removal of the wholesale taxes and imposition of the GST. In order to achieve passage through Parliament, several compromises were made to the scope of the GST base. The most notable of these was the removal of basic food and personal products from the GST base.

The introduction of capital gains, fringe benefits and the GST has meant that the government has been able to flatten the income tax rates. Australia's top marginal tax rate has decreased over the past 50 years from over 75 per cent in the 1950s to 47 per cent (including the Medicare levy) as of 1 July 2006 (see Table 17.3). The company tax rate, like personal income tax rates, has been progressively reduced in recent times, decreasing from a high of 49 per cent in 1986 to the current rate of 30 per cent. The rate reductions have largely corresponded with base broadening measures, such as the removal of accelerated depreciation.

Despite the replacement of the wholesale taxes with the GST some excise duties are still imposed in Australia. These include duties on the domestic manufacture of petroleum fuels, certain biofuels, alcoholic beverages other than wine, tobacco products, crude oil and oils and lubricants. Equivalent duties on identical imported products are imposed through customs duty, along with tariffs imposed on imported goods for the purpose of protecting domestically produced goods.

TABLE 17.3 Australian individual income tax rates (residents), 2016/17

Taxable income	Tax on this income	Effective tax rate
$1–$18,200	Nil	0%
$18,201–$37,000	19c for each $1 over $18,200	0–9.7%
$37,001–$80,000	$3,572 plus 32.5c for each $1 over $37,000	9.7–21.9%
$80,001–$180,000	$17,547 plus 37c for each $1 over $80,000	21.9–30.3%
$180,001 and over	$54,547 plus 45c for each $1 over $180,000	30.3–less than 45%

Note: The above rates do not include the Medicare levy of 2 per cent and the temporary budget repair levy, which is payable at a rate of 2 per cent for incomes over $180,000.

Current Australian excises are typically applied to goods with a relatively inelastic demand and where the number of manufacturers is limited. Excises on tobacco and alcohol are supported on the grounds that they help to reduce negative externalities that arise from harm to non-smokers and non-drinkers, and from higher health, medical and motor vehicle insurance costs. An additional important reason is that they all raise revenue.

In addition to excises there are tariffs on imports. These involve the imposition of customs duties at variable rates on selected imports. The major implication of these is that they penalise those industries that are efficient and are not protected from foreign competition. In recent years the amounts collected in revenue from them has declined as tariff rates have fallen.

Along with controversy about the introduction of the GST controversy has also surrounded the taxing of resource rents. In Australia, the Australian Government's responsibility for the extraction of resources is generally limited to waters between 3 and 200 nautical miles seaward of the low-water line along the coast. The states own most resources on land and within the coastal boundary and impose taxes and charges on the extraction of those resources using a variety of mechanisms. Where the Australian and relevant state governments have a joint interest in a petroleum resource, resource taxation occurs by way of royalty.

In the period up to 1975, petroleum royalties were also the main instrument for accruing a return to society for the extraction of offshore petroleum resources. In 1975, a flat per barrel crude oil excise was introduced. Later, to encourage exploration and production in new and remote areas, the Australian Government introduced progressive rates of excise based on total production from a field. In 1987, the petroleum resource rent tax (PRRT) was introduced to generate an equitable return to society from its offshore petroleum resources, while also reducing potential distortions to offshore petroleum exploration and development. The PRRT is a tax on 'above normal' profits derived from upstream petroleum production, defined by the point at which a saleable commodity is first produced (for example crude oil, condensate, natural gas and methane). Downstream processing or value adding activities, such as liquefaction of natural gas, are not subject to PRRT. A gas transfer pricing formula has been developed to establish the upstream value of gas produced and consumed in an integrated gas to liquids project. This tax was later used as the model for the development of a broader *Mineral Resources Rent Act*.

Various taxes

Goods and services tax

Consumption taxes are different from income taxes because, as the name implies, consumption taxes are indirect taxes imposed on that component of income not saved but instead spent on purchasing products (goods and services). Consumption taxes assume various forms, such as wholesale taxes, value added taxes and retail sales taxes. Many developed countries have introduced VAT or GST systems. This is a sales or commodity tax that applies at each stage of the production process. As its name implies the tax is confined to the incremental value added component. Since this involves taxation on several parties at each stage of the production–distribution chain it is more difficult to avoid.

As previously mentioned, when the GST was introduced into Australia in 2000 it replaced a range of wholesale taxes. These were taxes imposed on goods at the wholesale level. Generally wholesale taxes are regarded as distortionary because they penalise the consumption of the goods covered, generally manufactured goods rather than services. The GST in Australia is a value added tax of 10 per cent on most goods and services sales. It is levied on most transactions in the production process, but is refunded to all parties in the chain of production other than the final consumer.

The idea for a broad based consumption tax was proposed by the then Australian Government Treasurer Paul Keating at the 1985 Tax Summit but was dropped at the behest of then Labor Prime Minister Bob Hawke after pressure from the ACTU, welfare groups and business, which did not like its association with proposals for capital and fringe benefits taxes. The idea was revived in 1991 by the opposition Liberal–National Coalition led by John Hewson, and a GST was the centrepiece of the opposition's 'Fightback!' platform at the 1993 election. Hewson lost the election, and so at this stage the GST was not introduced. Later, at the 1998 election, John Howard proposed a GST that would replace all existing sales taxes, as well as applying to all goods and services. As he was re-elected at this election he could introduce the GST.

A prominent selling point of the tax was that all the revenue raised by the GST would be distributed to the states. In 1999 an agreement was reached with the state and territory governments that their various duties, levies and taxes on consumption would be removed over time, with the consequent budget shortfall being replaced by GST income distributed by the Commonwealth Grants Commission. Furthermore, the Australian Government levied personal income tax and company tax were reduced to offset the GST.

Critics have argued that the GST is a regressive tax, which has a more pronounced effect on lower-income earners, meaning that the tax consumes a higher proportion of their income, compared to those earning large incomes. However, owing to the corresponding reductions in personal income taxes, state banking taxes, Australian Government wholesale taxes and some fuel taxes that were implemented when the GST was introduced some have claimed that this effect is minimal.

Because a GST is generally imposed across all goods and services it is regarded as being less distortionary than a system of different wholesale taxes. A GST also eliminates a bias against exports, as these are zero rated under this sort of scheme. By broadening the tax bases as well, it reduces tax avoidance, especially by those in the cash economy. In the Australian case, when it was introduced the GST was also used to lower and flatten income tax rates. It does, however, create additional compliance costs.

Taxation of the mining industry

As mineral rights are vested in the Crown, the granting of rights to mine to private operators brings a requirement for payment to compensate the community for reduction of the mineral stock. The most practical taxation is for mining to be taxed once is has got under way with royalties (per unit of output) or on profits earned in mining production. Traditionally in Australia royalties have been paid by mining companies to the state governments at fixed rates on each commodity. In the case of states with large mining industries like Western Australia and Queensland, the royalties make up a significant proportion of state based revenue.

An alternative to royalties is a resource rent tax such as the previously mentioned one on petroleum. The resource rent tax allows for current and capital expenditures to be deducted from the revenue generated by a project on a cumulative basis and the tax applied to rents which occur above the threshold rate of return. Losses can be carried forward, and it is this feature which reduces its disincentive effects on investment decisions in comparison to a profit tax. The resource rent tax has been applied in Australia as an alternative to the crude oil levy.

The minerals resource rent tax (MRRT) was a tax on profits generated from the mining of non-renewable resources in Australia. The tax, levied on 30 per cent of the 'super-profits' from the mining of iron ore and coal in Australia, was introduced on 1 July 2012. A company was to pay the tax when its annual profits reach $75 million, a measure designed so as not to burden small business. A repeal of the Act was undertaken in 2014.

Carbon taxes

A carbon pricing scheme in Australia, commonly dubbed by its critics a 'carbon tax', was introduced by the Gillard Labor Government in 2011 as the *Clean Energy Act 2011*, which came into effect on 1 July 2012. It was in operation until it was repealed on 17 July 2014, backdated to 1 July 2014. In its place, the Abbott Government set up the Emissions Reduction Fund in December 2014.

The 2011 scheme required entities which emit over 25,000 tonnes per year of carbon dioxide equivalent greenhouse gases and which were not in the transport or agriculture sectors to obtain emissions permits, called carbon units. Carbon units were either purchased from the government or issued free as part of industry assistance measures. As part of the scheme, personal income tax was reduced for those earning less than $80,000 per year, and the tax free threshold was increased from $6,000 to $18,200. Initially the price of a permit for one tonne of carbon was fixed at $23 for the 2012/13 financial year, with unlimited permits being available from the government. The fixed price rose to $24.15 for 2013/14. The government had announced that the scheme was part of a transition to an emissions trading scheme in 2014/15, where the available permits would be limited in line with a pollution cap. The scheme primarily applied to electricity generators and industrial sectors. It did not apply to road transport and agriculture.

Tax incidence

The incidence of a tax describes who actually bears the burden of the tax. The incidence does not depend on who actually pays the money to a government; rather it depends on a range of market characteristics. In determining the incidence of the tax, it makes no difference whether the tax is levied on producers or consumers; they may be able to pass the cost on to the other. In competitive markets, for instance, the tax incidence depends on the elasticity of demand and supply. In these markets, an excise tax is not borne at all by consumers if the demand curve is perfectly elastic, or by producers if the supply curve is perfectly elastic. It is borne completely by consumers if the demand curve is perfectly inelastic, or by producers if the supply curve is perfectly inelastic.

Figure 17.3 gives an indication of how the incidence of tax might be distributed. In this case panel A of the figure shows the effect of an excise tax on the quantity supplied by a firm. At any price, p0, the firm will supply a lower quantity. The tax can be thought of as increasing the marginal cost of production, and the output supplied is reduced from q0 to q0'. Panel B of the figure shows the effect of the tax on the whole market supply curve and equilibrium. At each price, the market is willing to supply less (the supply curve shifts to the left), or, equivalently, the price required to elicit a given supply out of the market is higher, by an amount exactly equal to the tax. Figure 17.4 shows the distribution of the tax incidence between consumers and producers. An alternative way to look at it is to view the change brought about by the tax as a downward shift in the demand curve (see Figure 17.5). How the tax is distributed between the producers and consumers depends on the elasticity of supply and demand. If for instance there is a perfectly elastic supply curve (horizontal supply curve), the price rises by the full amount of the tax; the entire burden of the tax is on consumers. On the other hand, with a perfectly inelastic demand curve, the price rises by the full amount of the tax; the entire burden of the tax is on the consumers. With a perfectly inelastic supply curve, the price does not rise at all; the full burden of the tax is on producers. With a perfectly elastic demand curve (horizontal demand curve), the price does not rise at all; the entire burden of the tax is on the producer.

Generally speaking, the extremes of perfect inelasticity or elasticity do not exist, but often the curves can trend one way. For instance, in the case of a tax on cigarettes, the demand curve is fairly inelastic even if it is not perfectly inelastic. This means that the tax can be largely passed on by producers to consumers, who are not very responsive to the change in the price. Because of the importance of the elasticities the factors that influence the incidence are really those that affect the elasticity. These might include such things as:

- The time span (the short run versus the long run). Demand and supply curves are likely to be more elastic in the long run than in the short run. This means that the impact is different in the long run and in the short run.

- The degree of openness of the economy. Supply curves of factors are more elastic in an open economy.
- The degree of competition in the market. Monopolies tend to be able to pass on the cost of taxes to consumers. A tax on a monopolist may be shifted more than 100 per cent; that is, the price paid by consumers may rise by more than the tax.

The imposition of most taxes of these sorts introduces some inefficiencies. The magnitude of the inefficiencies is measured by the deadweight loss shown in a standard demand and supply diagram, that being the difference in revenues that could be obtained from a lump sum tax (which creates no inefficiencies) as compared to a distortionary tax, with the same effect on the level of welfare of consumers.

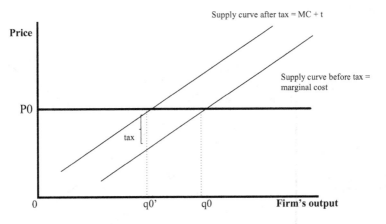
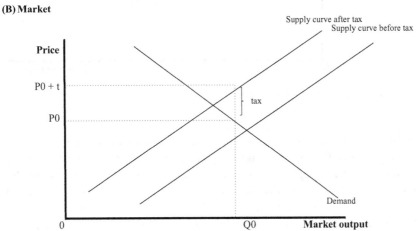

FIGURE 17.3 Effect of a commodity tax on supply

258 Social policies, environment and taxation

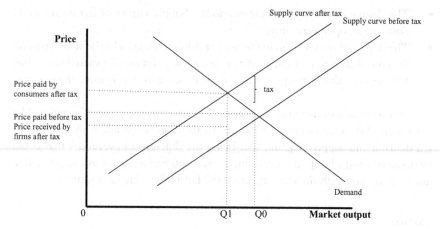

FIGURE 17.4 Effect of tax on prices and quantities

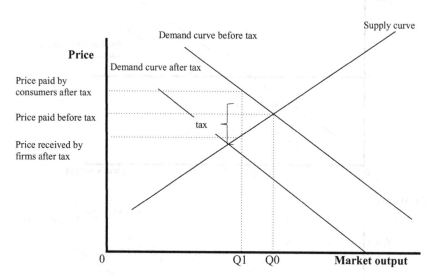

FIGURE 17.5 Alternative views of tax

When it comes to the taxing of capital some special conditions apply. There are both equity and efficiency reasons for arguing that income from capital should not be taxed. Some argue against the taxation of capital on the grounds that it involves heavy administrative costs. But there are perhaps even stronger equity arguments in favour of the taxation of capital, since without such taxes much of the income of the richest individuals in society would escape taxation. In terms of efficiency the taxation of the return to capital tends to reduce savings and investment. In a small open economy, in which only the returns to domestic investors are taxed, investment is unchanged but there is increased borrowing from abroad.

In the Australian case the capital gains tax is one of the main forms of wealth taxation. There are, however, serious problems in the measurement of both capital gains and losses. The fact that capital gains are taxed only when the asset is sold gives rise to the locked-in effect; individuals may retain an asset when, in the absence of taxation, they would have sold it.

The corporation tax is often viewed as a tax on capital in the corporate sector. The effective tax rate depends on a variety of details, including depreciation allowances and the fraction of debt financing. In the long run, if savings are fairly elastic or if capital is mobile internationally, most of the burden of the tax rests on consumers and workers.

Because the actual decrease in the value of an asset as it wears out or becomes obsolete cannot be easily measured, governments use simple rules to estimate depreciation (called depreciation allowances). Even the simplest rules, such as taking off one-tenth of the value of an asset each year for an asset that lasts ten years, tend to be excessively generous; that is, they provide allowances in early years that exceed true economic depreciation (the decrease in the value of the asset in a perfectly competitive capital market). As a result, they introduce distortions, with longer-lived assets typically being favoured. Tax neutrality requires either that depreciation allowances correspond to true economic depreciation or that the total value of the asset be depreciated in the year of purchase, in which case the tax becomes a tax on pure profits, not a tax on the return to capital.

In assessing the impact of the corporation income tax, one needs to consider the effect of the corporation tax simultaneously with the effect of the individual income tax. The total (corporate plus individual) tax liability associated with a marginal investment depends on how that investment is financed, whether through debt or through equity. The tax structure may affect how firms raise capital. With the growth of multinational firms, there are serious problems in administering a corporate income tax – in particular, in ascertaining how much income (profit) should be attributed to each country.

Conclusion

Given the large scale of the modern welfare state and the involvement of governments in financing the health care sector in Australia, one of the most important ongoing policy concerns is that of revenue raising. How the government raises money brings into sharp focus several issues of equity and efficiency. These two aspects, equity and efficiency, are often at odds with each other, and in many circumstances there is a trade-off between them. In the past few decades, reform of tax systems has been a consistent area of policy debate in most countries, including Australia. In the Australian case tax policy has been an area of major political controversy and looks likely to remain so for a number of years into the future. This debate will continue around efforts to achieve an optimal tax structure that balances the gains from additional redistribution of income through taxation and welfare spending with the costs in terms of loss in efficiency.

References

Abelson, Peter 2012, *Public Economics: Principles and Practice*, McGraw-Hill, Sydney.
Asprey, K., Lloyd, J., Parsons, R. and Wood, K. 1975, *Taxation Review Committee, Full Report*, AGPS, Canberra.
Australia, 1985, *Reform of the Australian Tax System: Draft White Paper*, AGPS, Canberra.
Australia, Treasury 1974, *Company Income Tax Systems*, Treasury Taxation Paper No. 9, November, AGPS, Canberra.
Australia, Treasury 2016, *Budget Paper No. 1: Budget Strategy and Outlook 2016/17*, Treasury, Canberra.
Freebairn, John 2005, *A Comparison of Alternative Tax Bases*, Working Paper No. 11/05, Melbourne Institute, Melbourne.
Groenewegen, Peter 1983, *Australian Wholesale Sales Tax in Perspective*, Australian Tax Research Foundation, Sydney.
Groenewegen, Peter 1985, *Everyone's Guide to Taxation in Australia*, Allen & Unwin, Sydney.
Mathews, R.L. and Grewal, B. 1997, *The Public Sector in Jeopardy: Australian Fiscal Federalism from Whitlam to Keating*, Centre for Strategic Economic Studies, Victoria University, Melbourne.
Mills, S. 1925, *Taxation in Australia*, Macmillan, London.
Organisation for Economic Co-operation and Development (OECD) 2016, *Government at a Glance*, OECD, Paris.
Pedrick, W.H. 1981, *Oh! To Die Down Under! Abolition of Death and Gift Duties in Australia*, Centre for Research on Federal Financial Relations, ANU, Canberra (reprint from *Tax Lawyer*, vol. 35, no. 1).
Saunders, Peter 2001, *The Ends and Means of Welfare: Coping with Economic and Social Change in Australia*, Cambridge University Press, Cambridge.
Smith, J. 1993, *Taxing Popularity: The Story of Taxation in Australia*, Federalism Research Centre, ANU, Canberra.
Smith, J. 1999, *Is the Only Good Tax an Old Tax? A Historical Perspective on the GST Debate*, Discussion Paper No. 398, Research School of Social Sciences, ANU, Canberra.

18
ENVIRONMENTAL POLICY

Introduction

In recent years environmental demands have presented novel challenges in public policy as governments in Australia have tried to juggle the conflicting interests of environmental protection and employment and economic development. The government at all three levels in Australia (federal, state and local) has long been involved in the formulation and application of environmental policy, and government action on behalf of the environment clearly can have a beneficial effect on it. The effects of these policies are easy to see. The quality of air in Australia's major cities, for instance, has been improved by the enforcement of emissions standards. Waterways are also cleaner because of the prohibitions on making use of them for the removal of waste products. Problems, however, still remain.

While it is increasingly agreed that government actions are required to preserve the environment, the extent and form of these actions remain a subject of debate. This chapter, therefore, will describe the economic rationale for government intervention in the environment and review some of the main government programmes and policy issues related to environmental policy.

Externalities

Environmental problems and policy responses represent a classic situation in which there is an externality being imposed on those not taking part in a transaction. This can be seen clearly in the case of pollution (Callan and Thomas 2010; Stiglitz and Rosengard 2015). To begin with, it must be recognised that the optimal level of pollution is not zero, but it is also not what will probably eventuate in a market context. This is because the party generating the pollution has inadequate incentives to reflect the social costs imposed by these decisions in the

Social policies, environment and taxation

prices charged or paid. The focus of public policy, therefore, should be on achieving an efficient pollution level, which is the level that would have arisen under a voluntary contractual situation if parties could contract costlessly, and incorporate all costs of production and consumption in pricing.

Where an individual or company undertakes an action that has an effect on another individual or company, for which the latter does not pay or is not paid, there is said to be an externality. If the externality confers a cost on the affected parties then it is said to be a negative externality. If it confers a benefit then it is a positive externality. Air and water pollution and traffic congestion are considered examples of negative environmental externalities.

Markets affected by significant externalities result in inefficient resource allocations. If there is a negative externality then the tendency would be for the level of production to exceed the optimally efficient level of production. Figure 18.1 shows a conventional supply and demand diagram. In the absence of externalities the market equilibrium at point Qm would be efficient. The demand curve would reflect the individual marginal benefits to consumers of an extra production of an item. At the intersection of the supply and demand curves the marginal costs and benefits would be equal. With negative externalities the supply curve would not reflect marginal social costs, only marginal private ones. From a social point of view the optimal level of output would be Qe. This would not be achieved.

An important type of externality arises from what is known as the common resources problem. Its central characteristic is that it pertains to a pool of scarce resources to which access is not restricted. Fisheries to which there is open access can be considered to be of this type. In this case each additional boat reduces the catch of other boats. This is the externality. The marginal social benefit of an additional boat is therefore less than the average catch of each boat (see Figure 18.2). Some of the fish caught by a new boat would come at the expense of existing ones. This means that the market equilibrium is at a level of production in excess of the efficient level of production.

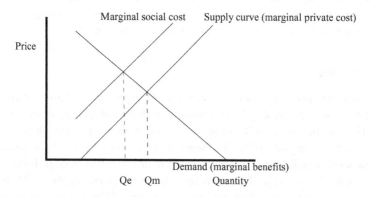

FIGURE 18.1 Production of a good with negative externalities

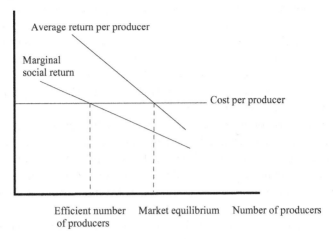

FIGURE 18.2 Common resources problem

Private solutions to externalities

Sometimes economic efficiency can be achieved where there are externalities without recourse to government intervention. This can be achieved by:

1. Establishing sufficiently large economic organisations such that the externalities are internalised. Large apartment complexes, for instance, can internalise the negative and positive externalities created by their inhabitants.
2. Establishing clear property rights so that private parties can bargain towards an efficient solution. This is known as the Coase theorem, where an allocation of property rights can internalise an externality.
3. Using the legal system whereby the imposers of externalities can be forced to compensate the victims through legal action.

There are important limitations to these private remedies. For instance, public goods problems and transaction costs can impede efficient bargaining solutions in the manner suggested by the Coase theorem. The costs associated with getting all the individuals together voluntarily might simply be too high to be readily feasible. Uncertainty and high litigation costs might also make it difficult to achieve legal solutions to problems. These failures necessitate a greater role of government intervention if efficient outcomes are to be achieved.

Government solutions

There are four methods by which governments have attempted to induce individuals and firms to act in a socially efficient manner: fines and taxes, subsidies, tradeable permits and regulation.

When there is good information about the marginal social cost of the externality (as with pollution) and the fines can be adjusted to reflect those costs, then a fine system can attain a Pareto efficient outcome. Figure 18.3 shows how this may be achieved. In the case of pollution, in the absence of a tax on pollution firms will set prices equal to the marginal private cost. There will therefore be excessive production (Qm). By setting a tax or fine equal to the marginal pollution cost, efficiency will be enhanced and the production level of Qe will be achieved. Effectively the external cost has been internalised.

Subsidies to pollution abatement while enabling the efficient level of pollution abatement to be attained will result in excessive production of the pollution generating commodity. In principle, the gainers under the fine system could more than compensate the losers, but in practice these compensations are seldom made. Thus the choice of system for controlling externalities has important distributional consequences.

An increasingly popular market based solution involves the creation of marketable permits, which allow a producer to pollute, but limits this to a set amount. A company therefore is permitted to emit so many units of pollutants. It then allows firms to trade these permits with other companies. A company that cuts its pollution can sell any surplus permits to someone else, creating an incentive for it to do so. One advantage of this approach is that the government can set the maximum level of pollution permitted and then let those most willing to pay to pollute do so. This means that the costs of pollution are incorporated into prices, and markets can allocate resources accordingly. Tradeable permits, therefore, can result in efficient pollution abatement. Making the initial assignments of permits can, however, create problems for the government, as the process can be the subject of political pressures.

Most economists favour market based solutions because they can curb the negative externalities while at the same time limiting the resource allocation problems. In contrast regulations focusing on inputs or standards, it is argued, are likely to result in inefficiency. Governments however have historically tended to use direct methods of regulation. Examples include such things as imposed restrictions on

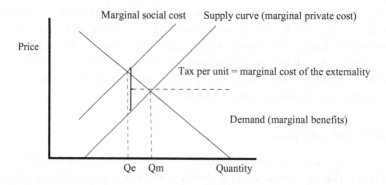

FIGURE 18.3 Market equilibrium with and without taxes

emissions from motor cars and factories, regulation of the disposal of toxic wastes, restrictions on cigarettes smoking, restrictions on fishing and so on. Advocates argue that these regulations create greater certainty in achieving their goals, whereas critics tend to point out the blunt and crude effects of this approach.

The Australian environment

In the Australian case many human activities, including the use of natural resources, have a direct impact on the environment. Environmental issues arose in Australia during the nineteenth century, and encouraged responses from the colonial governments. Australians' growing urban centres gave rise to sanitation problems, which led to colonial government subsidies to local authorities to build sewerage systems (Dingle and Rasmussen 1991; Birmingham 1999). In addition, so-called 'noxious' industries were regulated in terms of their location (zoning), and the first restrictions on waste disposal were introduced. Additional concerns at this time concerned the management of forestries and of the Murray River, both common resources problems (Butlin *et al.* 1982; Carron 1985; Cathcart 2009).

With the omission of environmental matters from the Australian constitution these remained until recent decades mainly with local and state governments. Campaigns for instance for the establishment of national parks were mainly conducted at the state or even local government level. The Australian Government became more involved in the 1970s but with no direct constitutional powers intervened mainly through indirect means such as the external powers of the constitution, its powers over corporations, taxes, commerce and fisheries and coastal powers.

In the first of these cases section 51(xxix) (external affairs) of the constitution allows the Commonwealth to make laws relevant to Australia's obligations under any international treaty. In 1974, for instance, Australia ratified the Convention for the Protection of the World Cultural and Natural Heritage, which later, in 1983, enabled it to prevent the Tasmanian Government from constructing a dam on the Gordon River in the south-west Tasmanian wilderness, an area listed by the Convention. The second power comes from section 51(xx) (corporations), which allows the Commonwealth to make laws with respect to foreign corporations and domestic, trading or financial corporations. In addition, section 51(i) (trade and commerce) allows the Commonwealth to make laws with respect to 'trade and commerce with other countries and among the States'. The environmental significance of this section is that many resource developments – forestry, mining, agriculture and fisheries – are carried out for the purpose of overseas and interstate trade. And, finally, section 51(26) (people of any race) allows the Commonwealth to make laws with respect to 'the people of any race for whom it is deemed necessary to make special laws'. This section protected Aboriginal sites, relics or artefacts. This formed the basis for the *Aboriginal and Torres Strait Islander Heritage (Protection) Act 1984.*

Despite the growth in the power over environmental policy of the Australian Government the states and territories still have a range of environmental responsibilities, including such things as the protection of catchments, waterways and groundwater, floodplain management, air quality, noise abatement, soil contamination, fire protection measures and the conservation of native flora and fauna. Standards of environmental quality are maintained through the use of work approvals, licences, abatement notices, unannounced inspections, collaboration with the public and private sectors, and co-regulation.

At the local level councils in the 1980s began to employ environmental officers, who would work with local groups, mainly with the control of planning and land use together with powers in the area of public nuisances, health and building control issues.

Despite the creation of negative externalities and efforts to negate them through government action, this action is still difficult to use in practice. Two main obstacles prevent effective government action (at all levels) in formulating environmental policy and are the cause of government failures. These are imperfect information possessed by regulators, who often rely on the industry they regulate for information, and the existence of the opportunity for political influence from bureaucrats and industry and environmental groups applying pressure.

After the initial problems of conservation in Australia in the nineteenth and early twentieth century, problems arose surrounding the introduction of noxious weeds and pests, such as prickly pear and rabbit plagues. Australia's geographical isolation has resulted in the evolution of many delicate ecological relationships that are sensitive to foreign invaders and in many instances provided no natural predators for many of the species subsequently introduced. Introduced plants that have caused widespread problems are lantana and the prickly pear bush. The introduction and spread of animals such as the cane toad or rabbit can disrupt the existing balances between populations and develop into environmental problems. The introduction of cattle into Australia, and to a lesser extent the dingo, shows how species can change the landscape. In some cases, the introduction of new species can lead to plagues and the extinction of indigenous species. State government departments of agriculture and later the CSIRO attempted to tackle these problems.

In more recent years a key conservation issue is the preservation of biodiversity, especially by protecting the remaining rainforests. The destruction of habitat by human activities, including land clearing, remains the major cause of biodiversity loss in Australia. Another of the notable issues with marine conservation in Australia is the protection of the Great Barrier Reef. The Great Barrier Reef's environmental pressures include water quality from run-off, climate change and mass coral bleaching, cyclic outbreaks of the crown-of-thorns starfish, overfishing and shipping accidents.

Politically the environmental movement began to form in Australia during the late 1960s owing to such things as a growing pride in the country's natural heritage, increased public apprehension about environmental decay and the formation of a small but dedicated group of activists who campaigned strongly for additional measures. The original environmental agenda focused on the wilderness and sought to preserve the Australian bush from all exploitation. From the wilderness, the desire to protect natural places spread to a range of other issues, such as oil drilling on the Great Barrier Reef, 'green bans' on urban development in Sydney, logging in various parts of the country, the 1972 damming of Lake Pedder in Tasmania, and gold and platinum mining at Coronation Hill in the Kakadu National Park.

The 1980s saw the environmental movement come together, taking action over the proposal to dam the Franklin River. This measure was prevented by the Hawke Government (1983–93). The Hawke Government was proactive and consensus oriented in the environmental area. In 1992 the Intergovernmental Agreement on the Environment was signed, which outlined the responsibilities and interests of the three levels of government, hence avoiding the duplication of environmental assessments and problems associated with such issues as nature conservation, World Heritage listings and planning approval processes.

The Keating Government (1993–96) began a process of devolving Commonwealth influence over environmental matters back to the states. The Howard Coalition Government (1996–2007) that followed promised to use funds from the partial privatisation of Telstra to finance a land conservation fund, and a Natural Heritage Trust was established, later spending money on programmes to improve water use efficiency and develop technologies to reduce carbon emissions. It also passed the *Environmental Protection and Biodiversity Conservation Act 1999* and the *Renewable Energy (Electricity) Act 2000*. In March 2008, the government achieved agreement on a $10 billion rescue package for the Murray–Darling Basin, involving all states and territories, and commissioned the economist Ross Garnaut to report on the impact of climate change on the Australian economy and review the government's climate change policy (Garnaut 2008). A carbon tax was also introduced in 2012 (subsequently abolished by the Abbott Government in 2014).

The Rudd/Gillard governments (2007–13) ratified the Kyoto Protocol in December 2007. The Kyoto Protocol is an international treaty which extends the 1992 United Nations Framework Convention on Climate Change (UNFCCC) that commits countries to reduce greenhouse gas emissions. The Kyoto Protocol was adopted in Kyoto, Japan on 11 December 1997 and entered into force on 16 February 2005. In April 2016 the Australian Government also signed up to the Paris Agreement, an agreement within the United Nations Framework Convention on Climate Change dealing with greenhouse gas emissions mitigation, adaptation and finance starting in the year 2020. The Agreement was negotiated by representatives of 196 parties at the 21st Conference of the Parties of the UNFCCC in Paris and adopted by consensus on 12 December 2015. Under the Agreement, each country determines its own contribution to mitigate global warming. No mechanism to force a country to reach a specific target by a specific date was established as part of the Agreement. In Australia's case the government set a target to reduce emissions by 26–28 per cent below 2005 levels by 2030. Also the government committed $US187 million to international efforts to reduce greenhouse gas emissions.

Government responses to environmental problems can also lead to government failures if the policies are rushed, badly implemented or distorted by political pressures. In the late 2000s, for instance, the Australian Government introduced a number of new programmes, many with dual economic and environmental objectives. A number were criticised for being government failures because of their implementation and management. These included the Australian Government Home Insulation Program and the Green Loans Program (Kortt and Dollery 2012a, 2012b). The Home Insulation Program was categorised as being an example of both political and bureaucratic failure, as the government rushed to implement the scheme without prudent fiscal and administrative controls and failed to establish an effective governance model. The Green Loans Program was characterised as a bureaucratic failure because of the poor political and public service leadership in designing the programme. It was argued government agencies did not possess the specialist skills required to implement it.

The future

Looking to the future, environmental policy will be an important part of government policy formulation. This will be both to preserve the national environment and to sustain Australia's economic base. One problem that will affect the rural sector is that of land degradation. Land degradation results from nine types of damaging environmental impacts such as the clearcutting of old growth forests that is continuing in parts of Australia. This often involves the destruction of natural ecosystems and their replacement with monoculture plantations. The clearing of native vegetation is controlled by federal laws (indirectly), state laws and local planning instruments. The precise details of regulation of vegetation clearing differ according to the location where clearing is proposed.

Another important issue will be that of the protection of waterways in Australia. The main concern here will be that of the Murray–Darling Basin, which is under threat owing to irrigation causing high levels of salinity that affect agriculture and biodiversity in New South Wales, Victoria and South Australia. These rivers are also affected by pesticide run-off and drought. Water use is a major sustainability issue in Australia. During times of drought water restrictions are used in Australia to conserve water. Water transportation and desalination plants often affect water catchments and put increasing pressure on the environment.

Australia is one of the most urbanised countries in the world. Many Australian cities have large urban footprints and are characterised by an unsustainable low-density urban sprawl. This places demand on infrastructure and services, which contributes to the problems of land clearing, pollution, transport related emissions, energy consumption, invasive species, automobile dependency and urban heat islands.

Finally, there is the issue of climate change, which will continue to be a contentious issue into the foreseeable future. There is concern about greenhouse gas emissions, which can lead to global warming. Australia is a major exporter and consumer of coal, the combustion of which liberates CO_2. Most of Australia's demand for electricity depends upon coal fired thermal generation, owing to the plentiful coal supply, and limited potential for hydroelectric generation.

Australia, therefore, is a major producer of carbon emissions per capita, and because of its fragile environment is one of the most at risk from climate change. Table 18.1 shows the level of CO_2 emissions for a range of countries, illustrating the relatively high level of Australia. The absolute level of CO_2 emissions in Australia has also risen considerable (see Figure 18.4), although it is notable that recently it has peaked and begun to fall.

Carbon taxes and permits

Greenhouse gases are gases which, when released into the atmosphere, result in the warming of the planet. The main types are: carbon dioxide (CO_2), from burning fossil fuels and deforestation; nitrous oxide (N_2O), from fertilisers and burning

TABLE 18.1 Carbon emissions (CO_2) in a range of countries, 2012

	Tonnes per capita	kt
Australia	17.7	373,740
China	5.0	6,533,018
Singapore	11.8	554,147
Japan	10.1	1,253,517
New Zealand	7.3	32,635
South Korea	9.8	502,910
United Kingdom	9.4	539,176
United States	19.3	5,832,194

Source: World Bank (2016).

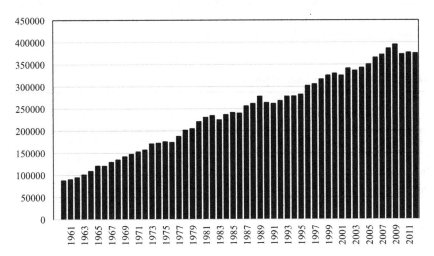

FIGURE 18.4 Australian CO_2 emissions, 1961 to 2012 (kt)

Source: World Bank (2016).

fossil fuels; methane (CH$_4$), from decomposition and landfills; and chlorofluorocarbons, from aerosol propellants, refrigerants and water vapour.

Under the international Kyoto Agreement in 1997 the industrial countries agreed to reduce gas emissions by at least 5 per cent below 1990 levels by 2008–12. To achieve this collective target, individual nations were allocated different targets. No agreement was reached on how to deal with non-compliance and the future involvement of developing countries. The Convention was based on sharing the burdens of coping with climate change. The atmosphere is a shared resource, part of the 'global commons'. Most countries subsequently, however, have failed to meet their targets.

In the Australian case, it was not originally a signatory of the Convention. A joint report by the CSIRO and the Bureau of Meteorology in October 2007 (CSIRO/Bureau of Meteorology 2007) claimed that Australia would face increasing temperatures, decreasing rainfall and worsening drought conditions, which in turn would create a decline in farm production and agricultural export earnings. The Rudd Government signed the Kyoto Protocol in December 2007 and committed the government to cutting greenhouse emissions by 60 per cent on 2000 levels by 2050 and a target of 5 to 15 per cent reduction in emissions by 2020.

Two possible responses that were strongly debated were those of fees/taxes and trade permits. A pollution charge is a fee that varies with the amount of pollution released. Three types are commonly proposed for climate change issues. The first of these is a petrol tax – a per unit tax levied on each litre of petrol consumed. The problem is that it only targets polluting sources using petrol. It also represents a disproportionate burden on (rural) communities lacking public transport. Table 18.2 provides the level of petrol taxes used across a range of countries. The second is a Btu tax – a per unit charge based on the energy content of fuel, measured in British thermal units (Btu), which encourages fuel switching and conservation by raising fuel prices. It is a tax on the consumption of fossil fuels (coal, oil and natural gas) to discourage consumption, reduce carbon

TABLE 18.2 Examples of taxes on petrol

	Tax on petrol US$ per litre
France	0.974
Germany	0.958
Italy	1.098
Spain	0.738
UK	1.003
Japan	0.593
Canada	0.108
USA	0.121
Australia	0.296

Source: IEA (2017).

dioxide emissions and promote other measures against the greenhouse effect. As the carbon content of fuels varies, fossil fuels would be taxed at different rates. Table 18.3 provides a list of the various countries that have carbon taxes, including Australia's scheme, which operated between 2012 and 2014.

In addition, an emissions trading (or cap and trade) plan is a method used to control pollution by providing economic incentives for achieving reductions in the emissions of pollution. A central authority or government will set a limit or cap on the amount of a pollutant that can be emitted. Companies or other groups that emit the pollutant are given credits or allowances which represent the right to emit a specific amount. The total amount of credits cannot exceed the cap, limiting

TABLE 18.3 Examples of emissions taxes and trading schemes, 2017

Country	Date	Detail
Australia	2012–14	$A23 per tonne of CO_2 generation, mining, business transport, waste and industrial processes.
Canada	2007	Quebec: $C3.5 per tonne of CO_2 from petrol ($A3.5) (0.8 cents per litre).
	2008	British Columbia: $C30 per tonne of CO_2 from petrol ($A30) (7.2 cents per litre).
Chile	2014	Emissions from the power sector.
Denmark	1992	100 DKK per tonne of CO_2 on fossil fuels ($A20).
Finland	1990	€20 per tonne of CO_2. Heat, electricity, transportation and heating fuels ($A30).
France	2014	€22 per tonne of CO_2 on fossil fuels ($A33).
Iceland	2010	Imports of liquid fossil fuels.
India	2010	100 rupees per tonne of coal ($A2.10).
Ireland	2010	€20 per tonne of CO_2 on fossil fuels ($A30).
Japan	2012	¥289 per tonne of CO_2 on fossil fuels ($A3.49).
Mexico	2014	Fossil fuel sales and imports.
Netherlands	1990	€26 per tonne of CO_2 on fossil fuels ($A39).
Norway	1991	NOK 253 per tonne CO_2, mineral oil, gasoline and natural gas ($A40).
South Africa	2016	Fuel combustion and non-energy industrial processes.
Switzerland	2008	CHF 36 per tonne CO_2 ($A41).
Sweden	1991	SEK 930 per ton of CO_2 ($A144).
Zimbabwe	2001	3 US cents per litre of petrol (4 Australian cents).
United Kingdom	2001	Fossil fuels for electricity generation.
New Zealand	2008	Emissions trading scheme from 2008 covering forestry, stationary energy, transport, liquid fossil fuels and industrial processes.
South Korea	2015	Emissions trading scheme covering facilities producing more than 25,000 tonnes of greenhouse gas emissions.
European Union	2005	Emissions trading scheme.

Source: Nadel (2016).

total emissions to that level. Companies that pollute beyond their allowances must buy credits from those that pollute less than their allowances. In effect, the buyer is being fined for polluting, while the seller is being rewarded for having reduced emissions. The more firms that need to buy credits, the higher the price of credits becomes, which makes reducing emissions cost effective in comparison. The overall goal of an emissions trading plan is to reduce pollution, and in some cases the cap may be lowered over time. In other systems, a portion of all traded credits must be retired, causing a net reduction in emissions each time a trade occurs. Trading schemes of this sort are in existence in many countries, including New Zealand and the countries of the European Union (see Table 18.3).

Conclusion

Environmental demands have created considerable problems in recent years for governments in attempting to balance the achievement of environmental goals with the goals of employment and economic development. The federal, state and local governments have for a long time been involved in the formulation and application of environmental policy. While it is increasingly agreed that government actions are required to preserve the environment, the extent and form of these actions remain a subject of debate. This will continue to be the case, especially concerning the issue of climate change and measures to reduce greenhouse gas emissions. Although environmental damage constitutes a classic case of the creation of a negative externality, externalities are notoriously difficult to quantify, a situation which will make resolution of these policy debates difficult.

References

Birmingham, J. 1999, *Leviathan: The Unauthorised Biography of Sydney*, Random House, Sydney.
Butlin, N.G., Barnard, A. and Pincus, J.J. 1982, *Government and Capitalism: Public and Private Choice in Twentieth Century Australia*, George Allen & Unwin, Sydney.
Callan, S.J. and Thomas, J.M. 2010, *Environmental Economics and Management: Theory, Policy and Applications*, 5th edn, South-Western Cengage Learning, Mason OH.
Carron, L.T. 1985, *A History of Forestry in Australia*, ANU Press, Canberra.
Cathcart, M. 2009, *The Water Dreamers: The Remarkable History of Our Dry Continent*, Text Publishing, Melbourne.
CSIRO/Bureau of Meteorology 2007, *Climate Change in Australia: Technical Report 2007*, CSIRO, Canberra.
Dingle, T. and Rasmussen, C. 1991, *Vital Connections: Melbourne and Its Board of Works*, McPhee Gribble (Penguin), Ringwood VIC.
Garnaut, R. 2008, *The Garnaut Climate Change Review: Final Report*, Cambridge University Press, Port Melbourne VIC.
International Energy Agency (IEA) 2017, *Monthly Oil Price Statistics*, IEA, Paris.
Kortt, Michael A. and Dollery, Brian 2012a, 'The Home Insulation Program: an example of Australian Government failure', *Australian Journal of Public Administration*, vol. 71, no. 1, pp. 65–75.

Kortt, Michael and Dollery, Brian E. 2012b, 'Australian Government failure and the Green Loans Program', *International Journal of Public Administration*, vol. 35, pp. 150–8.

Nadel, S. 2016, 'Learning from 19 carbon taxes: What does the evidence show?', 2016 ACEEE Summer Study on Energy Efficiency in Buildings, Pacific Grove CA.

Stiglitz, J.E. and Rosengard, J. 2015, *Economics of the Public Sector*, 4th edn, W.W. Norton, New York.

World Bank 2016, *World Development Indicators*, World Bank, Washington DC.

PART IV
Conclusion

19
CONCLUSION

Over the past 30 years Australian economists have scrutinised public policy using a market failure/government failure approach to policy evaluation, with considerable success in terms of creating insight into the nature of the measures and their impact on economic efficiency. Over the same period the nature of government policy has been the subject of considerable reform, with many long-standing policies being brought into question and finally being abolished. No longer is microeconomic policy in Australia based on the use of protective measures to support domestic manufacturing and agriculture, as it was in the early 1970s, along with support for substantial government business enterprises in the communications, transport and energy sectors of the economy. Instead a more market based and global approach has been adopted by most governments, including making use of microeconomic techniques to evaluate government policy proposals.

There is some indication that the programme of microeconomic reform in Australia provided some successes, evidenced by the long period of growth which began in 1991 and survived the twin external shocks of the Asian Economic Crisis of 1998 and the Global Financial Crisis ten years later.

Despite these changes and successes the use of microeconomic techniques to evaluate government policy in Australia is still critical. Since the turn of the century there has been a growing concern that the quality of government interventions is declining (see for instance Garnaut 2013; Edwards 2014). In particular, critics have concentrated on the growing tendency on the part of governments to run populist inspired programmes, with reduced levels of fiscal probity. These criticisms have become more telling given the failure of a range of government measures in the late 2000s, indicating that the capacity for Australian governments to create political and bureaucratic failures has not diminished. An additional driver has been the growing view that Australia has squandered the proceeds of another mining boom, which began to run down after 2015.

An additional concern has been that the increasingly internationalized nature of the Australian economy is leading to greater inequalities in Australian society, which along with an ageing population is putting additional strain on Australia's welfare and health sectors. The combination of these factors has meant that the use of economic analysis to evaluate microeconomic policies has not lost its urgency, although its future use looks destined to concentrate on the various tax and spending problems of the government rather than regulatory measures, as has been the case in the past.

In looking to the future a series of reports as part of the Securing Australia's Future programme of the Australian Council of Learned Academies (Took and Holper 2017) advocated that Australia concentrate more on higher value added commodities, using greater levels of investment in research and development, education and training, and investments in infrastructure. Many of the measures advocated in these reports are reminiscent of the sorts of measures advocated during the collapse of a previous mining boom in the 1980s, which led at the time to a greater emphasis in Australia on the support of research and development and education. The combined measures of research and development, education and infrastructure spending would appear to be destined to continue to attract the most attention from policy makers wishing to boost Australia's economic growth, although it should be remembered that these areas of endeavour are as prone to government failures as any other.

References

Edwards, John 2014, *Beyond the Boom*, Lowy Institute Paper, Penguin Australia Group, Sydney.
Garnaut, Ross 2013, *Dog Days: Australia after the Boom*, Redback, Collingwood VIC.
Took, Simon and Holper, Paul 2017, *Securing Australia's Future: Harnessing Interdisciplinary Prosperity*, CSIRO Publishing, Clayton South VIC.

INDEX

Abbott, M. 104, 108, 111, 112, 120, 121, 123–124, 125, 128, 129, 160, 169
Abbott Government 156, 255
Abelson, P. 109, 176
Aboriginal and Torres Strait Islander Heritage (Protection) Act (1984) 265
Access Economics 150
acquisitions and mergers 88–89, 91–92
ACT (Australia Capital Territory): energy industry reform 145, 149, 153; government business enterprises 115; land use regulation 180; utility price regulation 160, 169
adverse selection 220, 234
Advisory Committee on Prescription Medicines (ACPM) 236
Advisory Council of Science and Industry 77
ageing population 184, 194, 213, 218, 227, 278
Agham, R.F. 124
agriculture: agricultural policy 58–73; 'farm problem' 59–62; history of government policy 12, 13, 15; industry policy 52; productivity growth 99; research and development 77
Agriculture and Water Resources 21
airports: price regulation 165; privatisations 106–107, 113, 115, 117, 121–122, 128–132; utility price regulation 161, 166
air travel privatisations 17, 103, 104–108, 109, 113, 121–122
Akerlof, G.A. 37

allocative efficiency 29, 30, 31, 47, 71, 157, 162, 262
altruism 35
anti-competitive behaviour 37, 83, 84, 87–88, 92, 94, 97
arbitration 67, 186–189, 214
'arm's length' bodies 19, 101
Arrow, K. 199, 233
Asian Economic Crisis (1998) 277
Asia-Pacific Economic Cooperation Group 51
Asprey Report 249, 251
Assaf, A.G. 121, 122
Aulich, C. 127
Australian Bureau of Agriculture and Resource Economics 19
Australian compact/federation settlement 13
Australian Competition and Consumer Commission v Boral Ltd and Boral Masonry Ltd (formerly Boral Besser Masonry Ltd) (1999) 91
Australian Competition and Consumer Commission v Health Partners Inc. (1997) 91
Australian Competition and Consumer Commission v Pioneer International Ltd (1996) 92
Australian Competition and Consumer Commission v Roche Vitamins Australia, BASF Australia Ltd and Aventis Animal Nutrition Pty Ltd (2001) 90
Australian Competition and Consumer Commission v Visy Group (2007) 91
Australian Competition Tribunal 89, 97

Index

Australian Council of Learned Academies 278
Australian Dairy Industry Council 101
Australian Drug Evaluation Committee (ADEC) 236
Australian Energy Market Operator 145, 155
Australian Energy Regulator 89, 124, 148, 155, 160
Australian Industrial Relations Commission 183, 186–187, 189
Australian Industries Preservation Act (1906) 86
Australian National Railways 113
Australian National University 77, 202
Australian Nuclear Science and Technology Organisation 77
Australian Postal Commission 111
Australian Postal Corporation Act (1989) 128
Australian Research Council 205
Australian Soldiers Repatriation Act (1917) 214
Australian Telecommunications Commission 111
Australian Universities Commission 204
Australian Wheat Corporation 68
Australian Wool Corporation 64–65
Australia Post 127–128, 129, 161, 170
Averch-Johnson effect 165–166
aviation *see* airports; air travel privatisations
Avkiran, N.K. 120
award systems 186–189

banking 12, 17, 18, 91–92, 118–121
barley industry 68–69, 70
barriers to entry 32, 95, 164
Barton, R. 123, 126
basic wage 188
Bator, F.M. 33
Baumol, W.J. 163
Becker, G. 198, 204
beef industry 13, 52, 61
Begg, P. 178
benefits *see* welfare
benefits, external 33–34 *see also* externalities
Berg, C. 10
Berger, A.N. 119
best practice levels 141
Bhagwati, J. 55
bias 38
bid rigging 88
biodiversity 266, 268
biofuels 141, 156
Blaug, M. 199
Boehm, E.A. 50, 109
Bollard, A.E. 163
bond issues 174

Borenstein, S. 138
Borjas, G.J. 193
Bork, R.H. 86
bottleneck facilities 97
bracket creep 249
Britain *see* United Kingdom
Buchanan, J.M. 40
buffer stock/ buffer fund schemes 64–65, 68
building regulations 179–181
Building the Education Revolution programme 207–208
Bureau of Industry 123
Bureau of Industry Economics 53, 96, 125, 126
Bureau of Meteorology 270
Bureau of Resources and Energy Economics 155
Bushnell, J 138
Business Regulation Review Unit 53
Butlin, N.G. 7, 14, 15, 109, 110, 159, 229, 265
buyer power 63

Cabinet 18, 19, 20
Callan, S.J. 261
Campbell, K.O. 15
Campbell Committee of Inquiry (Australian Financial System Inquiry) 17, 18–19
Canada 155, 199, 202–203, 217, 219, 222–223, 226, 242, 271
capital dilution 193
capital gains taxation 240, 249, 250, 252, 254, 258–259
capital investment 152, 173–182
capital markets 109, 110
capture theory 39
carbon emissions tax 240, 244, 255, 267
carbon pricing 156–157, 255
Carrington, R. 125, 126
cartels 86, 90
Casey, A. 120
Centerlink 215
Centre of International Economics (CIE) 101
Chan, J. 120
Chester, L. 125
Child Endowment Act (1941/1942) 214
Chile 51
China 51, 79, 269
Civil Aviation Authority 130
Clayton Act (US) 86, 88
Clean Energy Act (2011) 255
Clean Energy Finance Corporation 157

climate change 156, 267, 268–272
coal 139, 140, 141, 146, 255
Coase, R.H. 34
Coase theorem 263
Cohen, B. 104, 108, 112
collective bargaining 187
collective refusals to deal 88
colleges of advanced education 203
collusion 87–88, 90–91
Collyer, F. 127
colonies 12, 49, 77, 181, 213, 245
Committee on the Future of Tertiary Education in Australia 204
common resources problem 262
common shock risks 220
Commonwealth Bank 14, 17, 103, 108, 113, 117, 120
Commonwealth Bank of Australia/Colonial Ltd (merger case) 91–92
Commonwealth Conciliation and Arbitration Commission 188
Commonwealth Court of Conciliation and Arbitration 188
Commonwealth Grants Commission 254
Commonwealth Industrial Court 188
Commonwealth Reconstruction Training Scheme 203
communications industry 99, 103, 104–108, 116, 170 *see also* postal services; telecommunications
comparative advantage 47–48
compensating wage differential theory 192
compensation 34, 62, 191
compensation principle 28
competition: agriculture 72; anti-competitive behaviour 37, 83, 84, 87–88, 92, 94, 97; competition law 85–90; economic efficiency 29–32, 95, 98; education and training 207; effects of tariffs 55; efficient cost of service approach 166–167; energy industry 141–142, 143–144, 145, 150, 153–154; health care 233–234, 235; Hilmer Report (1993) 17, 19; history of government policy 16; labour markets 184–186; National Competition Policy 94–102; natural monopolies 161, 163–164; non-traded goods 83; and R&D support 74; tax incidence 256; theory of the firm and markets 28–29; trade practices 83–93
Competition and Consumer Act (2010) 5, 17, 84, 85, 87–90, 165
Competition and Consumer Commission 87, 88–92, 97, 122, 148, 159, 167

Competition Principles Agreement (1995) 17, 96–99, 100
competitive bidding 161
competitive neutrality 97, 207
compulsory acquisition powers 63
Conciliation and Arbitration Act (1904) 188
conservation 266 *see also* environmental issues
Considine, M. 127
constitution, Australian 187, 213, 215, 229, 246, 265
consumer ignorance 200–201
consumer protection law 87
consumer sovereignty principle 29
consumer surplus 55, 85, 162
consumption taxing 243, 251–252, 253–254, 270–271
contestable markets, theory of 32
contracting out of services 161
Convention for the Protection of the World Cultural and Natural Heritage 265
Corden, W.M. 51
Cornish, S. 15
Corones, S.G. 85
corporation tax 259
corporatisation 111, 124, 132
corruption 244
cost/benefit approaches 22, 38, 175–178
cost of service approach 166–171
cotton industry 52, 63–64
Council of Australian Governments 96, 143, 153–154
Country Coalition 15
Country Party 67
CPI (consumer price index) 188, 231, 232
CPI-X 166, 169, 170
Crafts, N. 99
Crean Plan 100
Crisp, L.F. 6
cross-subsidisation 96, 109, 112, 128, 143
CSIRO (Council for Scientific and Industrial Research Organisation) 63, 77, 266, 270
currency floatations 17
customs and excise duties 215, 240, 241, 242, 243, 244, 245, 246, 252–253

dairy industry 15, 52, 63–64, 66, 68, 99–101
Dairy Industry Act (1992) 101
Davies, D.G. 121
deadweight losses 30–31, 55, 71, 88, 162, 257
Deakin Government 213
DEA Malmquist approach 121

Index

debt financing 167, 247
Defence Science and Technology Organisation 77
demand-boosting interventions 65
demerit goods 36
democracy 40
demographics 184, 194, 213, 218, 227, 278
Department of Aviation 128
Department of Health 236
Department of Human Services 215
Department of Natural Resources and Environment 101
Department of Social Services 215
deregulation: agriculture 68–69; aviation 121; banking 119–120; financial markets 17; history of government policy 16; labour markets 183; trend towards 5, 159
developmental approval 180
displacement 7
dollar, flotation of 17
Dollery, B. 38, 120, 268
dried fruits industry 67, 68
dynamic efficiency 29, 31

Eames, J. 129
ecology 266, 268
economic efficiency (concept of) 29–32
Economic Planning and Advisory Commission 53
economies of scale 31, 88, 154, 161, 193
economies of scope 31
education and training 21, 76, 197–208, 212
Edwards, J. 277
efficiency: and competition 84; CPI-X 166; economic policy and efficiency 24–43; in economic theory 28, 29–32; efficiency versus equity trade-off 32, 175, 242–245, 250, 258–259; and environmental policy 261–262, 263; government owned businesses 112; and infrastructure projects 175; market failures/ imperfections 33–37; and monopolies 163; and price discrimination 168; and privatisation 120, 127, 132–133; trade practices 83
efficiency wage hypothesis 185–186
efficient cost of service approach 166–171
eggs industry 68
electricity supply industry: efficiency 26, 152; energy policy 138–158; health and safety 149, 193; natural monopolies 109, 161–163; privatisations 104–108, 111, 113–116, 117, 123–126; productivity growth 99; utility price regulation 170
Eling, M. 120

Emissions Reduction Fund 255
employment 127, 151, 183–196 *see also* unemployment
energy industry: Australian Energy Regulator 89–90; energy policy 138–158; government business enterprises 103; industrial disputes 186; privatisations 113–116, 117, 123–126 *see also* electricity supply industry; gas supply industry
enterprise bargaining agreements 189, 191, 198
environmental issues 112, 156, 178, 244, 261–273
Environmental Protection and Biodiversity Conservation Act (1999) 267
equilibrium effects 50, 55
equity, vertical versus horizontal 242–243
equity costs 167
equity versus efficiency trade-off 32, 175, 242–245, 250, 258–259
Essential Services Commission 124
estate taxes 247, 249
Eureka Stockade 245
European Union 87, 271, 272
evaluation of policies 27
exclusive dealing 87, 88, 91
exclusive rights 146
exports: agriculture 59; dairy industry 100; effects of subsidies 55; evolution of trade policy 50, 51; and GST 254; history of government policy 12, 14, 15; industry policy 48; manufacturing 59; mining 59; services industry 59
externalities: agriculture 62; education and training 200–201, 207; environmental issues 261–265, 266; industry policy 56; infrastructure 175, 178; and market failure 33–34; research and development 76, 81; and the welfare state 221 *see also* negative externalities; positive externalities

Fair Pay Commission 189
Fair Work Act (2009) 189
Fair Work Commission 183, 187, 189
family reunion immigration 194
'farm problem' 59–62
favours, government 40–41
Federal Airports Corporation (FAC) 129–130
Federal Court 89
federation settlement 13
feed-in tariff schemes 157
Finance department 20–21

finance industry 103, 104–108, 116, 118–121 *see also* banking; insurance
fines 34, 263, 264
firm, theory of the 28–37
Fisher, B.S. 15
flotation of Australian dollar 17
food, demand for 61
food beverages tobacco industry 52
Foreign Affairs and Trade 21
Forster, C. 49
Forsyth, P. 121, 122
Franklin, B. 198
Franklin River dam 267
Fraser Government 215
Freedman, C. 53
free rider problem 35, 36, 40, 62, 69, 76, 77
Freestone, R. 122
free trade agreements 51, 246
free trade policies 47, 49
freeways 178–179
friendly societies 228
fringe benefits taxation 240, 241, 249, 250–251, 252, 254
fully distributed costs 167, 168
Fulmer, J. 174

gambling 5, 105, 107, 108, 109, 116, 240
Garnaut, R. 267, 277
gas supply industry: energy policy 138–142, 153–155; natural monopolies 109, 161–163; price regulation 166; privatisations 104–108, 113–116, 117, 123–126; productivity growth 99
GDP (gross domestic product): agriculture 59; aviation 131; education and training 206; fiscal surplus/ deficit 8; government business enterprises 117; government owned businesses 104; health expenditure 226, 231; and human capital 199; infrastructure 173–174, 181; manufacturing 50, 59; mining 59; per capita, growth in 99; productivity growth 98–99; research and development 78–81; rising government expenditure as proportion of 7–8, 15, 24–25; services industry 59; social spending 216–217; tax ratio 246, 247; tertiary education 202
Geelong Ring Road 178–179
Gillard Government 156–157, 255, 267
Gillen, D. 122
Gini coefficients 222, 223
GIO Australia 120
Global Financial Crisis (2008) 7–8, 174, 277
global public goods 36, 270

gold rushes 13, 245
goods and services tax (GST) 240, 241, 251–252, 253–254
government business enterprises 87, 92, 94–102, 103–137, 161, 170, 201, 202, 227
government structure 11
grant programmes 78, 229, 230, 246, 252, 254
Grattan Institute 124
Great Barrier Reef 266, 267
Great Depression 247
Green Loans Program 268
Green Paper on Higher Education 205
Green Papers, purpose of 18
Grewal, B. 248
Groenewegen, P. 246, 248, 249, 251
Gropp, L. 63
gross fixed capital formation (GFCF) 173

Harman, G. 203
Harris, E. 176
Harris, M. 127
Harrison, M. 22
Haszler, H.A. 65
Hawke Labor Government 17, 129, 188, 204–205, 215, 229, 254, 267
Hayek, F.A. 84
health and safety 148–149, 191–192, 235
health care 225–238 *see also* welfare
health funds 227
health insurance 215–216
Health Legislation Amendment Act (1983) 229
Hensher, D.A. 121
Hewson, J. 254
Higgins, H.B. 186
higher education 198, 200 *see also* universities
Higher Education Contribution Scheme 205
Hilmer Inquiry (Independent Committee of Inquiry into Competition Policy) 17, 19, 96
Hodge, G.A. 108
Holper, P. 278
Home Insulation Programme 268
Hong, C.H. 122
Hooper, P. 121
housing industry 104–108, 116, 179–181
Howard Government 17, 51, 130, 156, 189, 254, 267
human capital 198–200, 204, 207–208, 227, 237
Humphrey, D.B. 119
hydro-electric power 139, 140, 141, 143, 155–157, 268

immigration: history 13, 15; and labour markets 184, 185, 192–194; land use regulation 181; overseas students 206
impact evaluations 175
import markets 48, 50, 54–55, 65, 240, 244, 253
import quotas 55
imputation systems 250
Incomes Accord 188–189
income support measures 211, 252
income taxation 240, 241, 242, 243, 246–250, 252, 259
industrial disputes 186–190
industrialisation 13, 15
Industrial Relations Act (1988) 189
industrial tribunals 186, 187, 189
Industries Assistance Commission 16, 19, 50–51, 53, 54, 56, 96
Industry, Innovation and Science 21
Industry Commission 51, 52, 53, 96, 100, 141, 143–144, 153
industry policy 47–57
inelasticity of demand 61, 66, 168, 253, 256
inequality (social) 220, 222, 246, 278
infant industry argument for government intervention 48, 49, 53
inflation 15–16, 188–189, 191, 249
information 37
information, imperfect 37, 62, 186, 192, 233, 235, 266
information asymmetries 22, 236
infrastructure 97, 173–182, 268
Infrastructure and Regional Development 21
innovation 75–76, 96
inquiries 18–19, 96, 100
insolvency risks 110
insurance: health care 234, 235; health insurance 225–227, 231; insurance industry 120; and the welfare state 220–221; workers' compensation 191
intellectual property 75, 76, 235
interest groups: agriculture 65, 71–72; environmental issues 266; and 'government failure' 38; land use regulation 180; National Competition Policy 98; private interest theory 39–40; public choice theory 40; and public policy 22; and regulation 24
Intergovernmental Agreement on the Environment 267
international benchmarking 125
internationalization 278
international markets 50, 155
international treaties 265, 267, 270

Inter-State Commission 51
Invalid and Old-Age Pension Act (1908) 213
invisible hand 84
IPART 124, 125
Itoh, M. 47

Japan: carbon emissions 270, 271; free trade agreements 51; health expenditure 226; poverty rate 222–223; rate of return regulation 165; research and development 79; social spending 219; taxation 242; tertiary education 202–203
Jefferson, T. 36
Jones, R. 104

Keating Labor Government 130, 254, 267
Kerin Plan 100
Keynesian macroeconomics 14, 15, 41
Klapdor, M. 194
Knopke, P. 61
Korea 51, 202, 203, 223, 226, 242, 269, 271
Kortt, M.A. 268
Kreuger, A. 40
Kyoto Protocol 267, 270

labour markets 17, 67, 183–196, 221, 247
land degradation 268
land taxes 246–247
land use regulation 174, 179–181, 266
Lawrence, D. 124, 125, 126
legislation: growth over time of 10–11; passage through stages 18–19
levies: agriculture 64, 65, 67; dairy industry 100; health care 229; Medicare 226, 229–230, 252; research and development 78; training levies 201
Lewis, C. 208
Liberal/National Party Coalition Government 130, 189, 254
Liberal Party 13, 15
lifetime consumption 243
Lin, L.C. 122
Littlechild, S. 124
living standards 99, 222–223
LNG (liquified natural gas) 155
lobby groups *see* interest groups
local government: environmental issues 265, 266; land use regulation 180; national-state-local government demarcations 5; range of powers 5; taxation 240
Lorenz curves 223
Luhnen, M. 120
Lye, J.N. 127

Maddock, R. 173
Maglen, L.R. 200
Malaysia 51
Mandatory Renewable Energy Target (MRET) 156
manufacturing: history of government policy 13, 15; industry policy 47–57; privatisations 104–108, 116; productivity growth 99
marketable permits 34, 263, 264, 270–272
market failures/ imperfections: agricultural policy 58, 61, 63, 70; education and training 200–201, 207–208; health care 232–233; industry policy 48, 53; infrastructure projects 175; land use regulation 179; and R&D support 74–75; and social policy 220; and unemployment 198; workplace health and safety 192
marketing: agriculture 65, 66; consumer protection law 87; health care 233; safety promotional campaigns 148
Marshall, A. 198
Martin Committee 205
Maternity Allowances Act (1912) 213
Mathews, R.L. 248
McIntyre, S. 187
McLean, I. 12, 173
meat industry 67, 68, 69
media role in public policy 21
Medibank 215, 227, 229
Medicare 215–216, 226, 229, 230, 231, 252
Melville, L. 15
Menzies, R. 13
mergers and acquisitions 88–89, 91–92
merit goods 36, 200–201
Meyrick and Associates 125
middlemen 63
migration 192–194
milk industry 15, 52, 63–64, 66, 68, 99–101
Mill, J.S. 49
Mills, S. 245
Mincer, J. 198, 204
Mineral Resources Rent Act 253
mineral resources rent tax 240, 255
minimum wages 185, 187, 188, 189
mining: contribution to GDP 59; exports 59; infrastructure 174, 176; mining booms 277, 278; privatisations 117; productivity growth 99; tax 245; taxation 255
Ministerial Council meetings 21
misuse of market power 88, 91, 117, 150–151, 161, 164

mixed economy, Australian economy as 6, 15
monetarist approaches 16
monetary policy 14
monopolies: agriculture 68, 71; airports 121; anti-trust law 86; Australia Post 128; and competition 84; and economic efficiency 30–31; energy industry 138–139, 140, 141, 151, 154; government business enterprises 108, 117; and industry policy 48, 49, 53; legal monopolies 161; mergers and acquisitions 88–89; misuse of market power 88, 91; natural monopolies 36, 97, 109, 139, 141, 154, 161–163, 164, 201; pharmaceuticals 235; and privatisation 132; rate of return regulation 165–166; and regulation 163; social costs of 162; and taxation 257; and trade practices 84–85; utility price regulation 159–172
monopsonies 48, 53, 67
moral hazards 220, 234, 235
motor vehicle industry 51, 52, 53, 77
Mountain, B. 124
Murray Committee 77–78, 203, 205
Murray-Darling Basin 267, 268
Murray River 265

Nadel, S. 271
National Competition Council 89, 97–98
National Competition Policy 19, 94–102, 143
National Electricity Market (NEM) 124, 141, 145
National Health and Pension Insurance Act (1938) 214
national independence, symbolisation of 53
National Insurance Commission 214
nationalisation 110
National Party 67
national-state-local government demarcations 5
Natural Heritage Trust 267
natural monopolies 36, 97, 109, 139, 141, 154, 161–163, 164, 201
natural resource exploitation 12, 253, 265 *see also* utilities
Natural Resources 21
Neal, P. 120
negative externalities 33–34, 35, 253, 262, 266
NERA Economic Consulting 160, 169, 171

New Public Management 20
New South Wales: agricultural policy 67, 68, 69, 70; dairy industry 100; energy industry 125, 141, 143, 144, 145, 148, 153, 154; government business enterprises 113, 116; land use regulation 180; privatisations 117; telecommunications 124; utility price regulation 160, 165, 169; welfare 213
New Zealand: carbon emissions 269, 271, 272; electricity industry reform 138; energy industry 146, 149; free trade agreements 51; health expenditure 226; human capital 199; poverty rate 222–223; price regulation 163; privatisations 118–119; social policy and the welfare state 213; taxation 242; tertiary education 202–203; utility price regulation 166
Nieuwenhuysen, J.P. 87
non-contractibility 109
non-excludability 35, 178
non-rival goods 35, 36, 178
non-transferability 110
Norris, K. 184
Northern Territory: energy industry reform 149, 155; government business enterprises 115; land use regulation 180; utility price regulation 169

occupational health and safety Acts 191–192
occupational superannuation 215–216, 221
O'Donnell, M. 122
OECD (Organisation for Economic Co-operation and Development): competition 99; government business enterprises 104; health expenditure 226, 231; labour markets 199, 202; research and development 79; social policy and the welfare state 216, 217, 218, 219, 222–223; taxation 242, 248
oil 139, 140, 141, 253, 255
oligopolies 37, 85
open access 155
optimal tariffs 48
Otchere, I. 120
Oum, T.H. 122
ownership transfer 110

Pacific Economics Group 124, 125, 126
Pareto principle 28–29, 34, 36, 243, 264
Paris Agreement 267
Parsons Brinckerhoff 124
partial equilibrium effects 55

partial factor productivity (PFP) 126
path dependency 181
PAYE (pay as you earn) 248
payroll taxes 248, 249
peaking plant 152, 157
Pedrick, W.H. 249
Pember Reeves, W. 14, 49
pensions 213, 214, 215, 216, 248, 252
performance monitoring 171, 176
pests 266
petroleum resource rent tax (PRRT) 253
petroleum royalties 253
Pharmaceutical Benefits Scheme (PBS) 226, 236
pharmaceuticals 234–237
philanthropy 228 *see also* third sector
Phillips, J. 194
Pickford, M. 163
Piggott, R.H. 64, 67
Pigou, A. 34
Pindyck, R.S. 28, 30, 31
planning permission 180, 266
Pollitt, M.G. 103, 138, 166
pollution 34, 35, 261–262, 264, 272
Pomfret, R. 51
Pope, A. 84
population growth 180, 184, 213
populism 277
positive externalities 33–34, 56, 109, 178, 201, 262
Posner, R. 25, 39, 86
Posner, R.A. 161, 168
postal services 127–128, 129, 170
potatoes 70
poverty alleviation 63, 218, 220
poverty rate 222–223
power to coerce 25
predatory pricing 88, 91
Premier, role of 20
Preston, A. 189
price discrimination 168
price fixing 67, 68, 86, 87–88, 90–91, 100
price-raising schemes 67
price regulation: and competition 97; efficient cost of service approach 166–171; light handed approach 163–165; rate of return regulation 165–166; utilities 159–172
price review bodies, independent 97
Prices Surveillance Act (1983) 130
price stabilisation mechanisms 64–65
price takers 30, 47, 48
pricing mechanisms 30
Priest, G.L. 39
primary education, as merit good 201

Primary Industries 21
Prime Minister 18, 20
principal-agent problems 38, 110
Private Health Insurance Administration Council 226
private interest theory 39–41, 65
private litigation 87
privatisations 103–137; electricity supply industry 26; energy industry 139, 141, 144, 148, 152, 154; history of government policy 17; utility price regulation 161
probate duties 247
producer surplus 55
Productivity Commission 52, 53, 78, 81, 100, 123, 124, 150
productivity growth: agricultural policy 61; airports 130; aviation 121, 122; banking 119; competition policy 95–96, 98–99; education and training 200–201; energy industry 150; and labour markets 184–185, 188, 189, 191, 193, 197; telecommunications 124
professions 87, 92, 94, 97
property rights 263
protectionism 49, 54–55, 245 *see also* tariffs
public choice theory 40
public goods 35–36, 75, 178, 186, 189, 201, 206, 235, 263
public interest 38–39, 87, 97, 98
public policy: formation of 17–22; history of 12–17; overview 6–11
public-private partnerships 112, 175
Public Services Commission 20
public utilities 14 *see also* utilities; *specific utilities*
pure public goods 35–36, 41, 186, 189

Qantas 17, 109, 113, 117, 121
Queensland: agricultural policy 65, 67, 68, 69, 70; dairy industry 100; energy industry 125, 141, 143, 144, 145, 148, 149, 154; government business enterprises 114, 116; infrastructure 174; land use regulation 180; mining royalties 255; privatisations 117; tax 249; telecommunications 124; utility price regulation 160, 165, 169
Quiggin, J. 200
quotas 50, 55, 65

railways: infrastructure 173–182; pricing models 168; privatisations 111, 113, 117, 163; utility price regulation 170
Ramsay pricing 168

rate of return regulation 165–166, 170
rationality 84
Rattigan, G.A. 50
Razor Gang 204
redistribution: and agricultural policy 58, 71; government roles in 25; health care 227; poverty alleviation 220; revenue raising and tax policy 239–260
referee/umpire role of government in markets 25
regulation: defined 25; and economic efficiency 37–41; economic policy and efficiency 24–43; education and training 201; energy industry 141, 142–143, 148, 154, 155; environmental issues 263, 264–265, 266; health care 227, 231–232, 235–237; as inducement to social efficiency 34; land use planning 179–181; performance monitoring 171; private interest theory 39–41; versus privatisations 133; privatised industries 112; public interest theory 38–39; and public policy 7, 9–10; rate of return regulation 165–166; utility price regulation 159–172; water industry 169; workplace health and safety 191–192
regulatory impact analysis (RIA) 21–22
renewable energy 139, 140, 141, 155–157
Renewable Energy (Electricity) Act (2000) 267
rent seeking behaviours 38, 40, 49, 55, 71, 84, 89, 162
Repatriation Commission 214
repatriation services 229, 247
resale price maintenance 88
research and development 56, 62, 63, 68, 71, 74–82, 235–236, 244
Reserve Bank 14
reserved services 128, 161
reserve plant margin 151
resource rent taxation 253, 255
revenue raising 239–260
revenue sharing arrangements 246
rice 69, 70
ring-fencing 163, 164
risk, concepts of 201, 219, 220, 232–233
risk mitigation 220
roads 178–179
Rosengard, J. 234, 261
royalties 253, 255
Rubinfeld, D.L. 28, 30, 31
Rudd Government 17, 189, 267, 270
Rushdi, A. 123, 125

safety regulation 148–149, 191–192, 235
sales taxes 240, 241, 247, 251, 253–254

Salvatore, D. 48, 54
Samuelson, P. 35
Sathye, M. 120
savings 221
scarcity 26–27
Schedvin, C.B. 14
Schultz, T.W. 198, 204
Schuster, D. 122
Science and Industry Research Act (1926) 77
screening hypothesis 199–200
Second World War 13, 68, 203, 213–214, 248, 250
Securing Australia's Future 278
self-interest 40, 110
Serebrisky, T. 122
services industry: competition law 87, 97; contribution to GDP 59; exports 59; research and development 80; tax 245
Shanks, S. 81
Shann, E. 67
sheep industry 61
Sheffrin, S. 174
Shenefield, J.H. 84, 86
Sherman Act (US) 86
Sidak, G. 163
Sieper, E. 64
Singapore 51, 149, 269
single desks 63, 66, 68, 70, 71
skills, labour 109, 193, 194, 197–198
Small, R. 121
small businesses 87, 92
Small-Scale Renewable Energy Scheme 156
Smart, D. 203
Smith, A. 84, 192, 198
Smith, J. 247
social cost-benefit analysis 176–178
socialism 109
social policy 211–224
social policy and the welfare state 112, 243, 252
social return on investment 200
solar energy 141, 156–157
South Australia: agricultural policy 67, 68, 70; dairy industry 100, 101; energy industry 125, 141, 143, 144, 145, 146, 148, 149, 153, 154; government business enterprises 114; land use regulation 180; privatisations 116, 118; utility price regulation 160, 169
South-East Asia 181
spillover effects *see* externalities
squatting 12
Standard for the Uniform Scheduling of Drugs and Poisons (SUSDP) 236
standards of living 99, 222–223

state banks 108
state governments: agriculture tariffs 69; competition law 87; energy industry 140, 142–143; environmental issues 265–266, 267; health care 225, 228–229, 230–232, 237; land use regulation 180; mining royalties 255; national-state-local government demarcations 5; price regulation of utilities 159–160; range of powers 5; reform of state owned businesses 96; regulation of energy industry 148–149; social policy and the welfare state 213, 214, 215; tax 245–246, 247, 248, 249, 252, 254; taxation 240; water industry 169
statutory authorities 19, 111
statutory marketing authorities 63, 66, 67–71
statutory planning 179–181
Steiner, F. 138
Stelzer, I. 84, 86
Stigler, G.J. 25, 39
Stiglitz, J. 9–10, 25, 37, 110, 234, 261
Stonecash, R. 53
strategic trade argument for government intervention 48–49, 53
structure of Australian government 11, 18
Sturm, J.E. 120
subsidies: agriculture 63–64; dairy industry 100; education and training 201; effects of 55; environmental issues 263, 264; evolution of trade policy 50; history (agriculture) 67–69; as inducement to social efficiency 34; infrastructure 175, 177; research and development 76; welfare state 213
sugar 52, 65, 68, 70
Sullivan, A. 174
sunk costs 168
sunset clauses 77
superannuation 216, 221, 244, 251
super fund taxes 241
super-profits 162, 255
supply restriction interventions 65
Sydney airport 107, 117, 122, 130

takeovers 110 *see also* mergers and acquisitions
Tariff Act (1908) 49
Tariff Board 50, 56
tariffs: agriculture 65, 67–69; effects of tariffs 54–55; evolution of trade policy 49–54; history of government policy 15, 67–69; optimal tariffs 48; versus R&D support 77; renewable energy 157;

revenue raising and tax policy 253; tariff reductions 17, 50, 51
task forces 129
Tasmania: agricultural policy 65, 67; dairy industry 100, 101; energy industry reform 141, 143, 144, 148, 149; environmental issues 265; government business enterprises 115; land use regulation 180; utility price regulation 169
taxation: environmental issues 264, 270; and health care 229; history of 244–253; as inducement to social efficiency 34; and infrastructure projects 174; limits on powers 213–214; progressive 220, 246, 247, 248, 252; and pure public goods 35; and R&D support 74, 76, 78, 80; regressive taxation 215, 245, 246, 254; revenue raising and tax policy 239–260; social policy and the welfare state 215, 218; tax concessions 56, 76, 78, 80, 244–245; tax incidence 256–259; tax reform 249–253; and the welfare state 211
Taxation Review Committee 249
technical and further education (TAFE) 202
technical/productive efficiency 29, 30, 31, 157
technological change: health and safety 192; and health care 227, 231; and the telecommunications industry 122–123
telecommunications: government business enterprises 103; privatisations 17, 113–116, 122–123; utility price regulation 161, 167
Telstra 17, 113, 117, 122–123, 267
terms of trade 48, 58, 60, 95, 193
textiles/clothing/footwear (TCF) 51, 52, 53, 77
TFP indexes 121, 124, 125
Thailand 51
Therapeutic Goods Act (1989) 236
Therapeutic Goods Administration 236
third sector 6, 212–213
Thomas, G. 122
Thomas, J.M. 261
Thorelli, H.B. 86
tobacco industry 52, 65, 252–253
tolls 174, 178
Toner, P. 127
Took, S. 278
total service long-run incremental costs (TSLRIC) 167
Tourism and Transport Forum Australia 121

town planning 179–181
tradable permits 34, 263, 264, 270–272
trade agreements, history of 14 *see also* free trade agreements
trade policy, evolution of 49–54
trade practices 83–93
Trade Practices Act (1965) 86
Trade Practices Act (1974) 16, 17, 85, 87, 92, 94, 97, 164 *see also Competition and Consumer Act* (2010)
Trade Practices Commission 87, 97
Trade Practices Commission v TNT Australia Pty Ltd, Mayne Nickless and Ansett Transport Industries (1995) 90
trade unions 13, 185, 186, 187–189, 197
training and education markets 197–208
transactions costs 34, 37, 127
transport: industrial disputes 186; infrastructure 173–182; Inter-State Commission 51; and oil 139; privatisations 104–108, 116, 117 *see also* air travel privatisations; railways; roads
Treasury, role of 20
Treaty of Rome 87
Tsai, H.C. 123
Tullock, G. 40
two-price schemes 66, 68–69, 70–71

unemployment: energy industry 151; history of government policy 15–16; and labour markets 185; trends in 189–190, 197; welfare state 213, 214, 221, 248
Unemployment and Sickness Benefits Act (1944) 214
Unified National System 203, 205
Uniform Tax Case (1942) 240
United Kingdom: carbon emissions 269, 270; energy industry 138, 149; health expenditure 225, 226; and the history of Australian government policy 16; history of government policy 12–13; human capital 199; poverty rate 222–223; privatisations 118–119; social spending 217, 219; taxation 242; tertiary education 202–203
United Nations Framework Convention on Climate Change (UNFCCC) 267
United States: anti-trust law 85–86, 164; carbon emissions 269, 270, 271; Clayton Act (US) 86, 88; competition law 85–86; energy industry 138, 149, 155; free trade agreements 51; health expenditure 226; and the history of Australian government policy 16; human capital 199; poverty

rate 222–223; privatisations 118–119; rate of return regulation 165; research and development 79; Sherman Act 85–86; social spending 217, 219; taxation 242; tertiary education 202–203; utility price regulation 166
universities 77–78, 197–208, 235–236
urbanisation 180, 181, 265, 268
urban planning 180–181
utilities: energy policy 138–158; price regulation 97–98; utility price regulation 159–172 *see also* energy industry

value, in economic theory 28, 31
value added tax (VAT) 240, 252, 253–254
vehicle industry 51, 52, 53, 77
Victoria: agricultural policy 67, 68; dairy industry 100, 101; energy industry 124, 125–126, 141, 143–145, 146–147, 148, 149, 152, 154, 155; infrastructure 175–176, 178–179; land use regulation 180; privatisations 111, 113, 116, 117; utility price regulation 160, 169; welfare 213
Ville, S. 12
vocational education and training (VET) 198, 200, 202
voluntariness 25
voluntary exchange, discipline of 38
voluntary schemes 67, 88

wage indexation 188
wages policies 183, 184–185, 186–191
Walker, B.C. 127
Walker, R.G. 127
Wallis, J. 38
water industry 99, 113, 169, 174, 175–176, 268
wealth creation 28, 31, 54–55
wealth destruction 54, 55
wealth distribution 211
wealth taxation 240, 246–247, 249, 259

weighted average cost of capital (WACC) 167
welfare: effects of tariffs 56; Gini coefficients 222, 223; infrastructure 177; and monopolies 162; Pareto principle 28–29, 34, 36, 243, 264; social policy and the welfare state 211–224
Western Australia: agricultural policy 67, 69, 70; dairy industry 100; energy industry 125, 143, 148, 149, 154, 155; government business enterprises 114; infrastructure 174; land use regulation 180; mining royalties 255; privatisations 113, 116, 118; telecommunications 124; utility price regulation 169
Wettenhall, R. 127
whaling 12
wheat 52, 68, 69, 70
White Australia Policy 13
White Paper on Higher Education 205
White Papers, purpose of 18
Whitlam Labor Government 50–51, 215, 229
Whitwell, G. 14, 15, 50
wholesale markets 141, 144, 145, 148, 150, 154–155
wholesale taxes 240, 241, 247, 251–252, 254
Widows Pension Act (1942/1943) 214
Williams, B. 120
Wilson Cook & Co 124
wind power 156, 157, 252
Withers, G. 12
wool industry 13, 15, 52, 64, 68, 69
workable competition 32
Work Choices 189
workplace health and safety 191–192
Workplace Relations and Other Legislation Amendment Act (1996) 189
World Health Organization 228
Wu, S. 120, 121, 129

Zheng, S. 81
zoning 180, 265